Hi Babe, it's me. You.

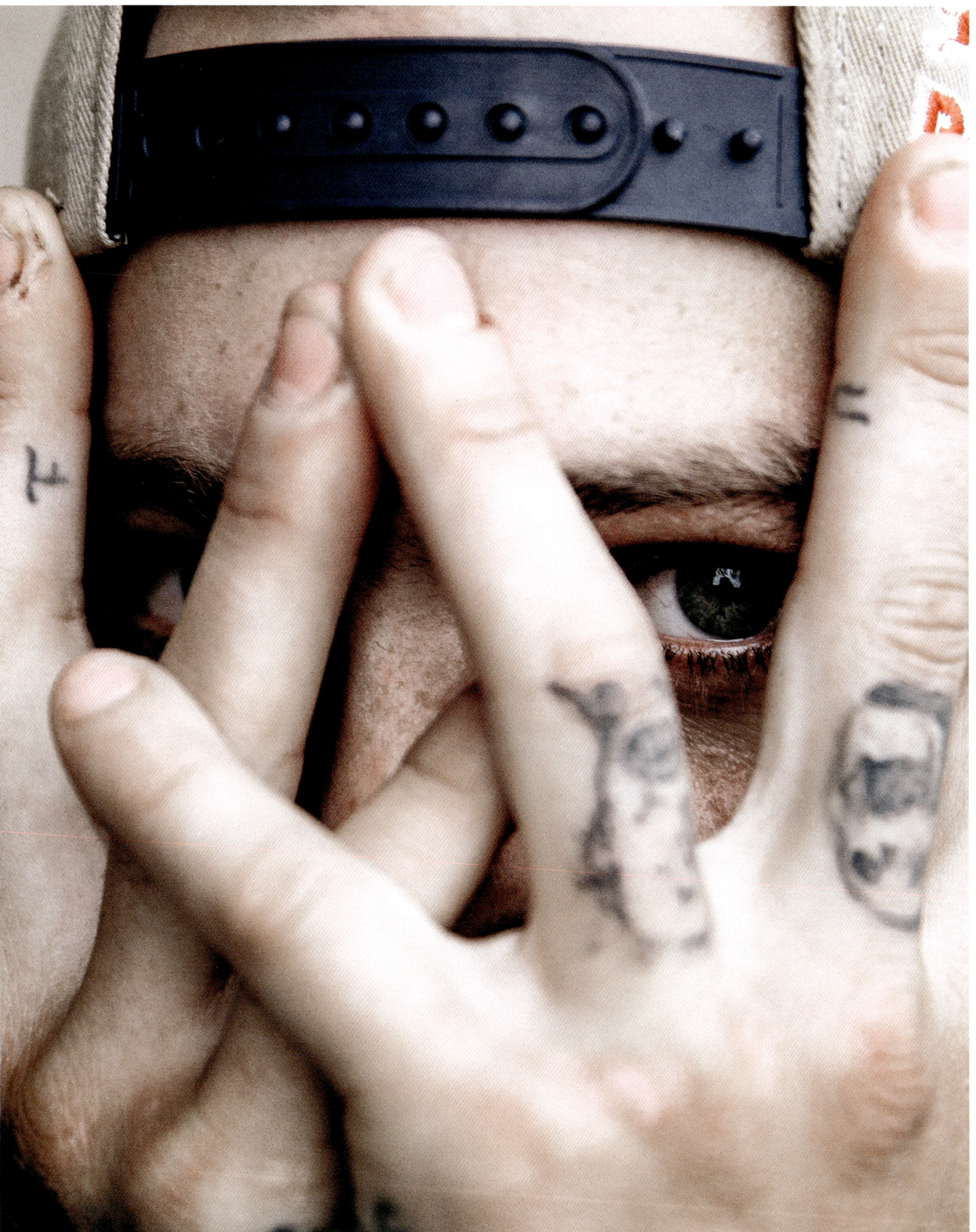

Hi Babe, it's me. You.

(aka Letters to A Younger Self)

Photographs by Sam McGuire

PARAGON BOOKS

Sam McGuire —
Hi Babe, It's Me. You.

First Printing
September, 2023

Hardcover Edition of 300
Softcover Edition of 1000

ISBN: 978-1-952251-23-8
Library of Congress Control Number: 2023915341

Designer & Editor: Shaun Roberts

The text was composed using *Helvetica Neue* designed by Max Miedinger from Linotype, *Albertshal Typewriter* by Lukas Krakora, and *Have Heart Two* by Set Sail Studios.

Designed in Oakland, California.
Printed in China.

Paragon Books
929 Camelia St.
Berkeley, CA 94710

www.samuelmcguire.com
www.paragon-books.com

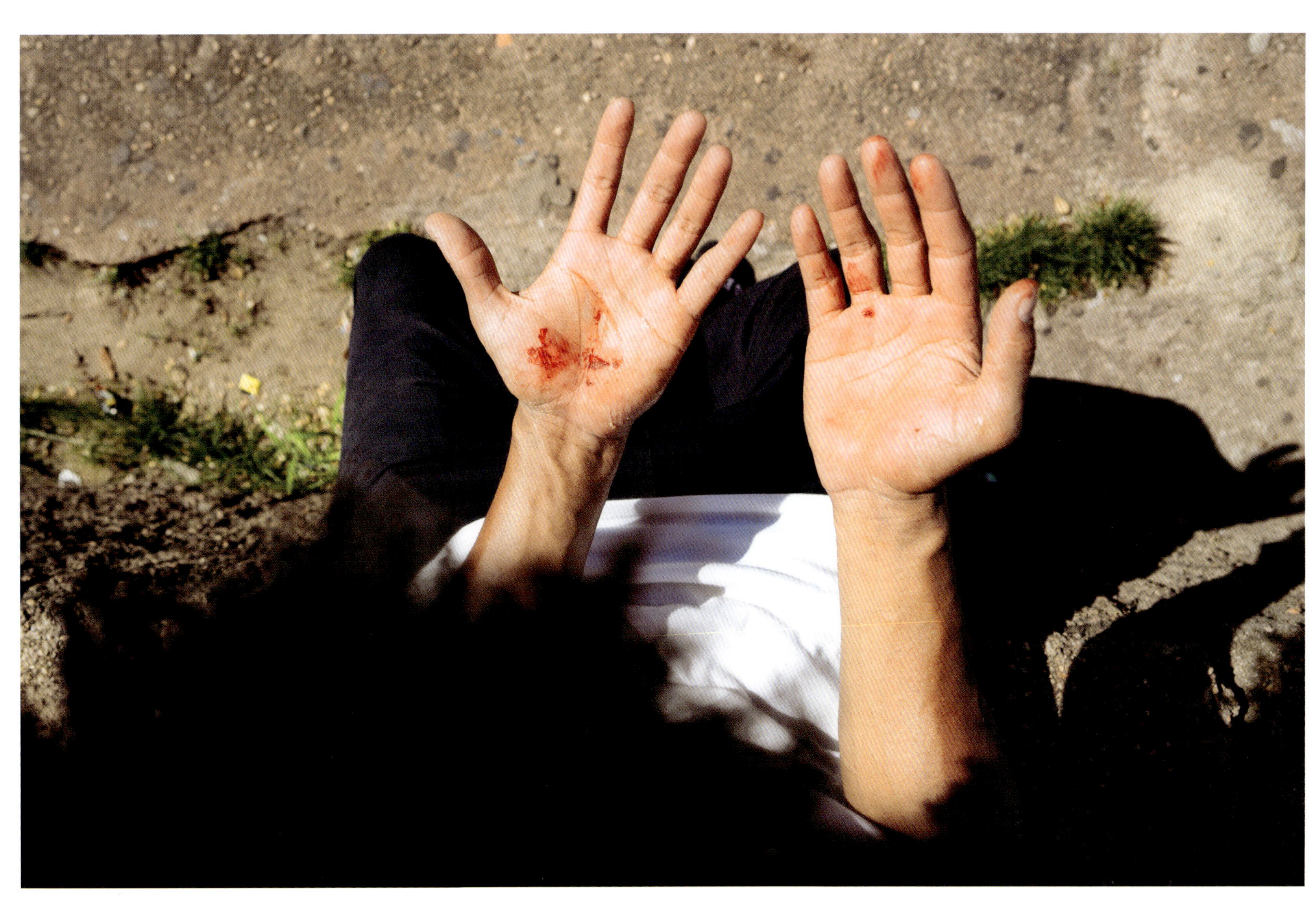

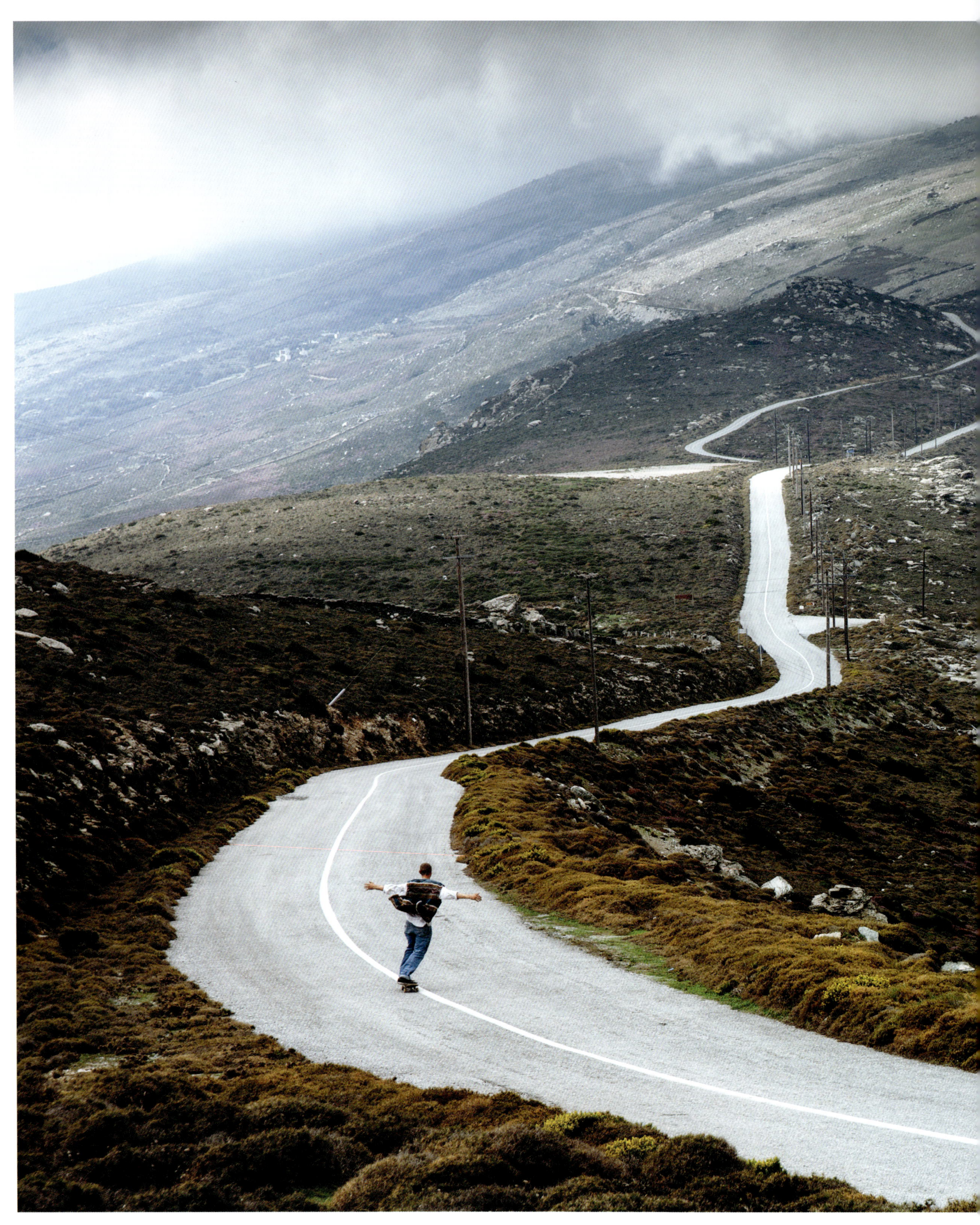

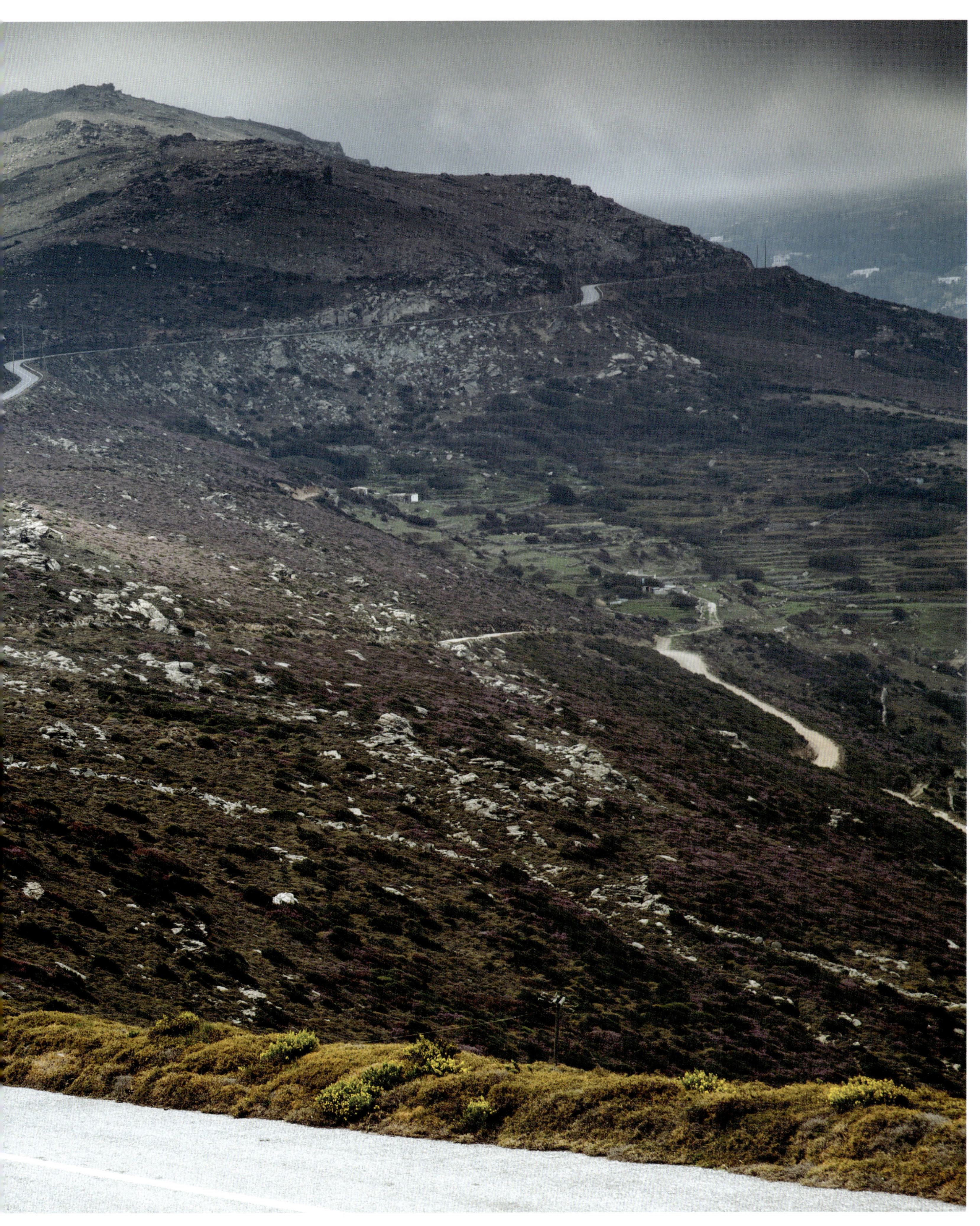

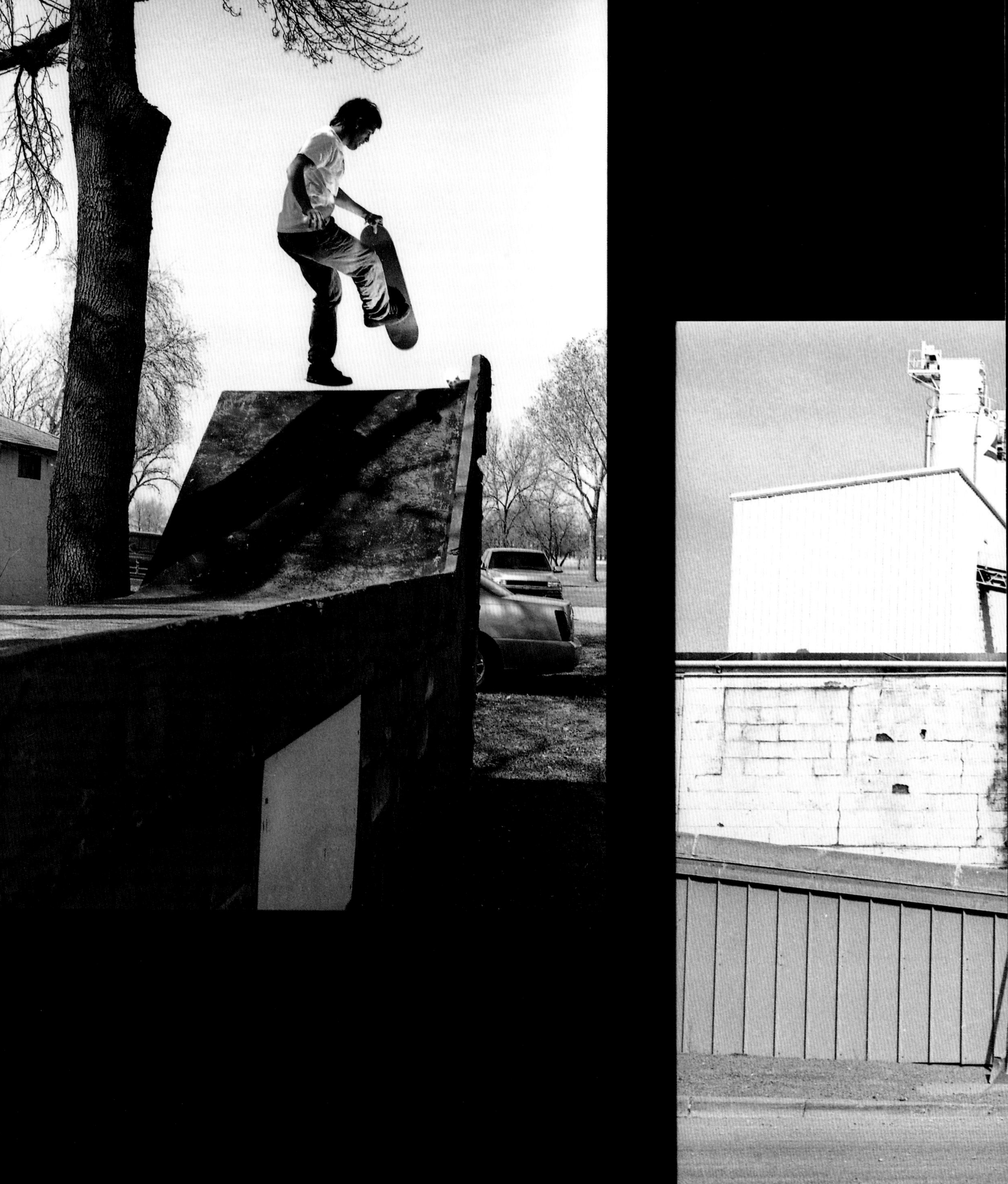

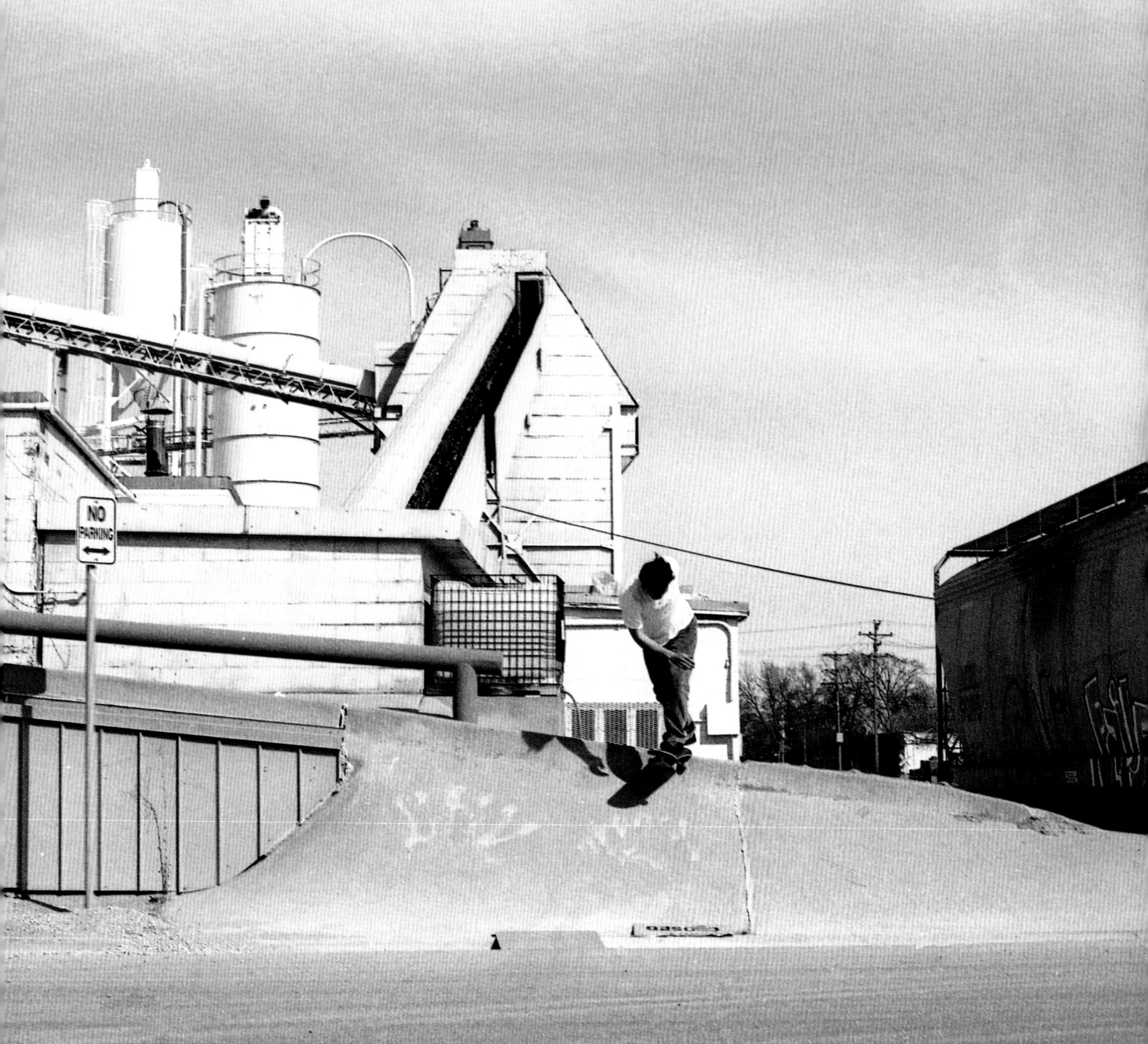
NO
PARKING

CHRIS VANDERWALL IOWA CITY, IA

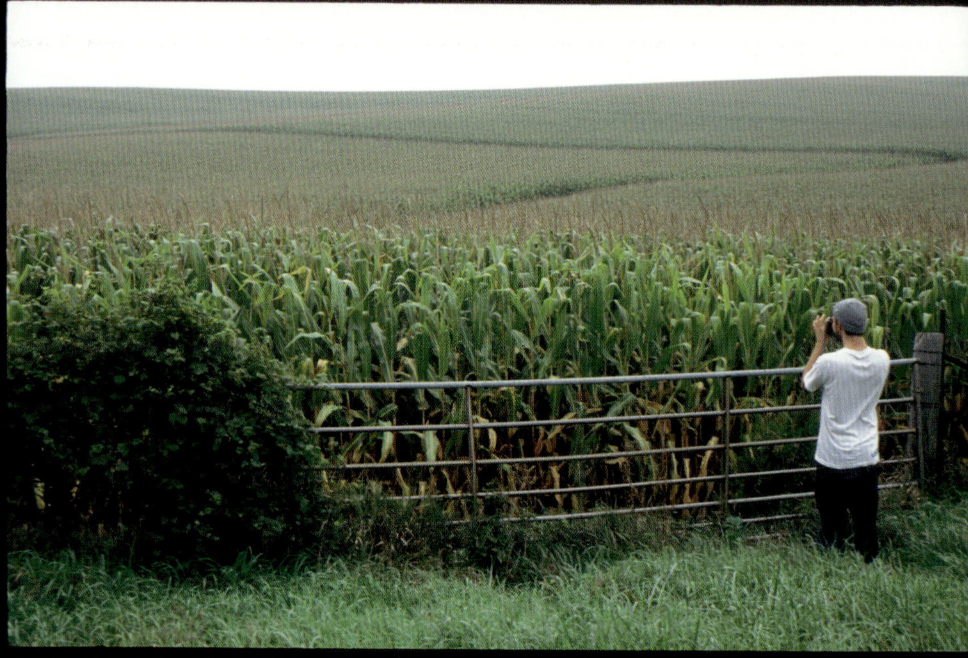

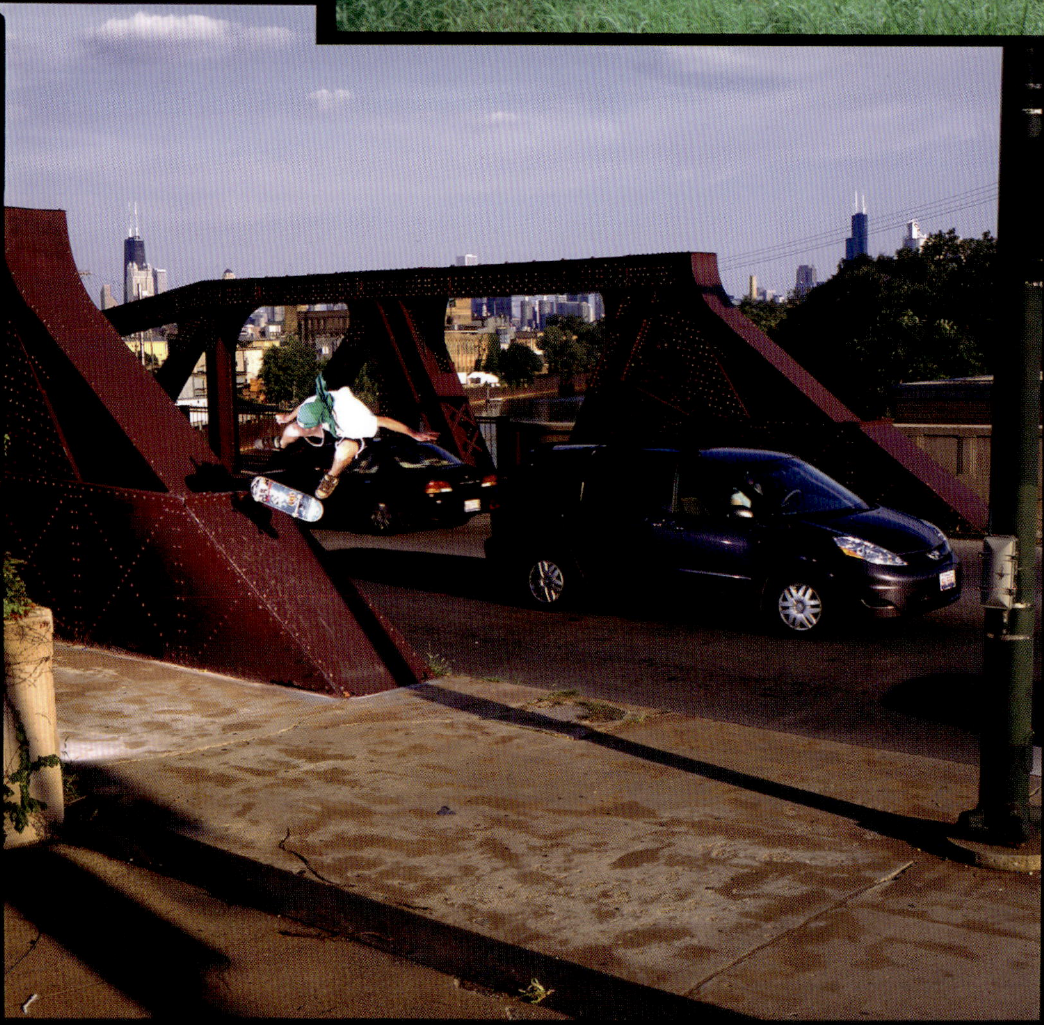

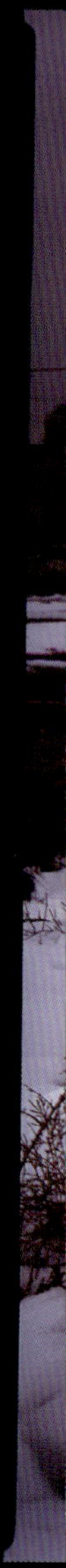

HENRIQUE PORTO CHICAGO, IL

NICK RILEY IOWA CITY, IA

SETH McCALLUM
MINNEAPOLIS, MN

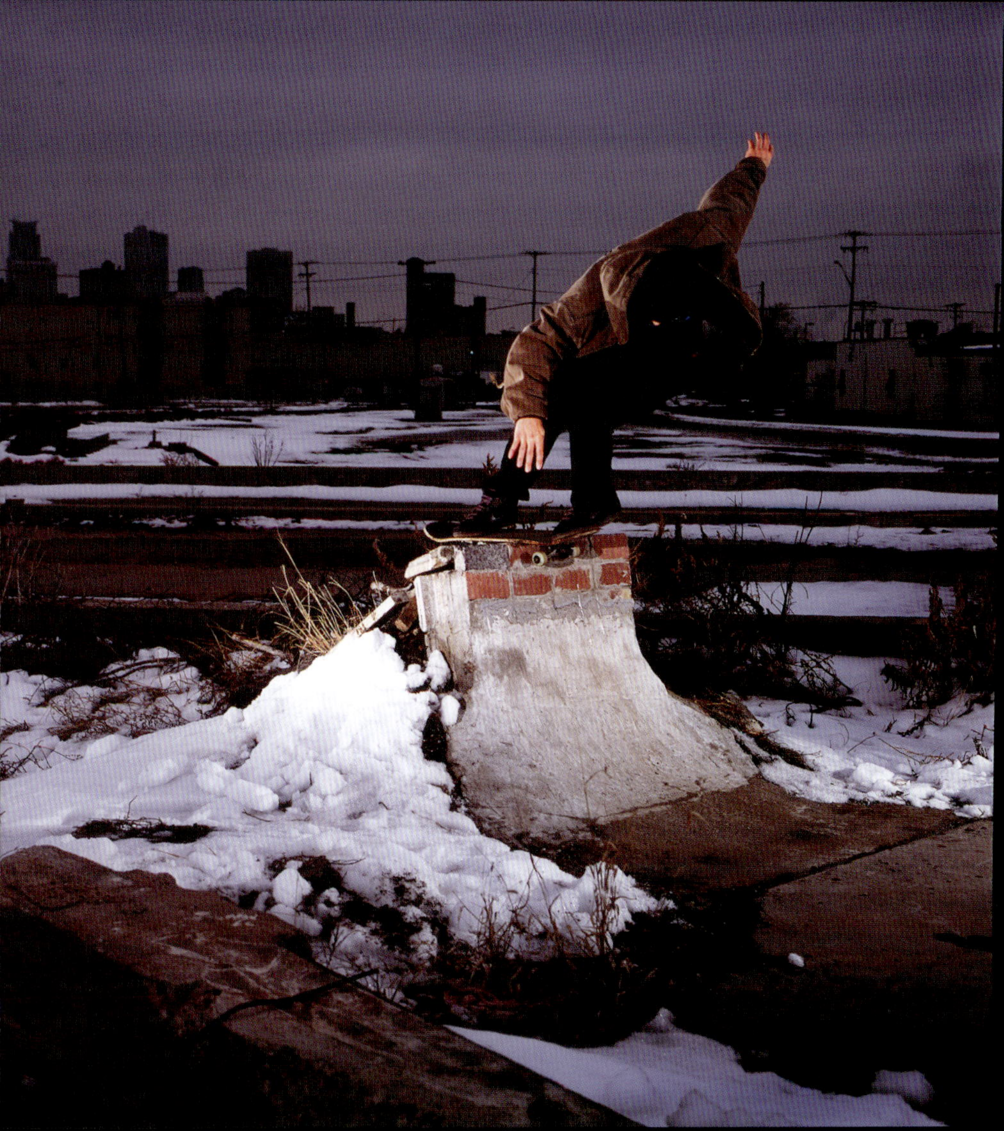

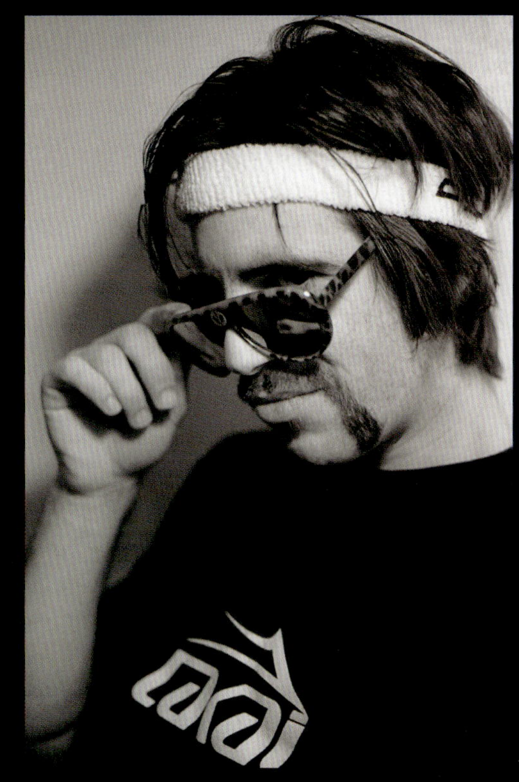

JACKSON ROMAN IOWA CITY, IA

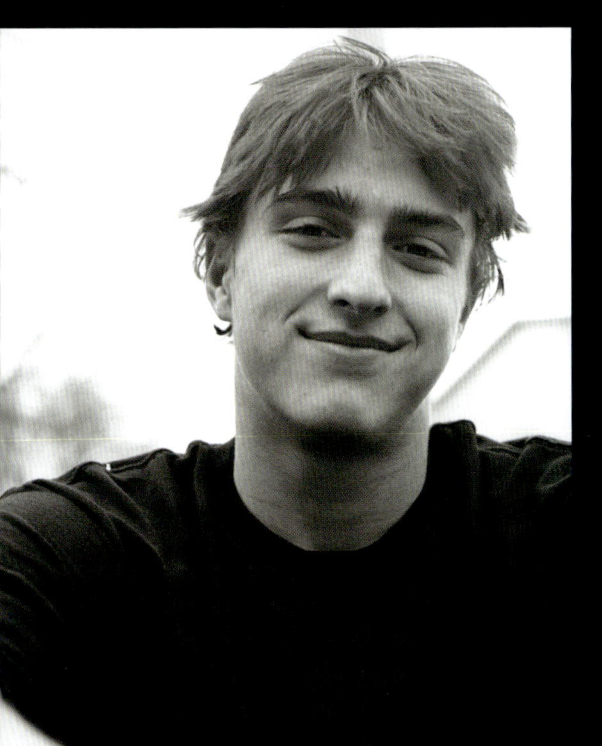

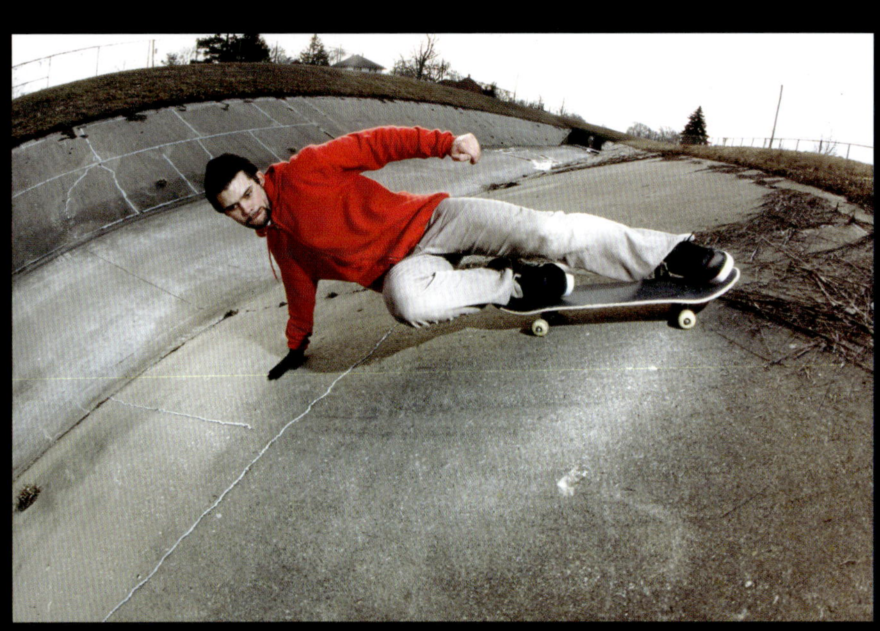

CHRIS VANDERWALL WATERLOO, IA

LUKE HUNT MINNEAPOLIS, MN

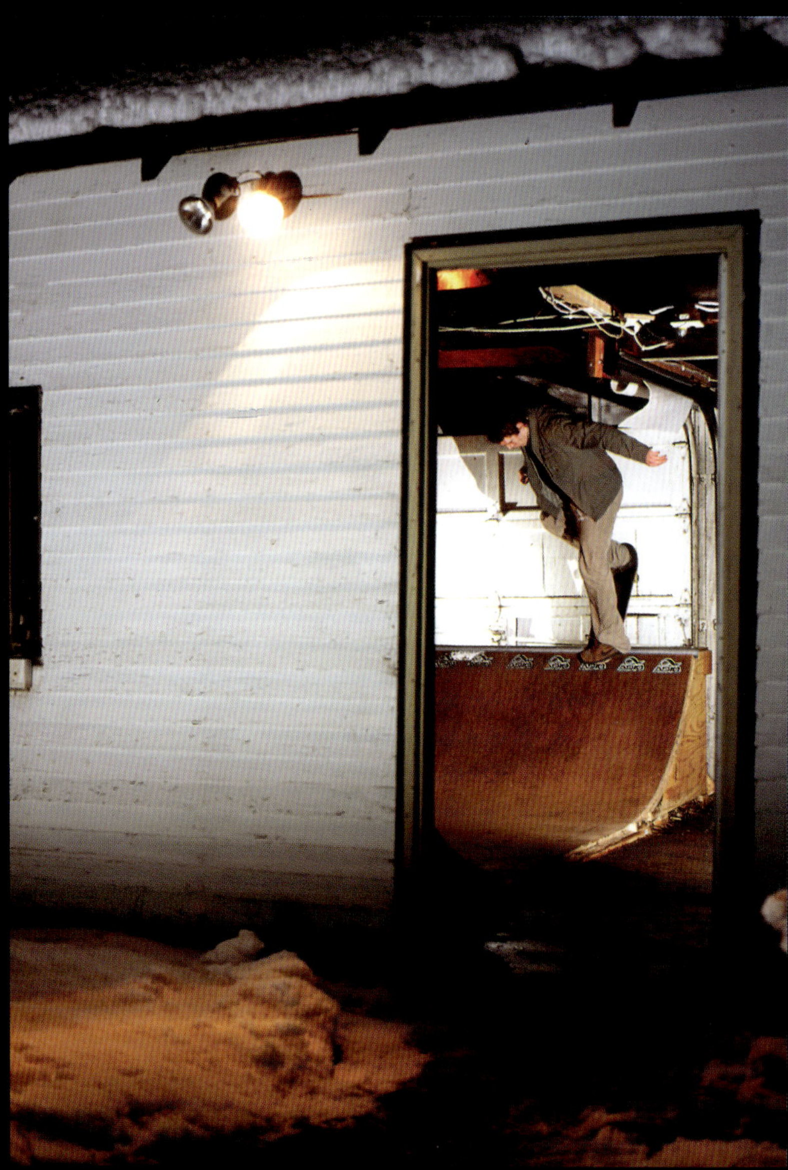

NEEN WILLIAMS CHICAGO, IL

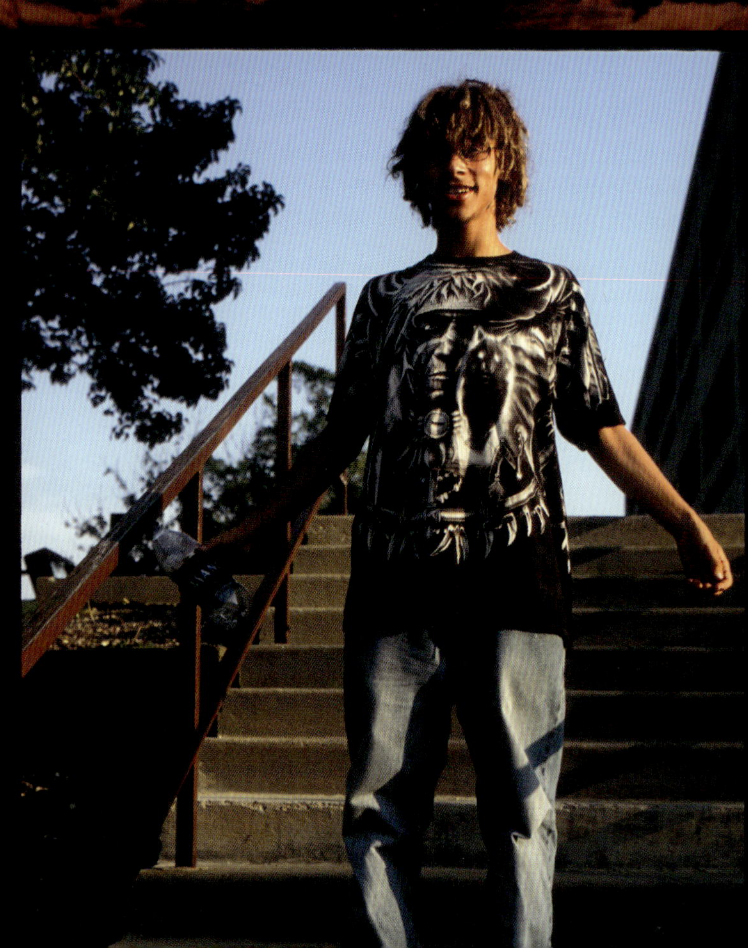

DONNIE BANDY IOWA CITY, IA

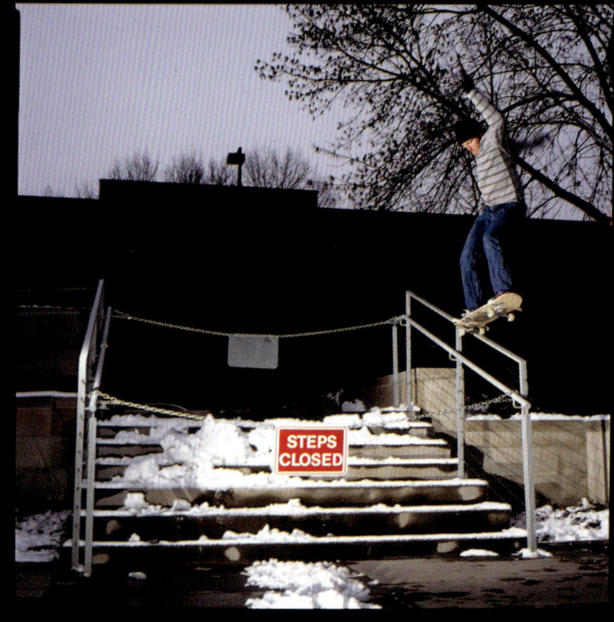

EDDIE KOLHENDORFER MINNEAPOLIS, MN

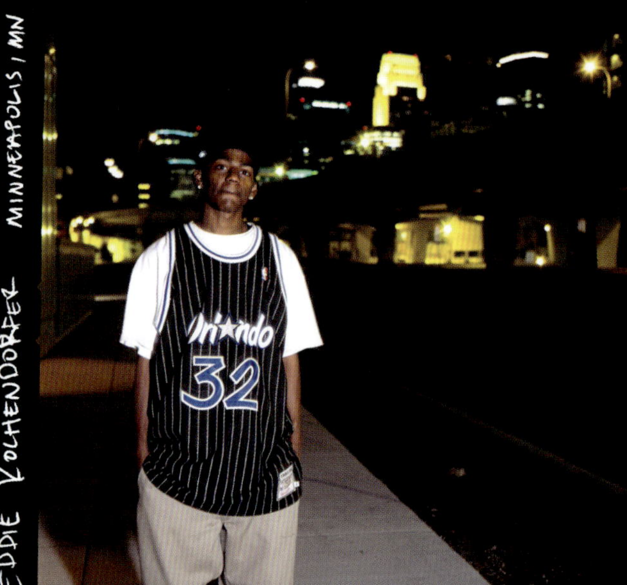

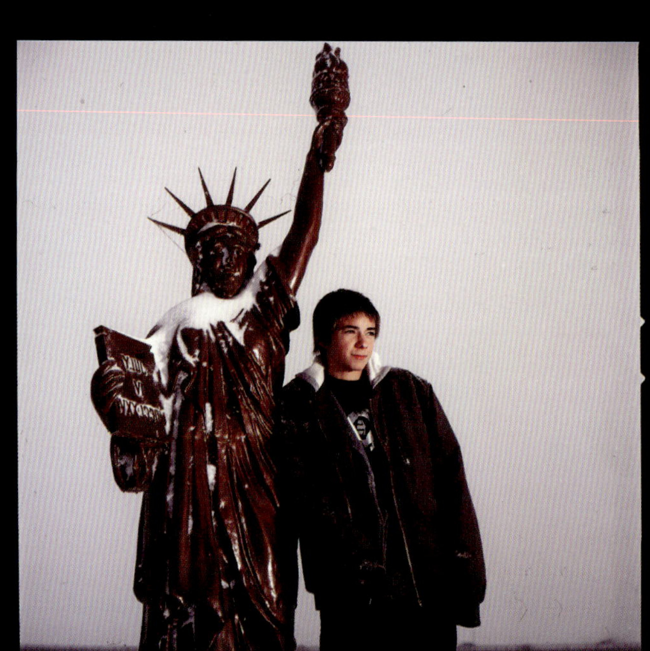

NICK RILEY CEDAR RAPIDS, IA

MITCH DETTMAN

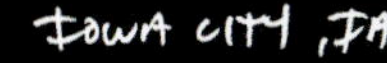

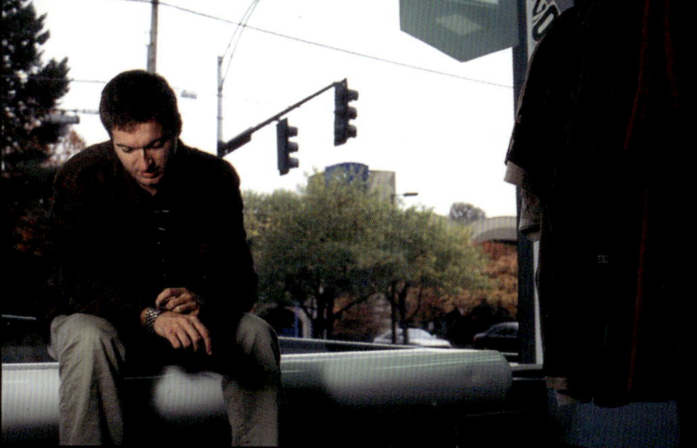

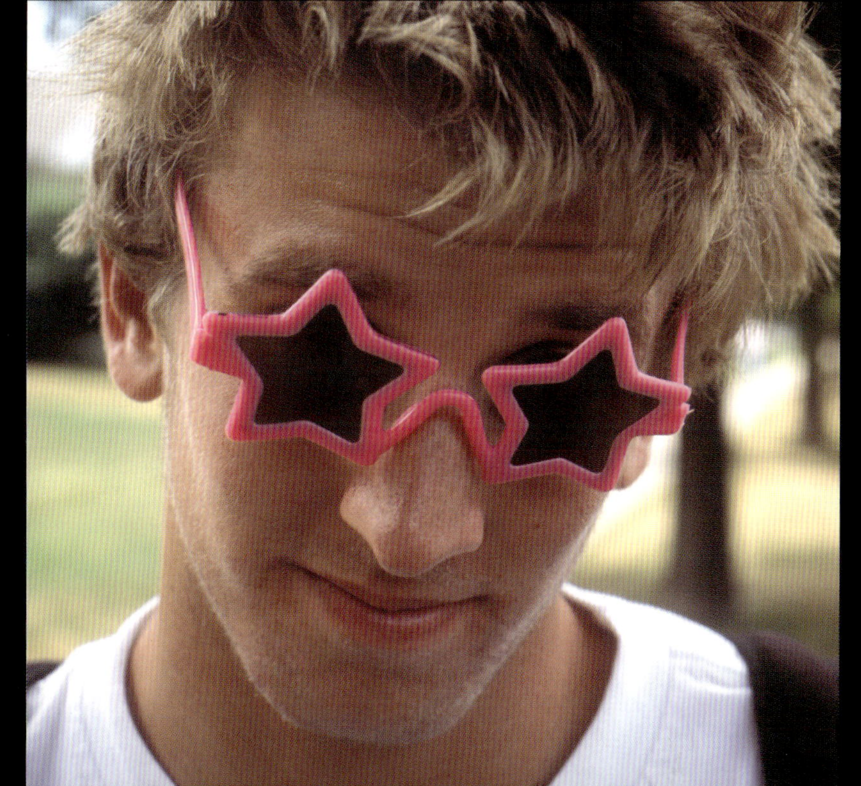

SPENCER PRATT MADISON, WI

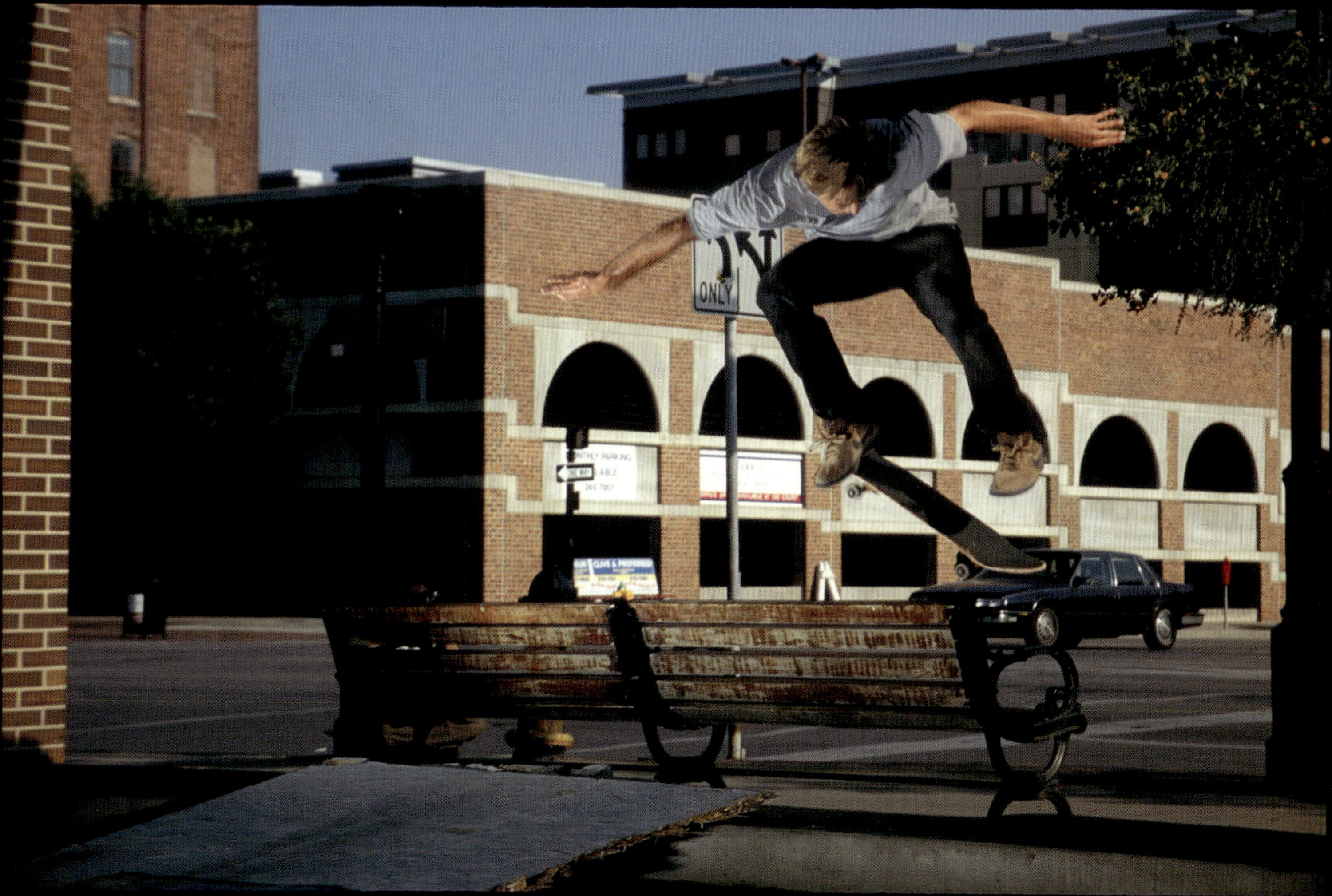

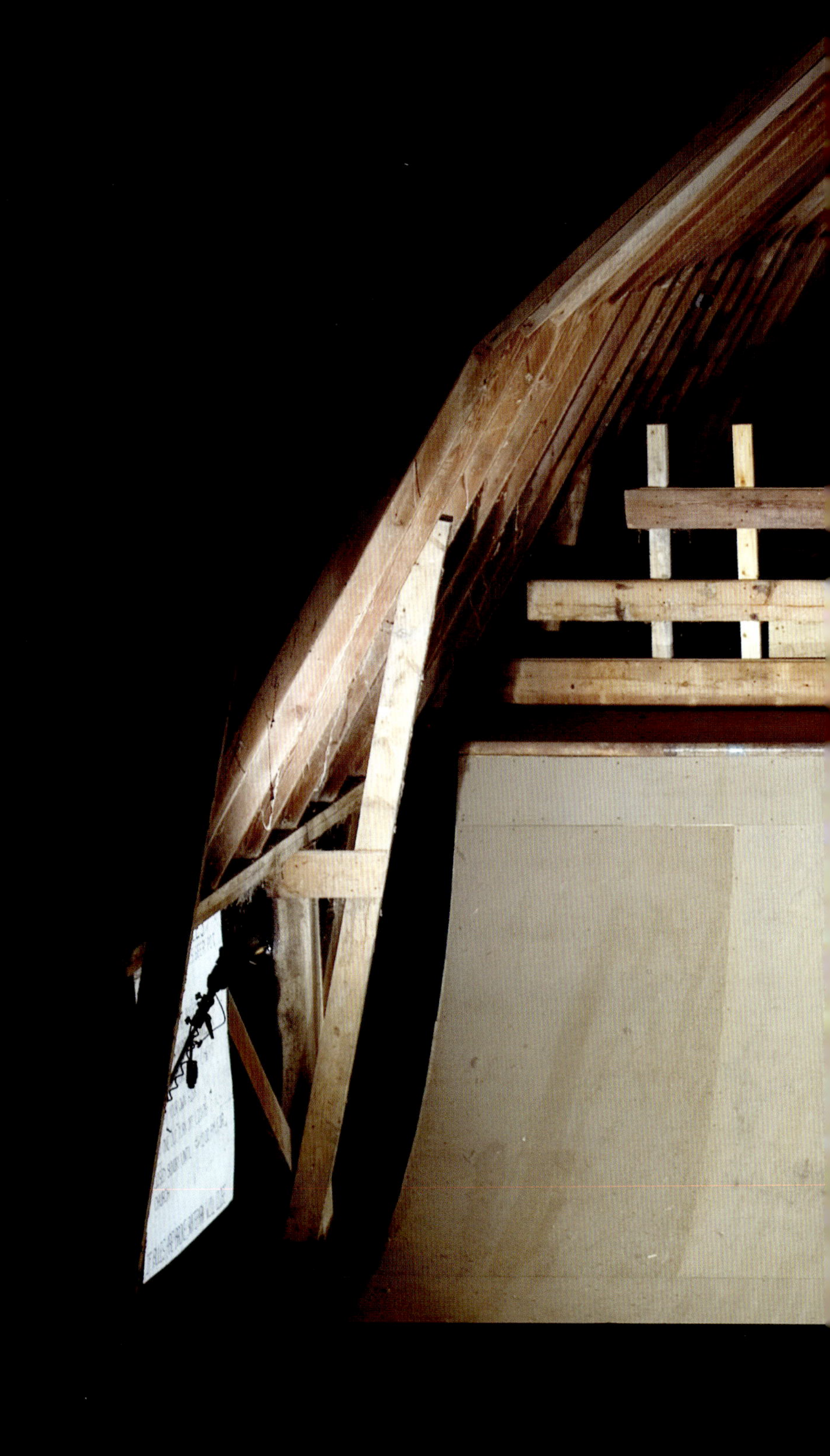

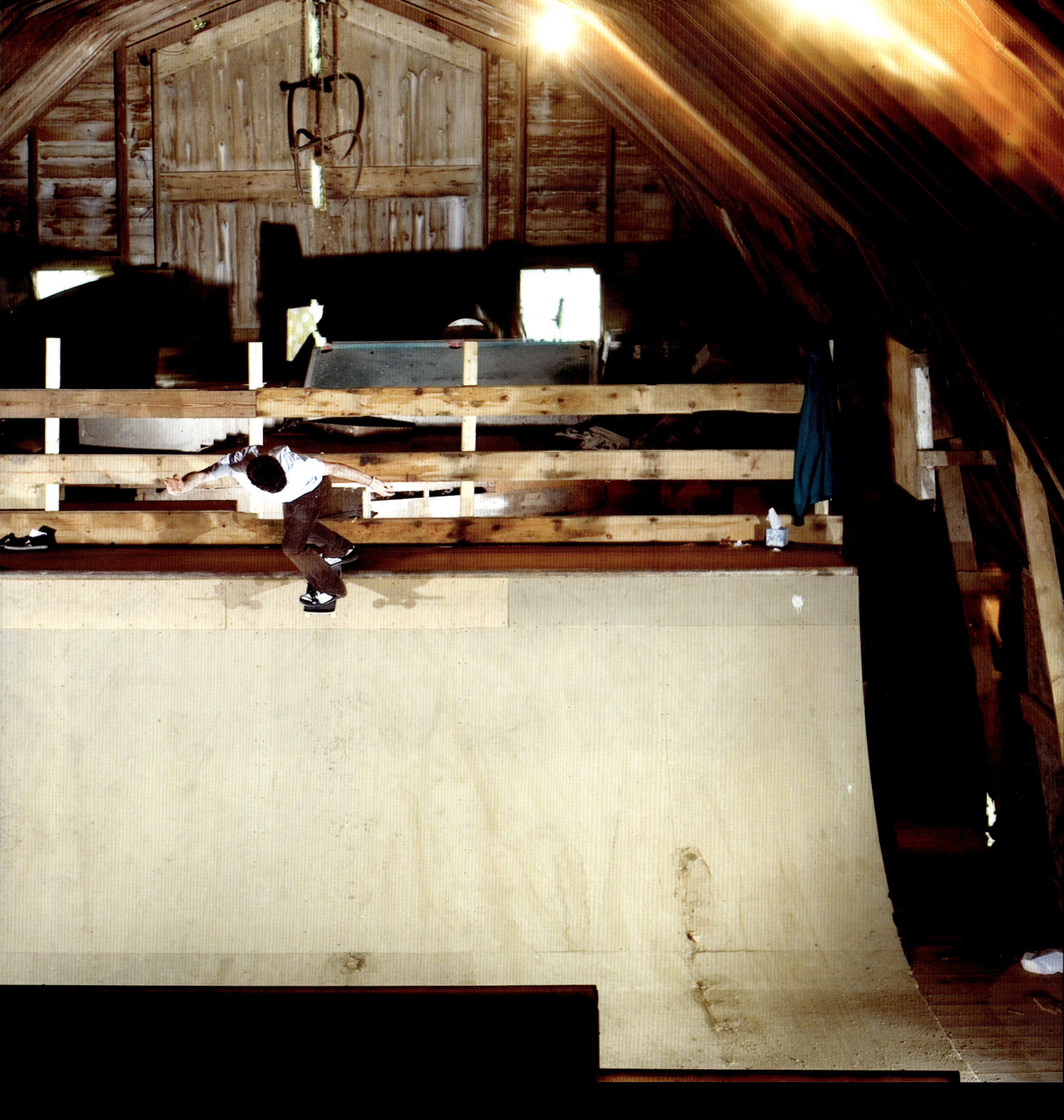

JACKSON ROMAN WASHINGTON, PA

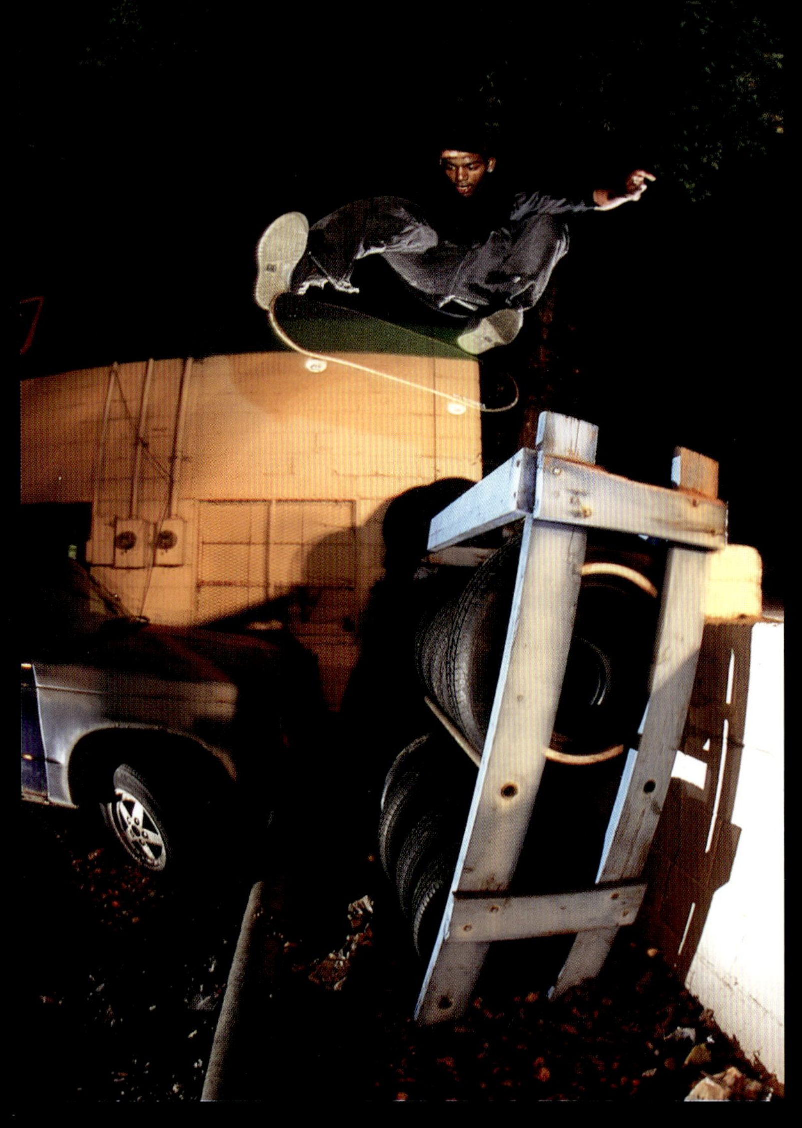

EDDIE KOLHENDORFER ST. PAUL, MN

NICK RILEY IOWA CITY, IA

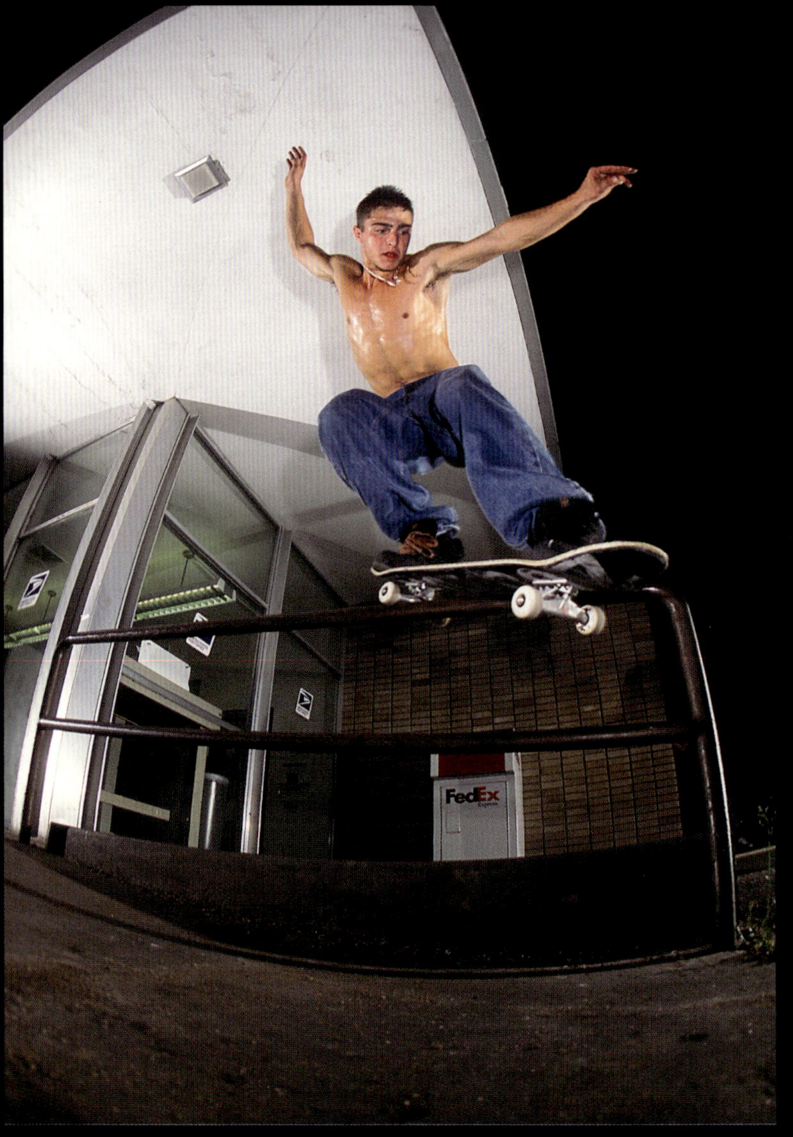

SEAN MALTO WINNIPEG, CANADA

BRAD HENDRICKSON CHICAGO, IL

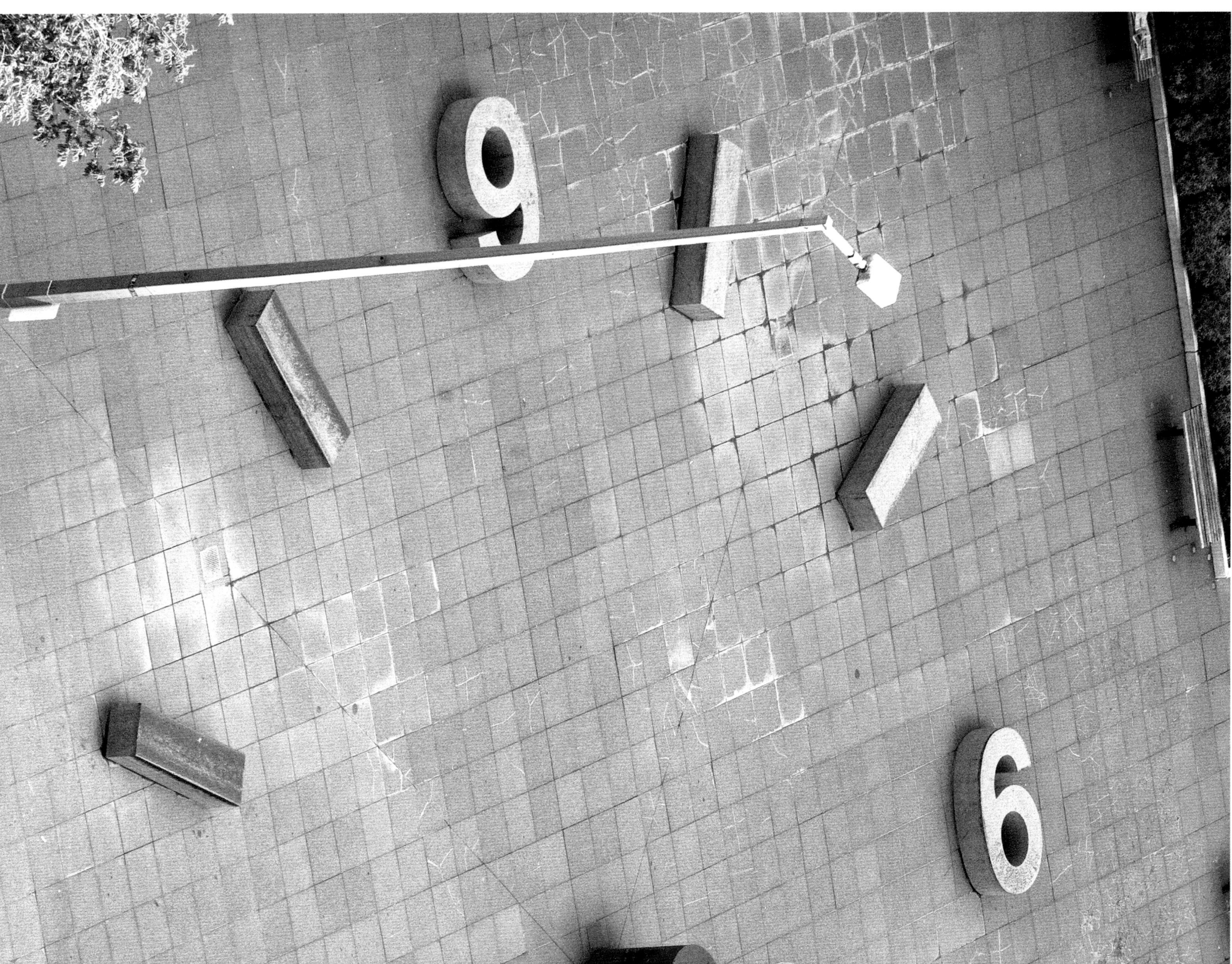

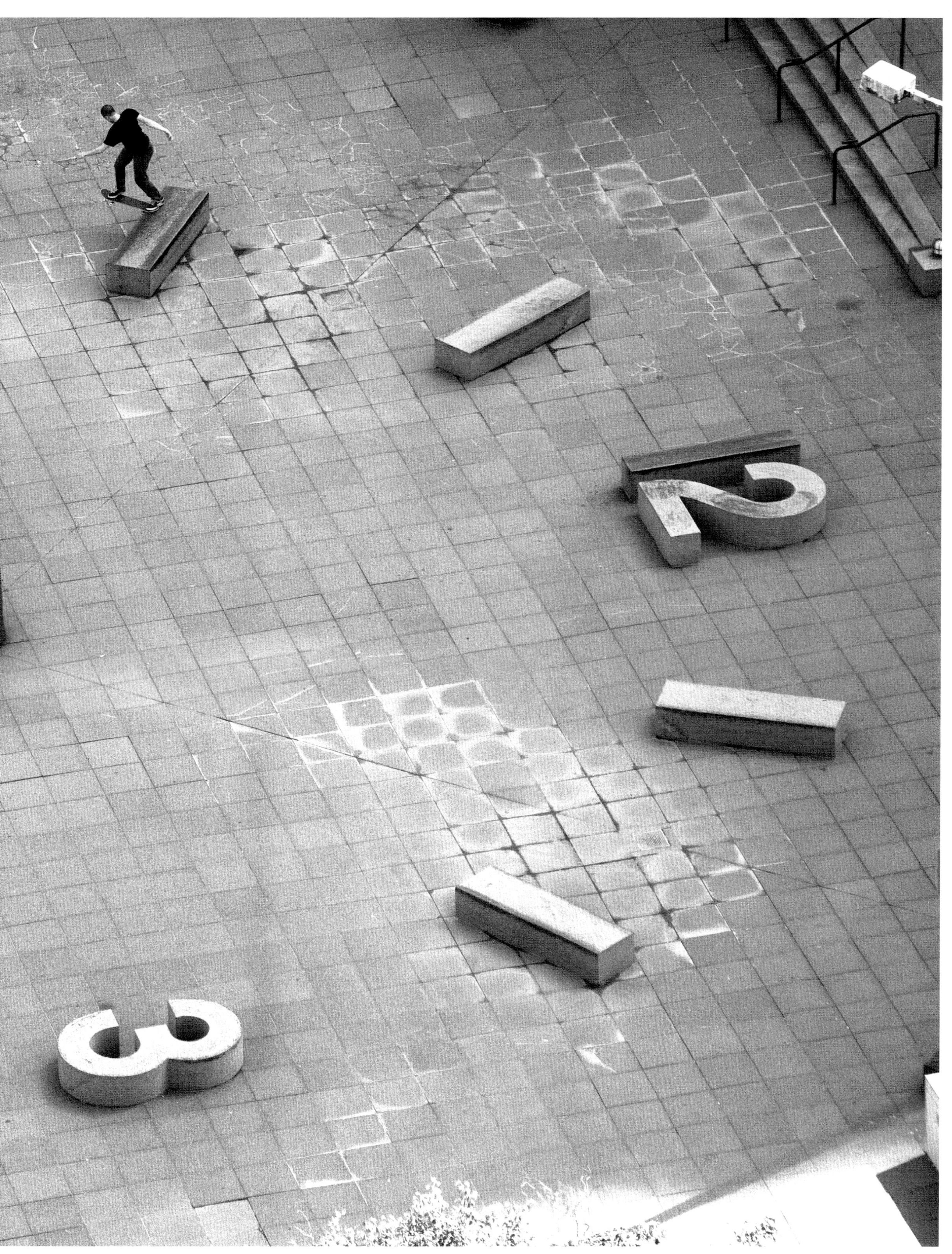

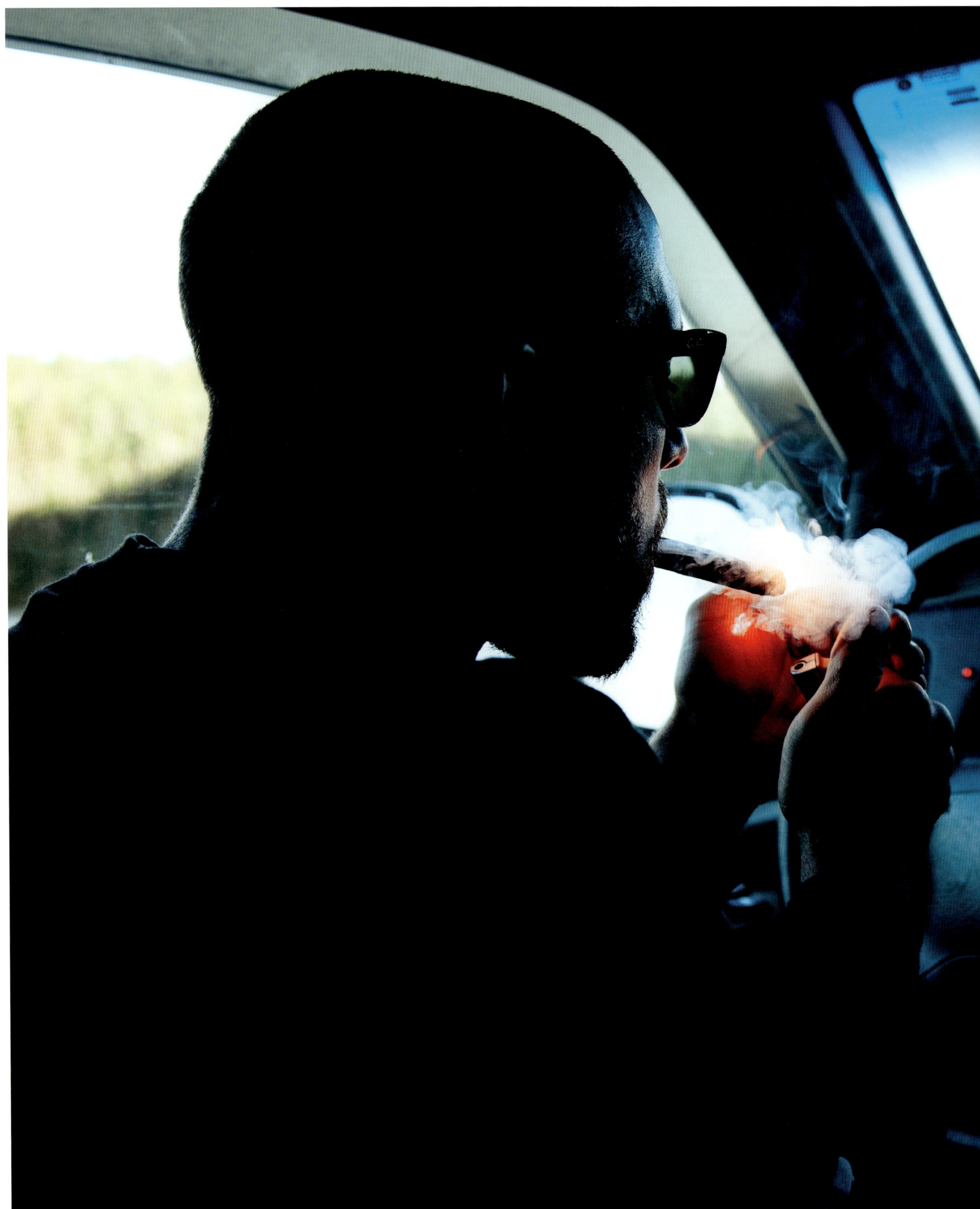

JOE TOOKMANIAN NOVA SCOTIA, CANADA

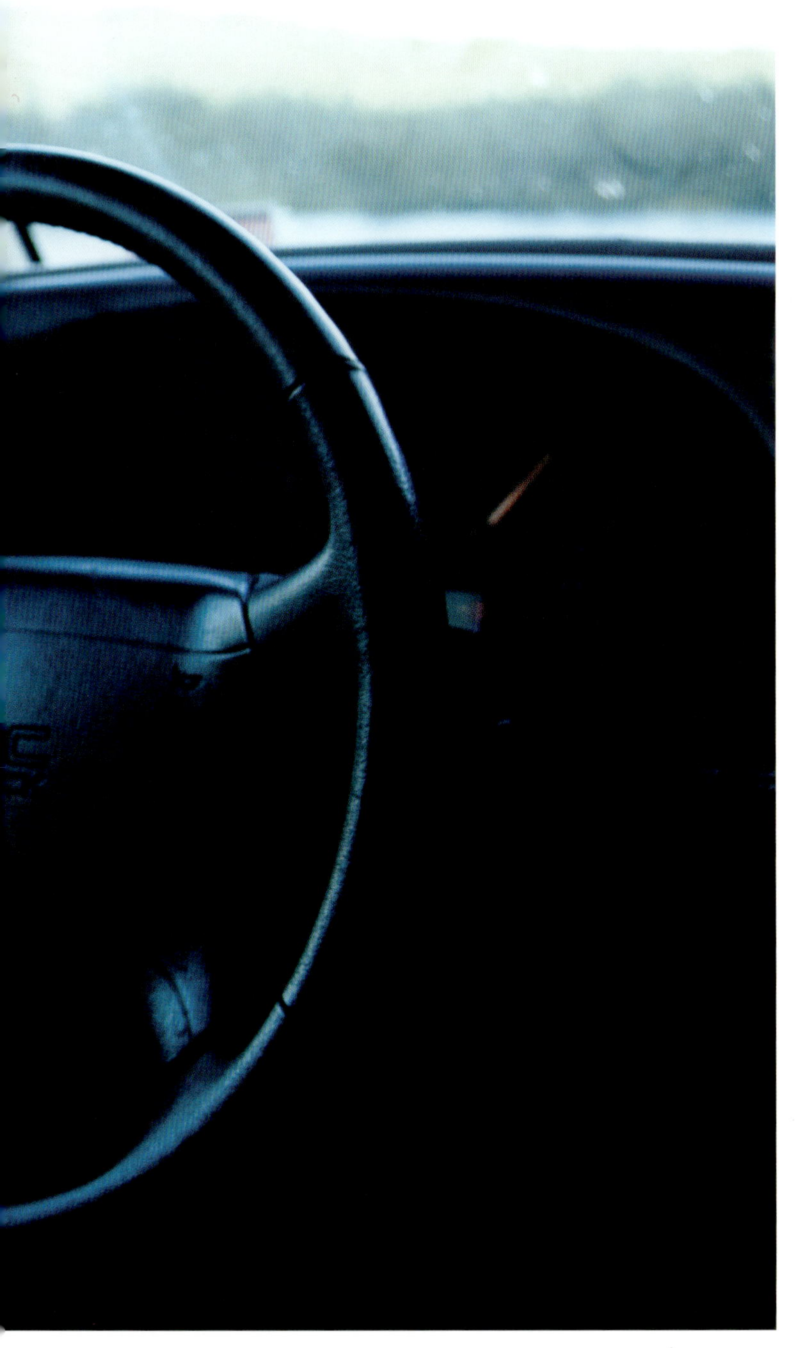

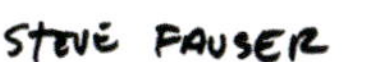

STEVE FAUSER HELL, MI

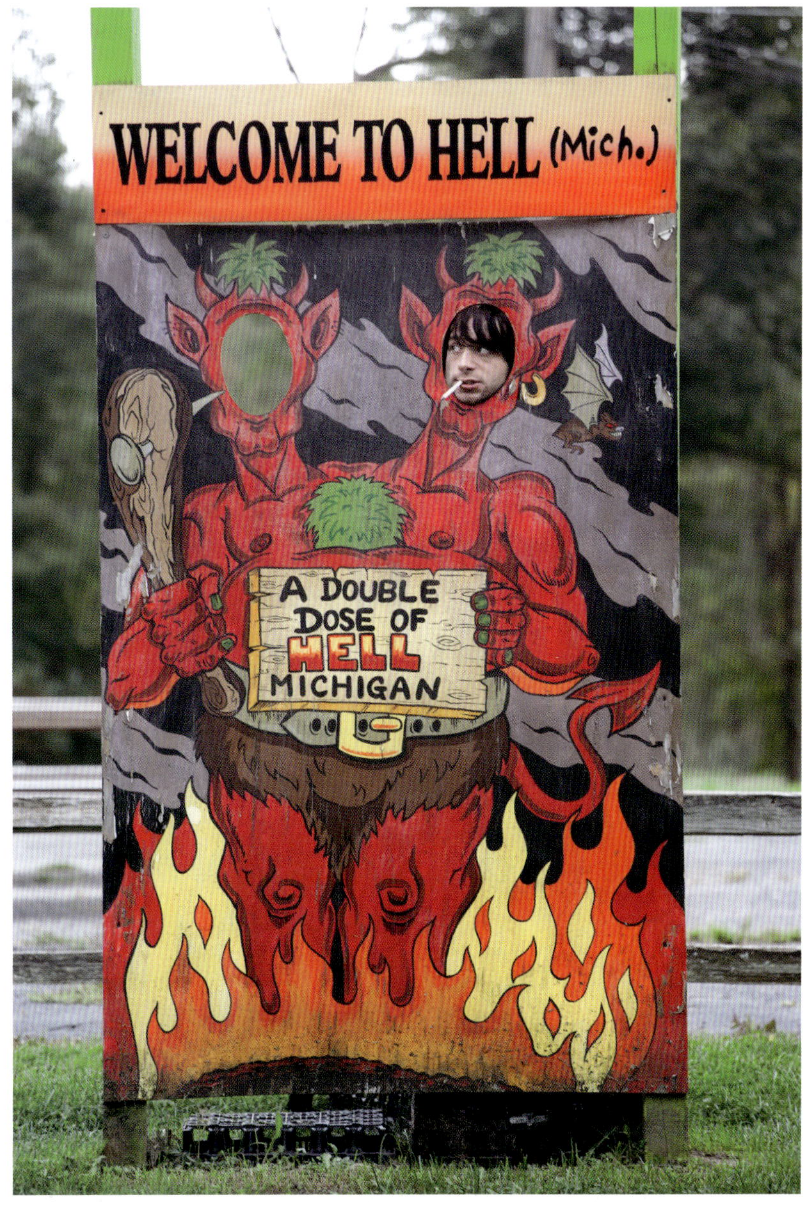

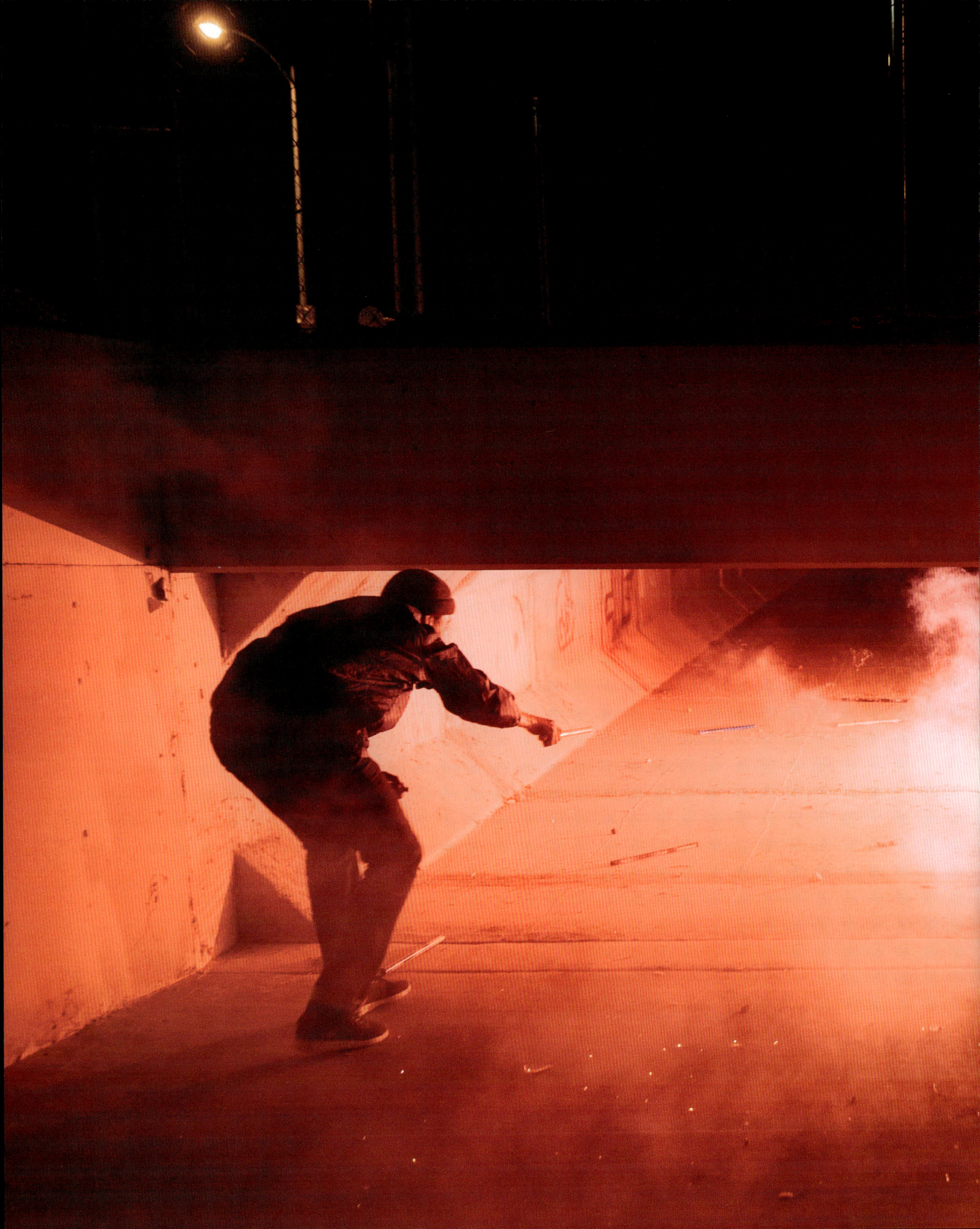

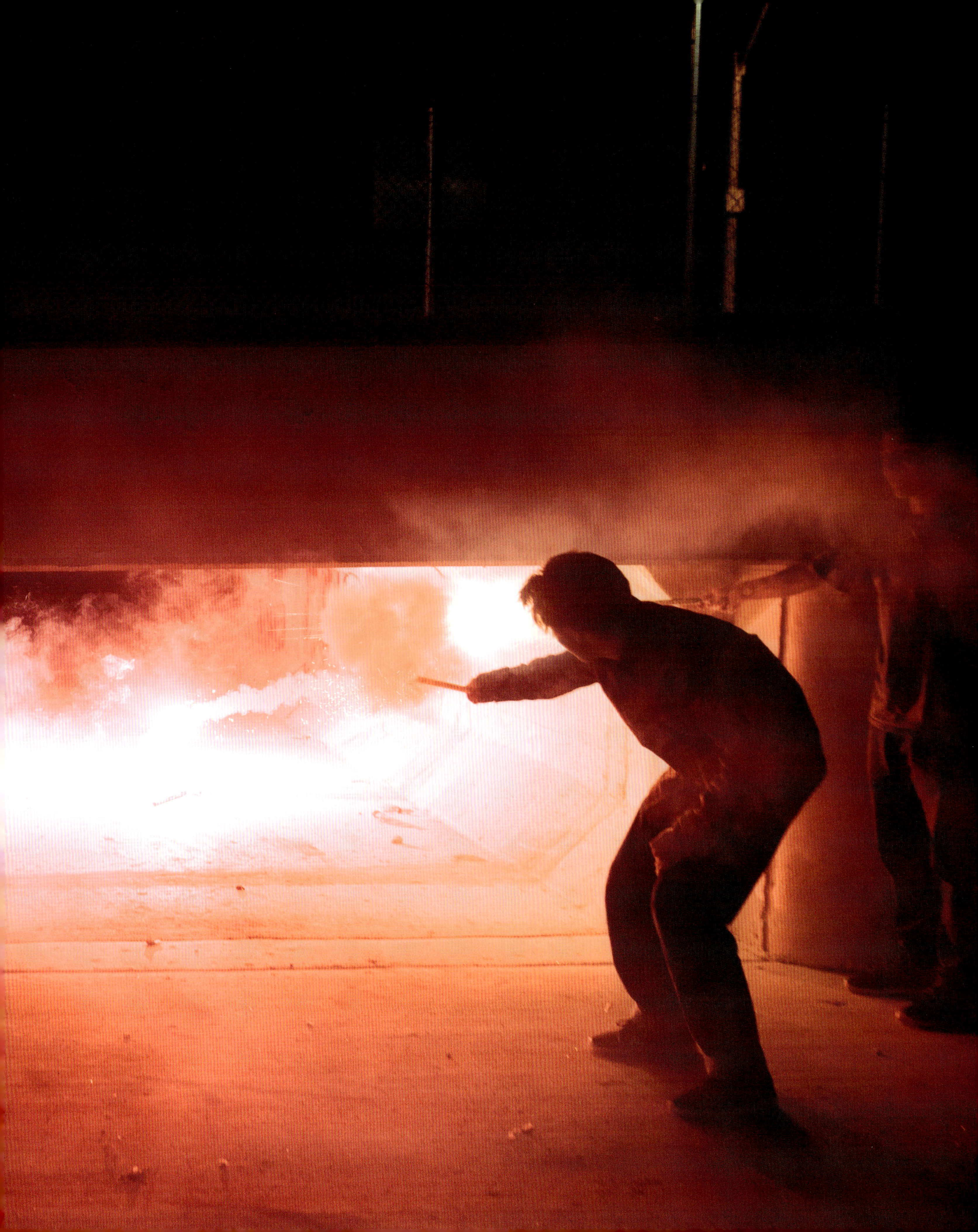

SEAN MALTO WYOMING

MIKEY TAYLOR PHOENIX, AZ

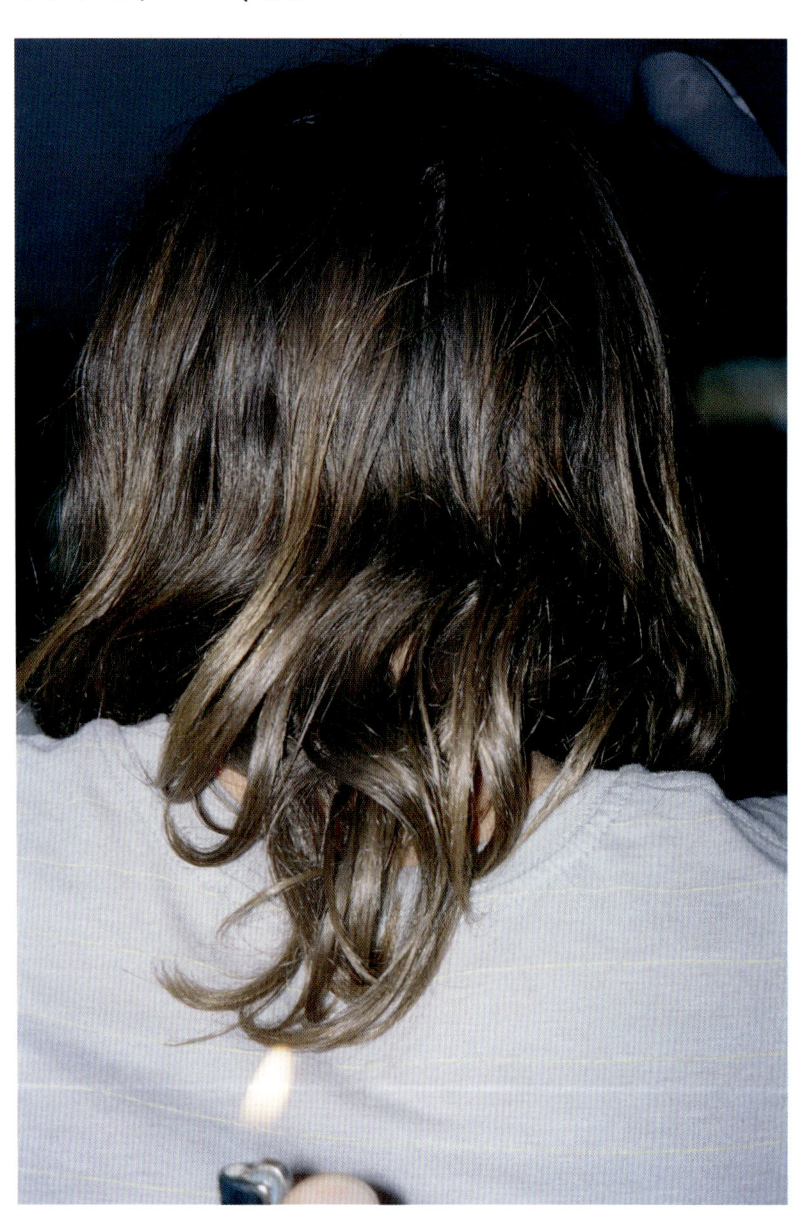

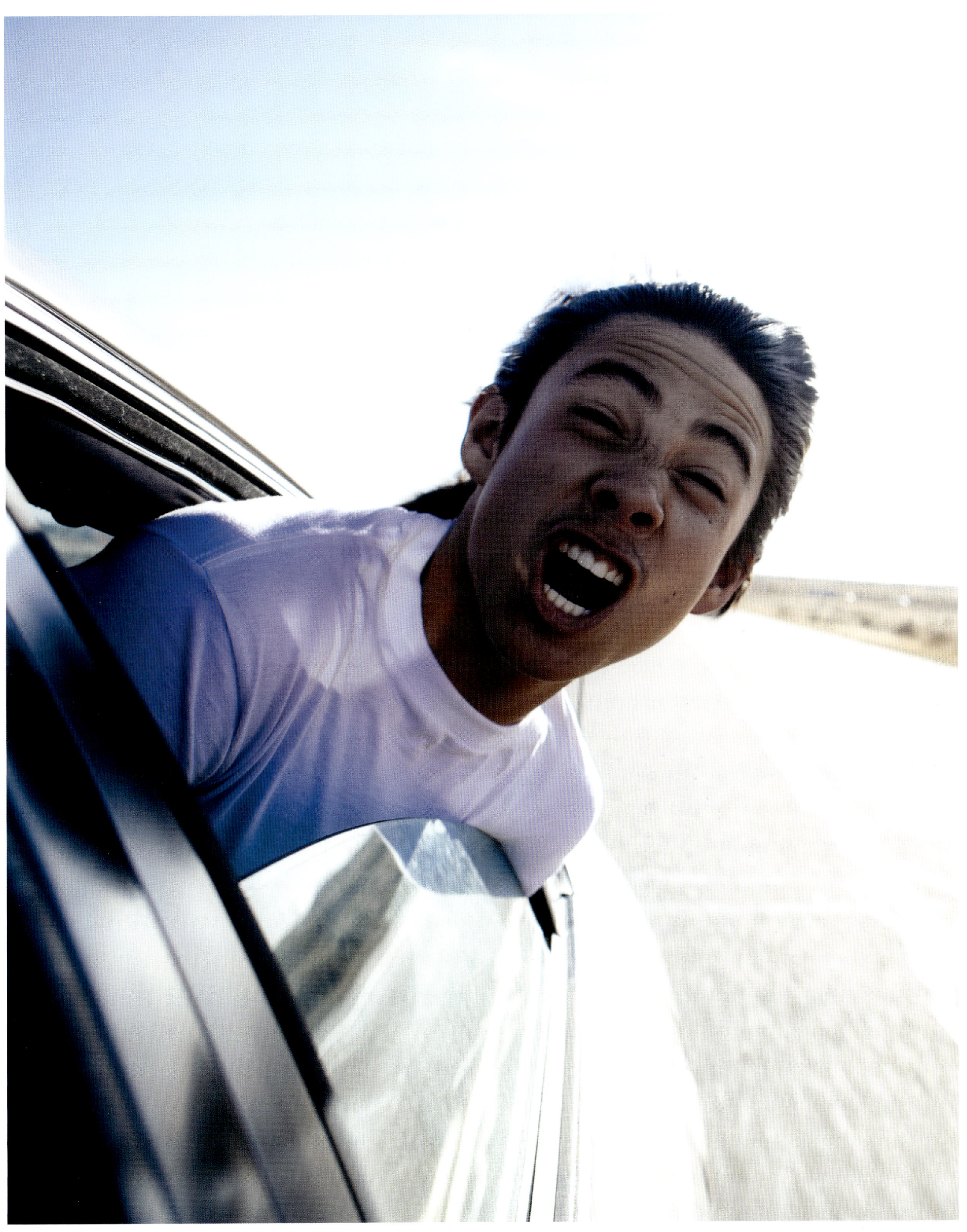

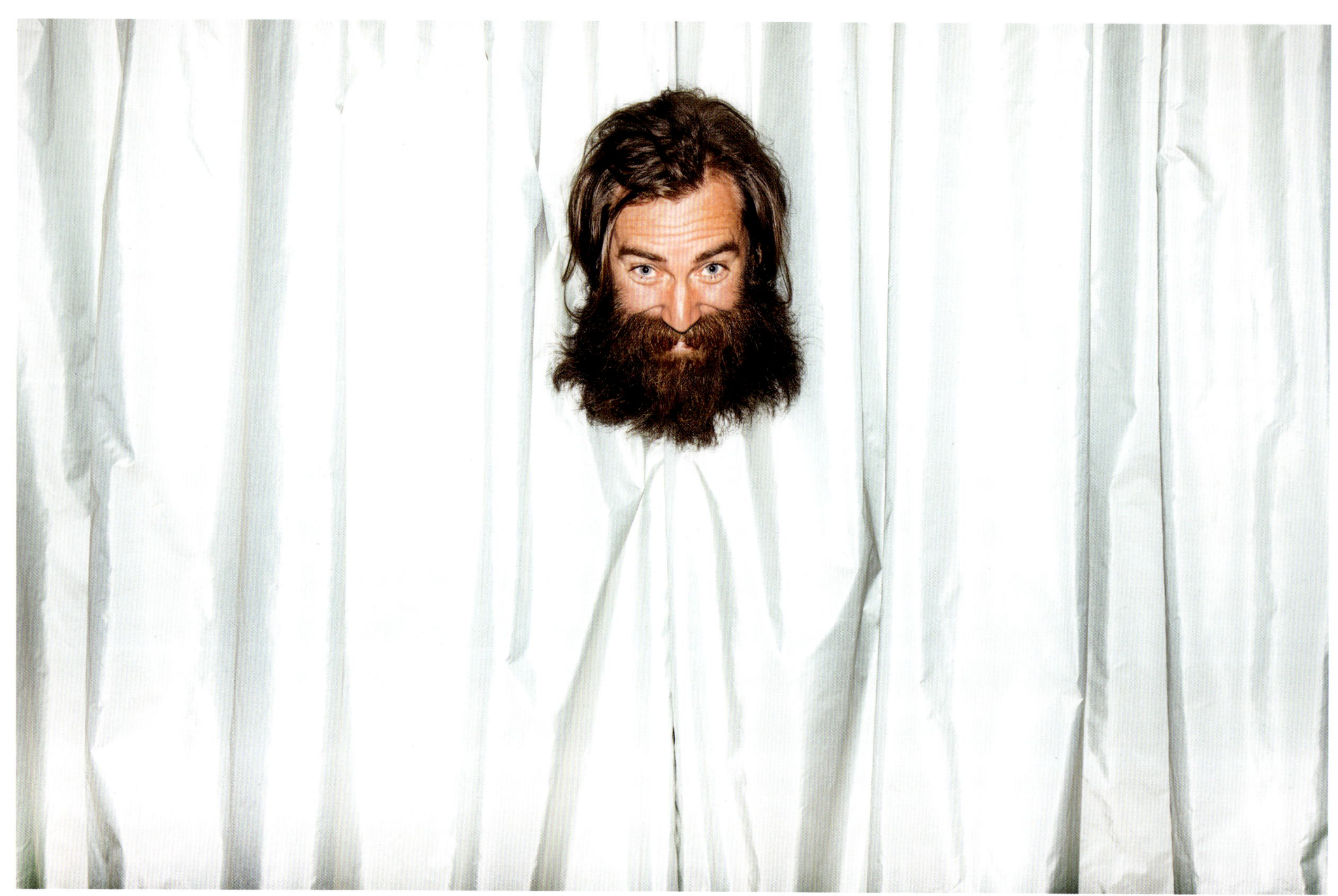

CHRIS HASLAM PARIS, FRANCE

RYAN PEARCE PARIS, FRANCE

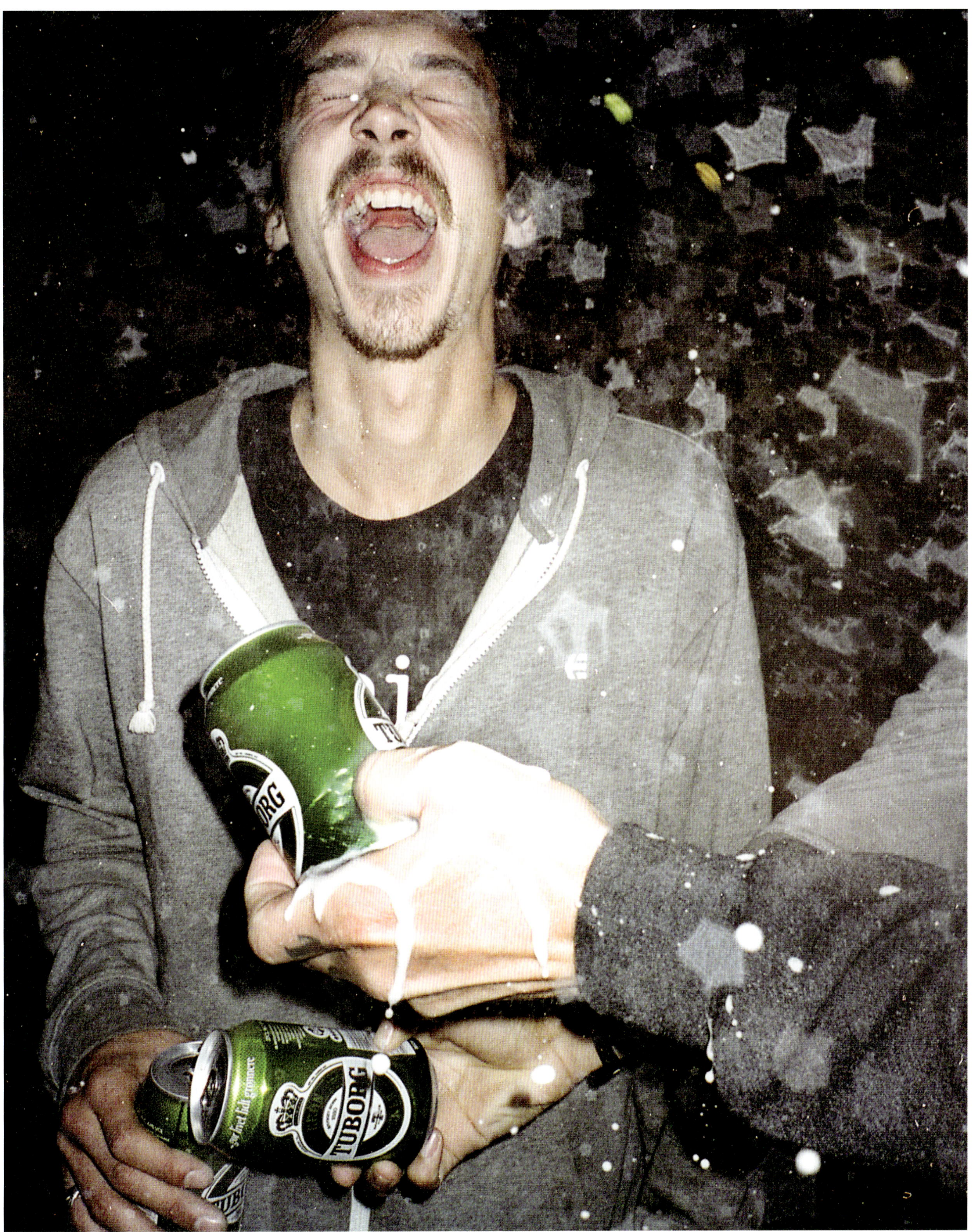
TUBORG

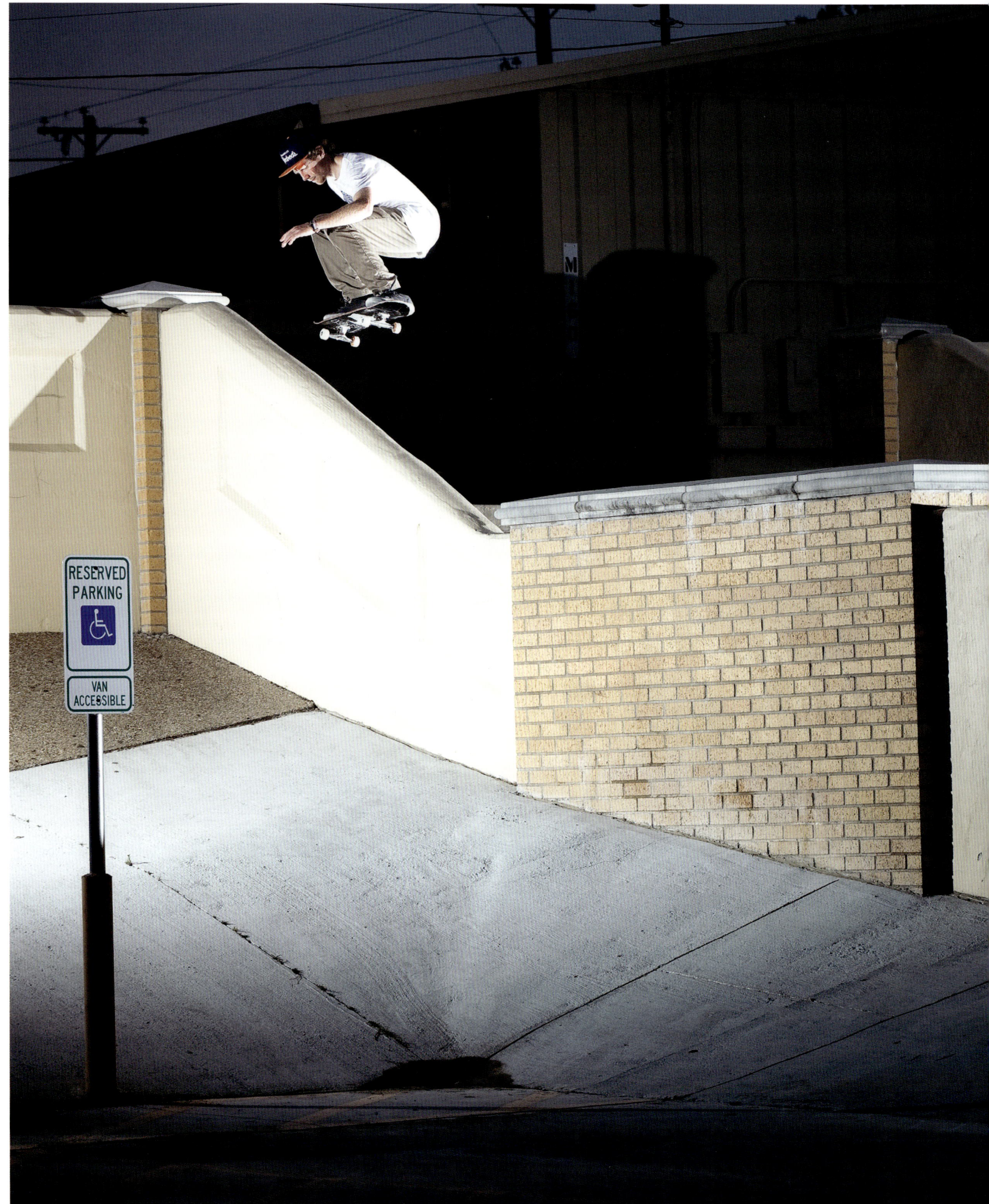
RESERVED
PARKING
VAN
ACCESSIBLE

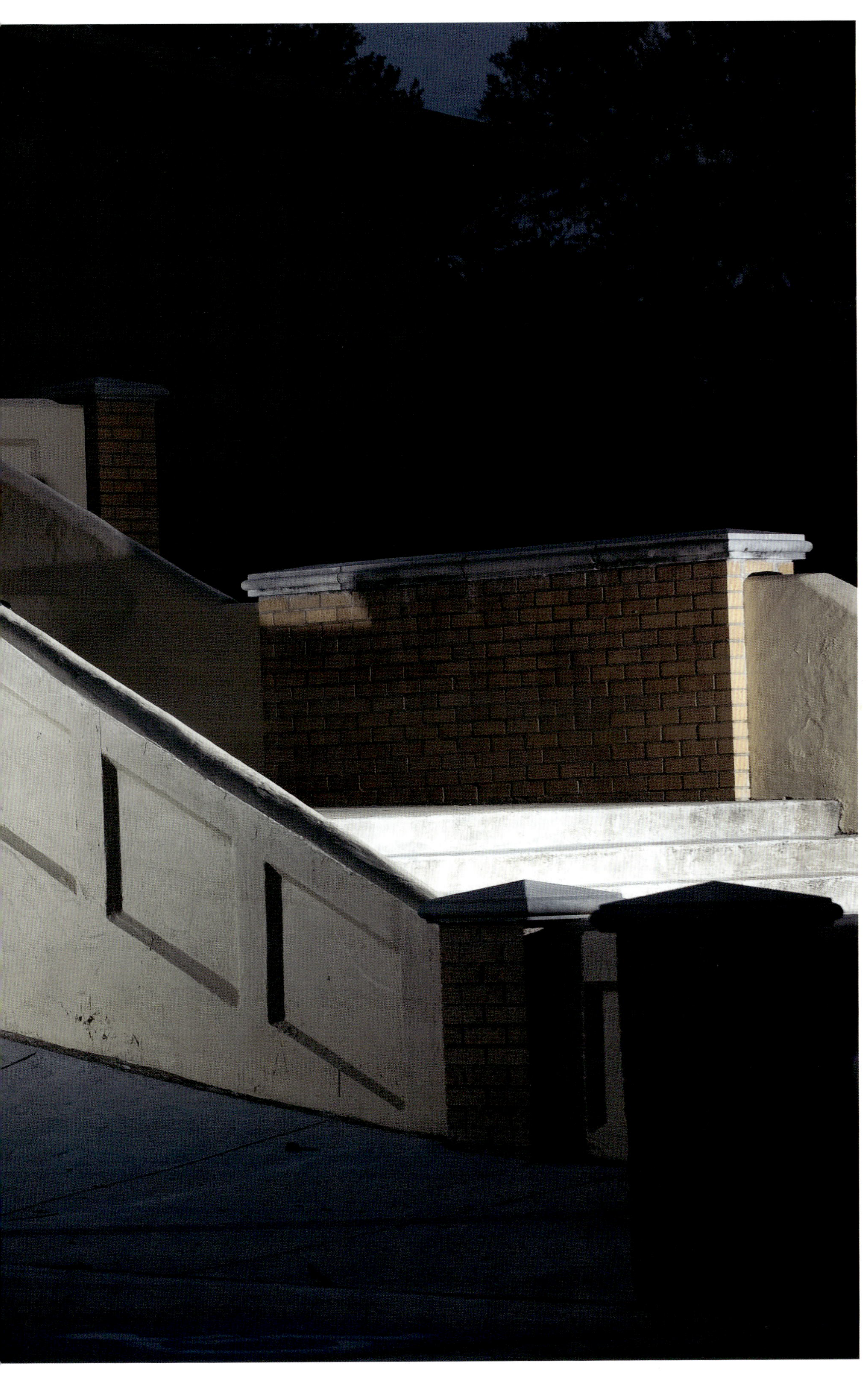

BARNEY PAGE ATLANTA, GA

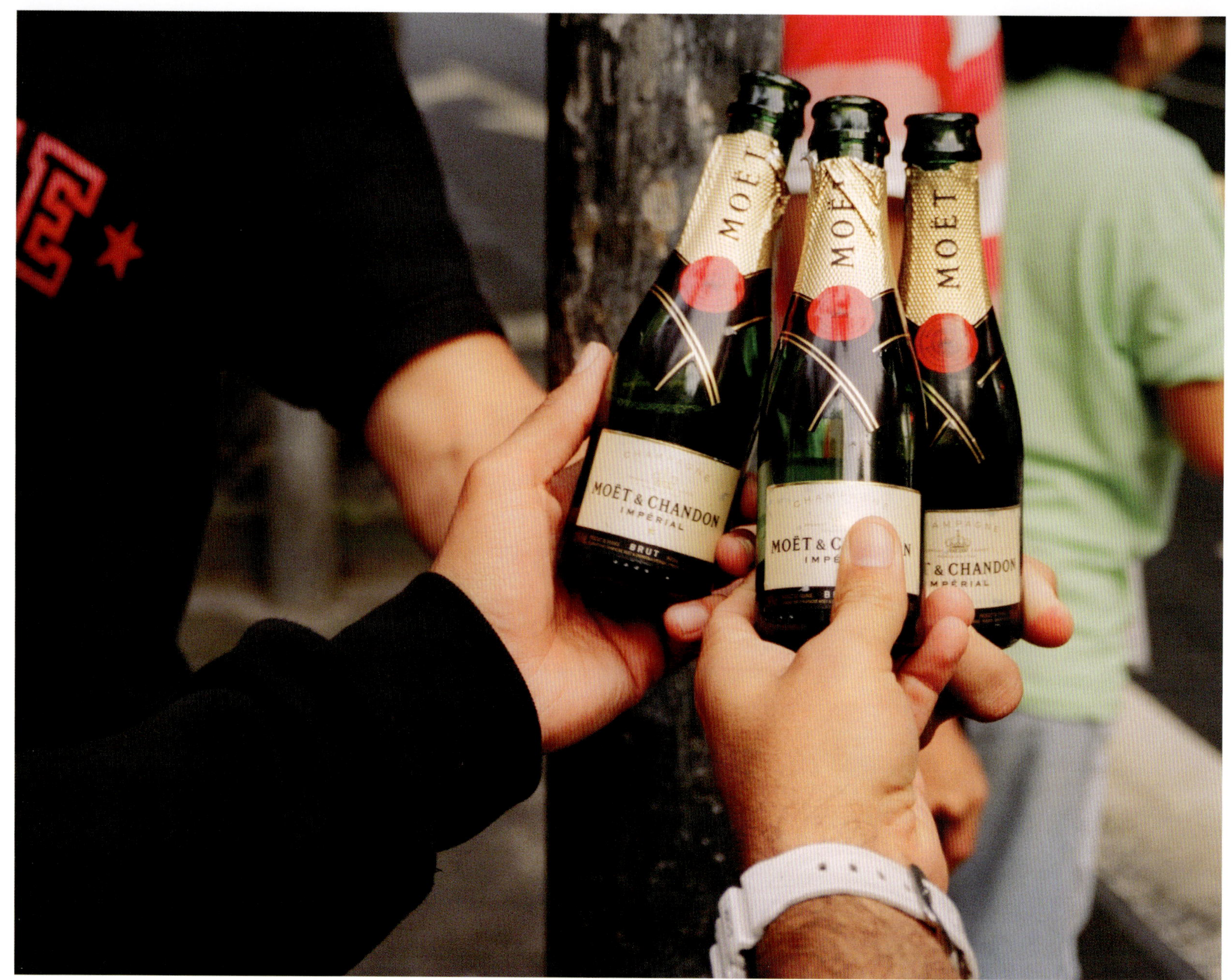

CHAMPS RIO, BRAZIL

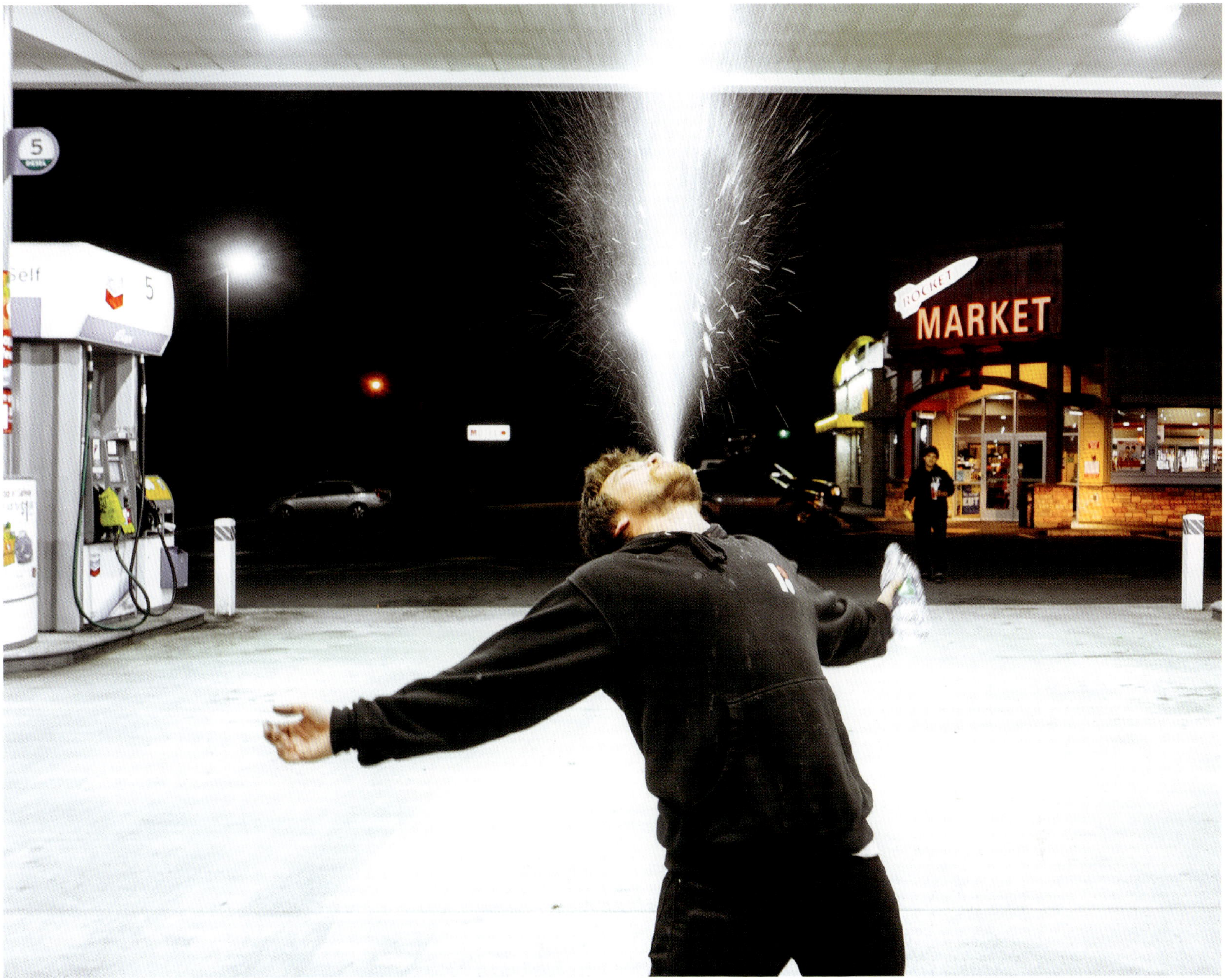

DAVID REYES OKC, OK

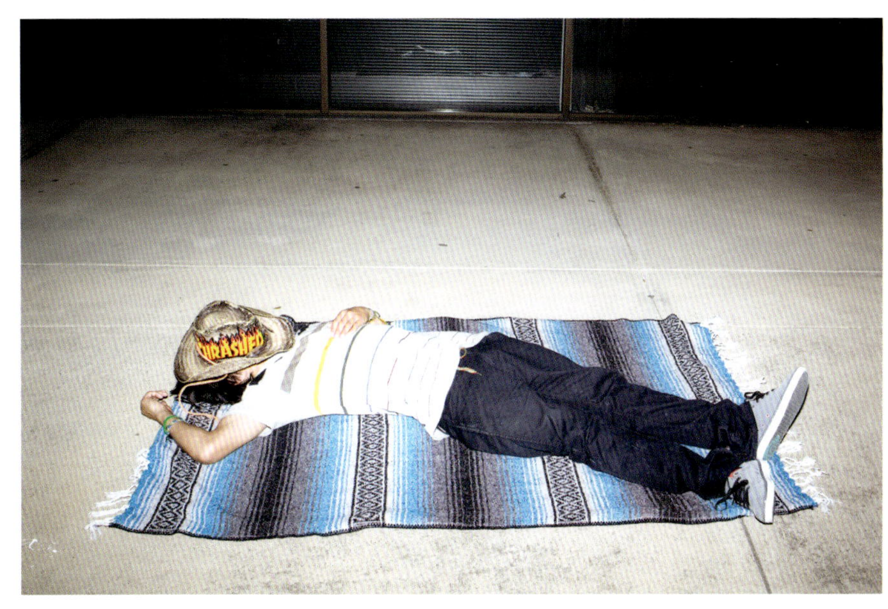

SEAN MALTO OKC, OK

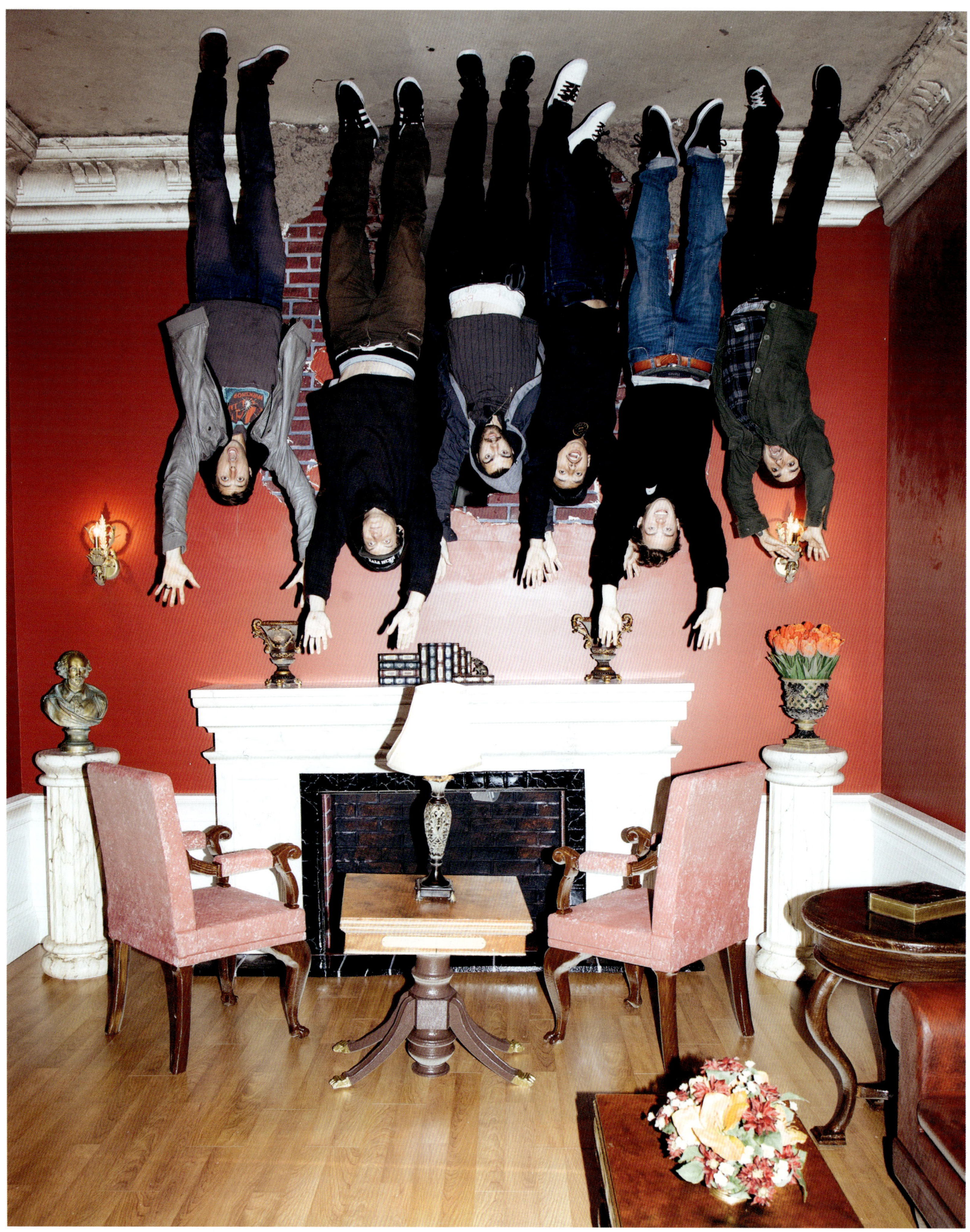

CLINT WALKER WISCONSIN DELLS, WI

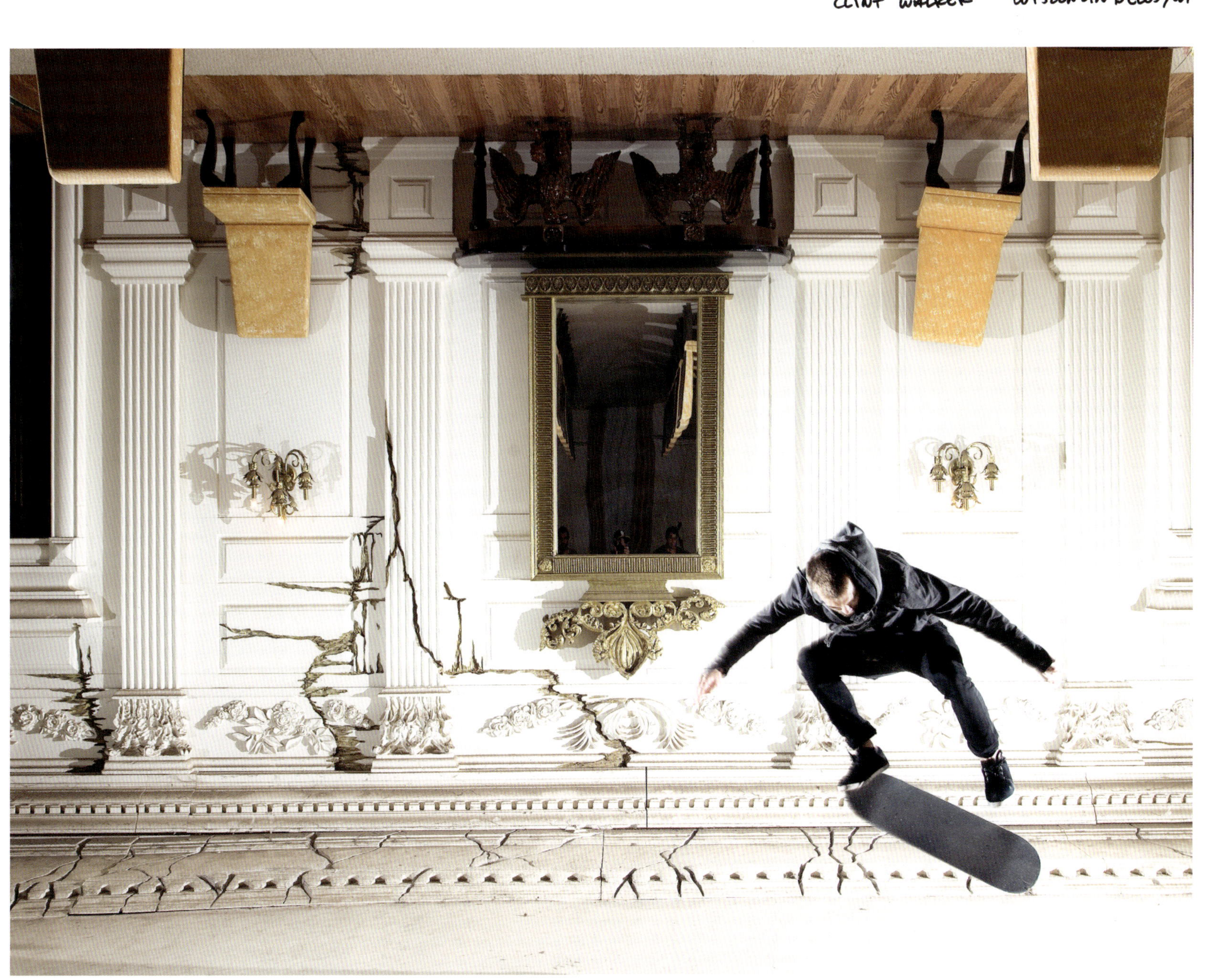

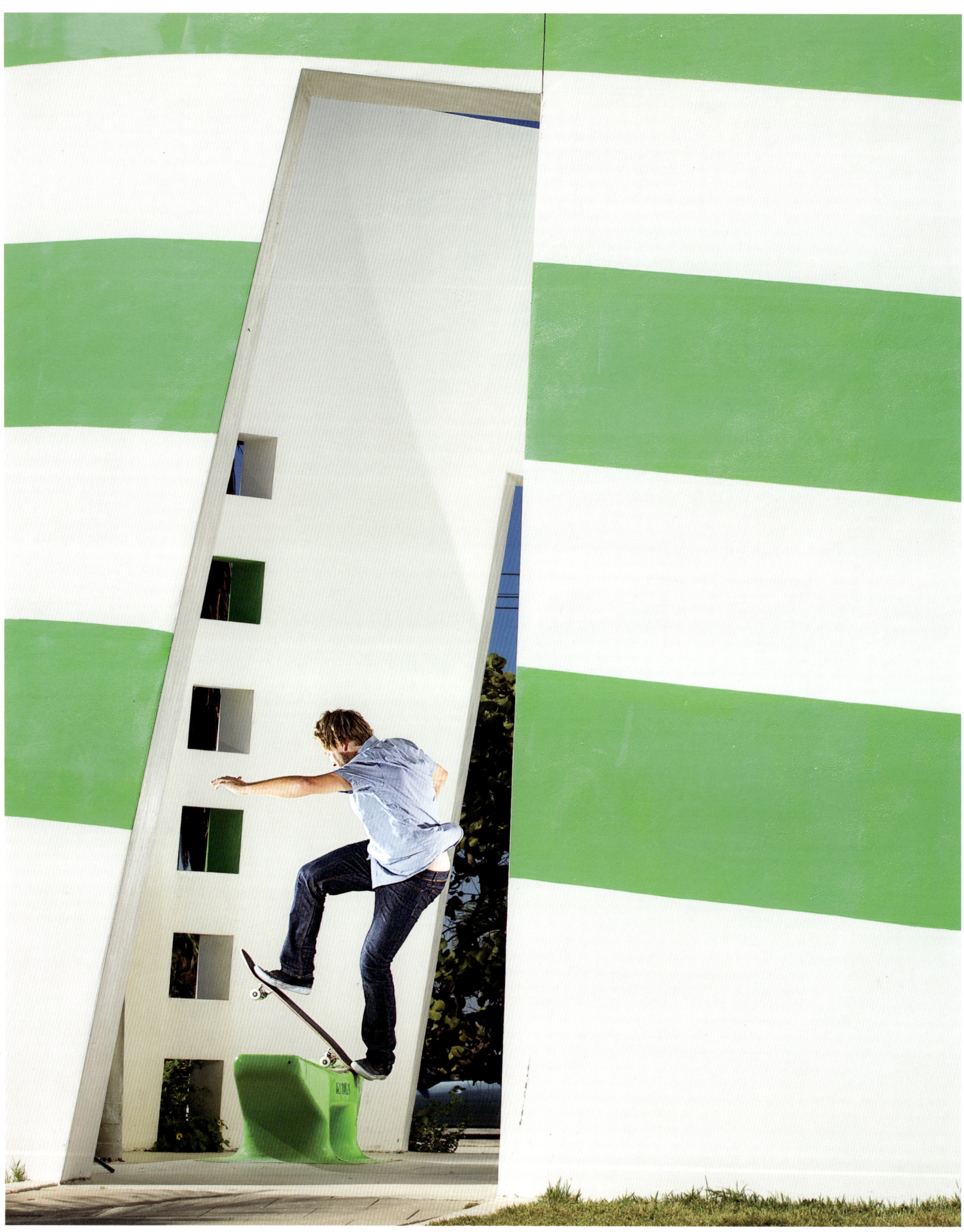

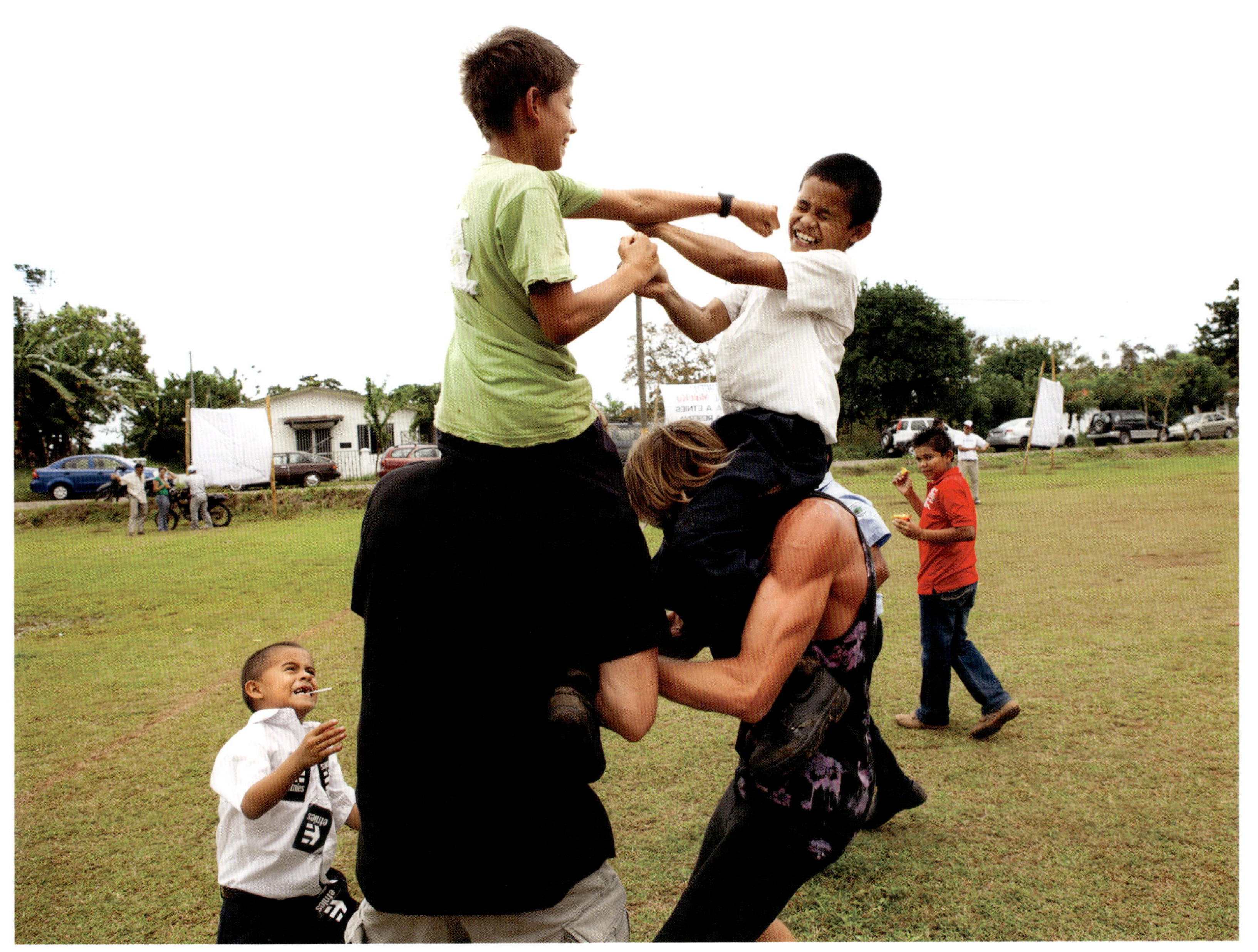

KIDS FIGHTING COSTA RICA

KYLE LEEPER MIAMI, FL

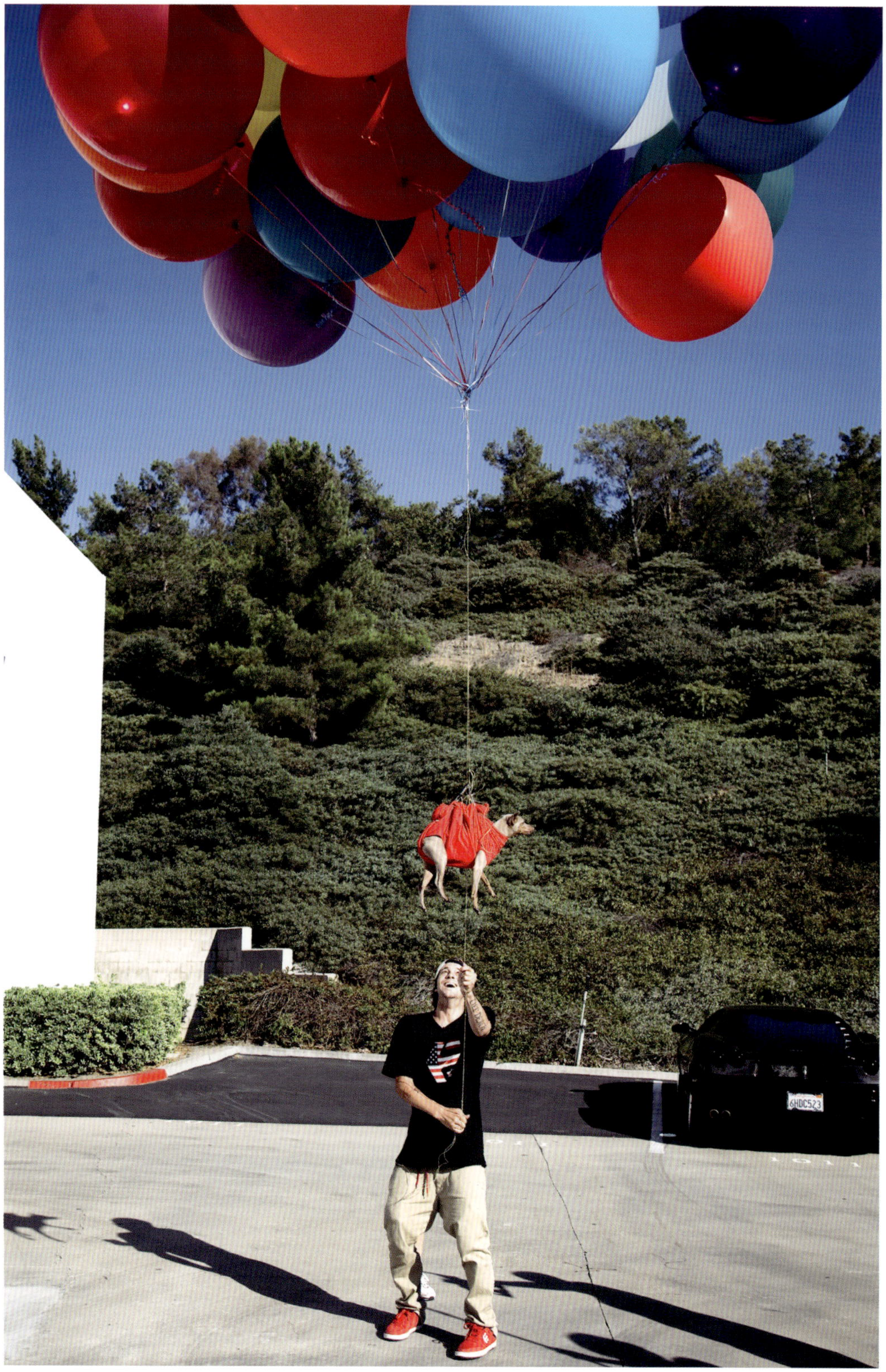

RYAN SHECKLER LAKE FORREST, CA

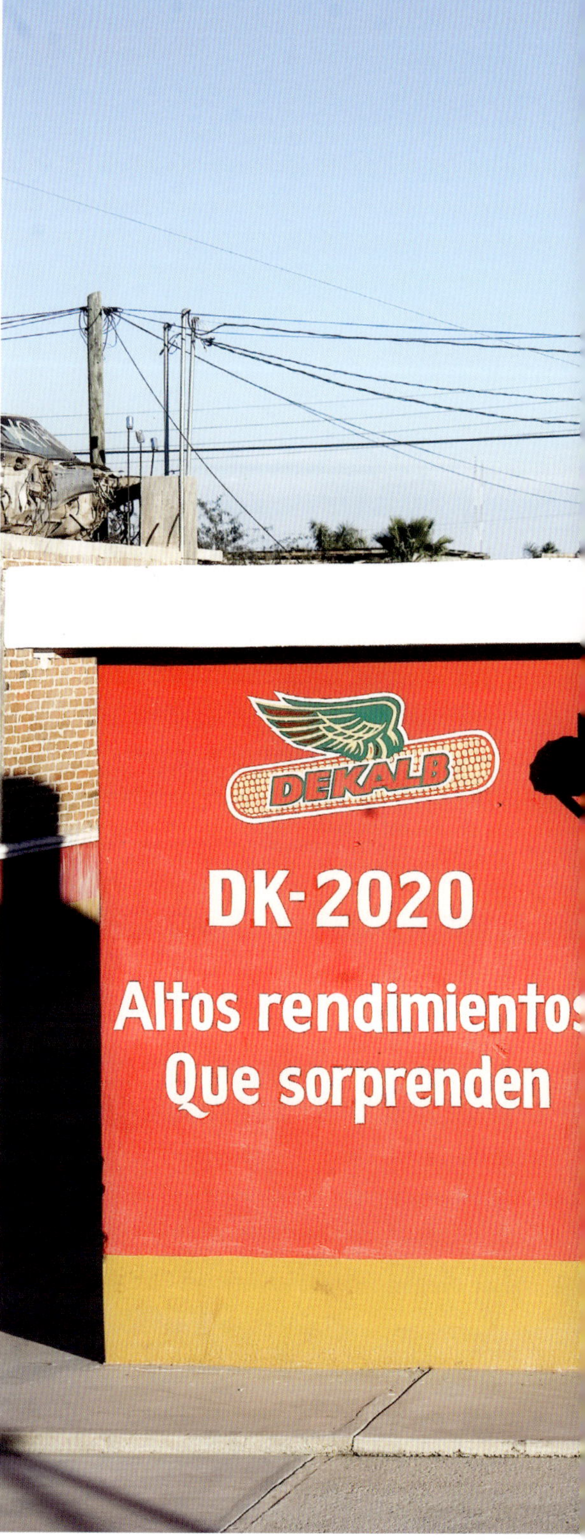

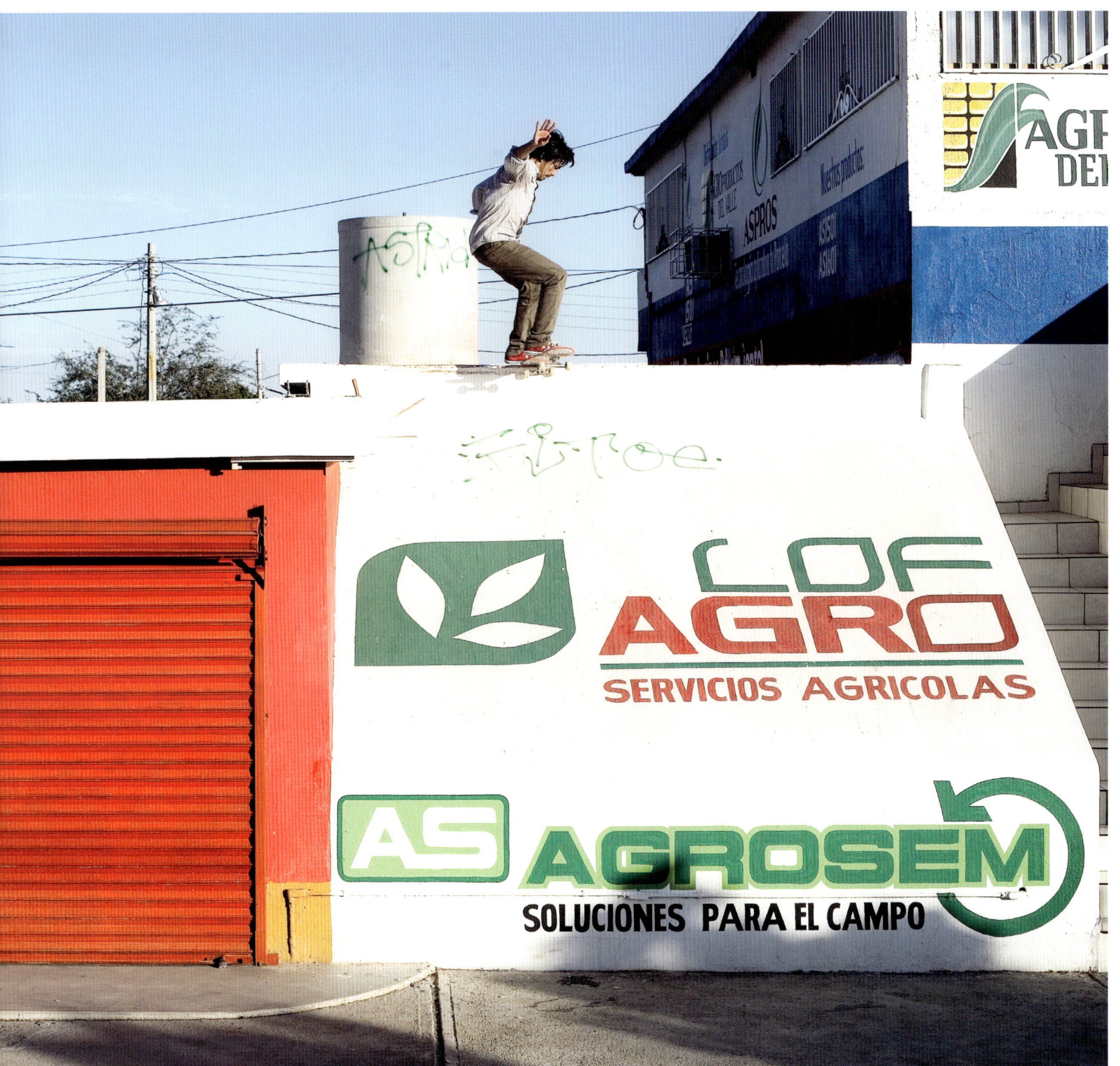

KENNY ANDERSON MEXICO

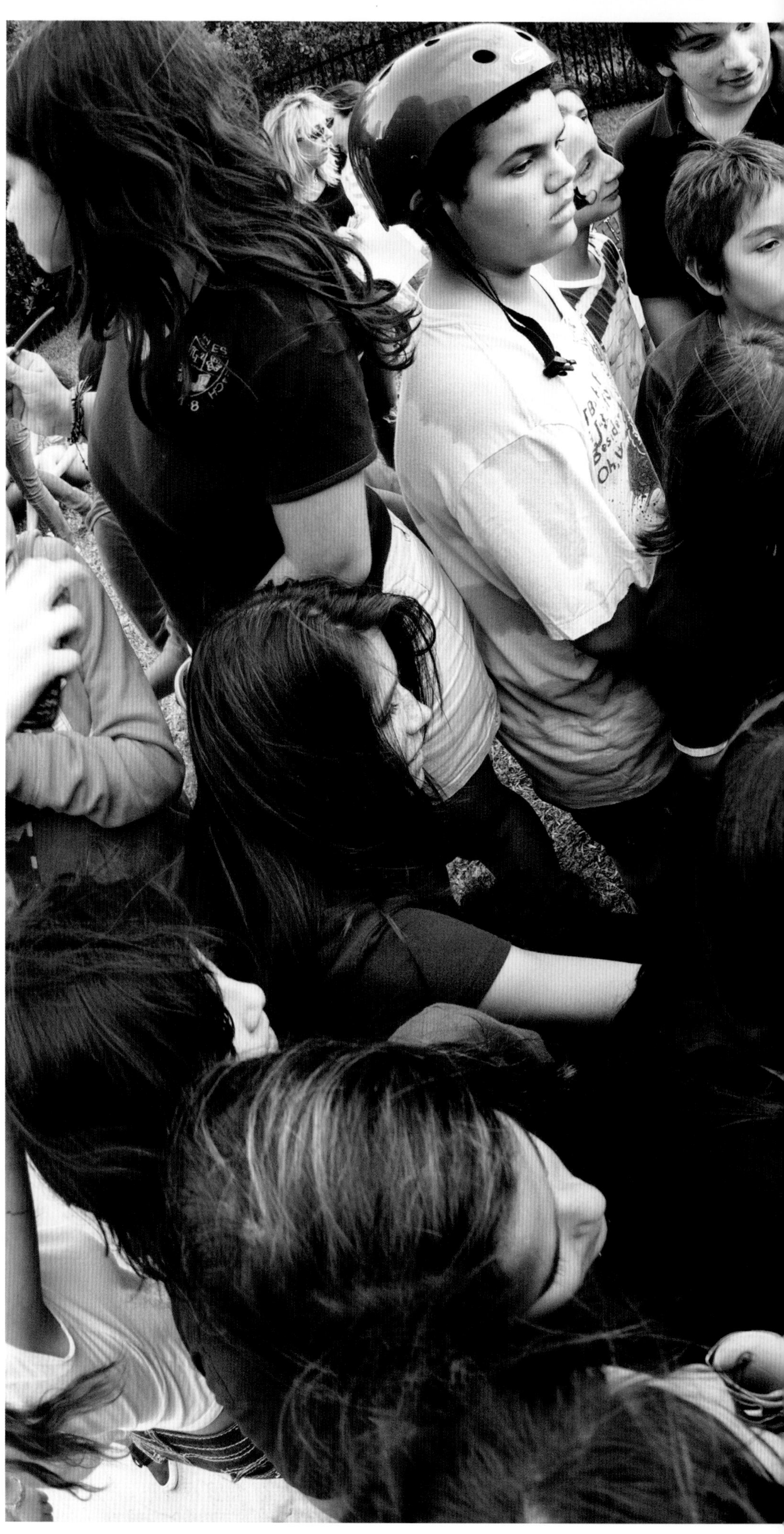

RYAN SHECKLER MIAMI, FL

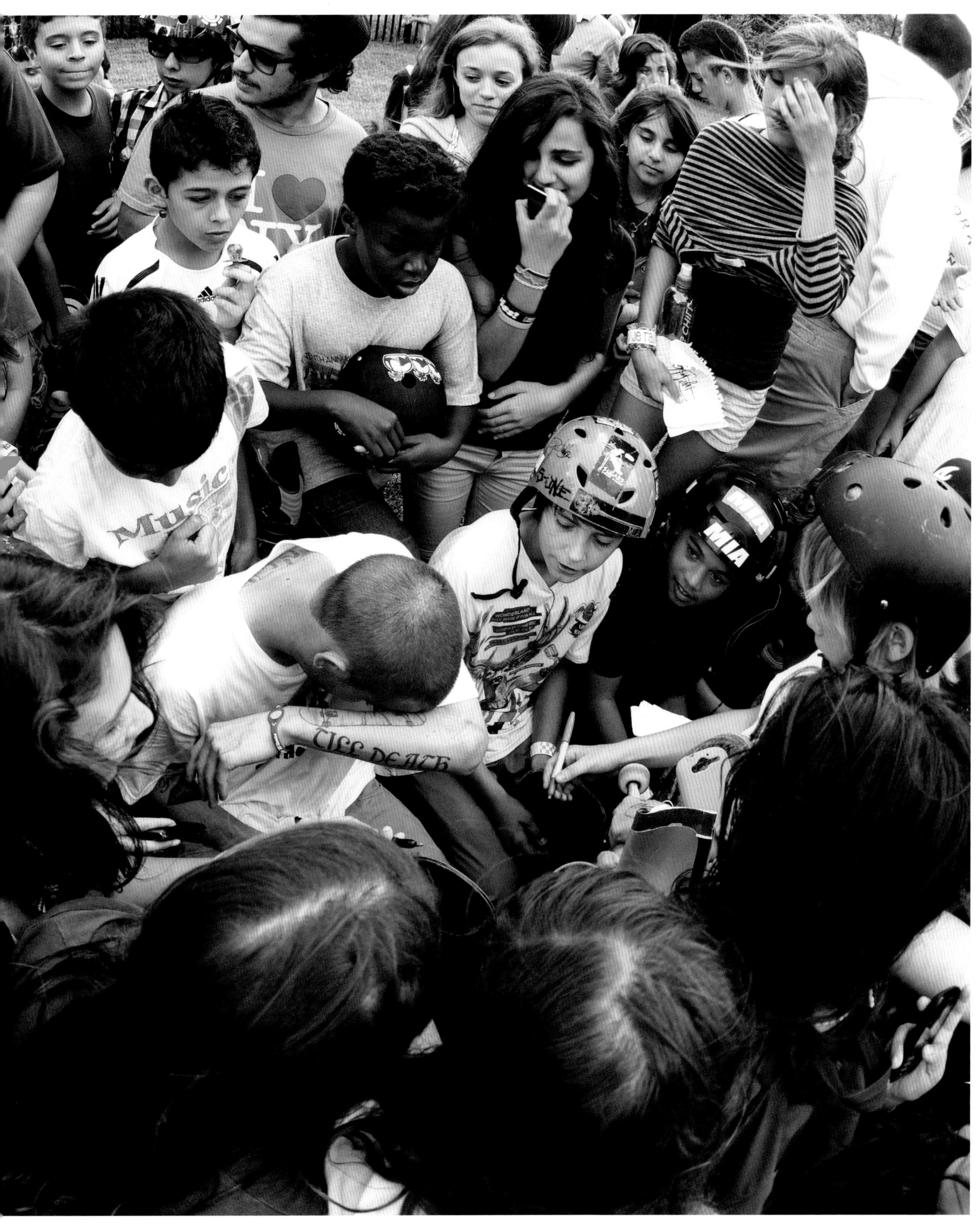
Music
MIA
MIA
TILL DEATH

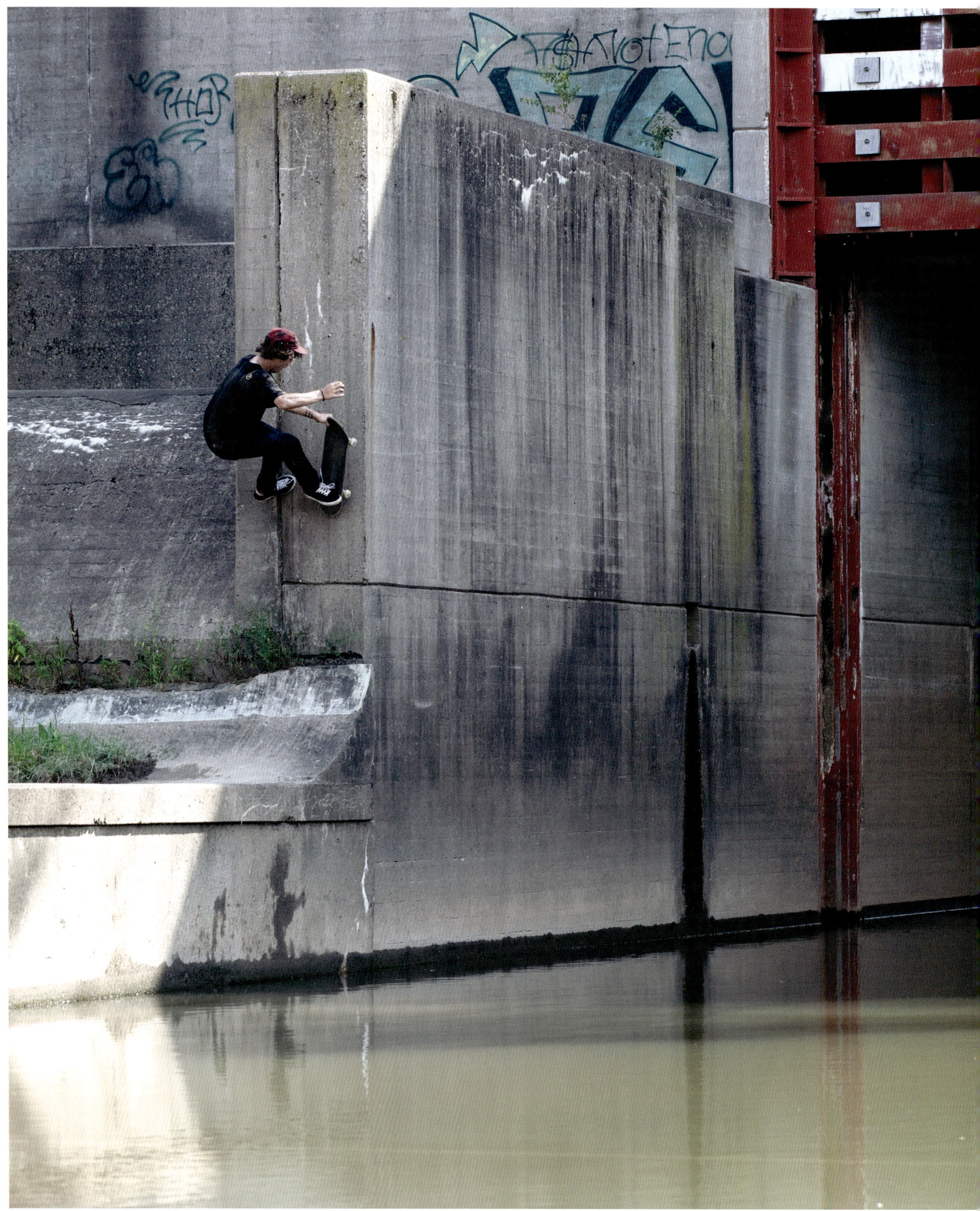

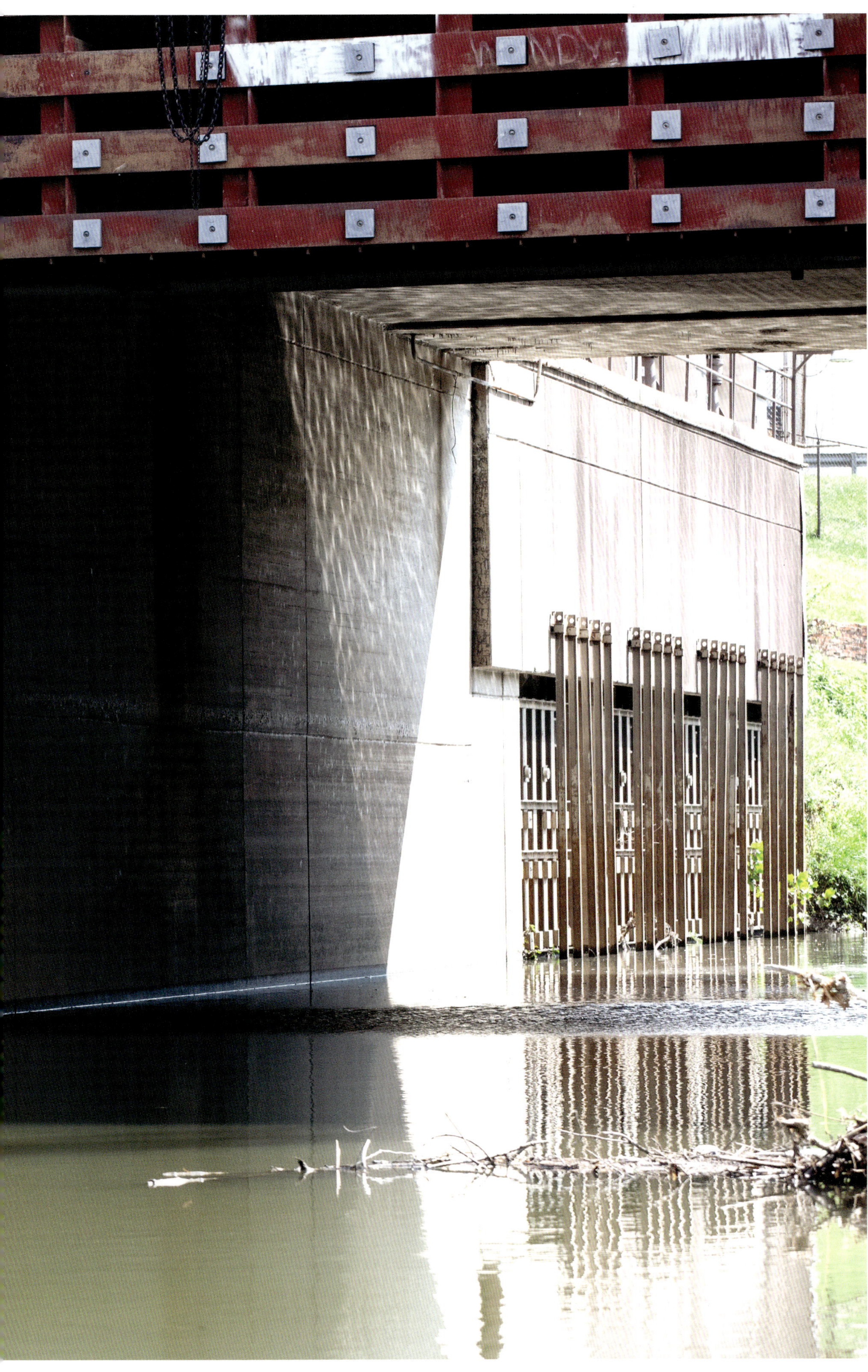

BEN RAEMERS BATON ROUGE, LA

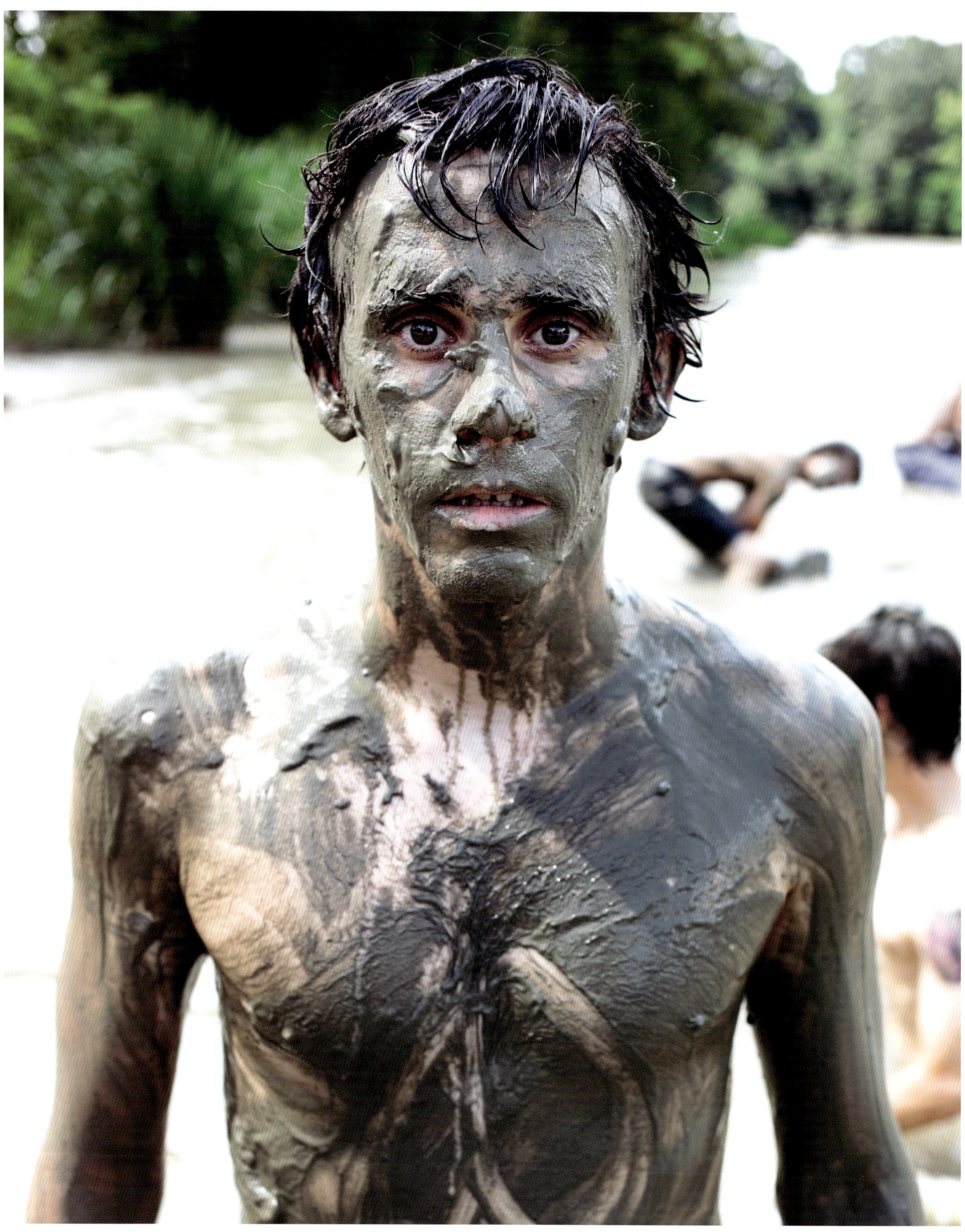

RICK McCRANK BATON ROUGE, LA

STEVE FAUSER CINCINNATI, OH

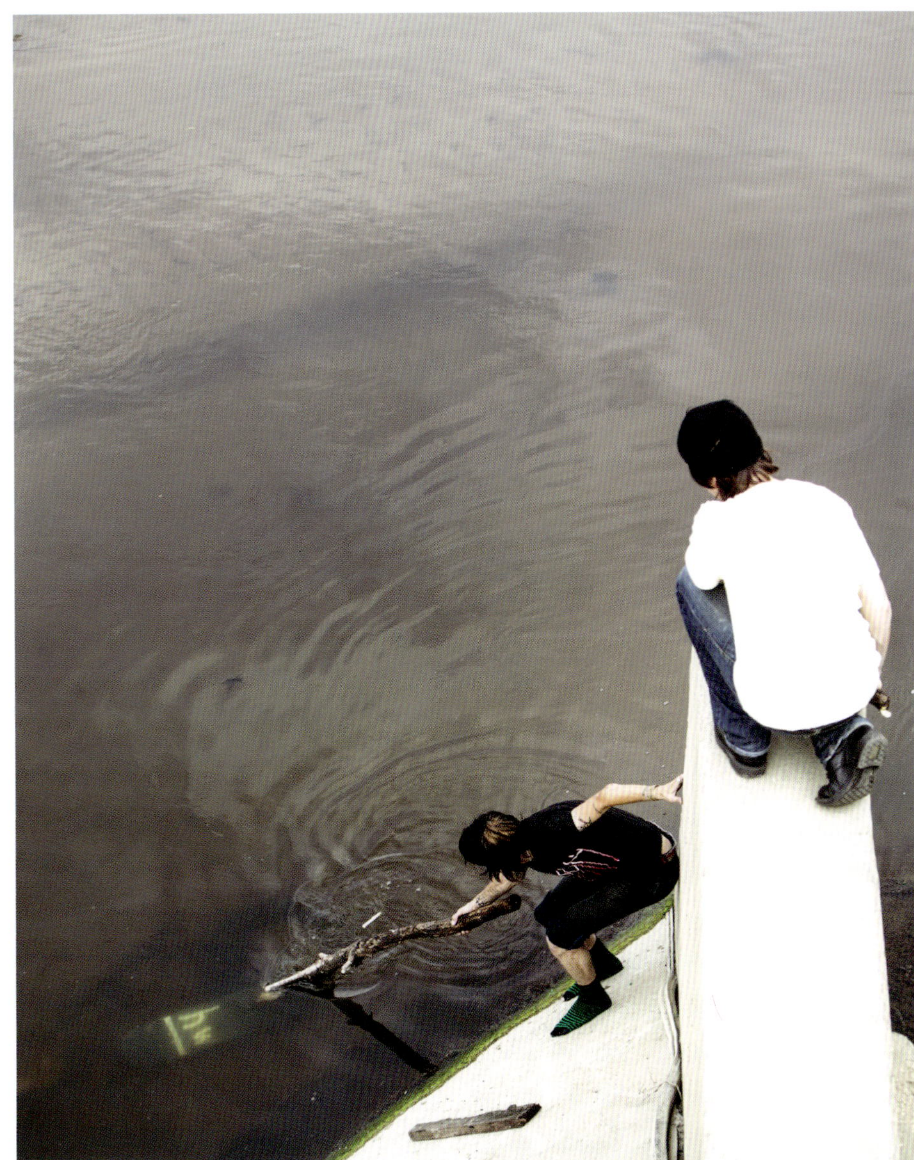

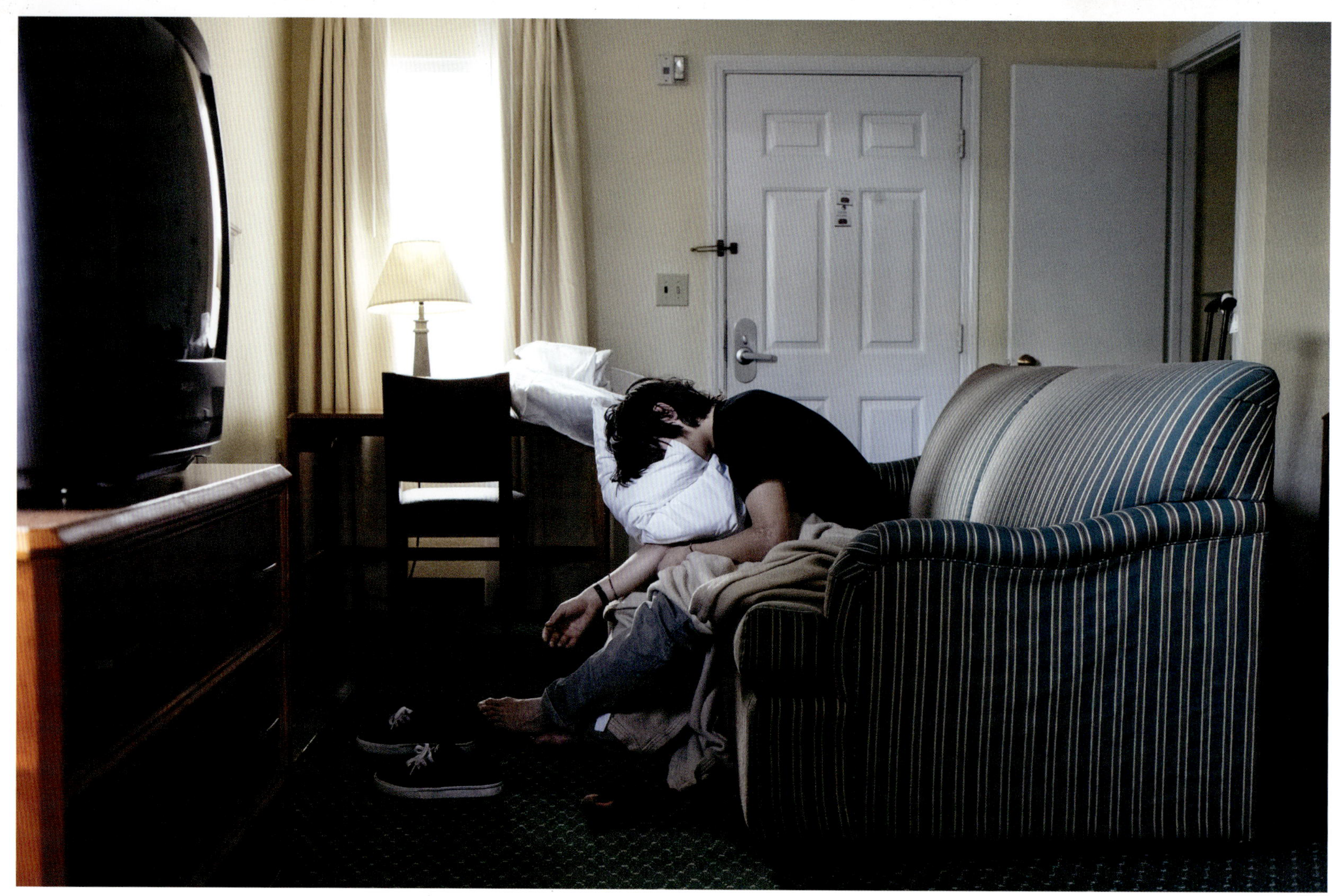

SEAN MALTO ATLANTA, GA

DOOGIE BAY OF FUNDY

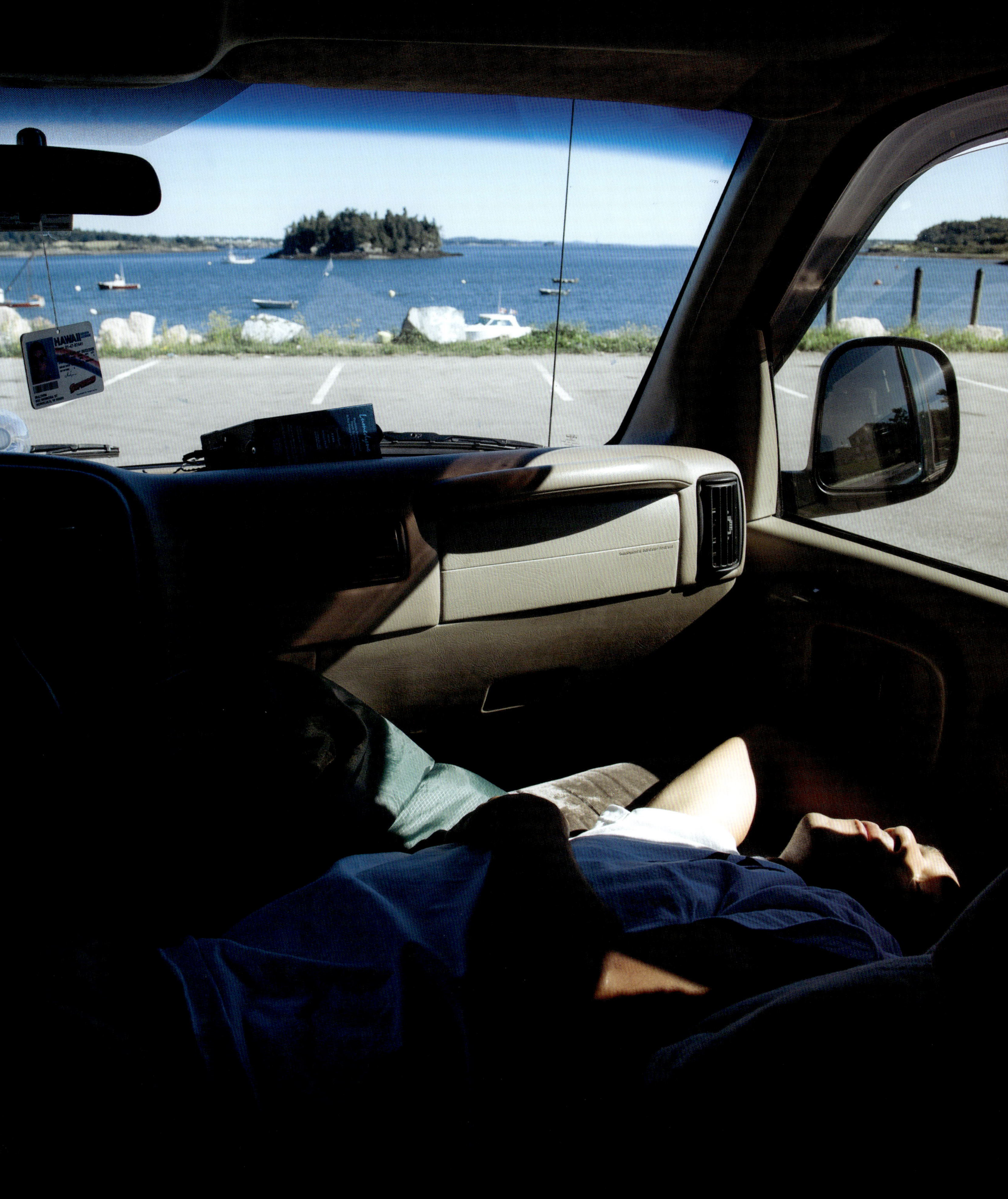
HAWAII

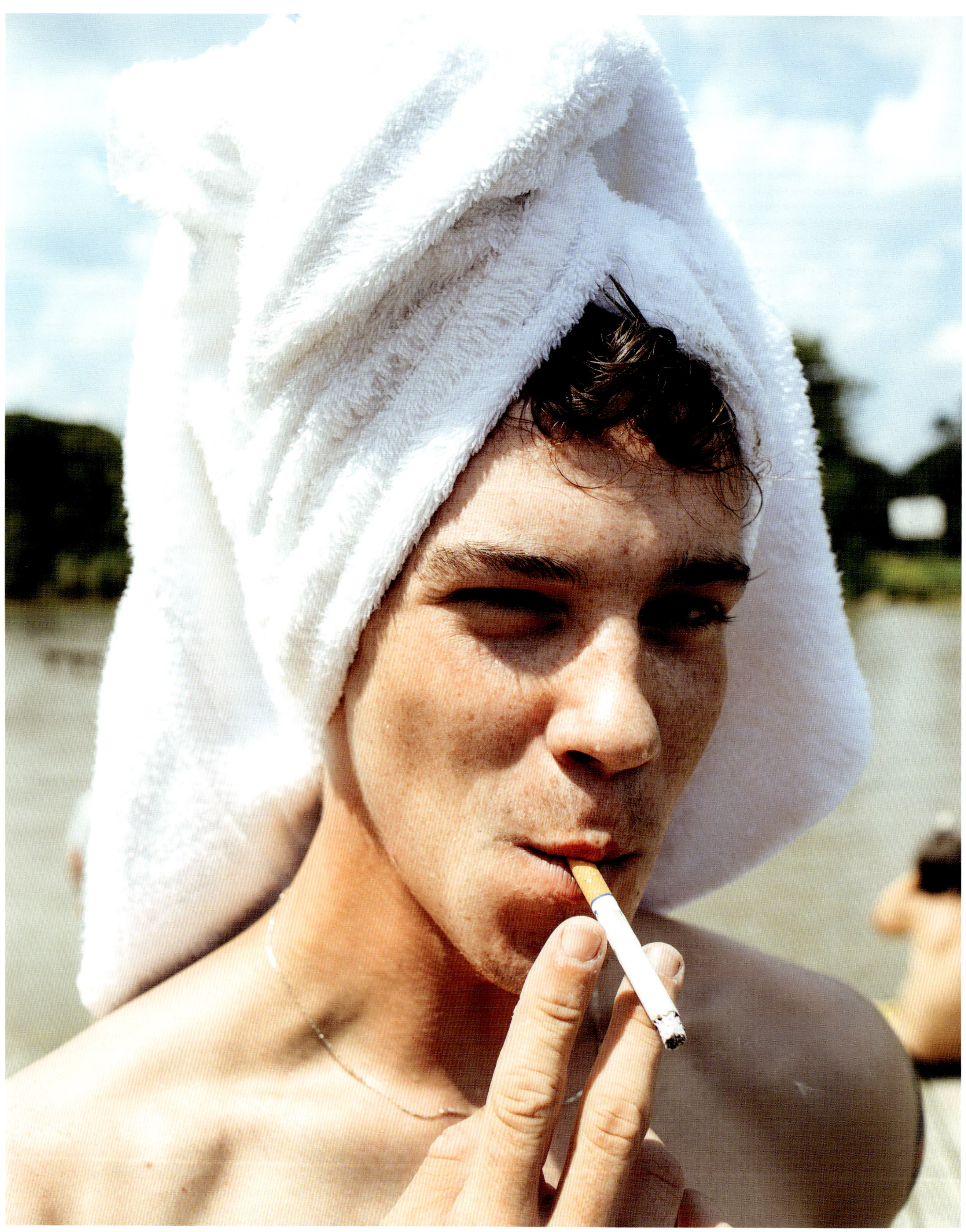

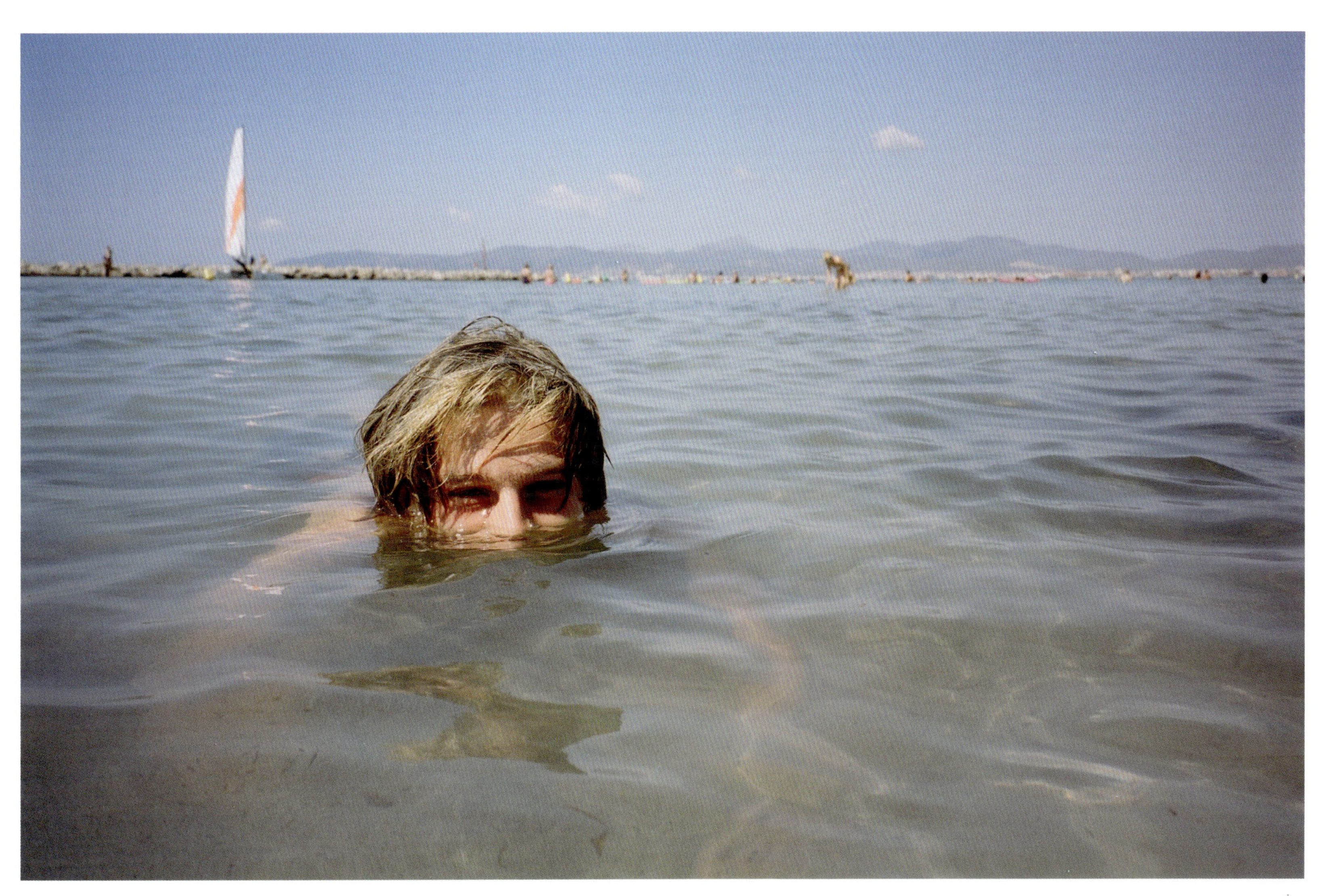

NICK GARCIA BCN, SPAIN

BEN RAEMERS BATON ROUGE, LA

SEAN MALTO MILAN, IT

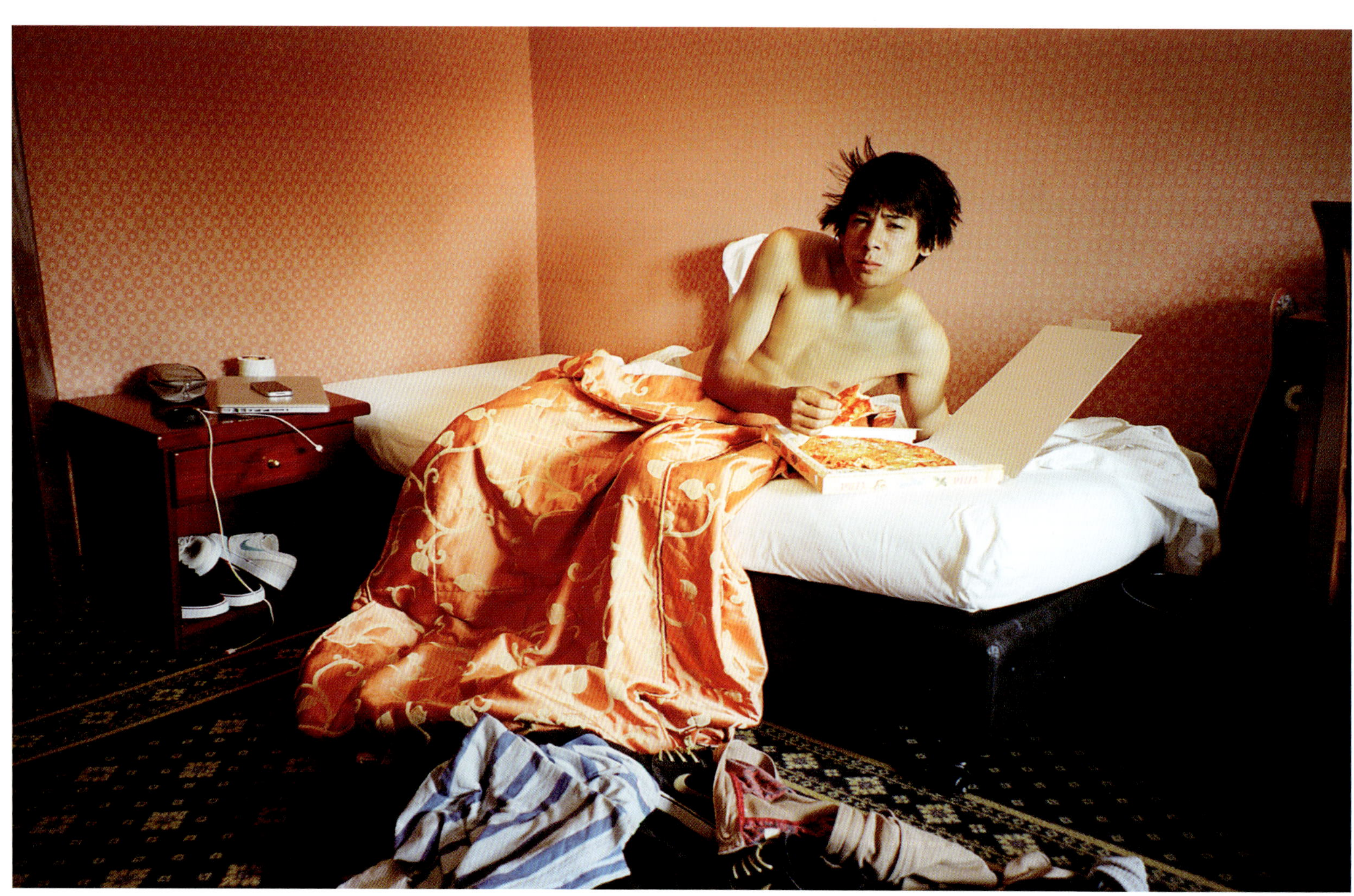

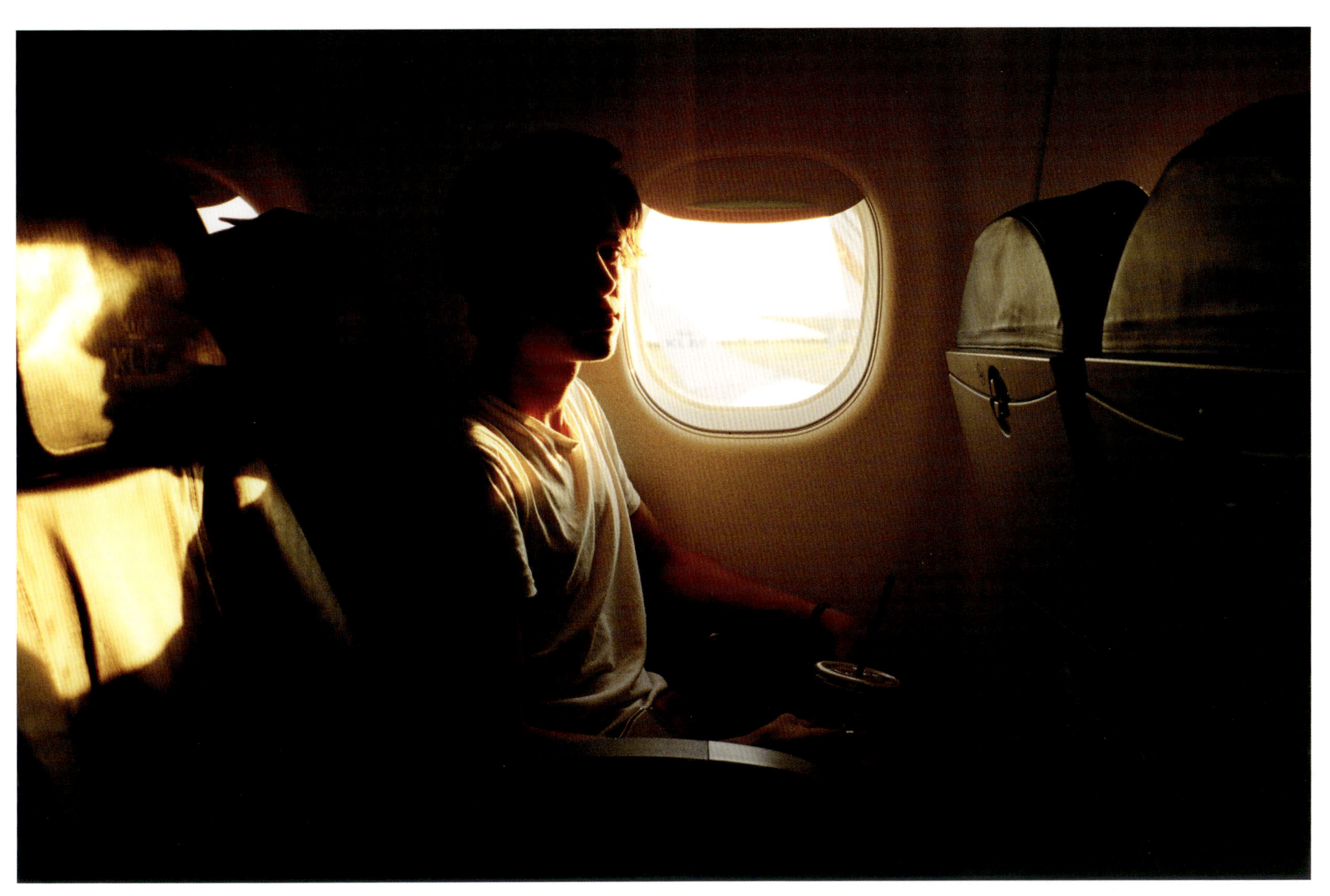

AXEL CRUYSBERGHS GERMANY

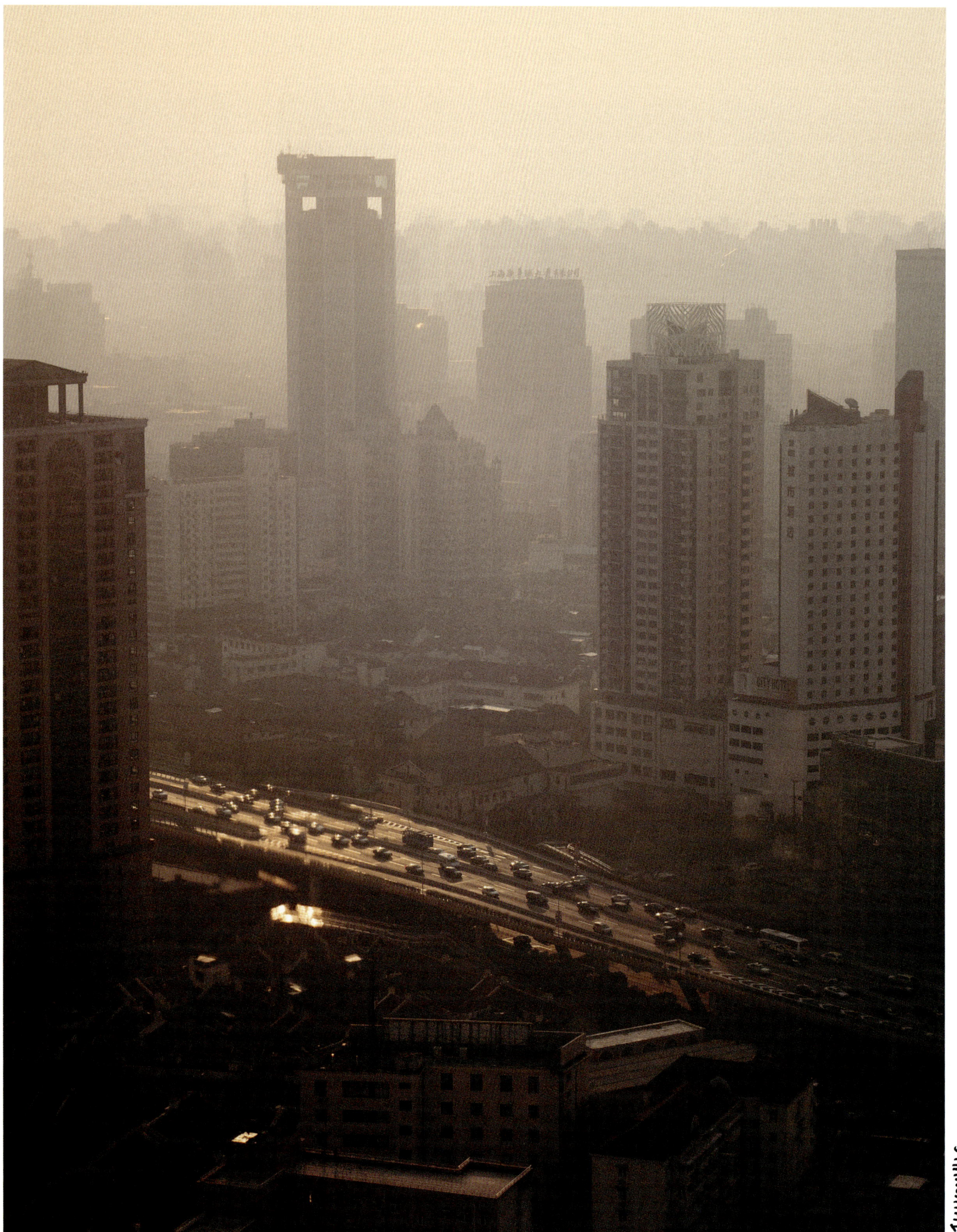

SHANGHAI

KENNY ANDERSON BEIJING, CHINA

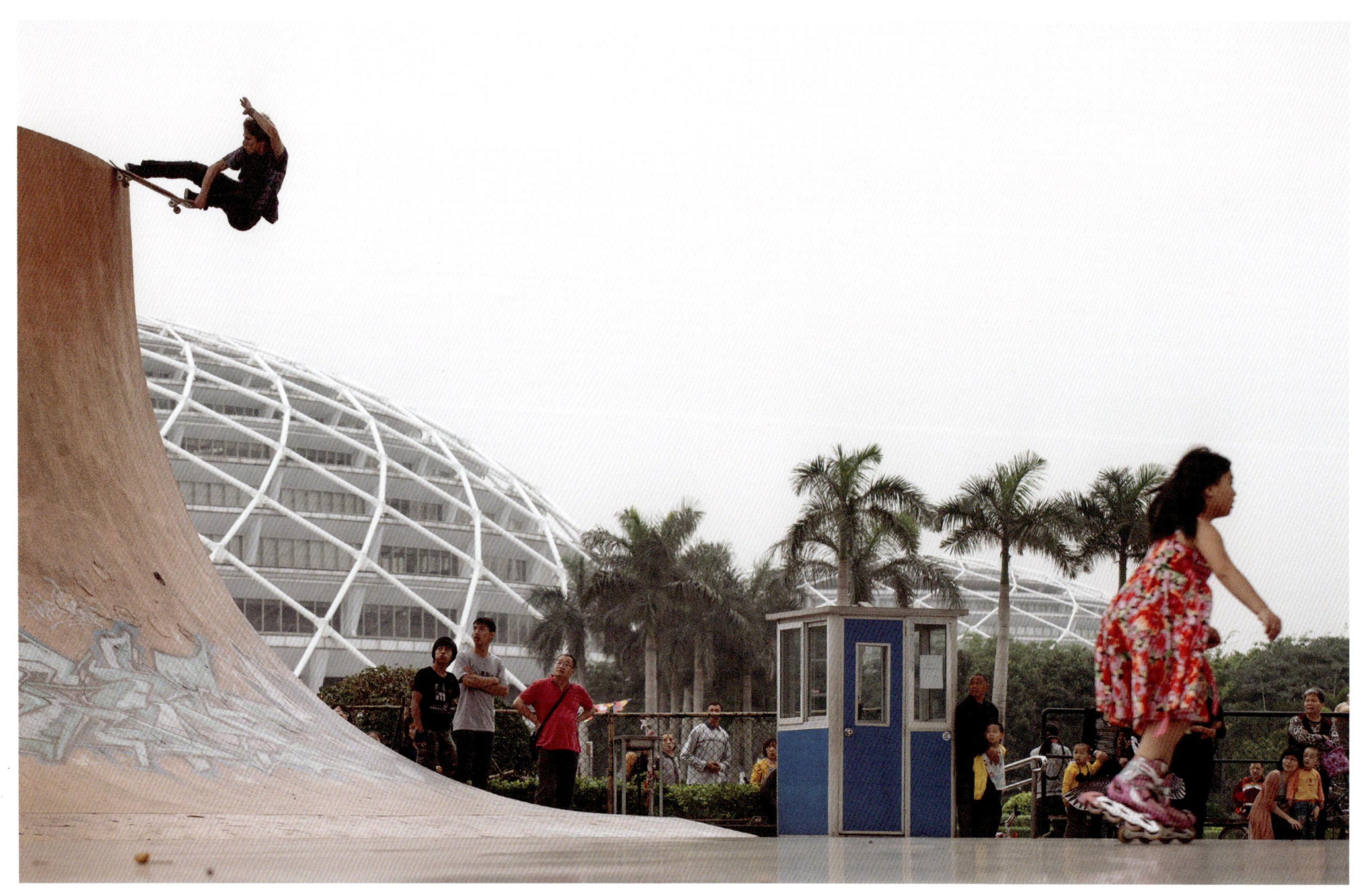

NICK GARCIA CHINA

DAVE HOANG CHINA

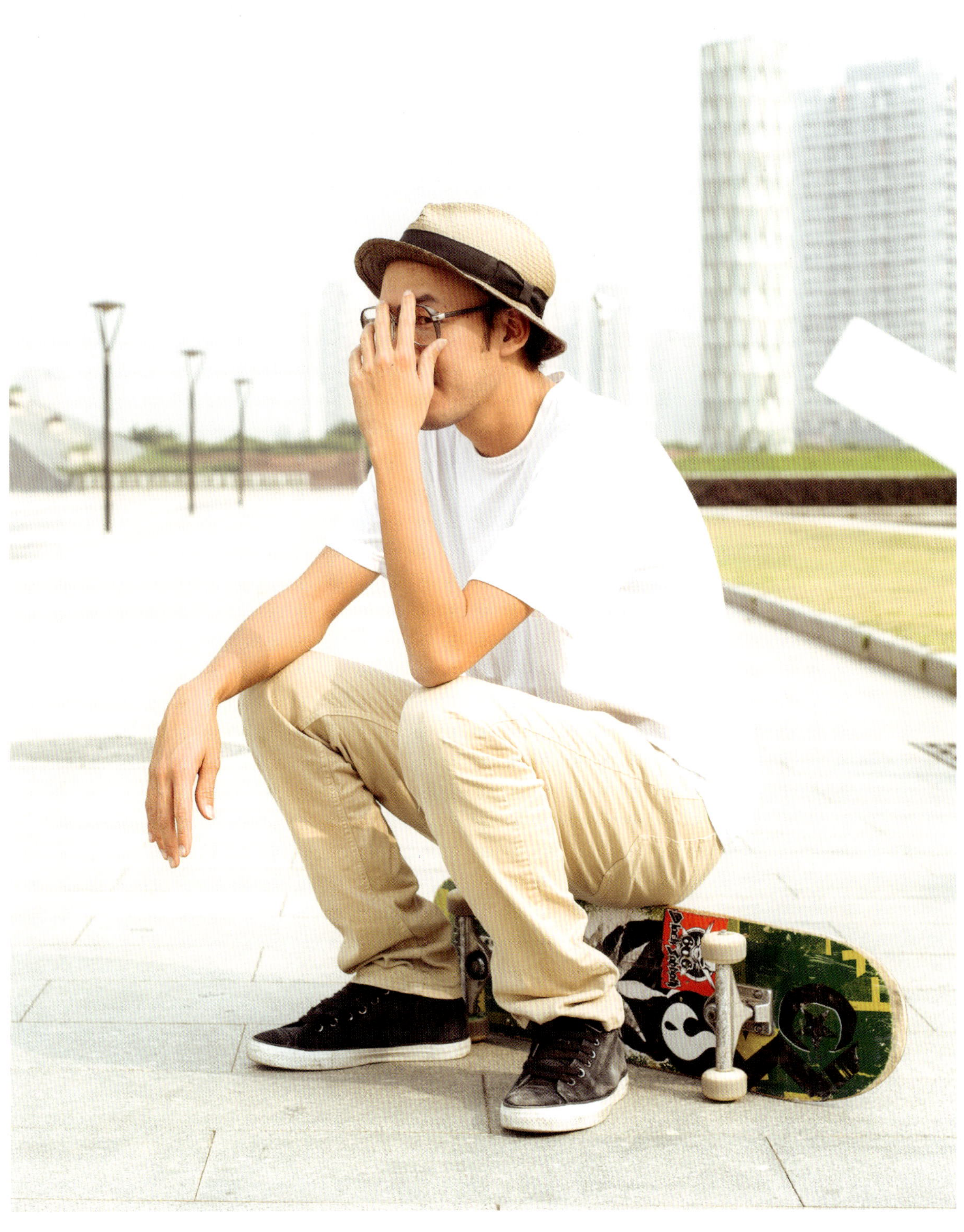

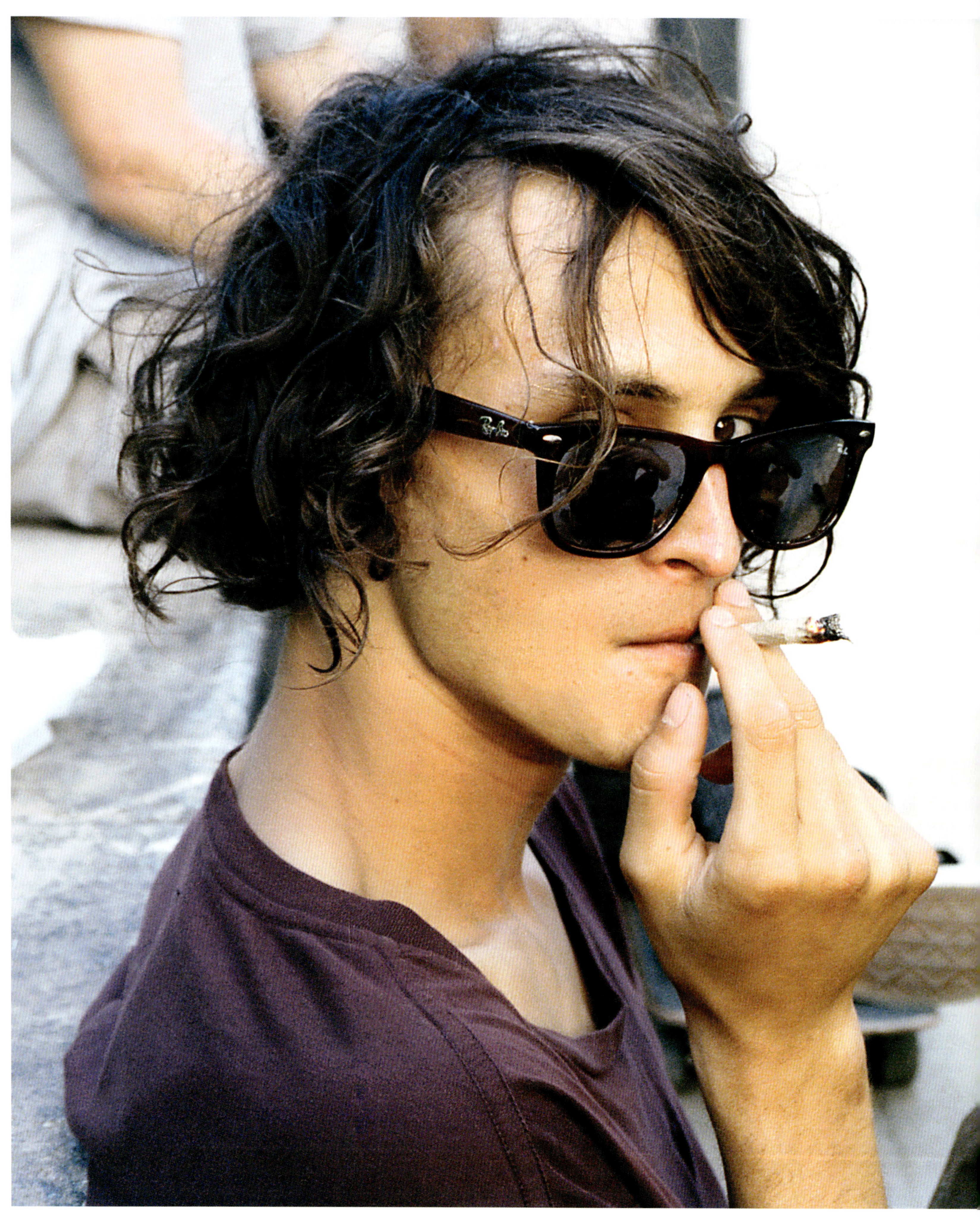

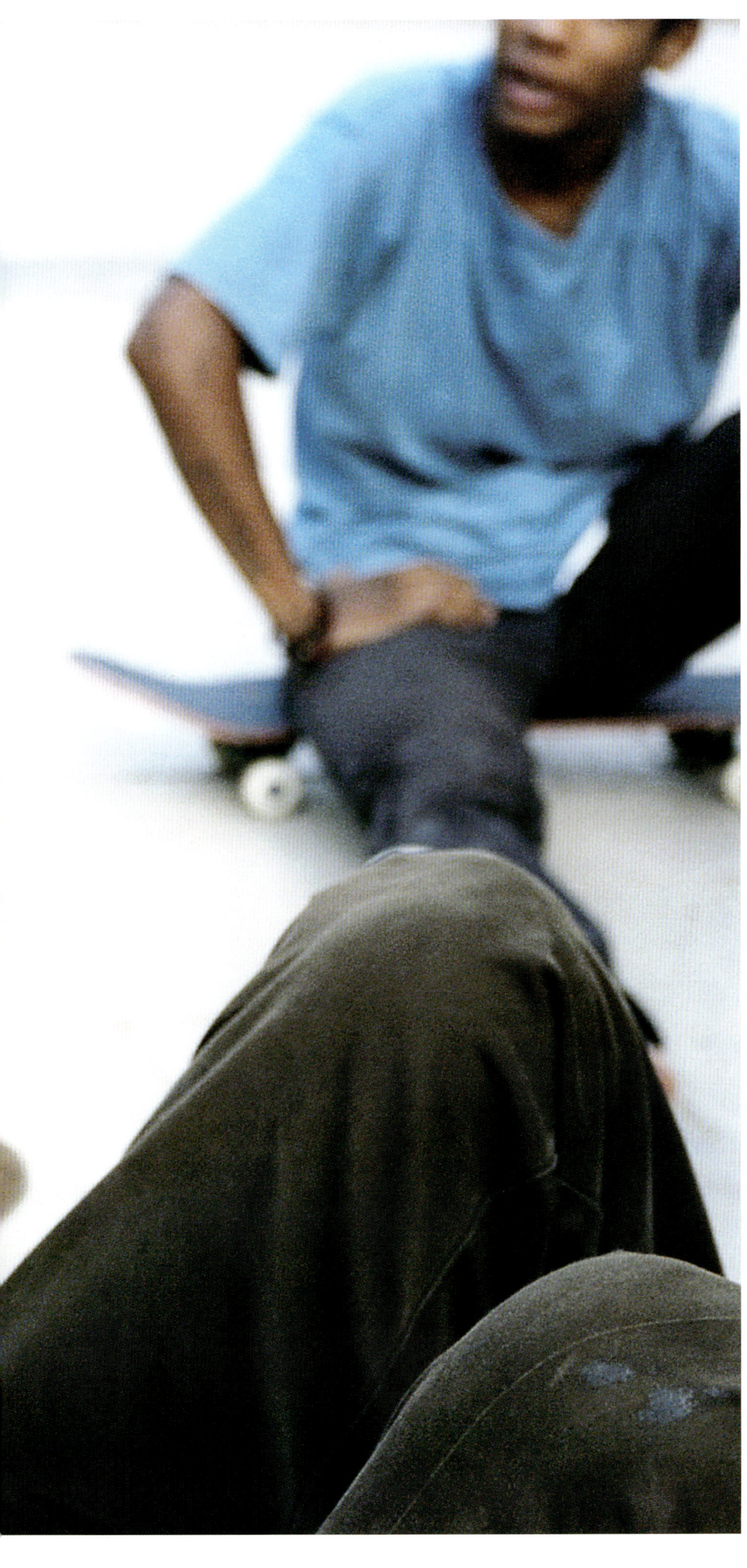

EVAN SMITH MALLORCA, SPAIN

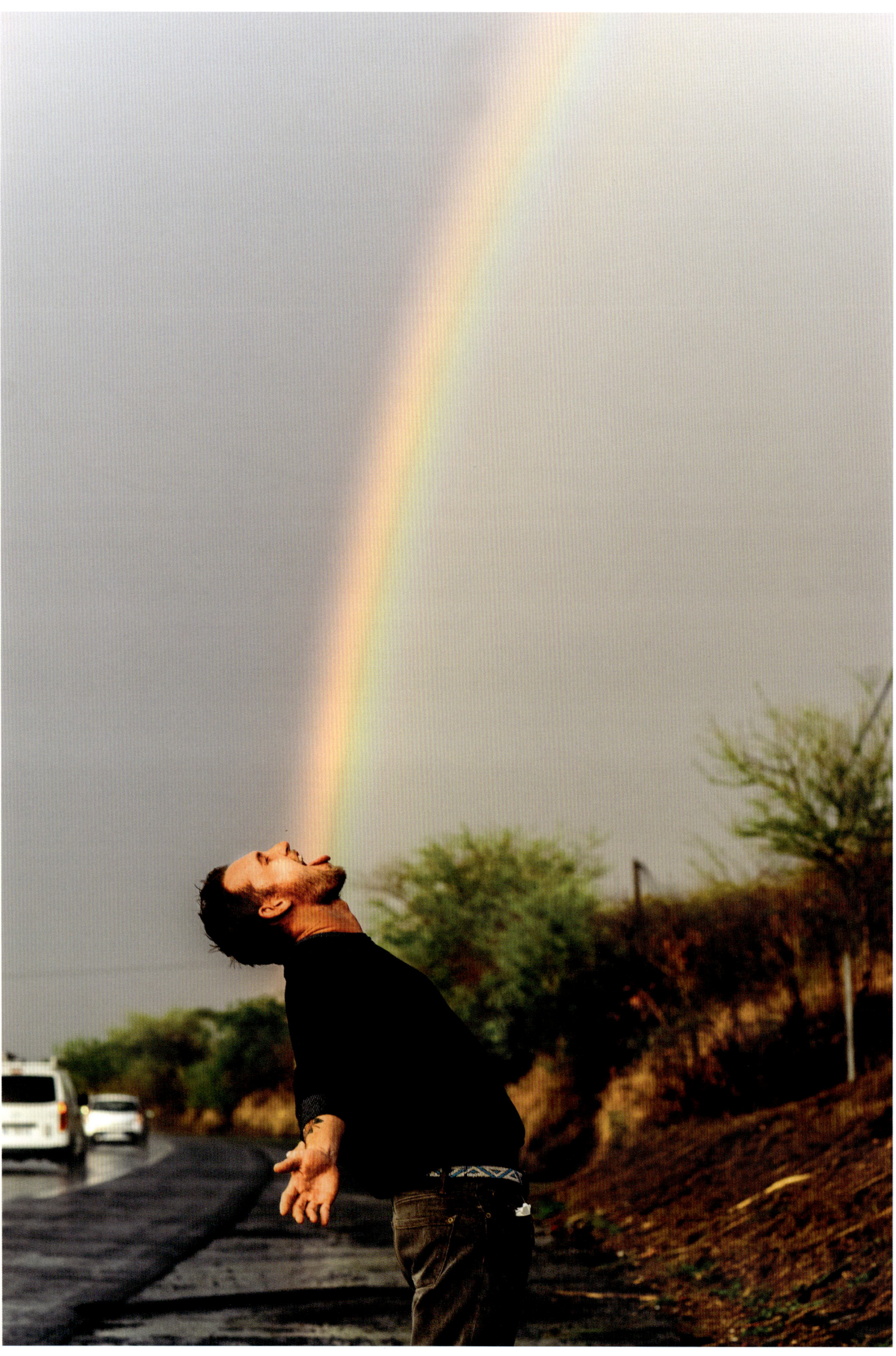

YANN HOROWITZ RÉUNION, FRANCE

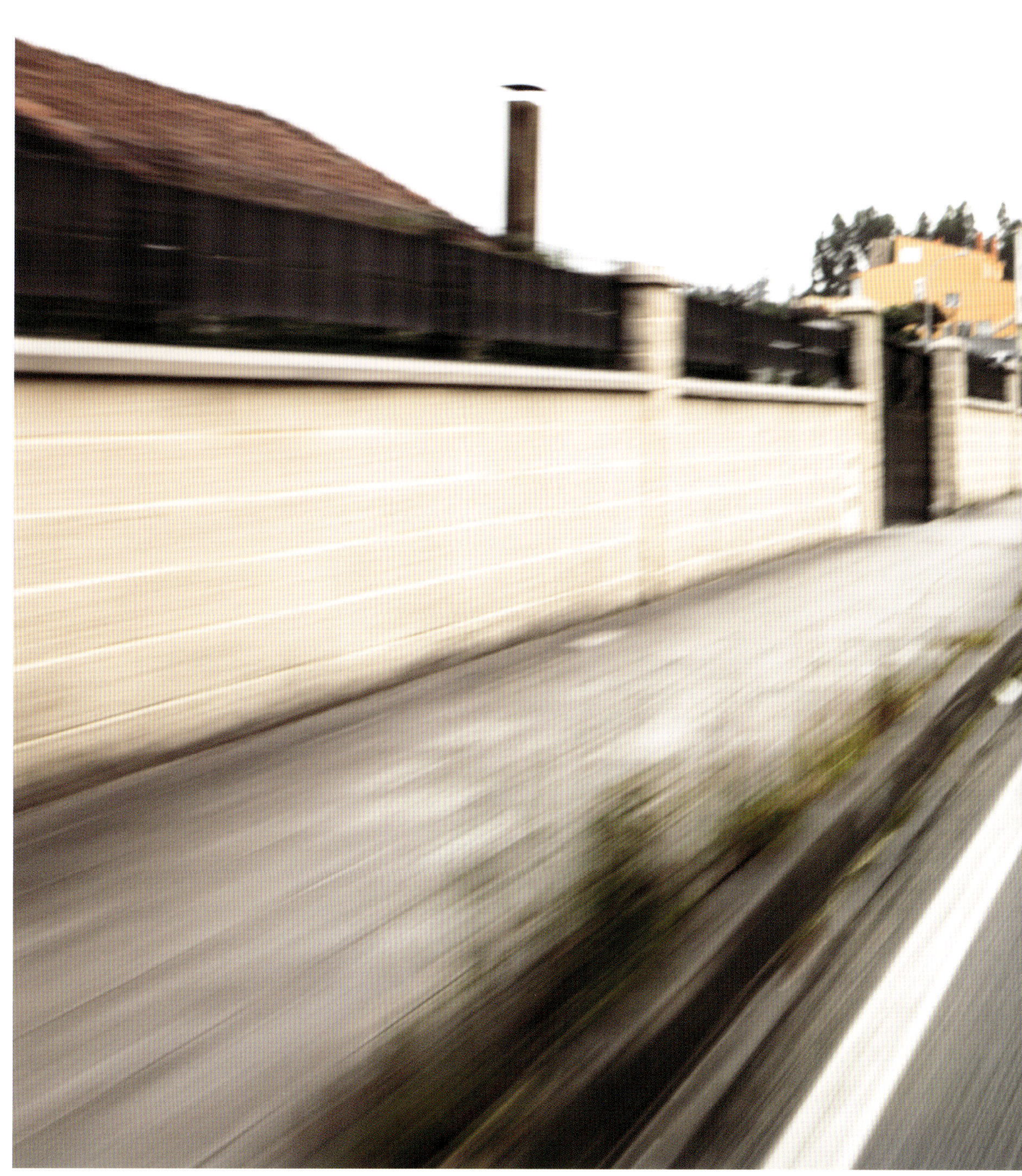

NORA VASCONCELLOS LISBON, PORTUGAL

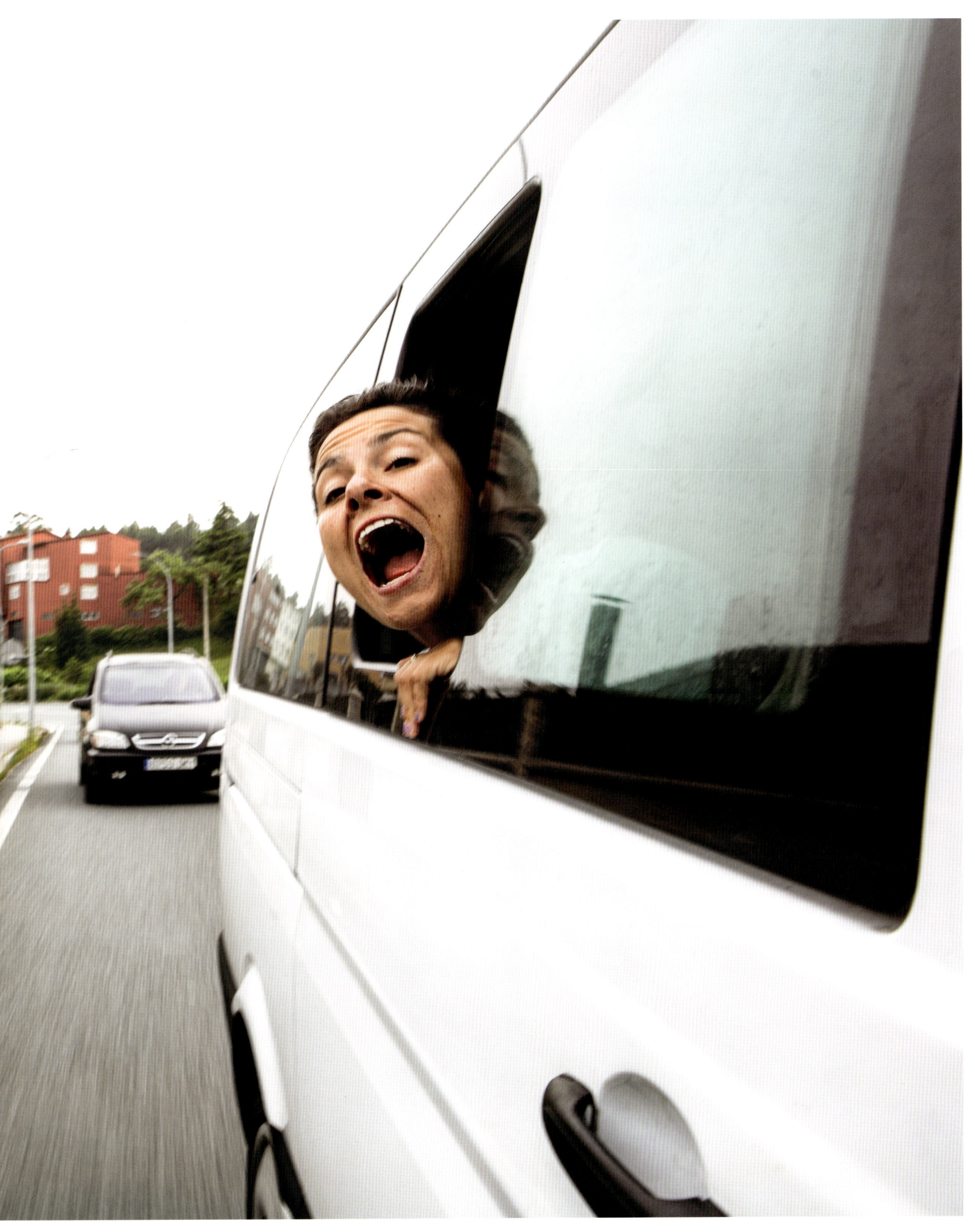

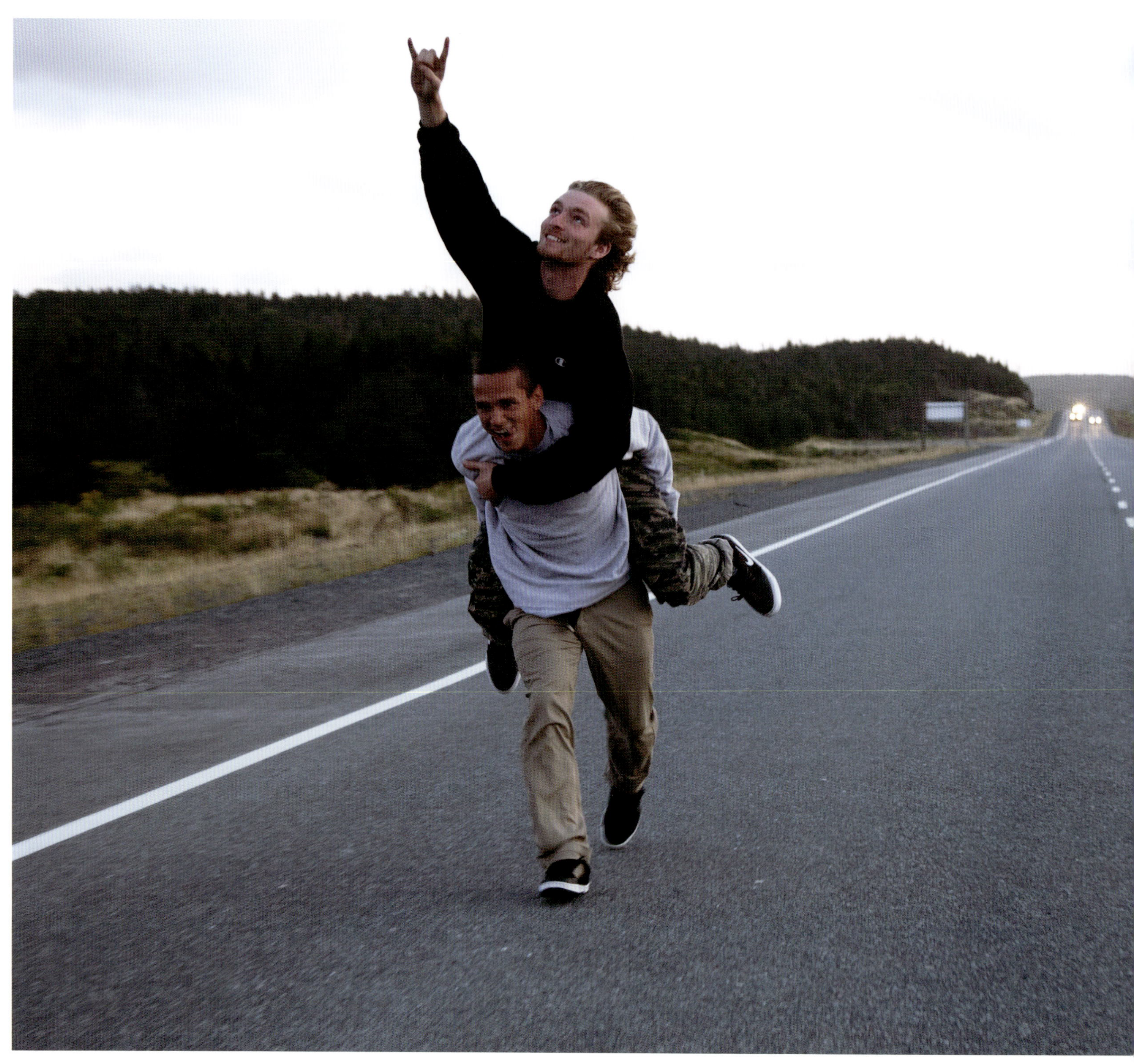

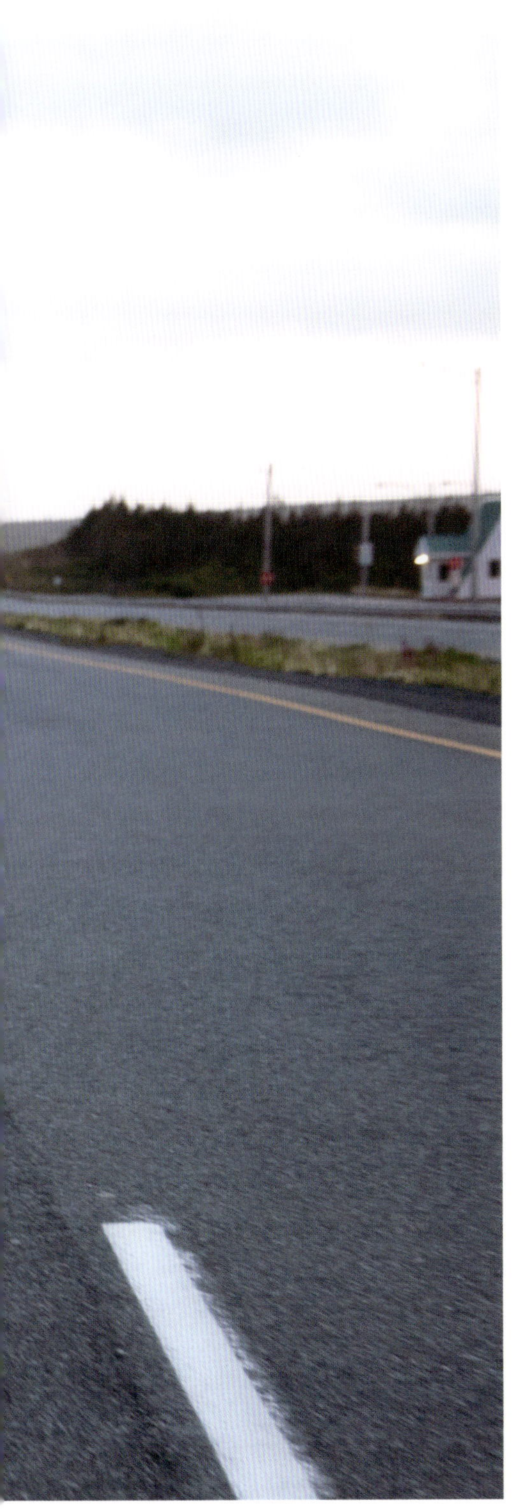

DOOGIE + GONYON NEW FOUNDLAND

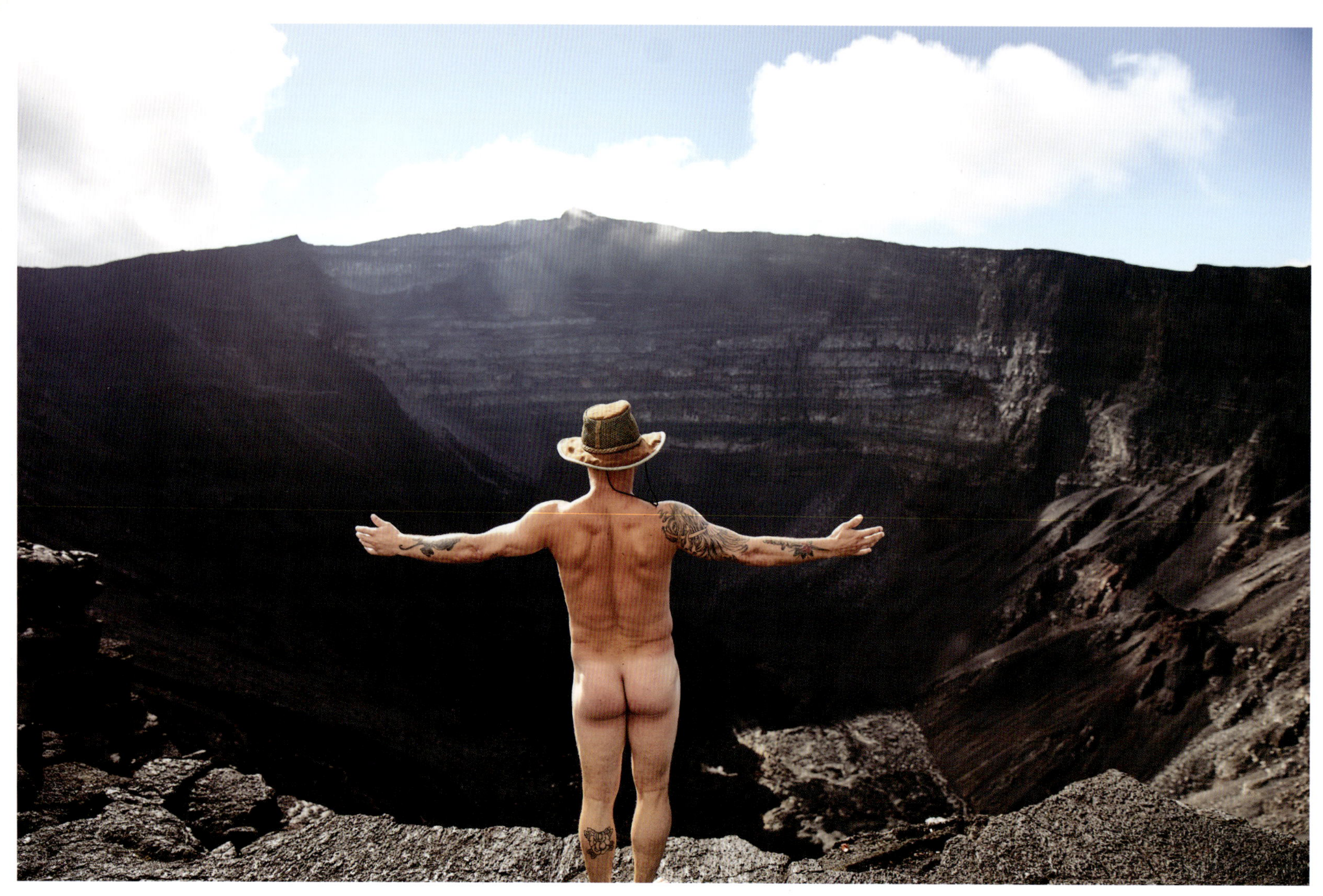

YANN HOROWITZ RÉUNION, FRANCE

CLINT WALKER MANAUS, BRAZIL

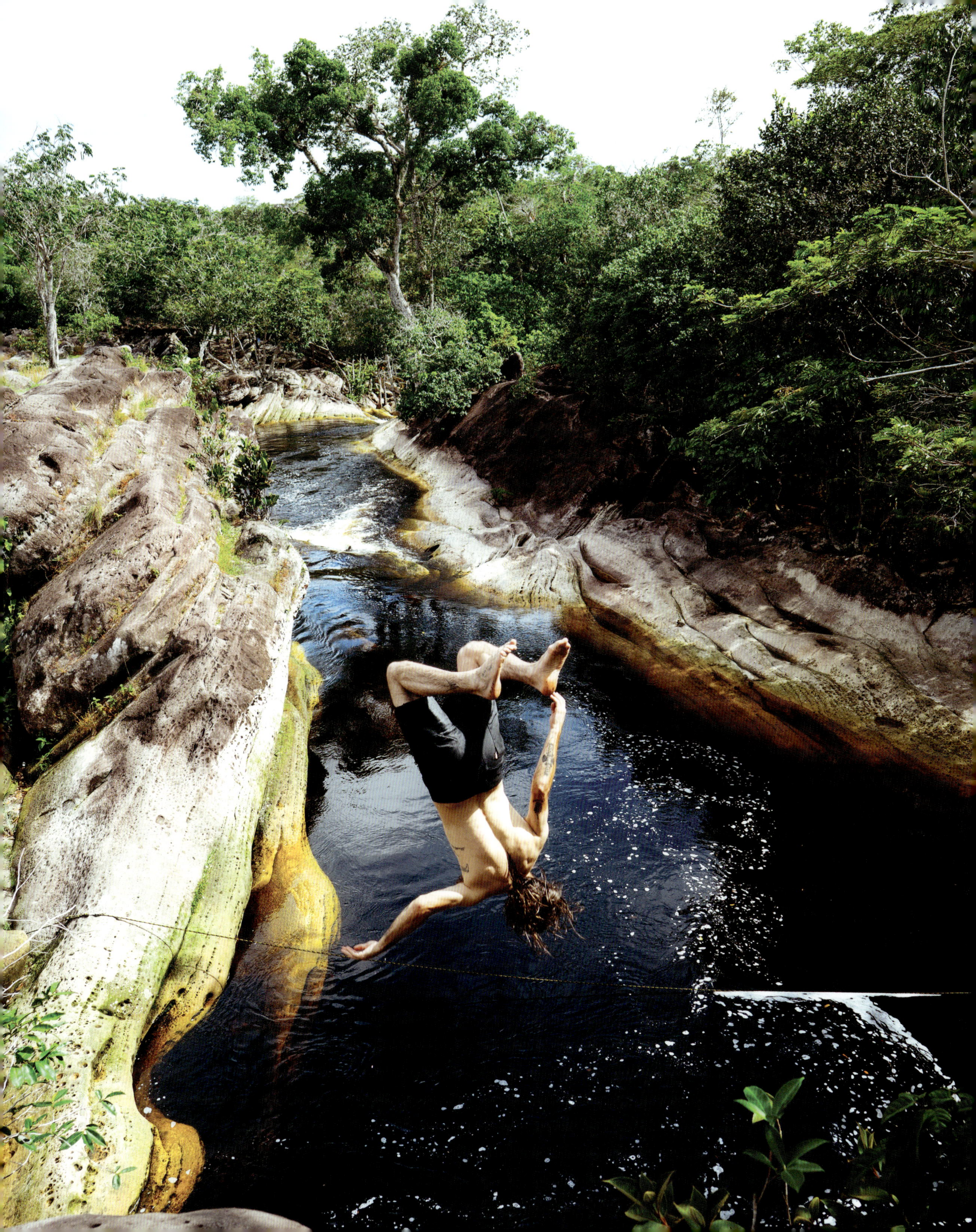

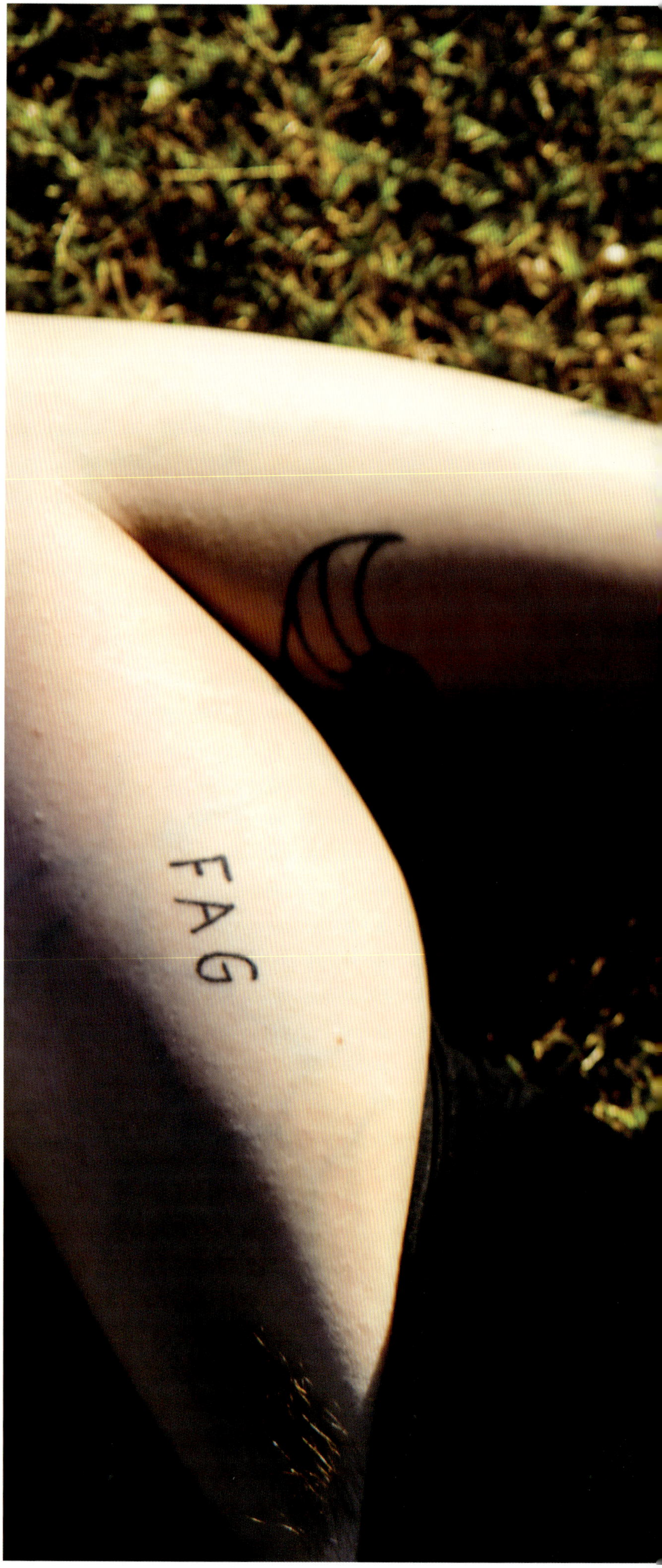

LEO BAKER SPAIN

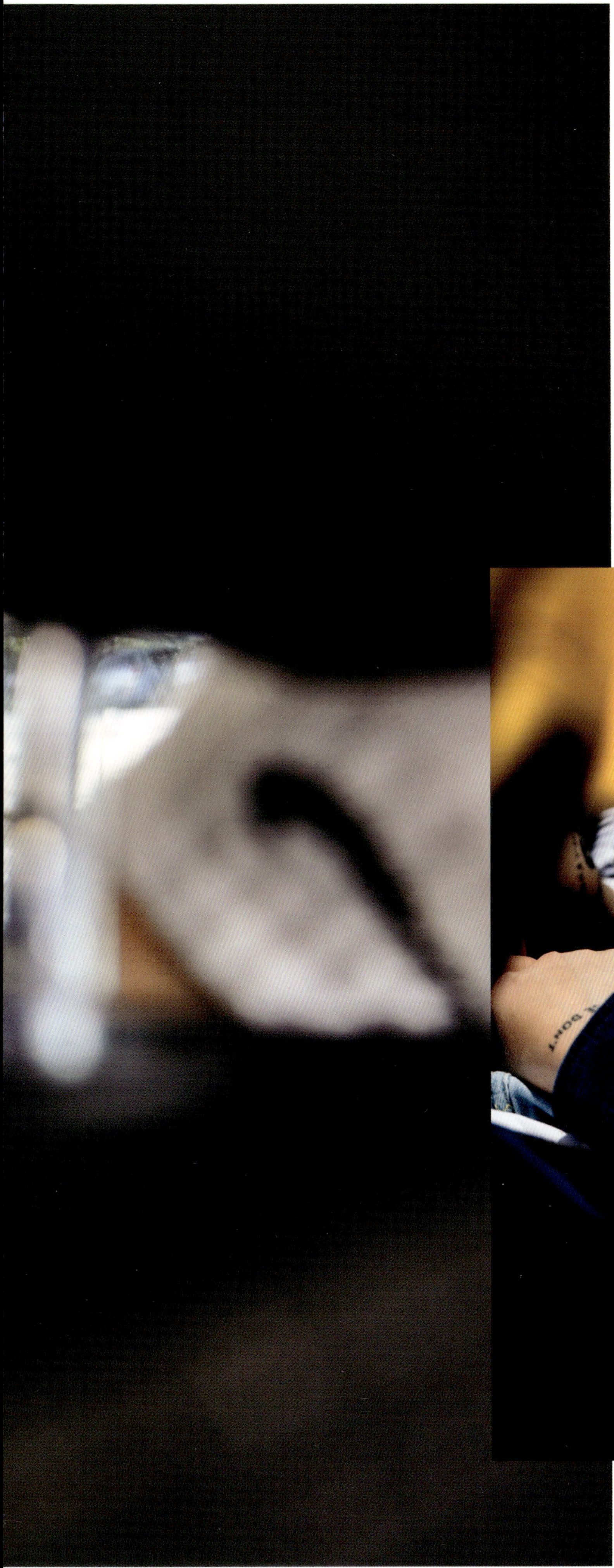

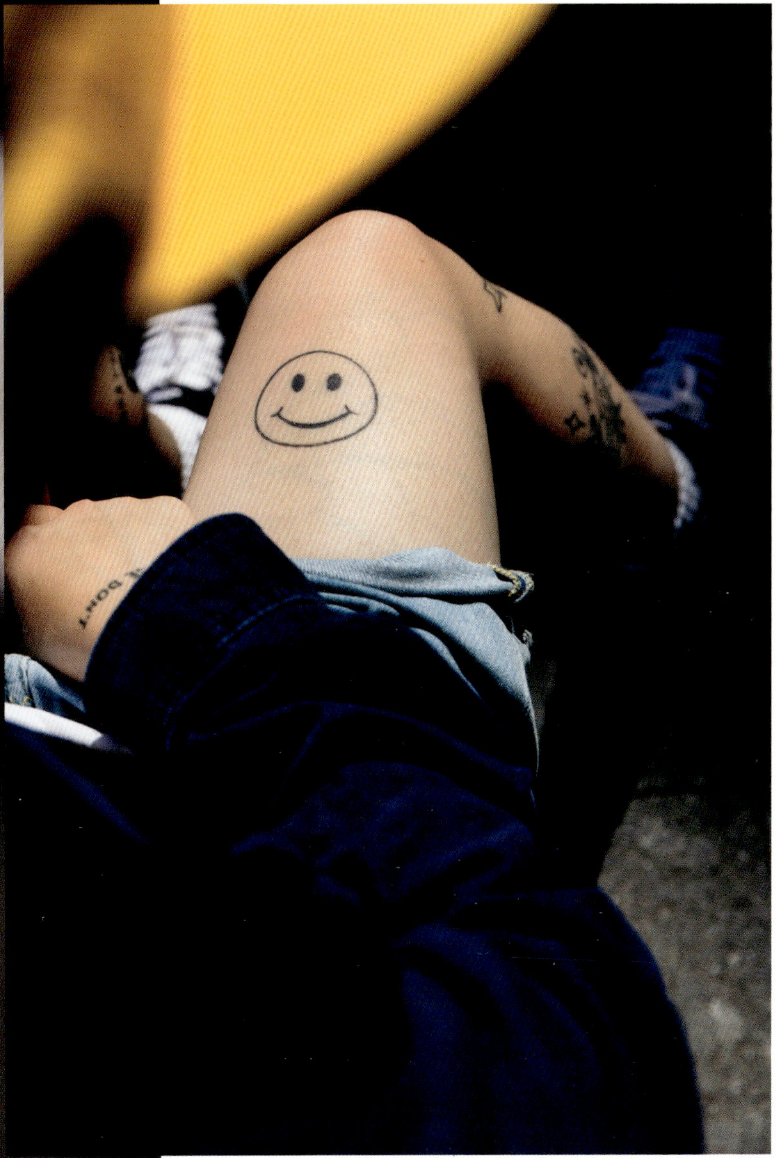

LEO BAKER SPAIN

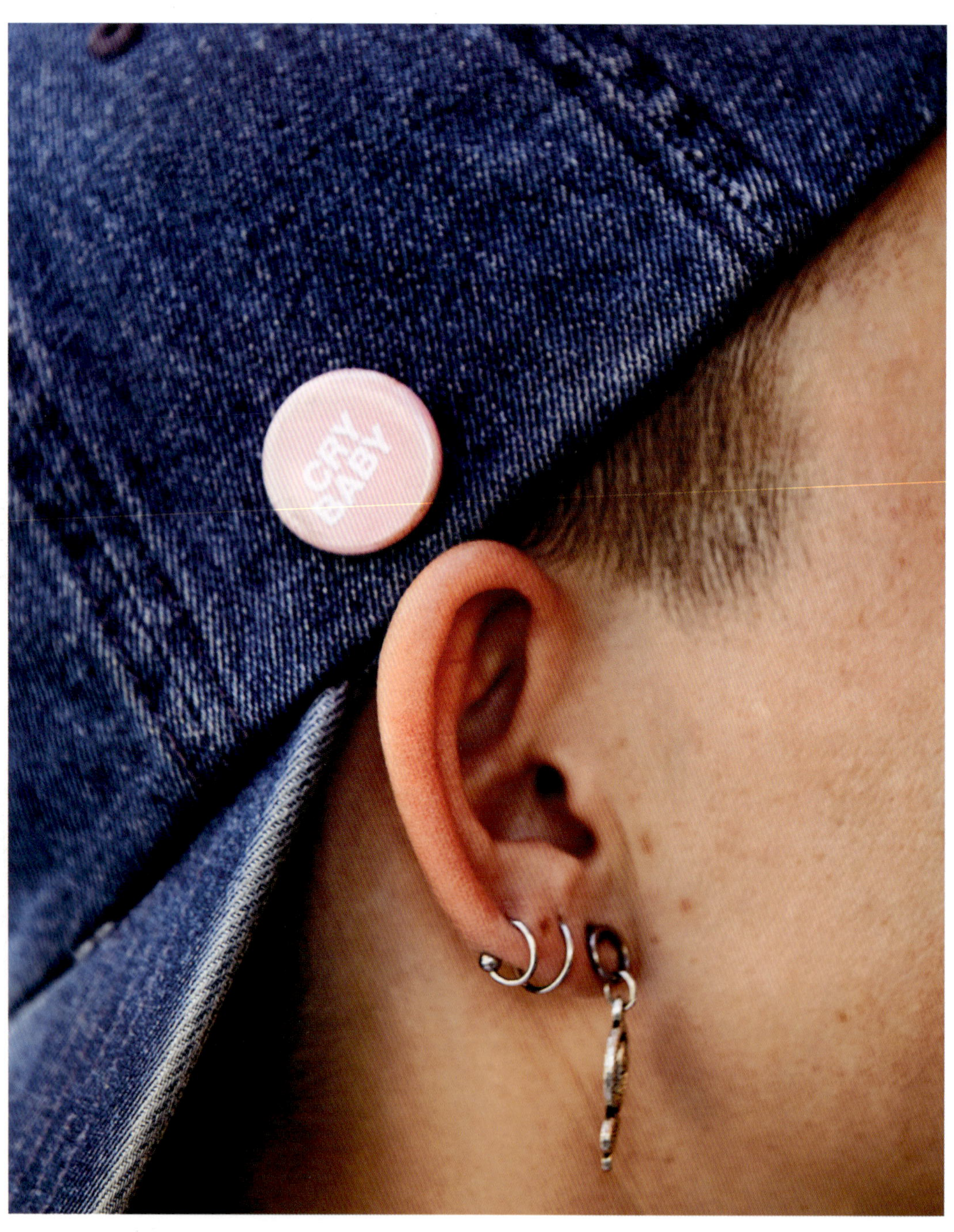

LEO BAKER LOS ANGELES

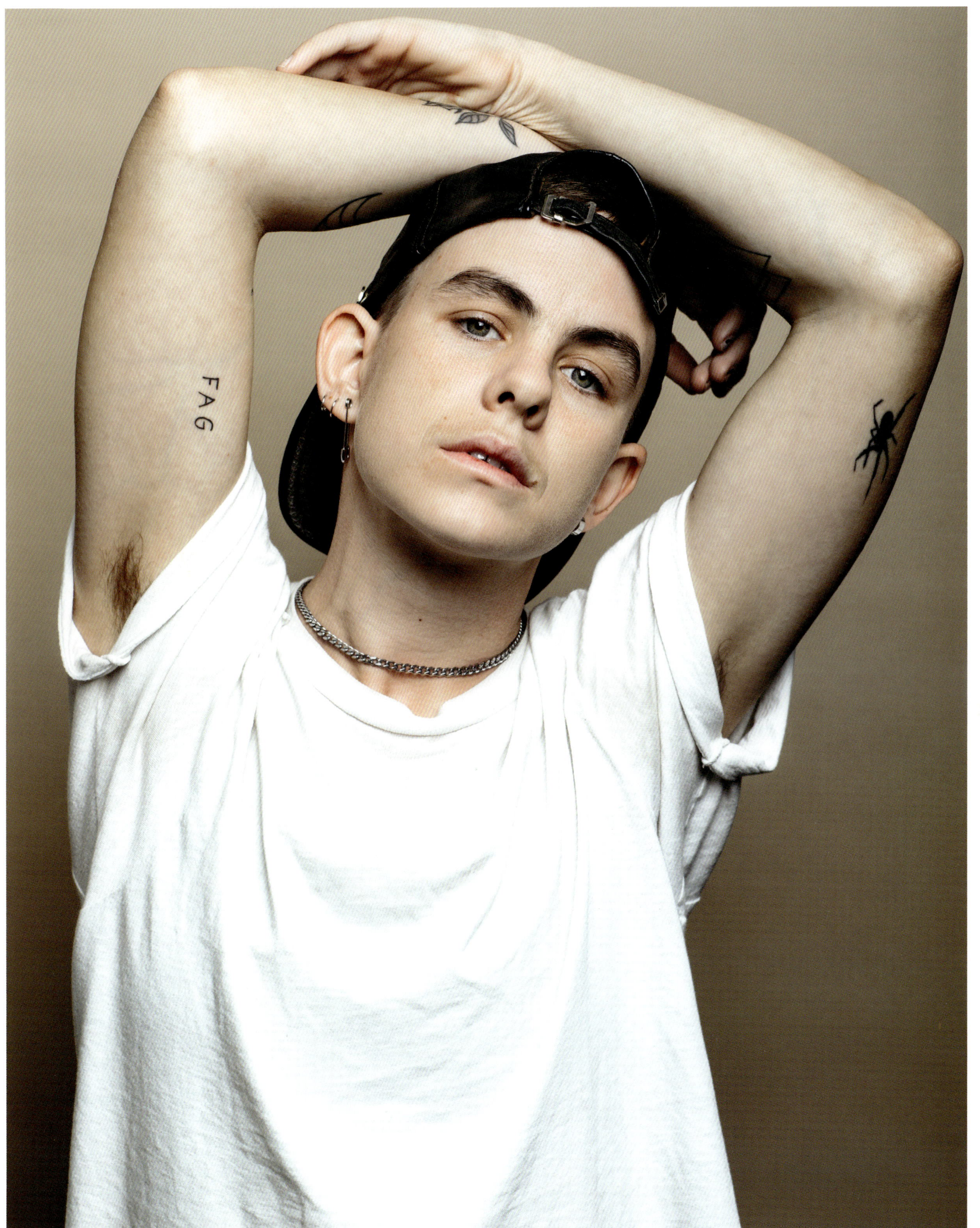
FAG

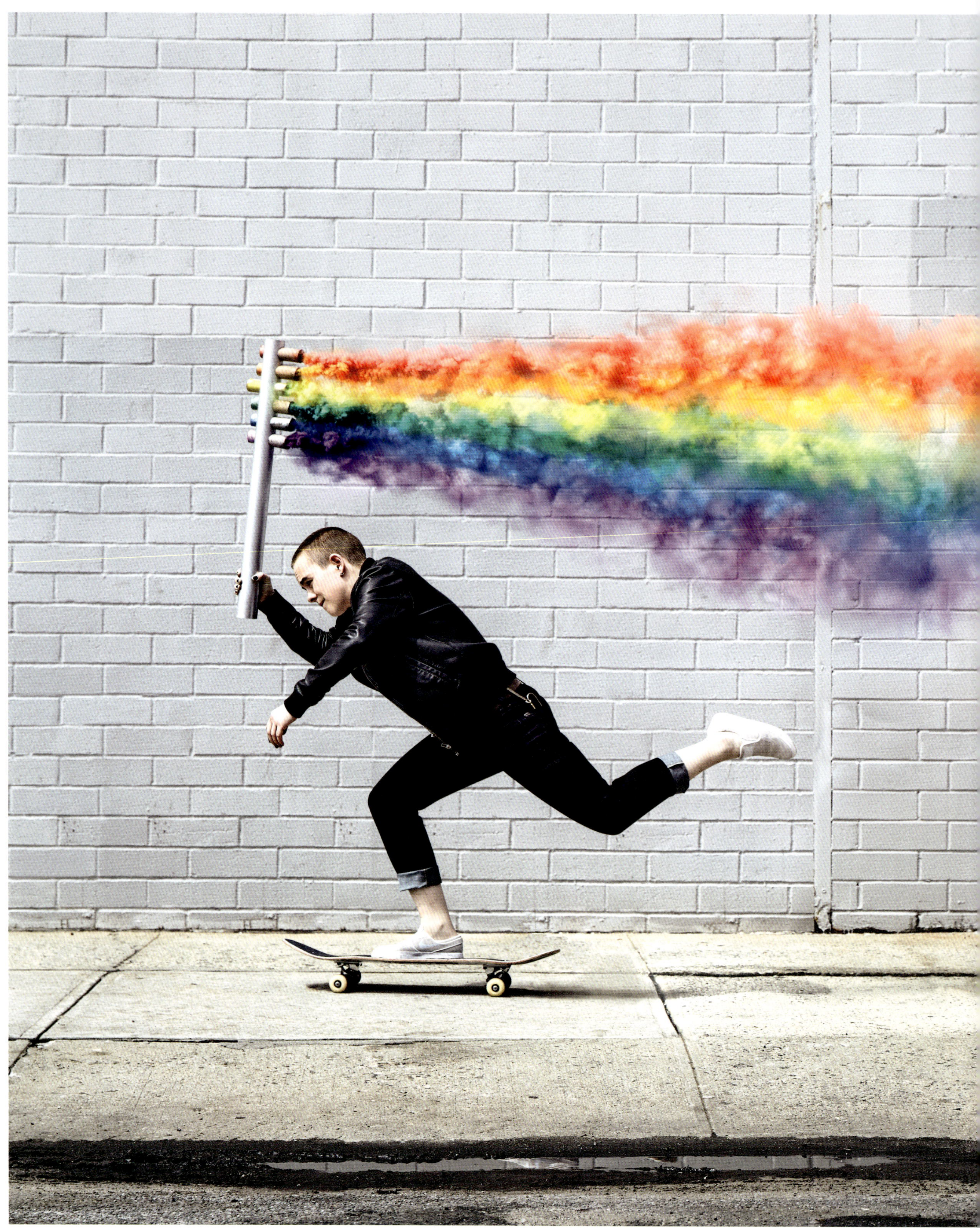

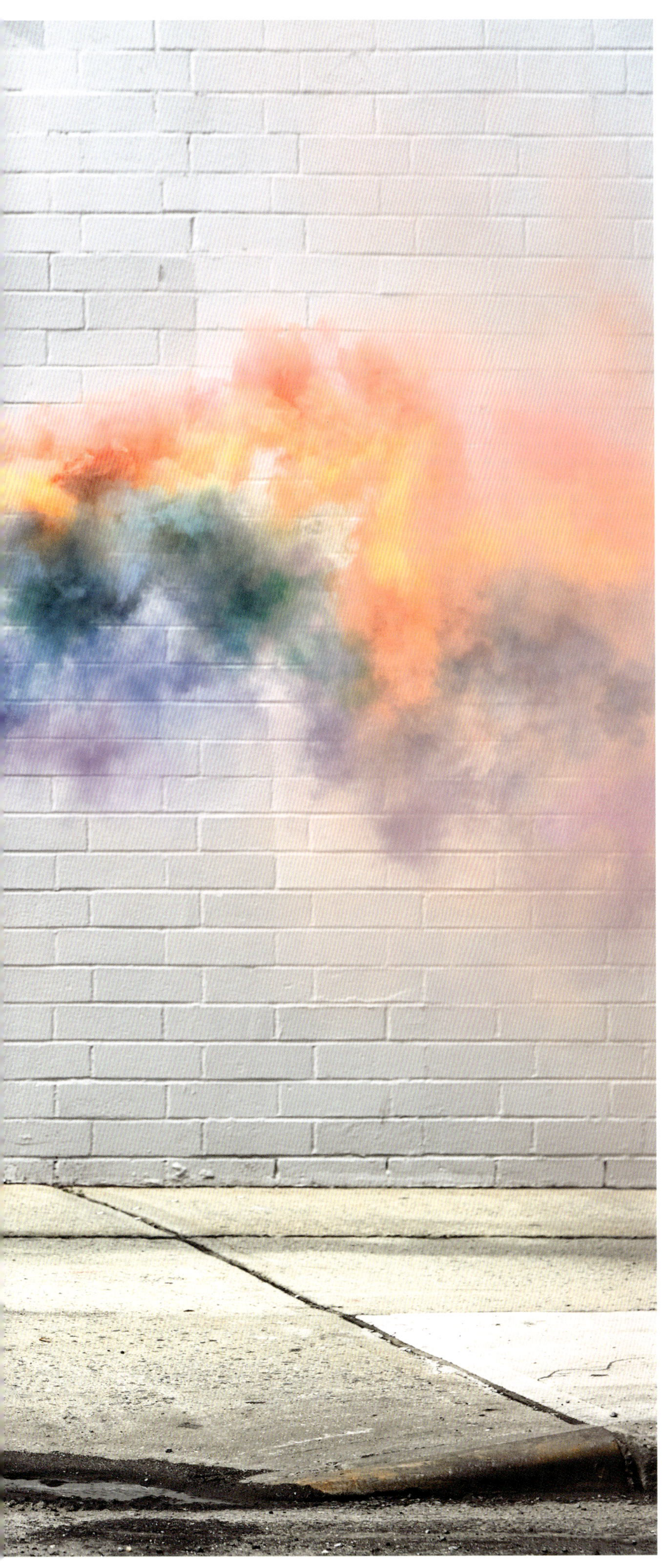

LEO BAKER NYC

JAMIE TANCOWNY MIAMI

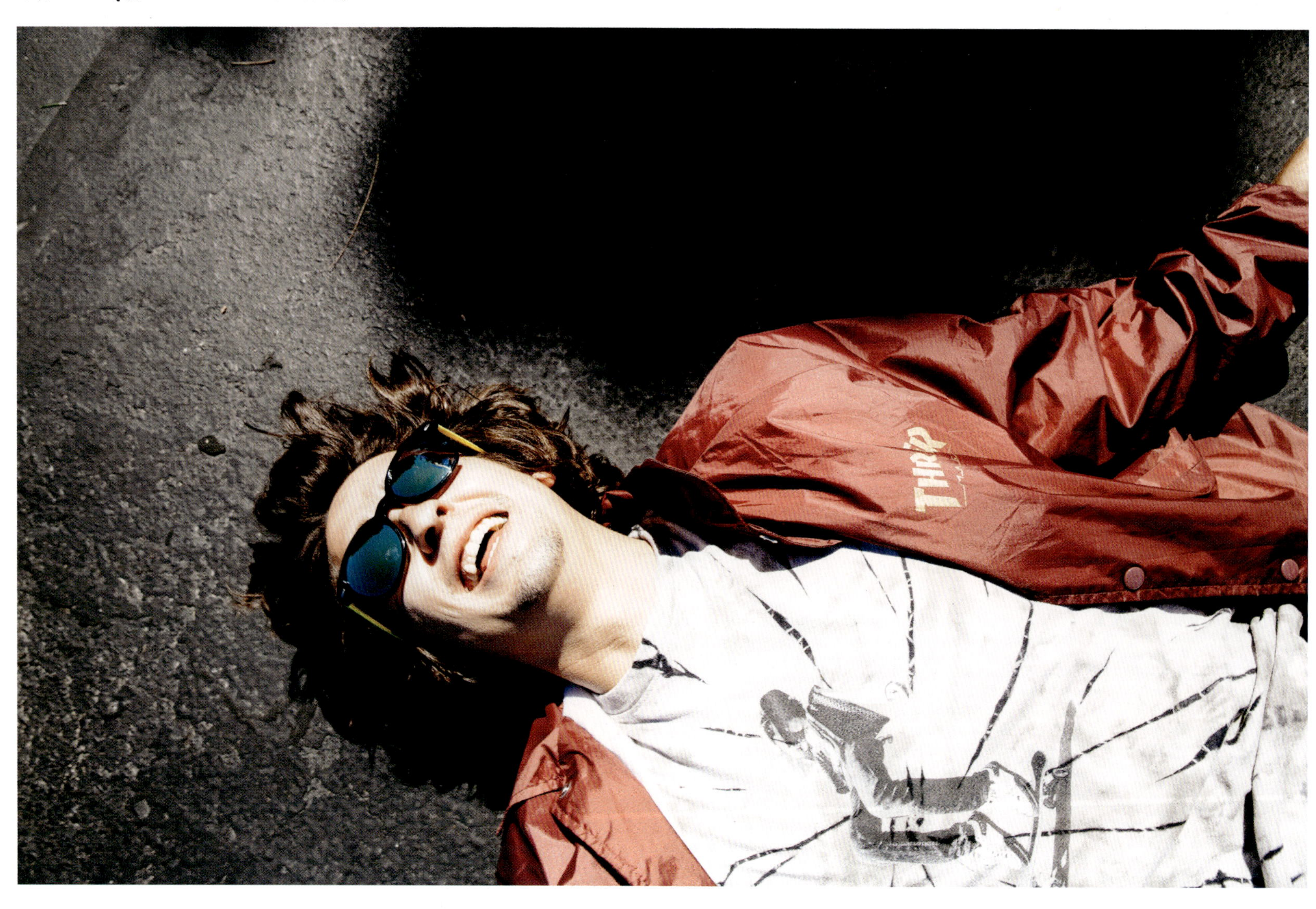

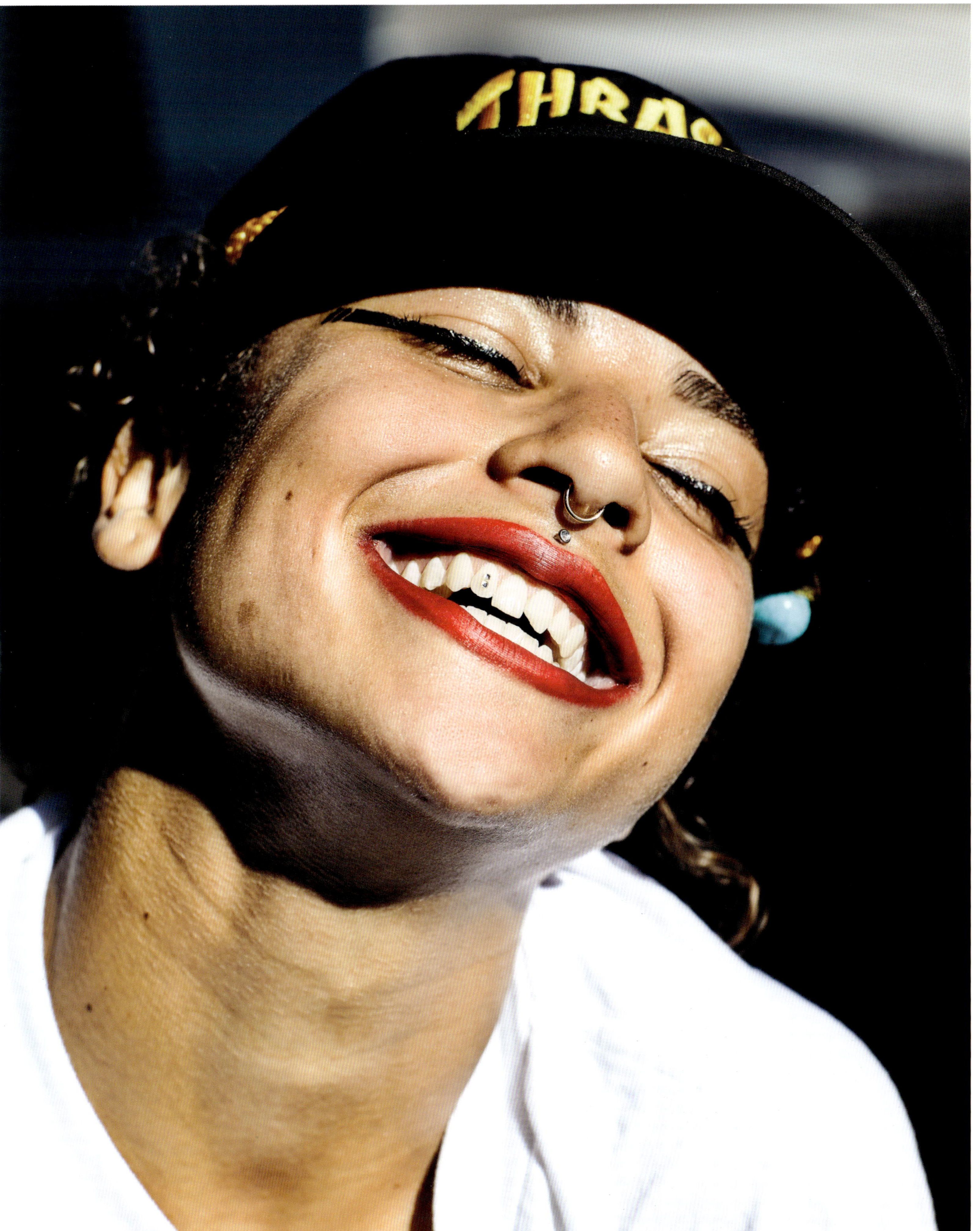

OAKLAND, CA

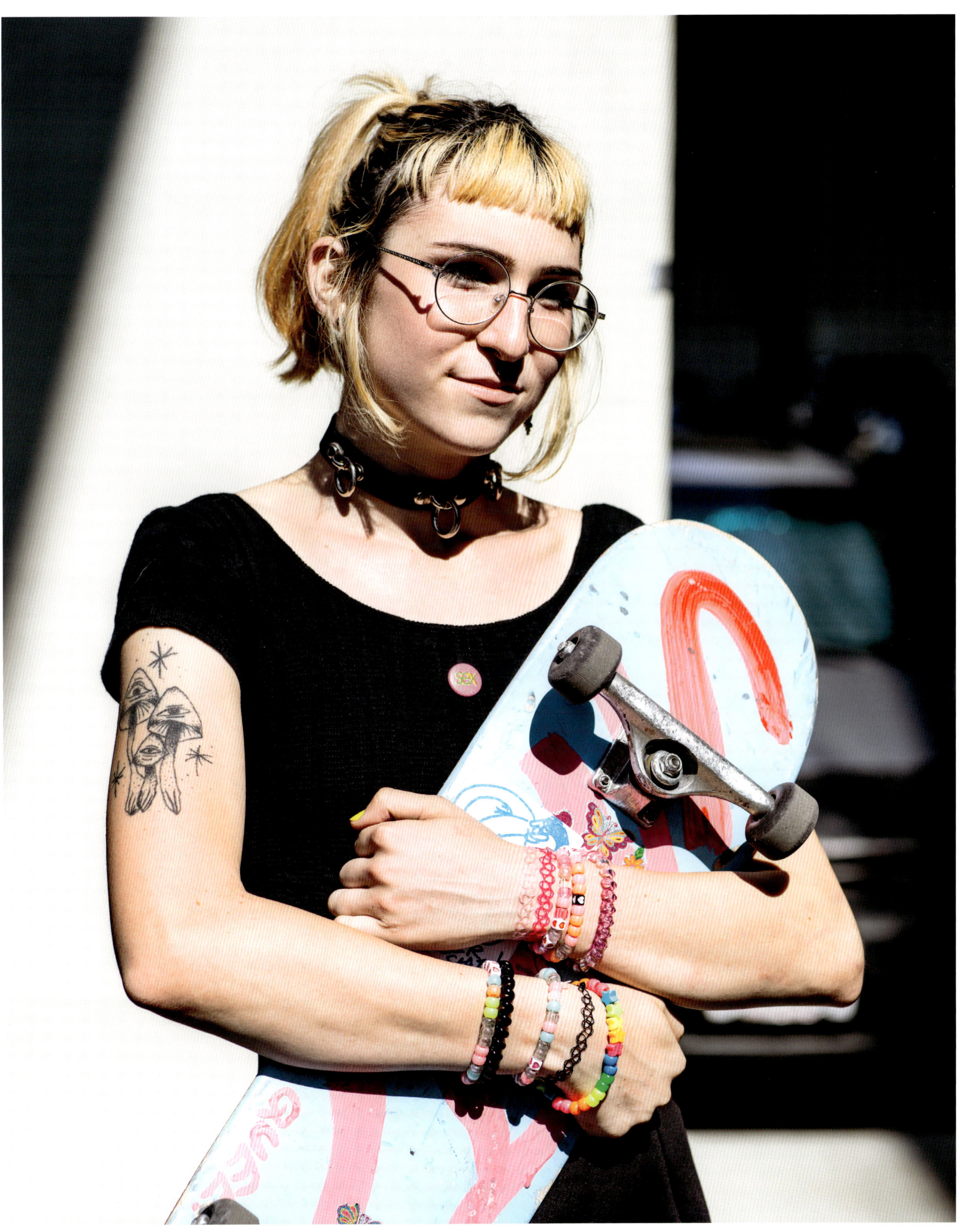
sex

MAE OAKLAND, CA

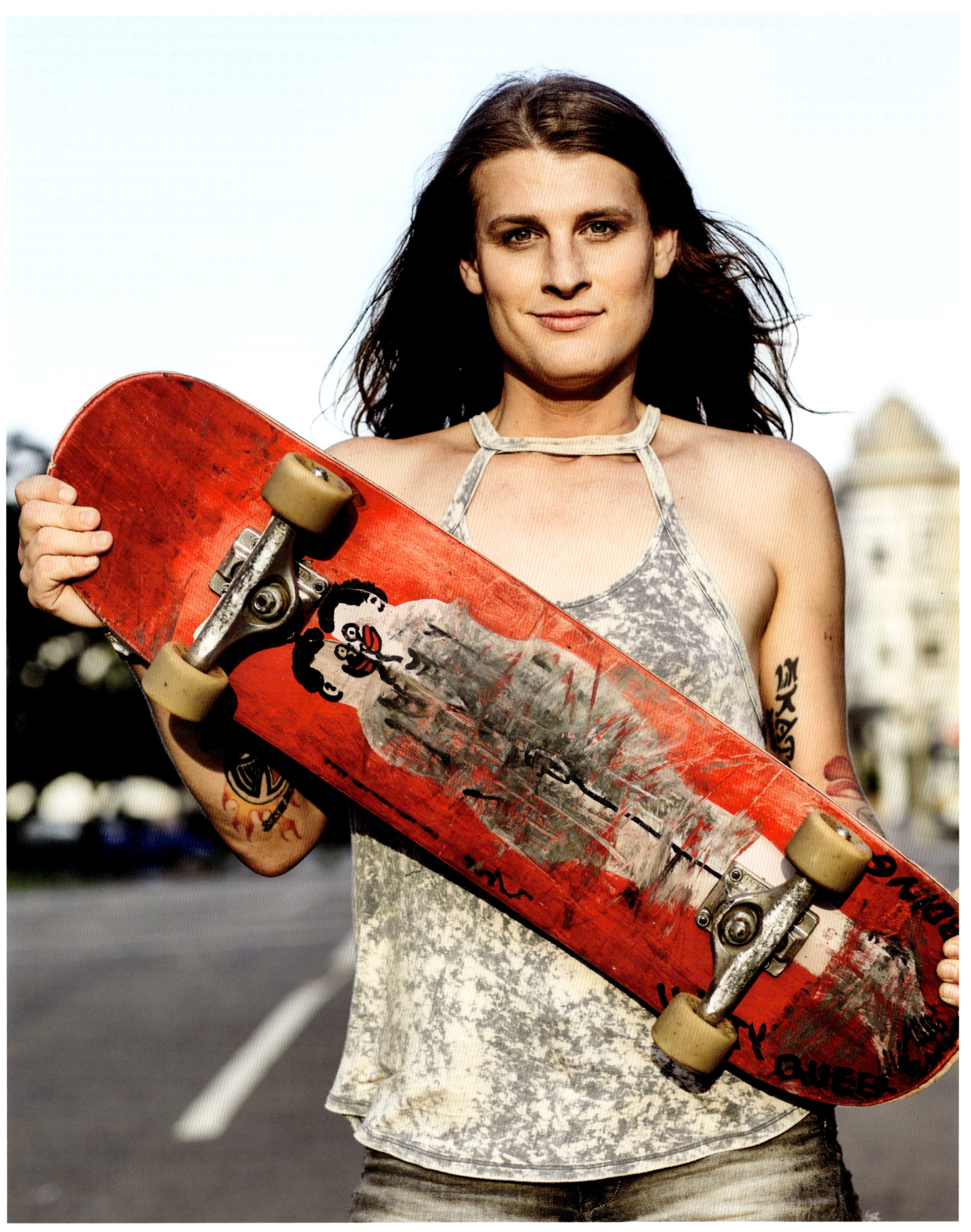

JEFF + GABE OAKLAND, CA

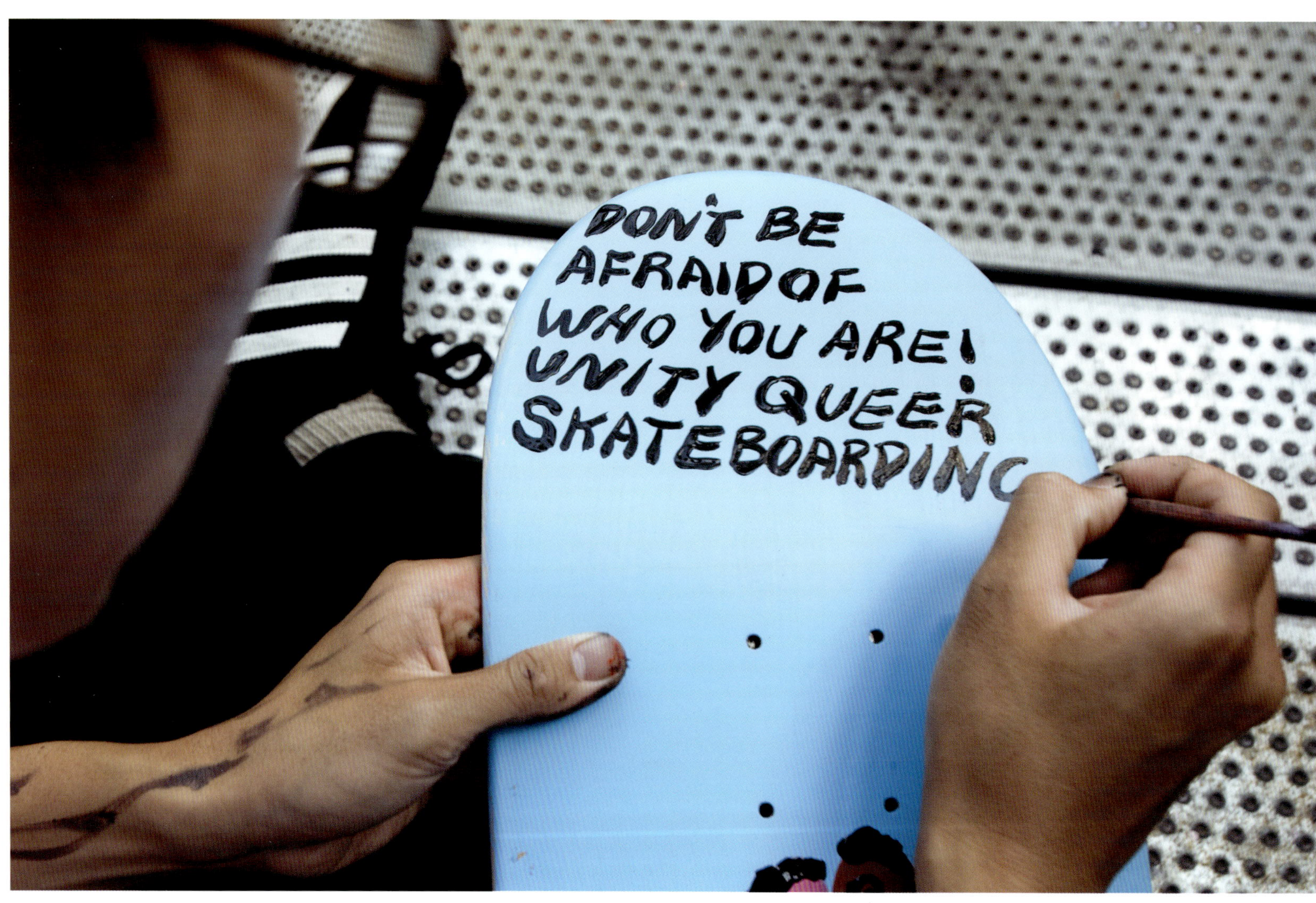

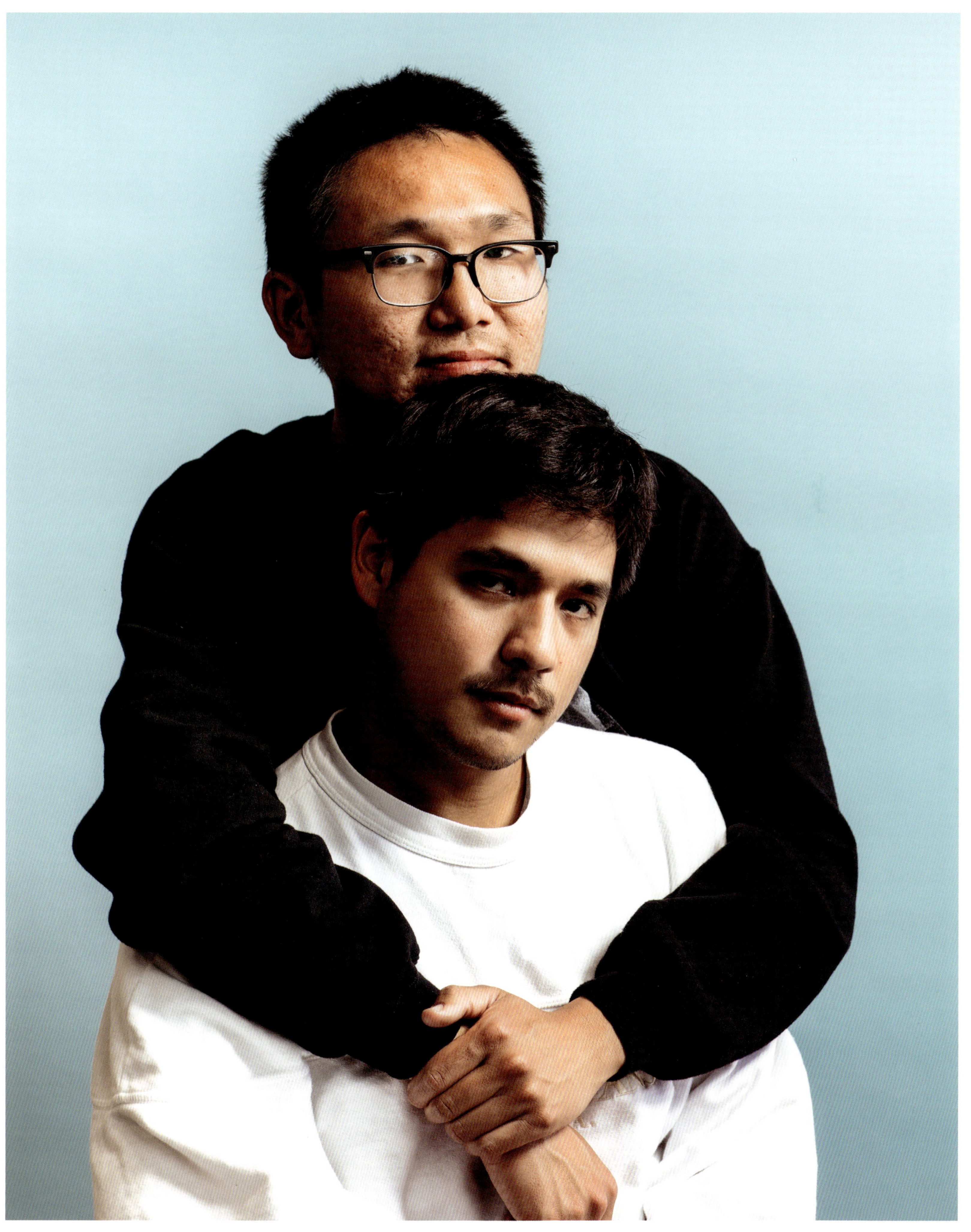

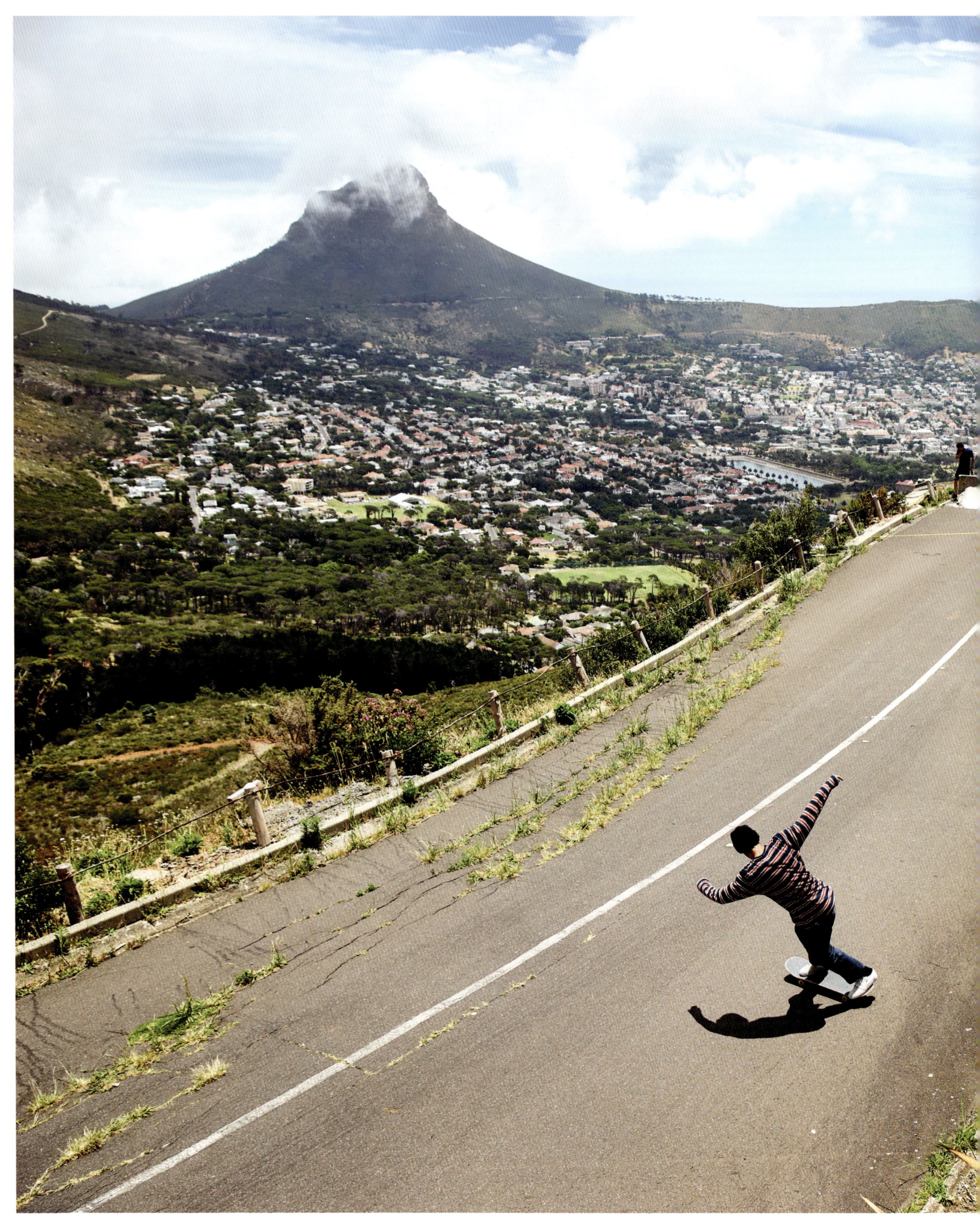

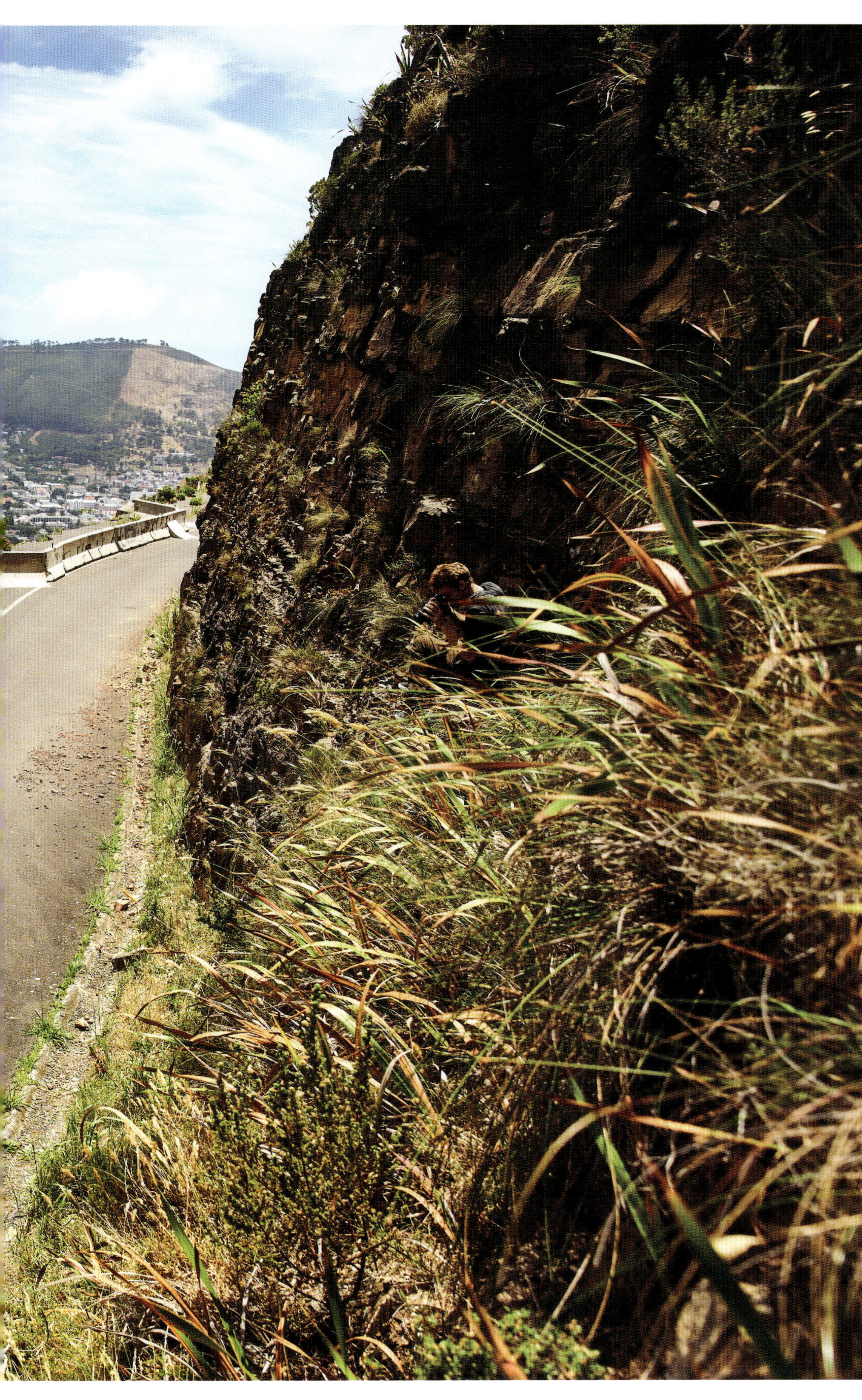

SEBO WALKER CAPE TOWN, SA

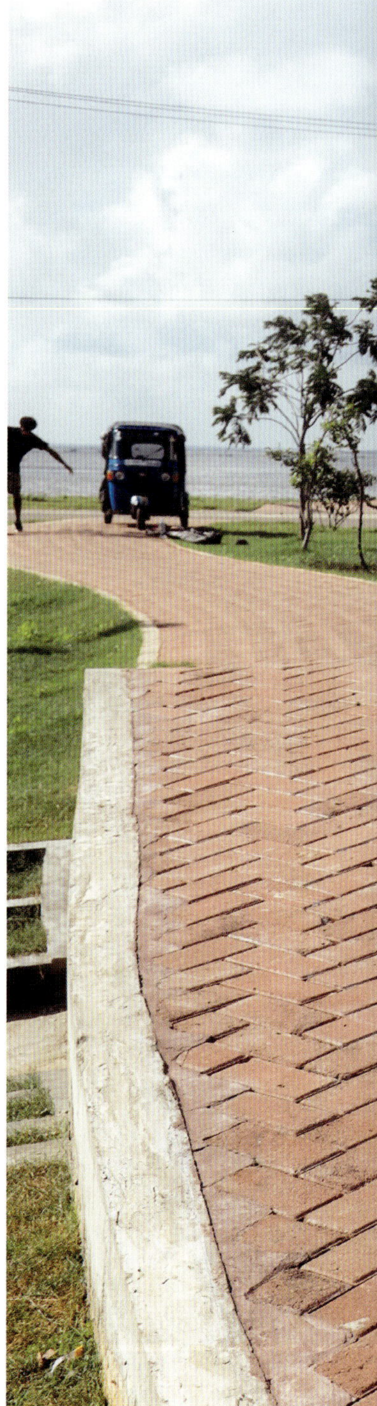

KIDS SKATING JAFFNA, SRI LANKA

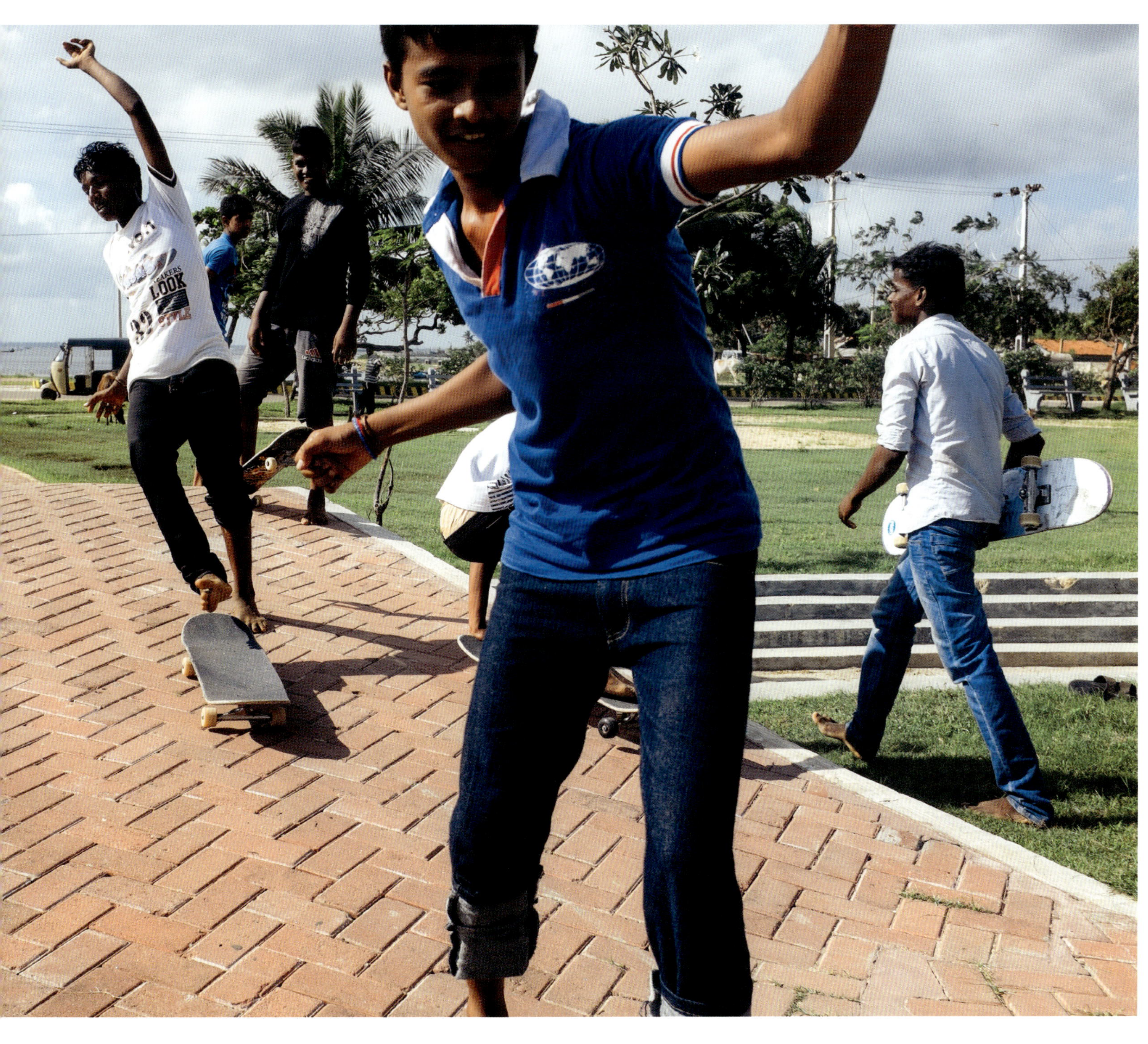
LOOK

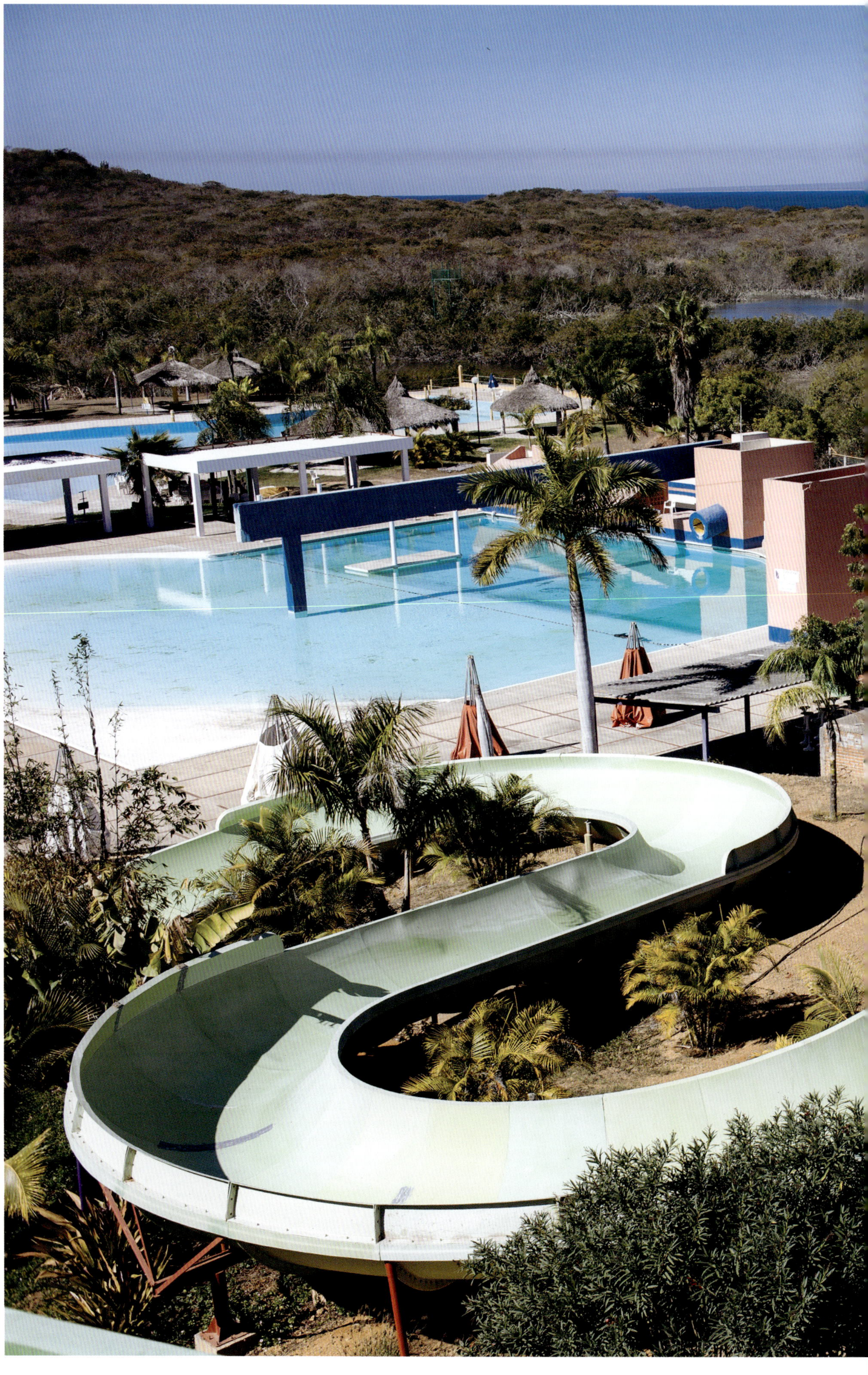

STEVE NESSER MAZATLAN, MX

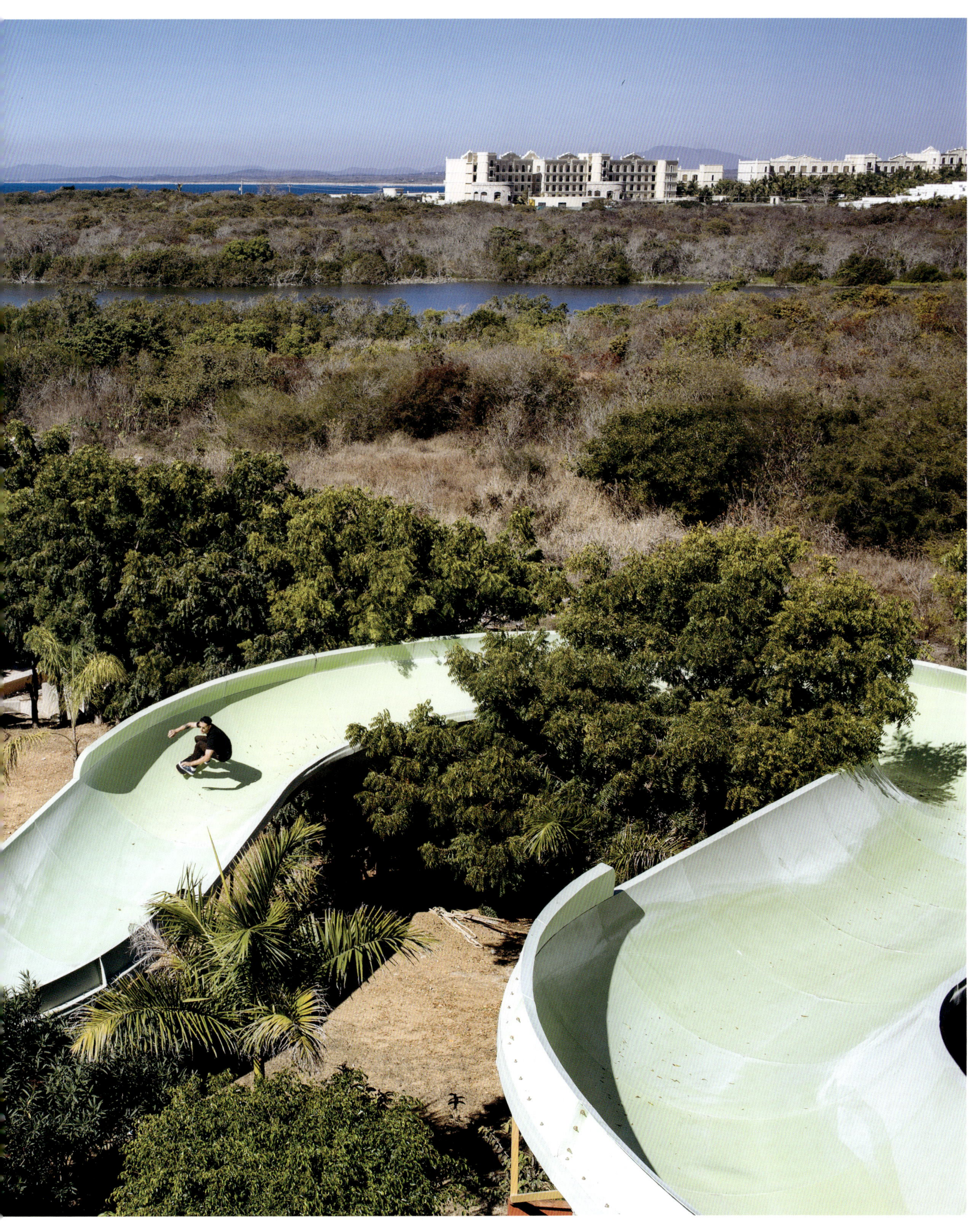

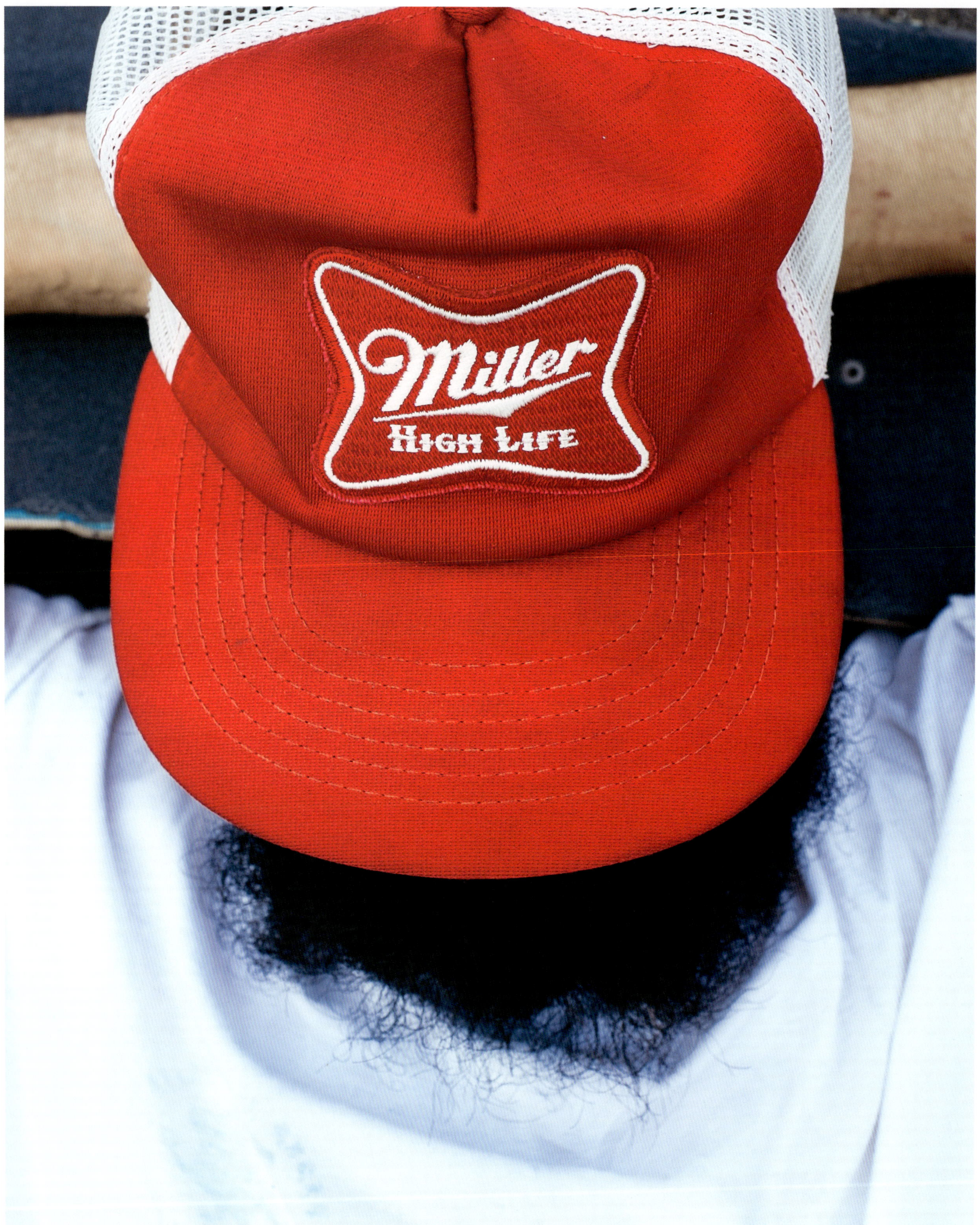
Miller
High Life

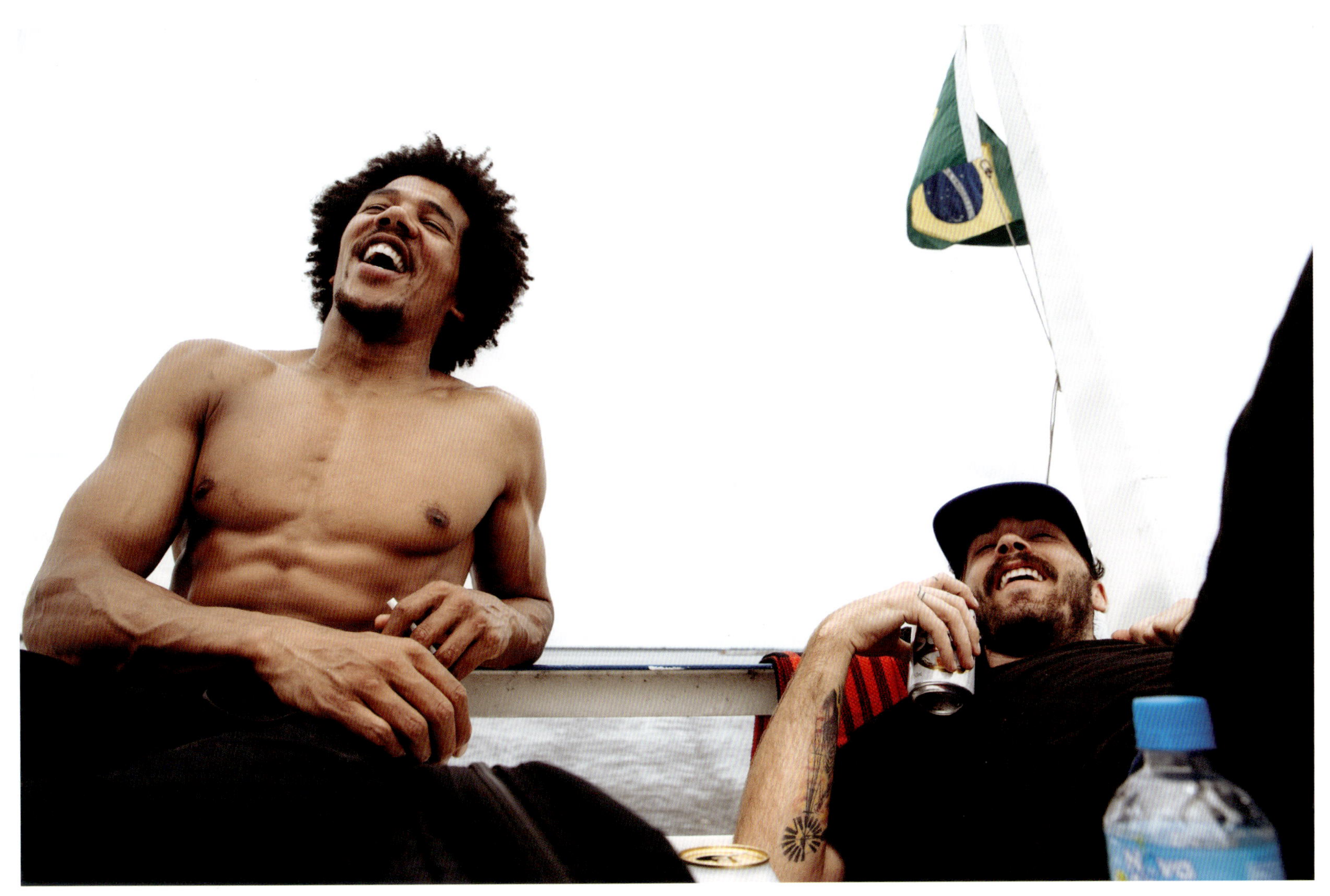

KORAHN GAYLE + CLINT WALKER   MANAUS, BRAZIL

NICK BOSERIO   SRI LANKA

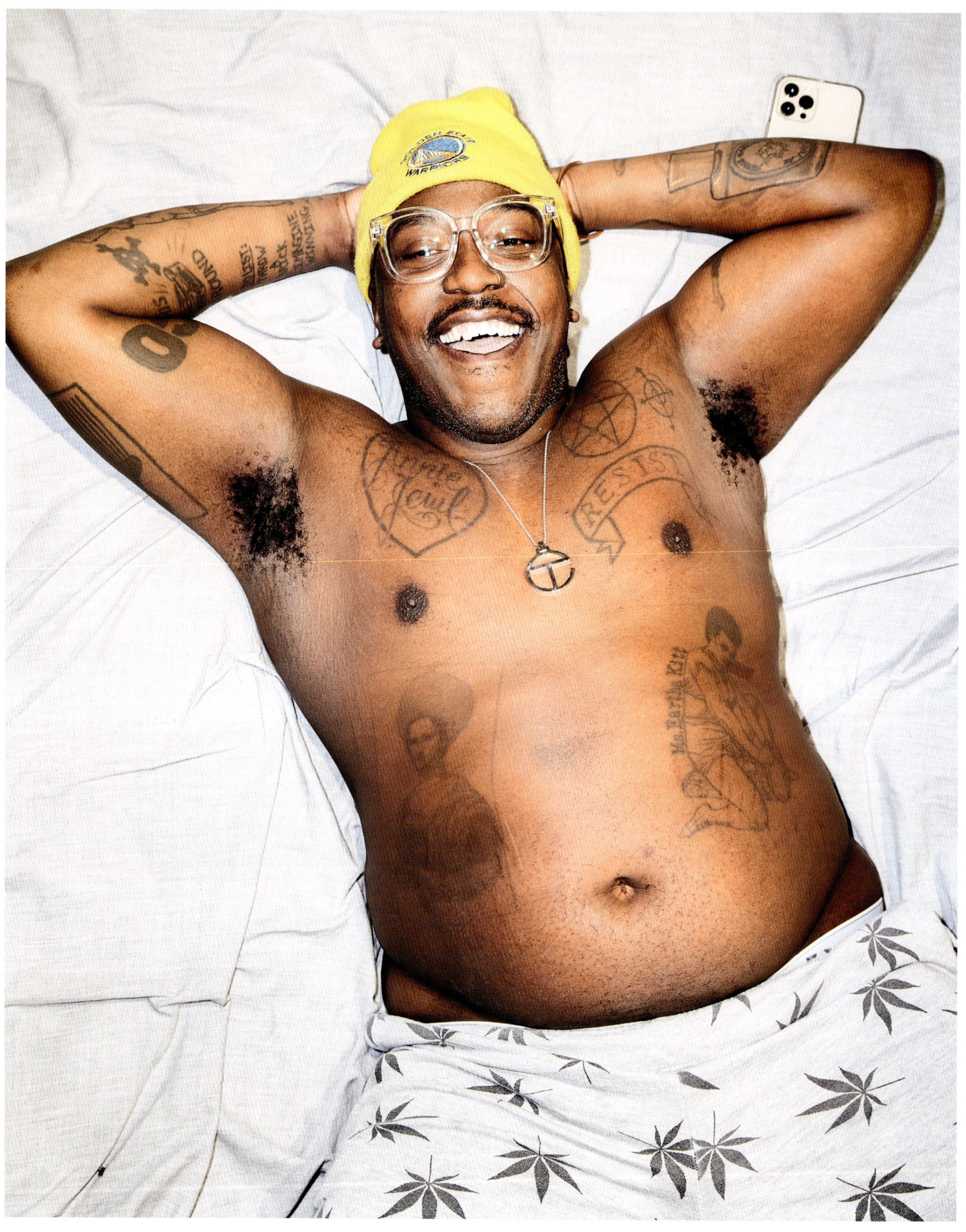
WARRIORS
RESIST

BRONTEZ PURWELL
OAKLAND, CA

MALDIVES

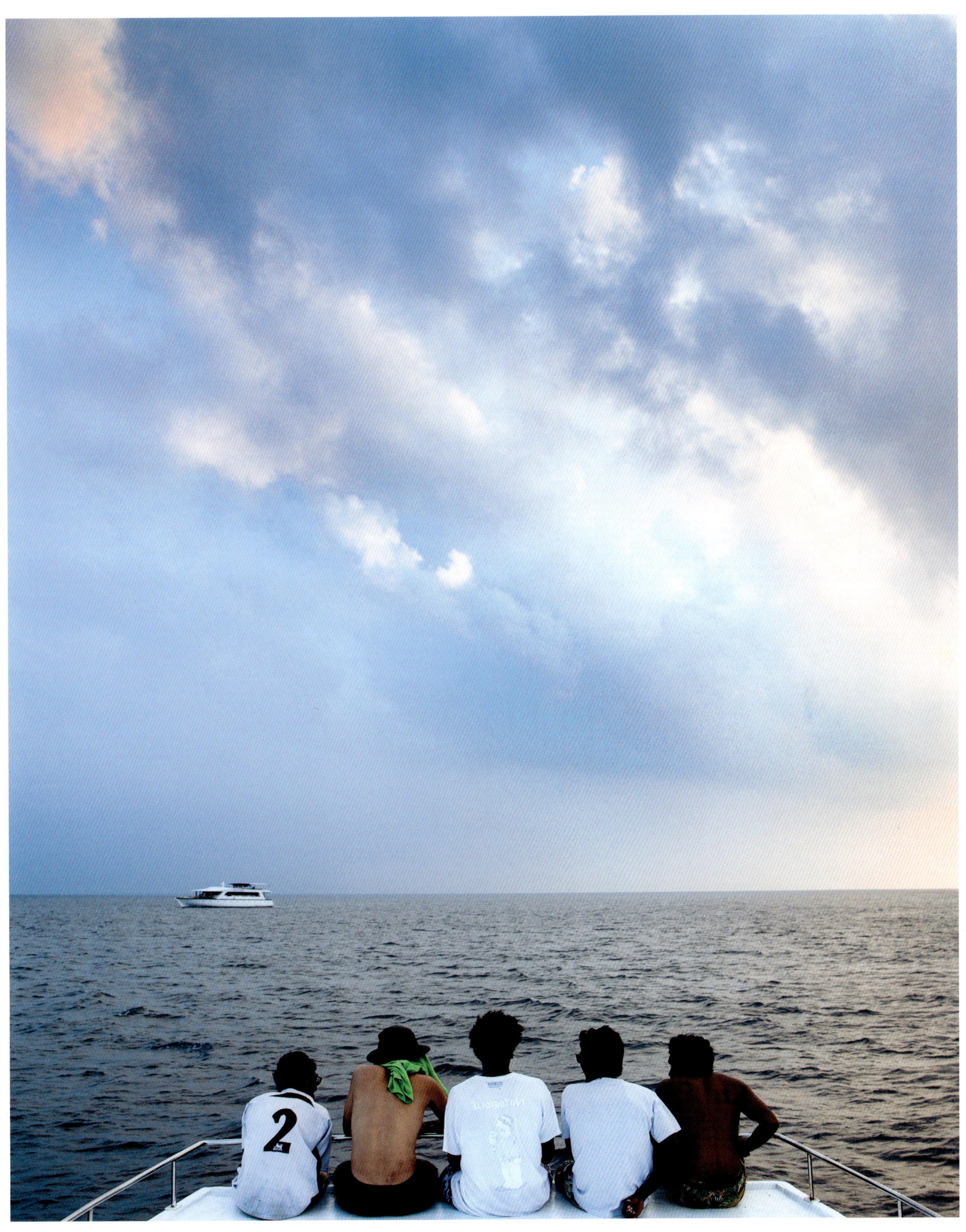
2

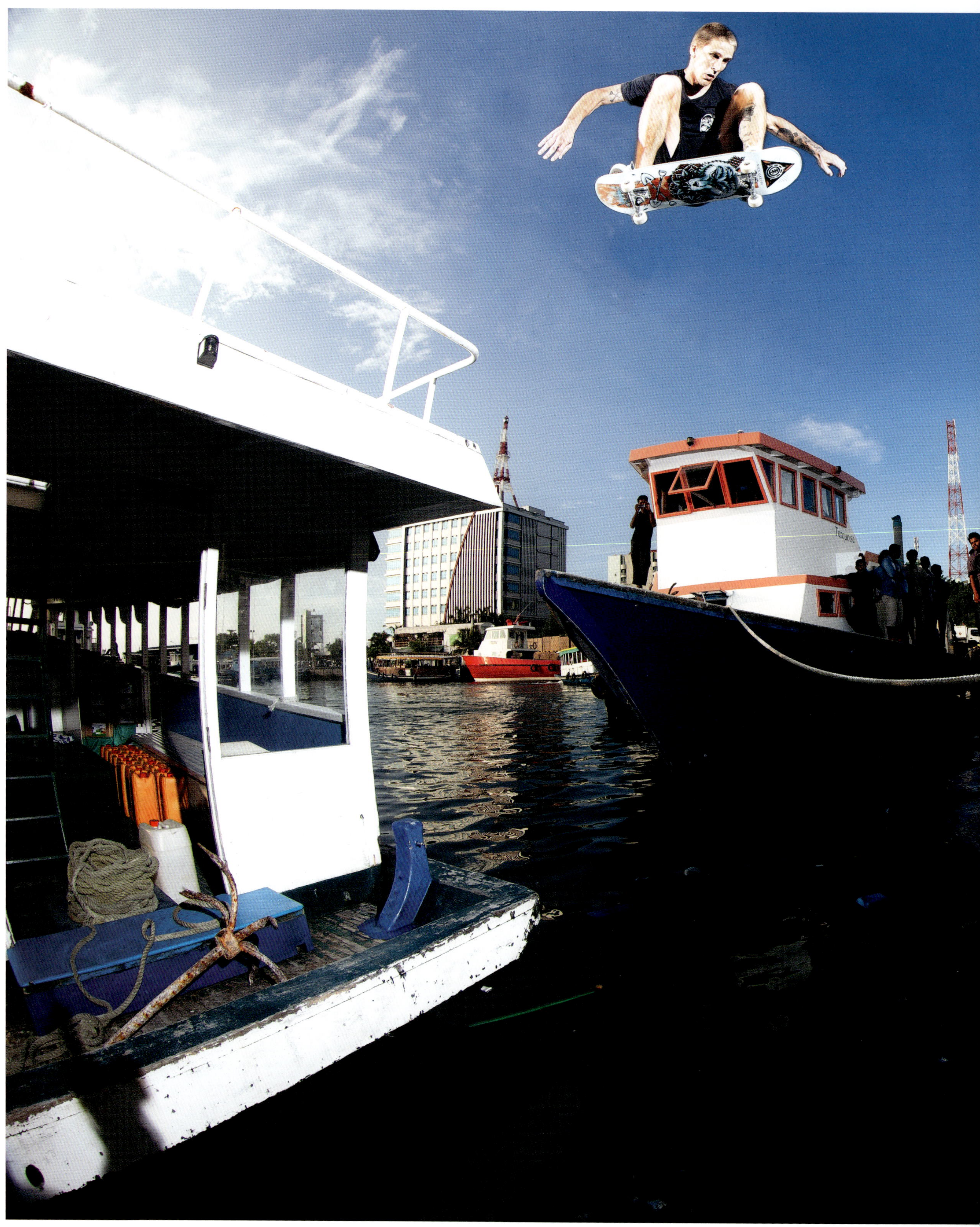
Turquoise

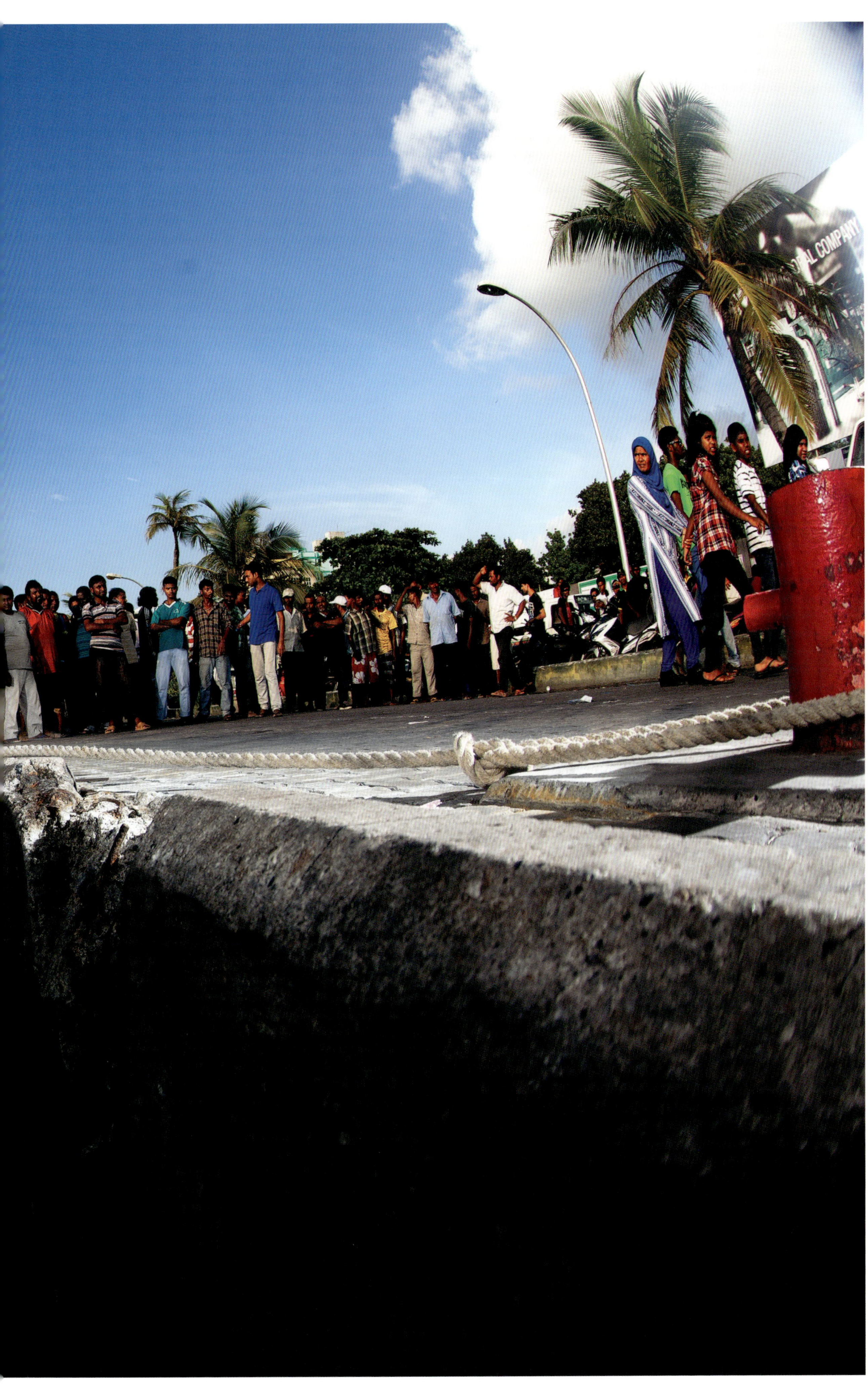

NICK GARCIA

MALÉ, MALDIVES

CYRUS BENNETT SARAJEVO, BOSNIA

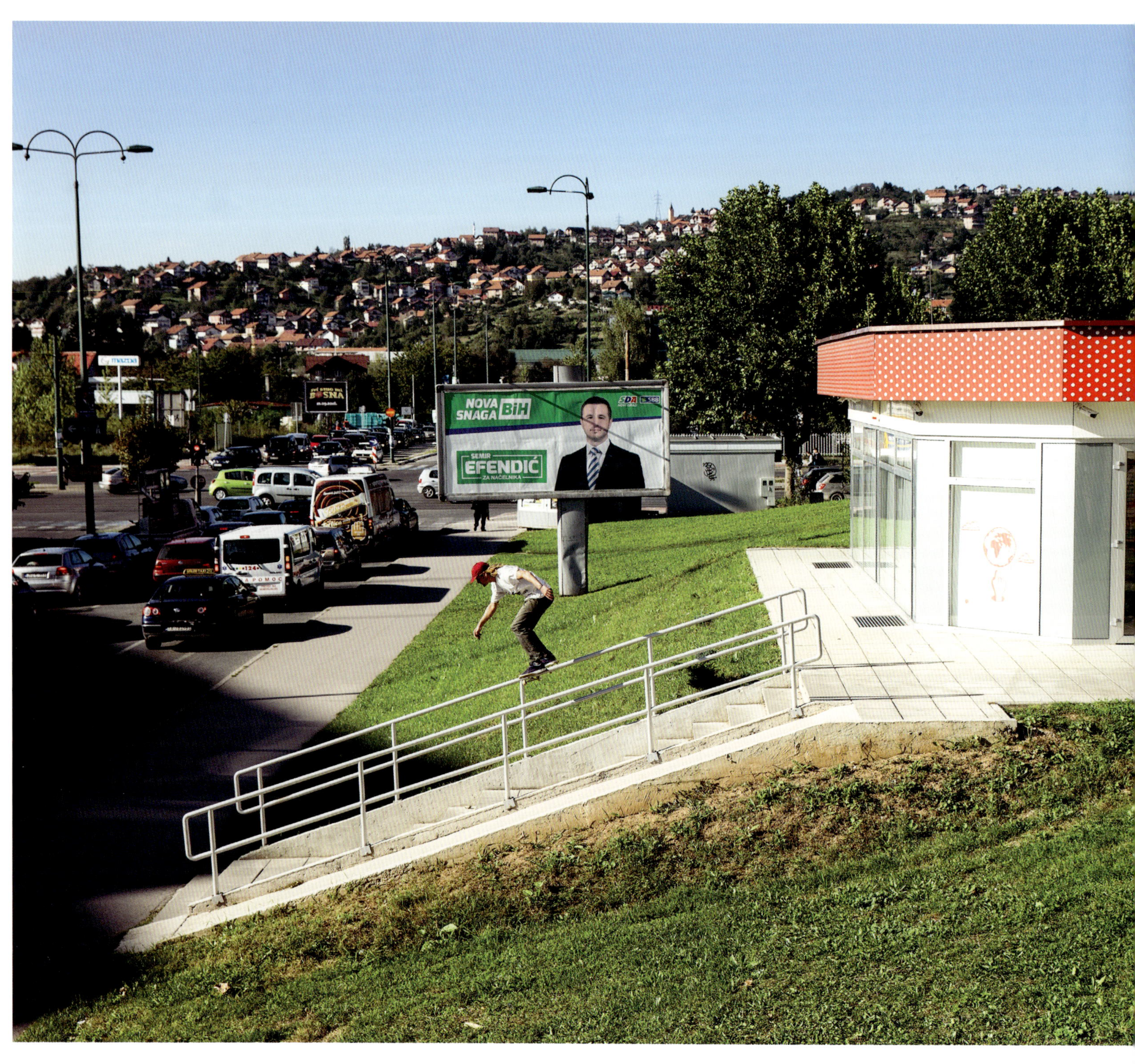

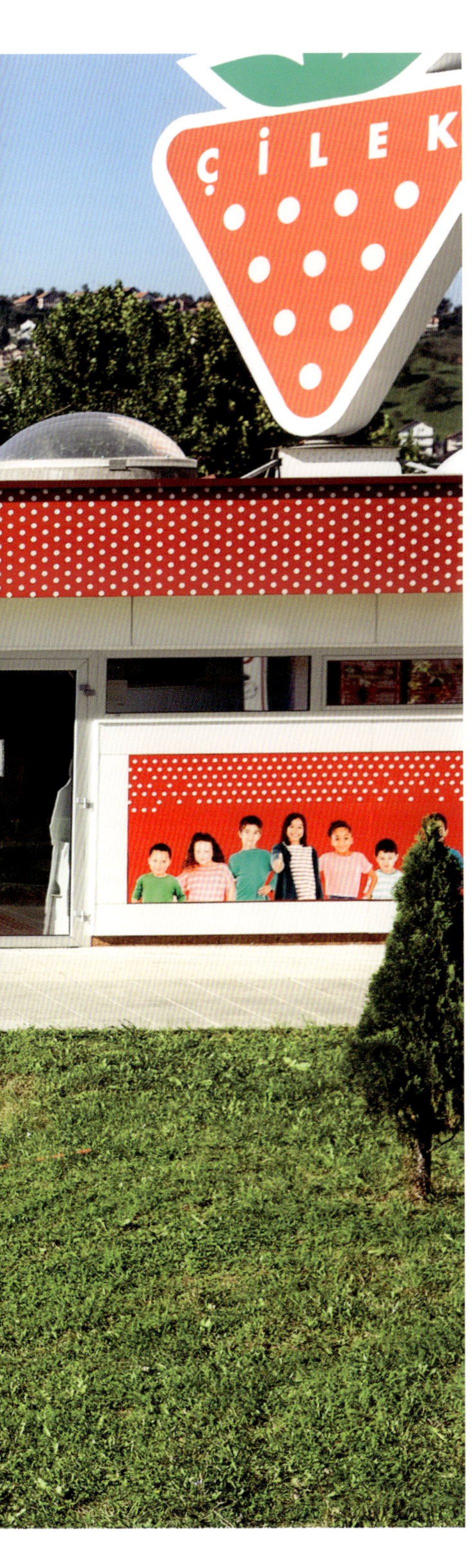
ÇİLEK

RYAN LAY TANGIER, MOROCCO

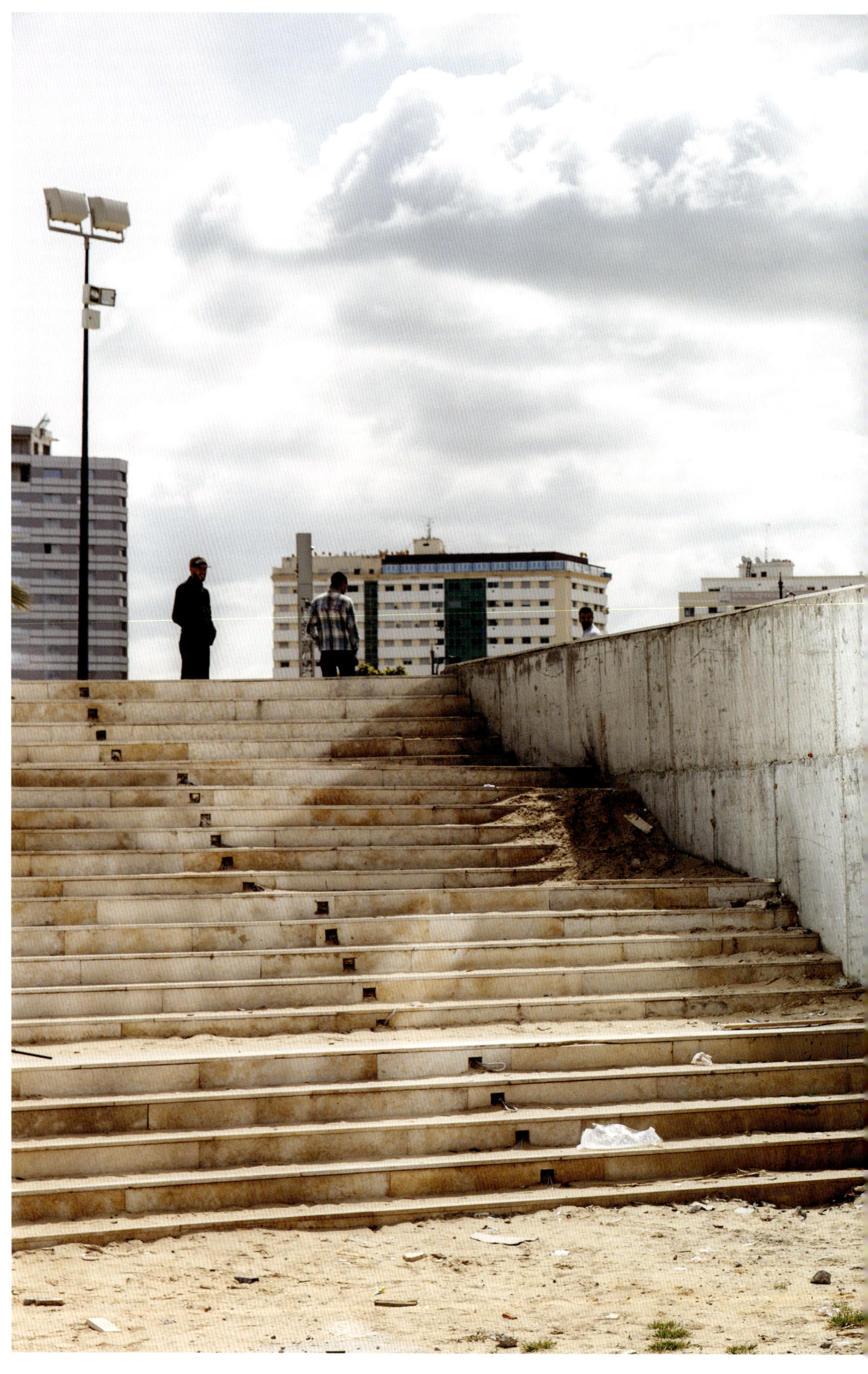

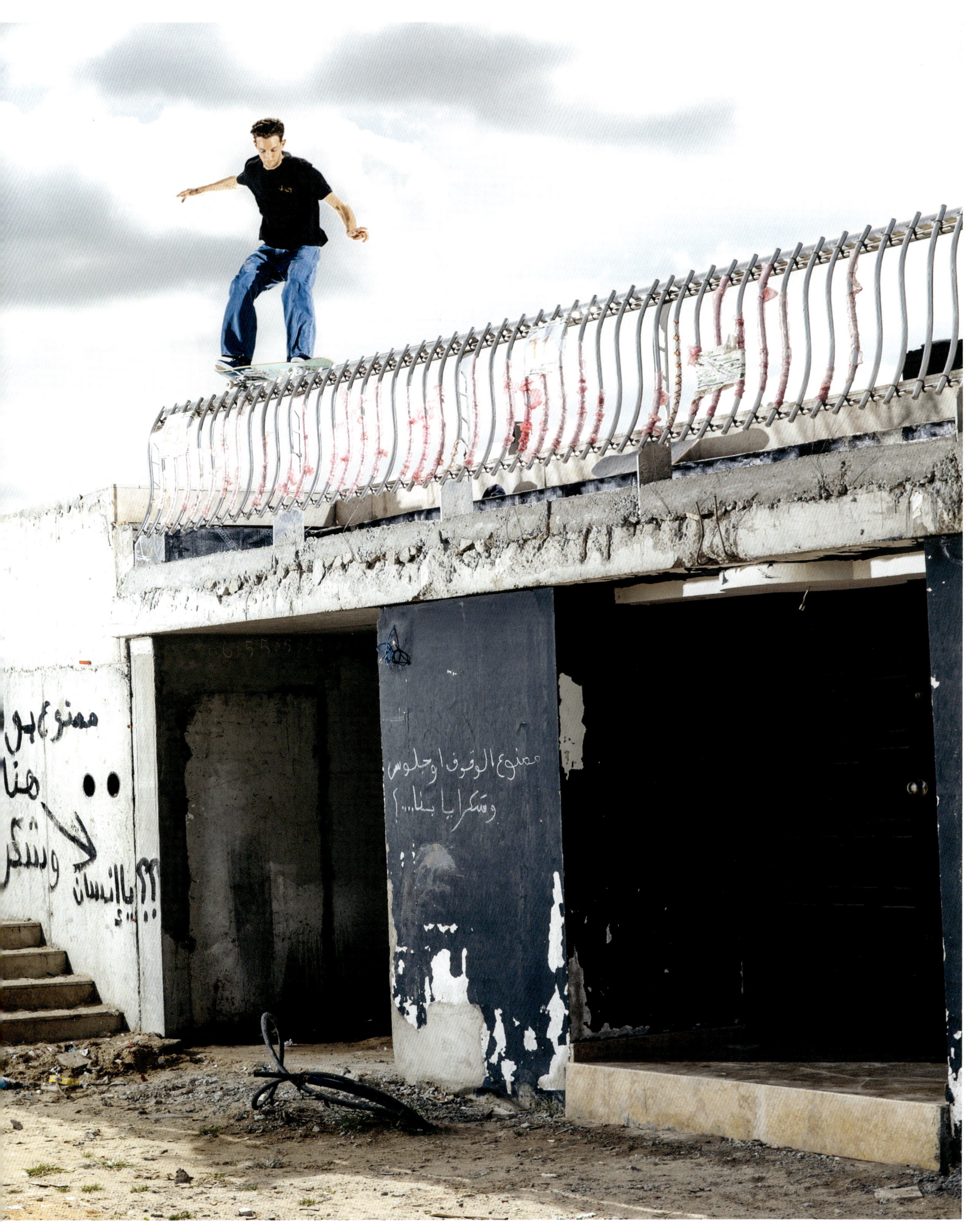
ممنوع الوقوف والجلوس

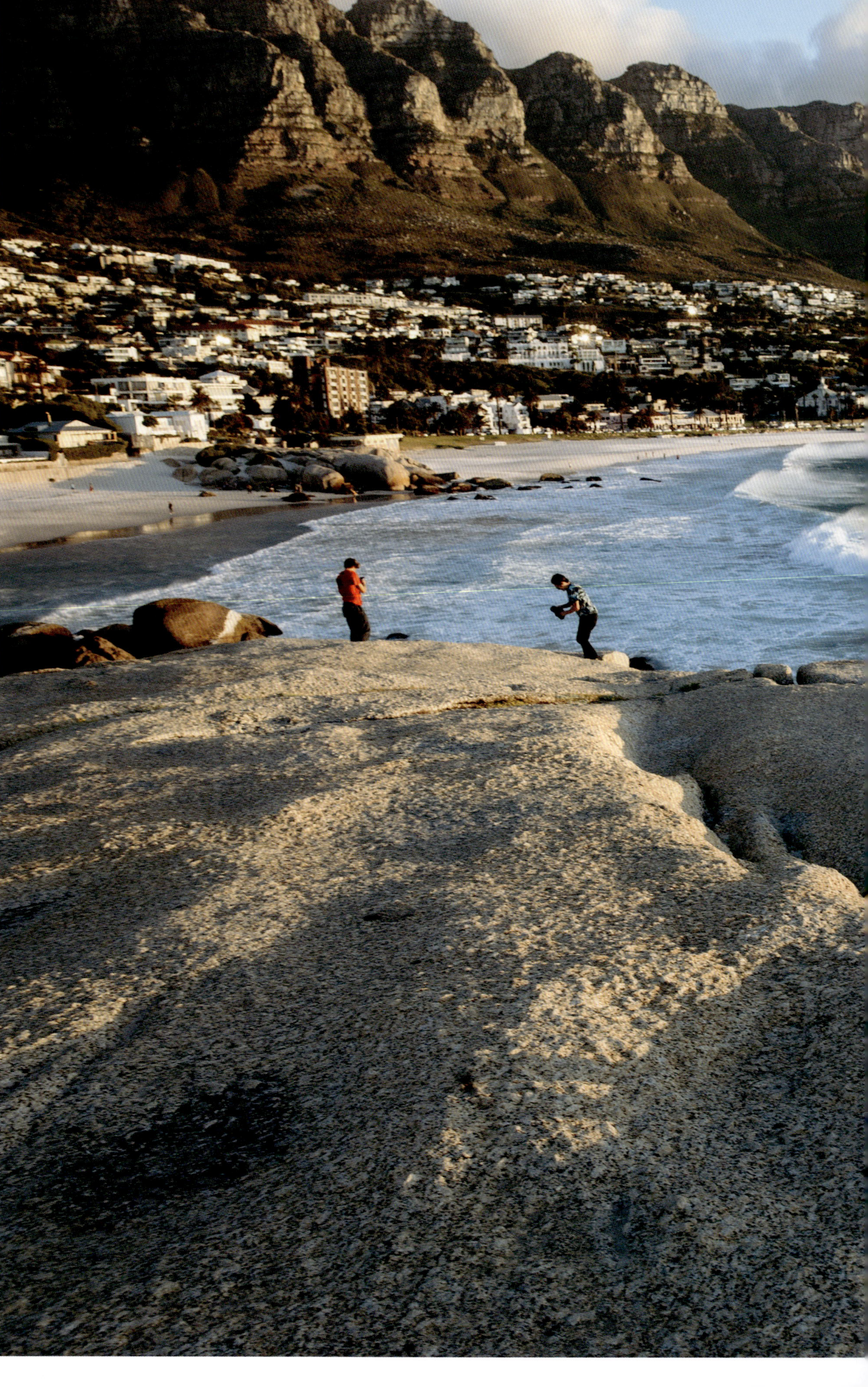

WALKER RYAN CAPE TOWN, SA

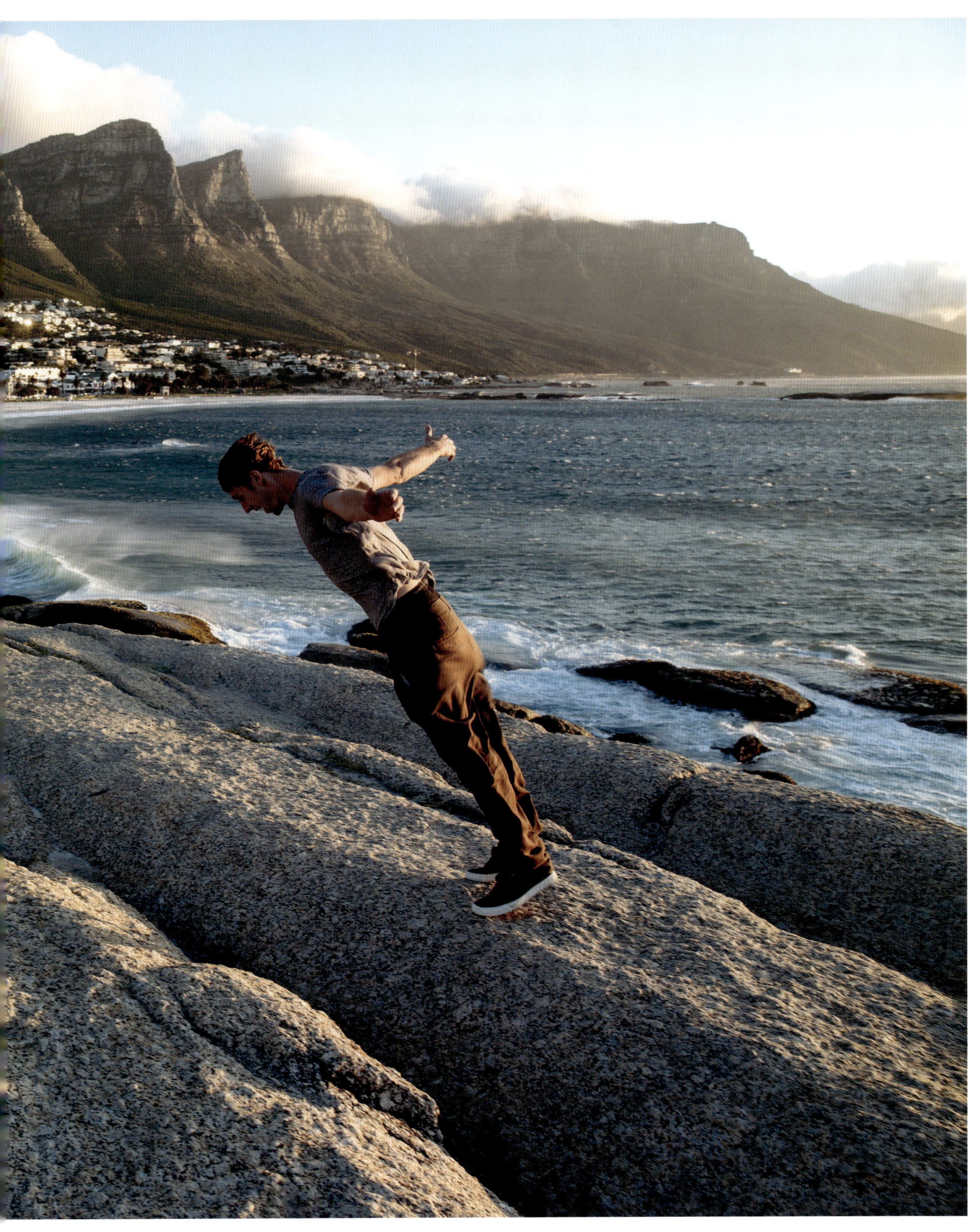

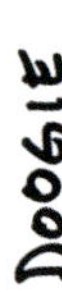

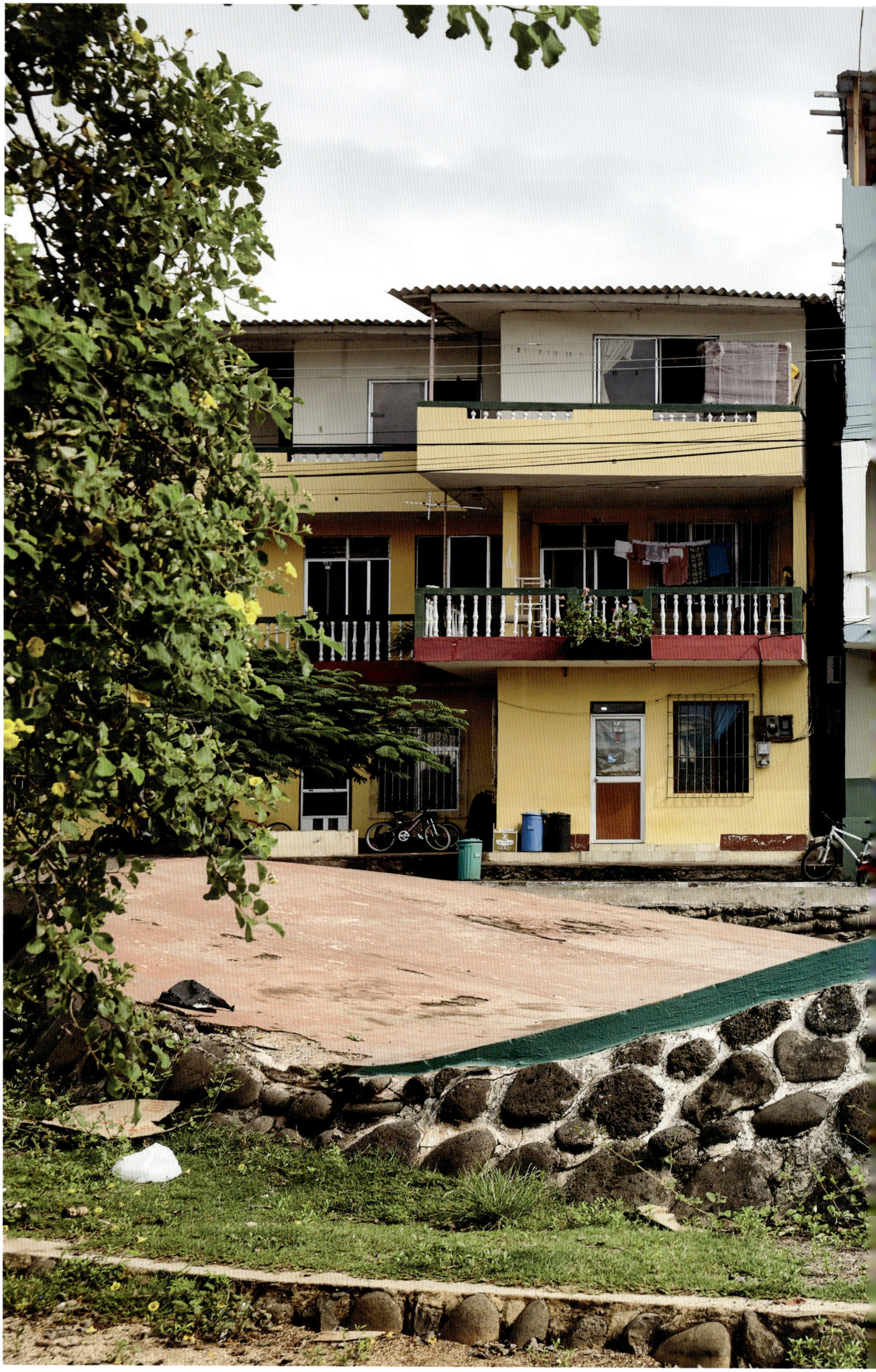

GALAPAGOS

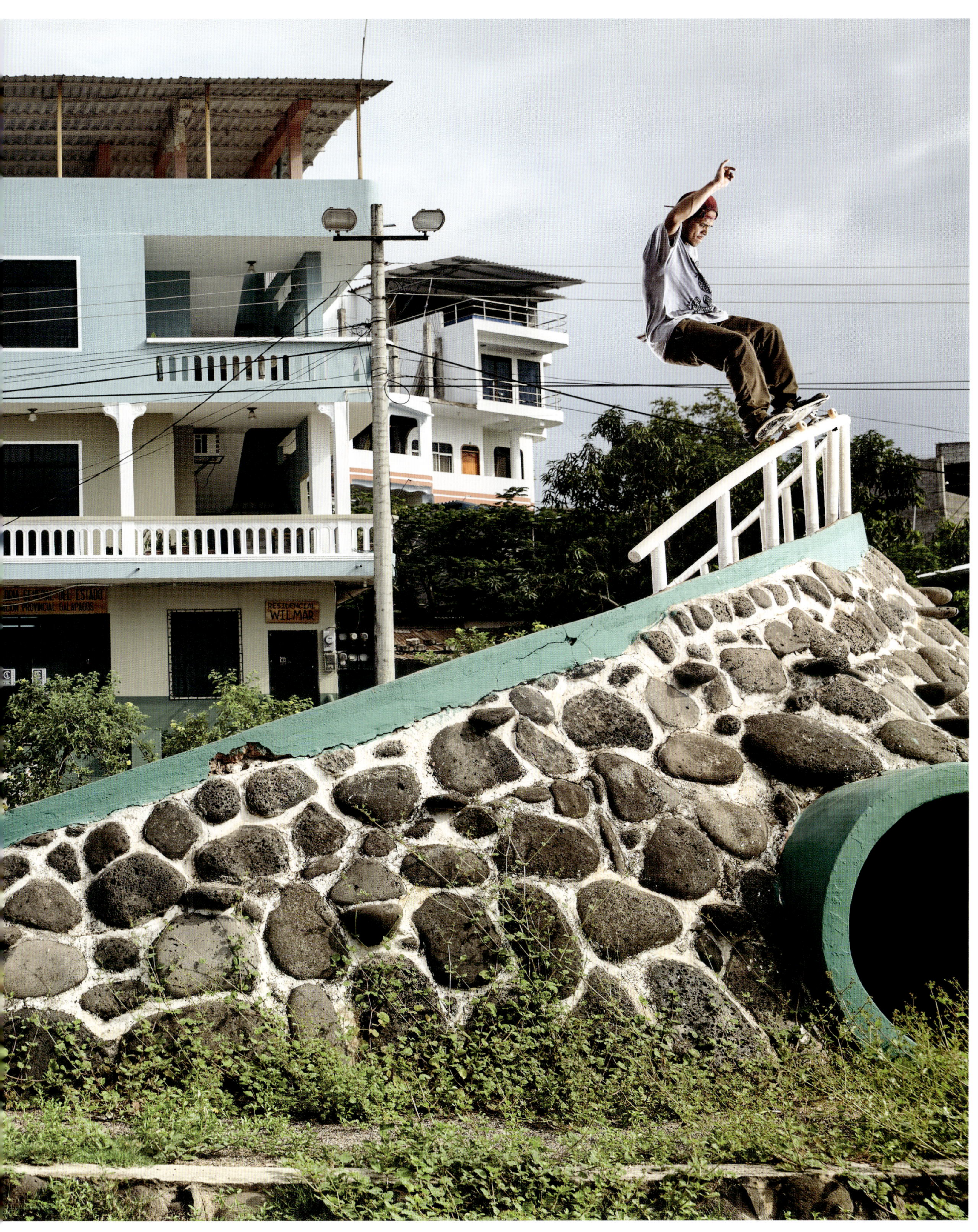
DEL ESTADO
PROVINCIAL GALAPAGOS
RESIDENCIAL
WILMAR

MALDIVES

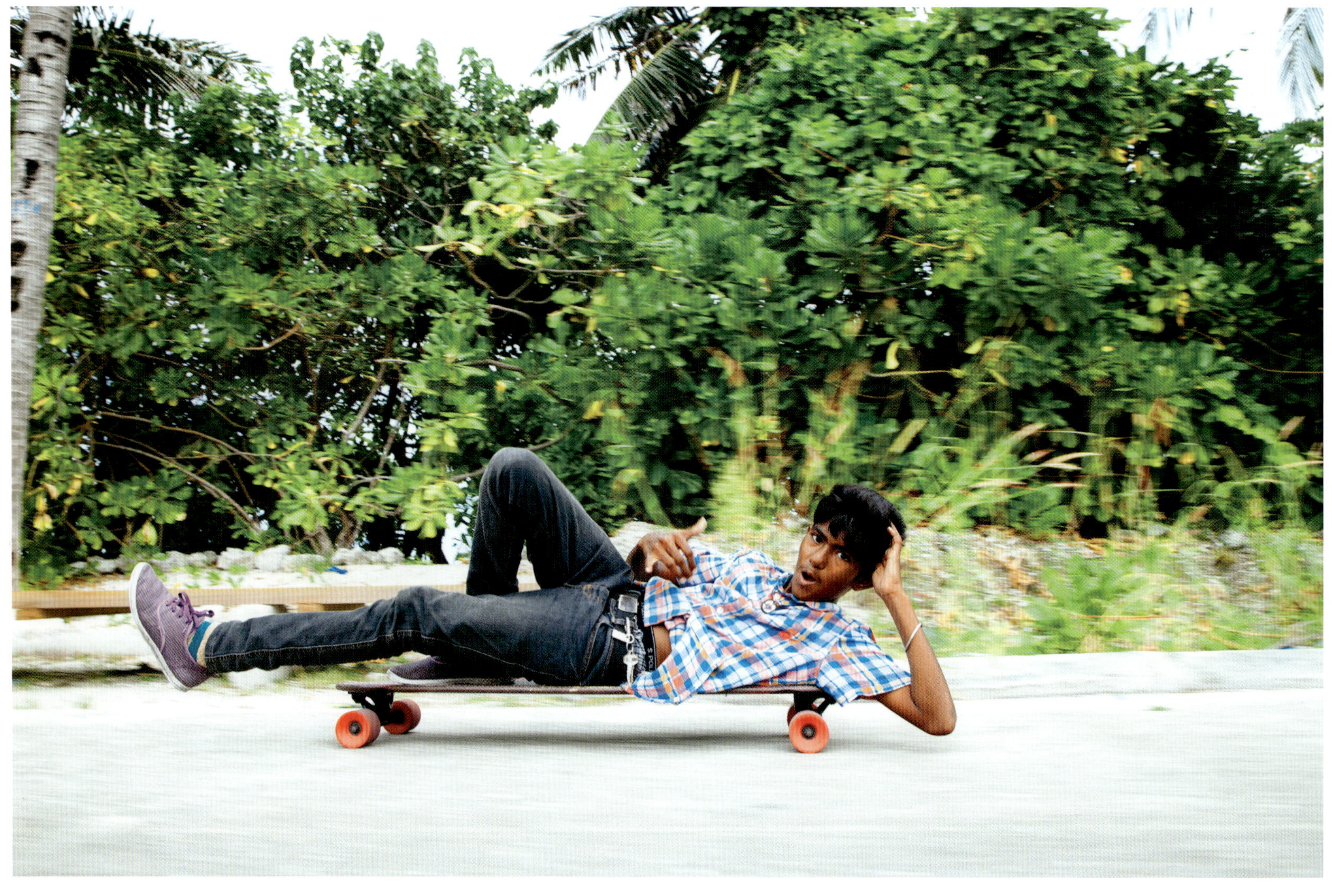

MASERU, LESOTHO

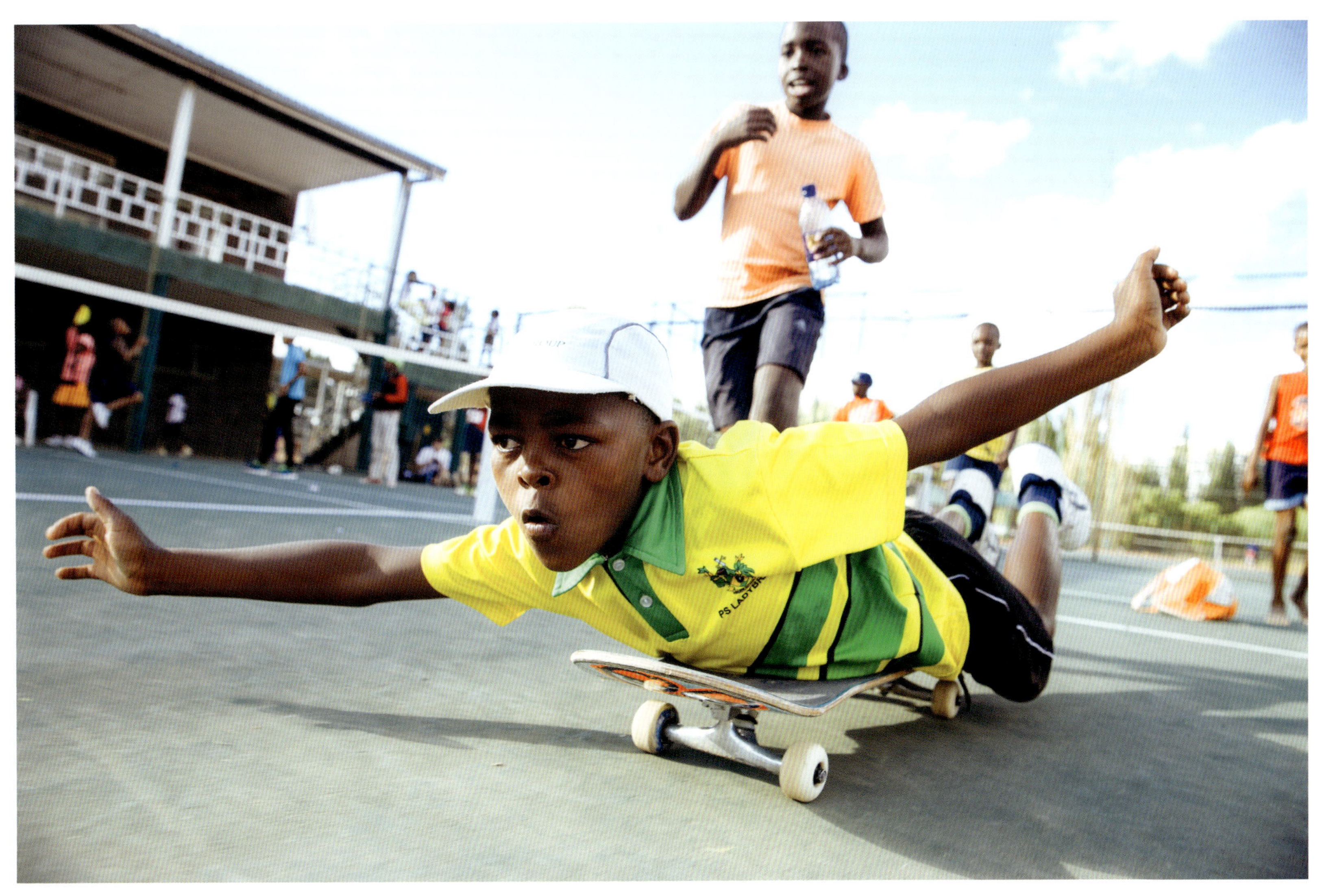

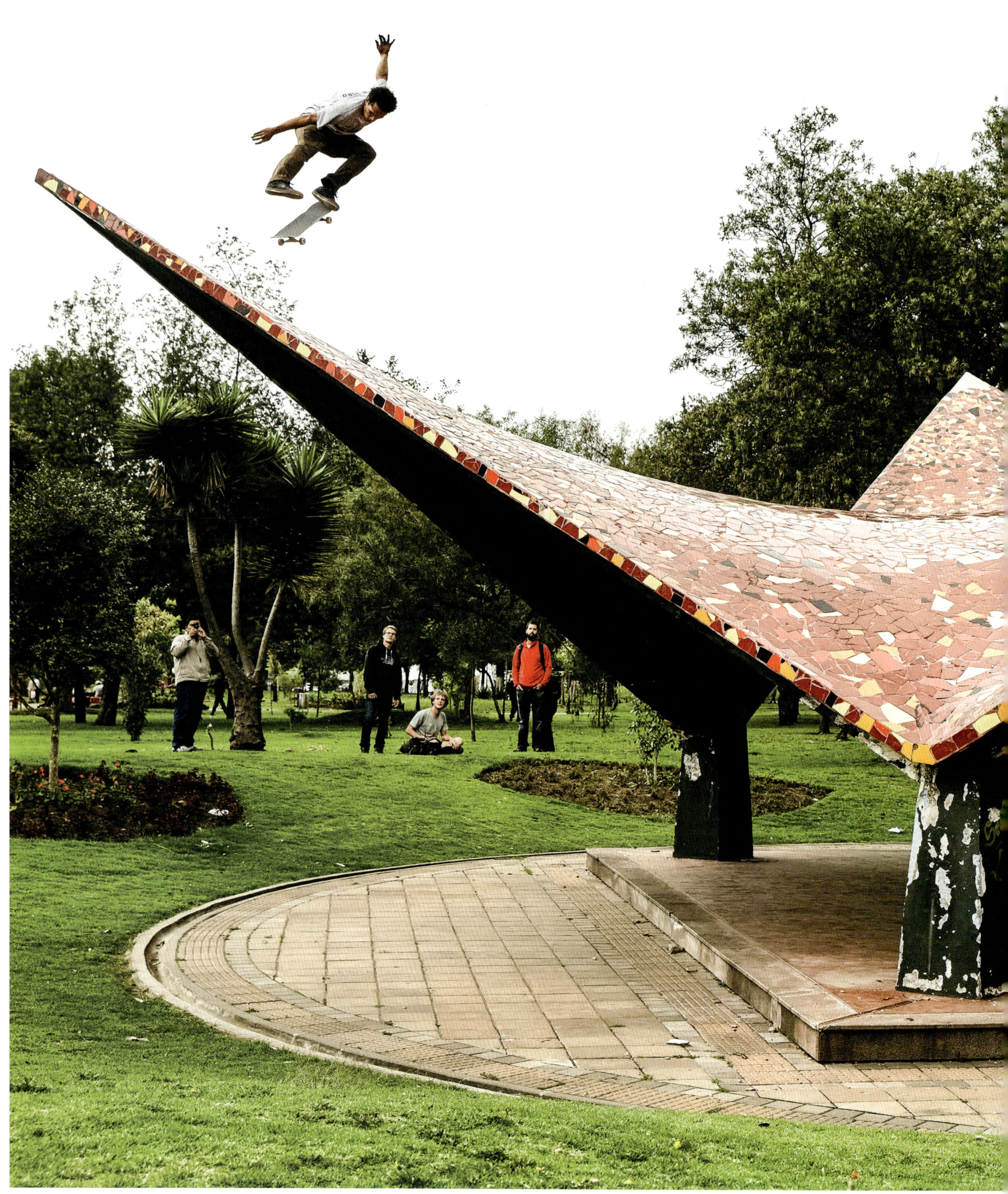

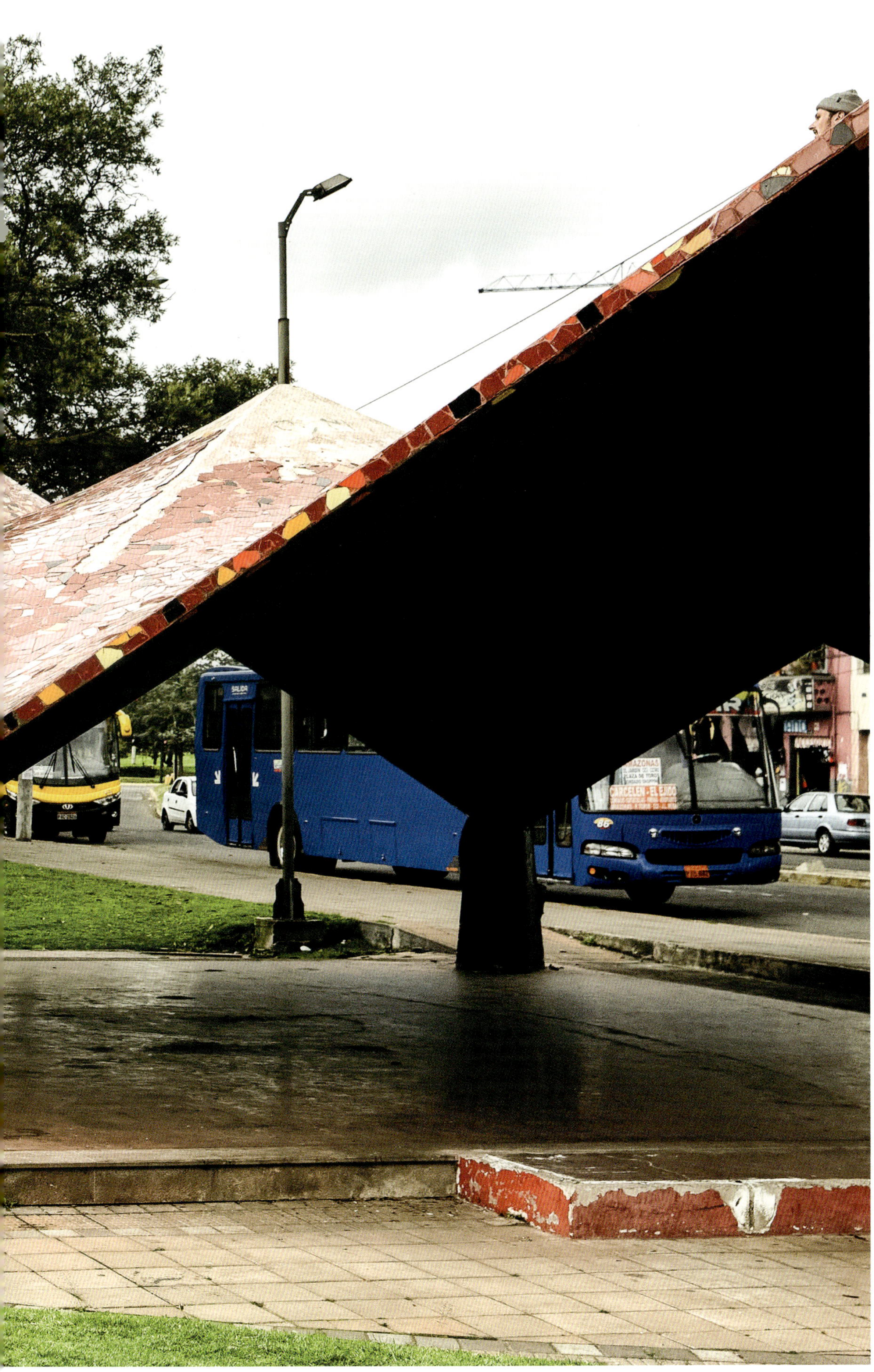

DOOGIE QUITO, ECUADOR

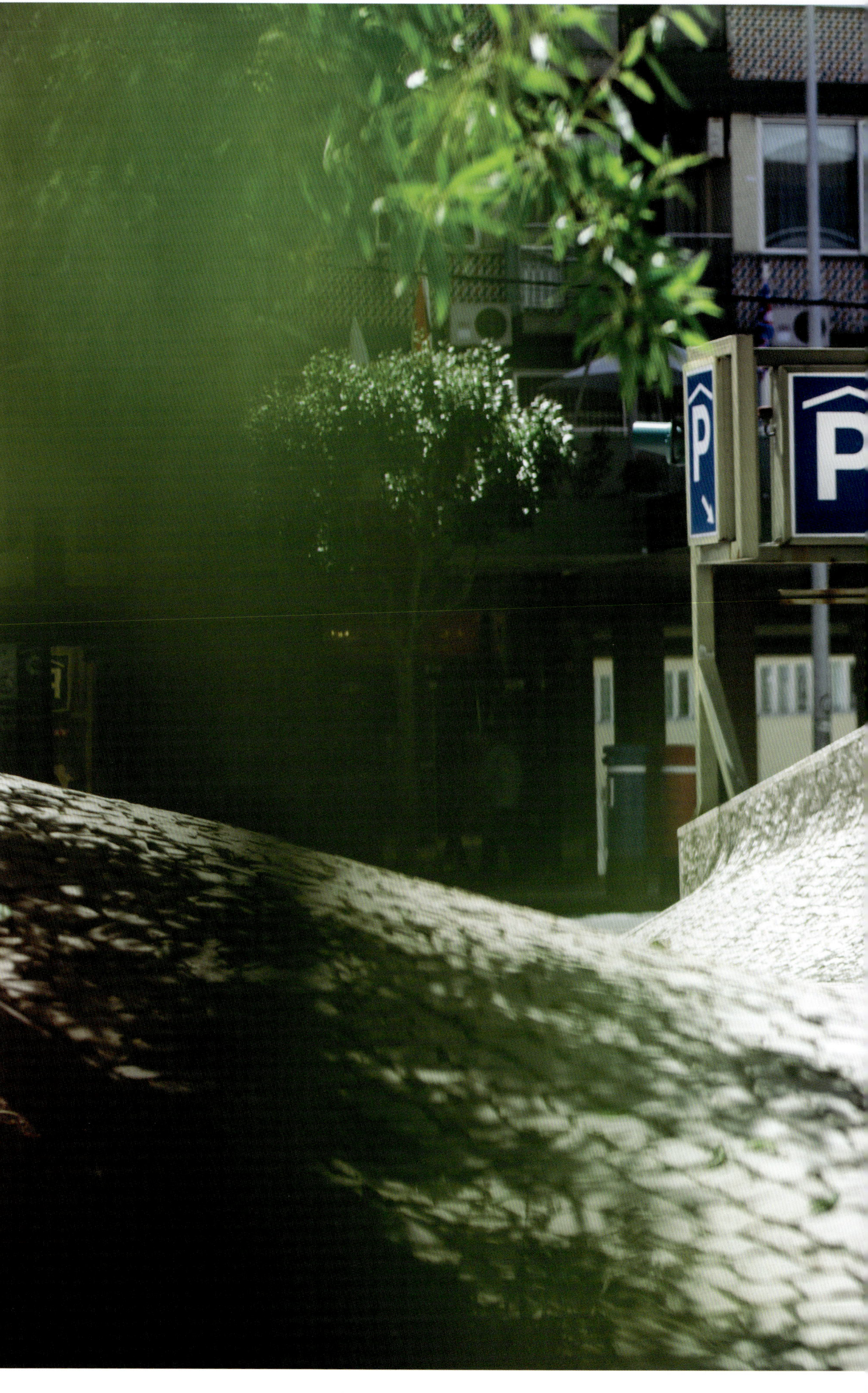

NORA VASCONCELLOS LISBON, PORTUGAL

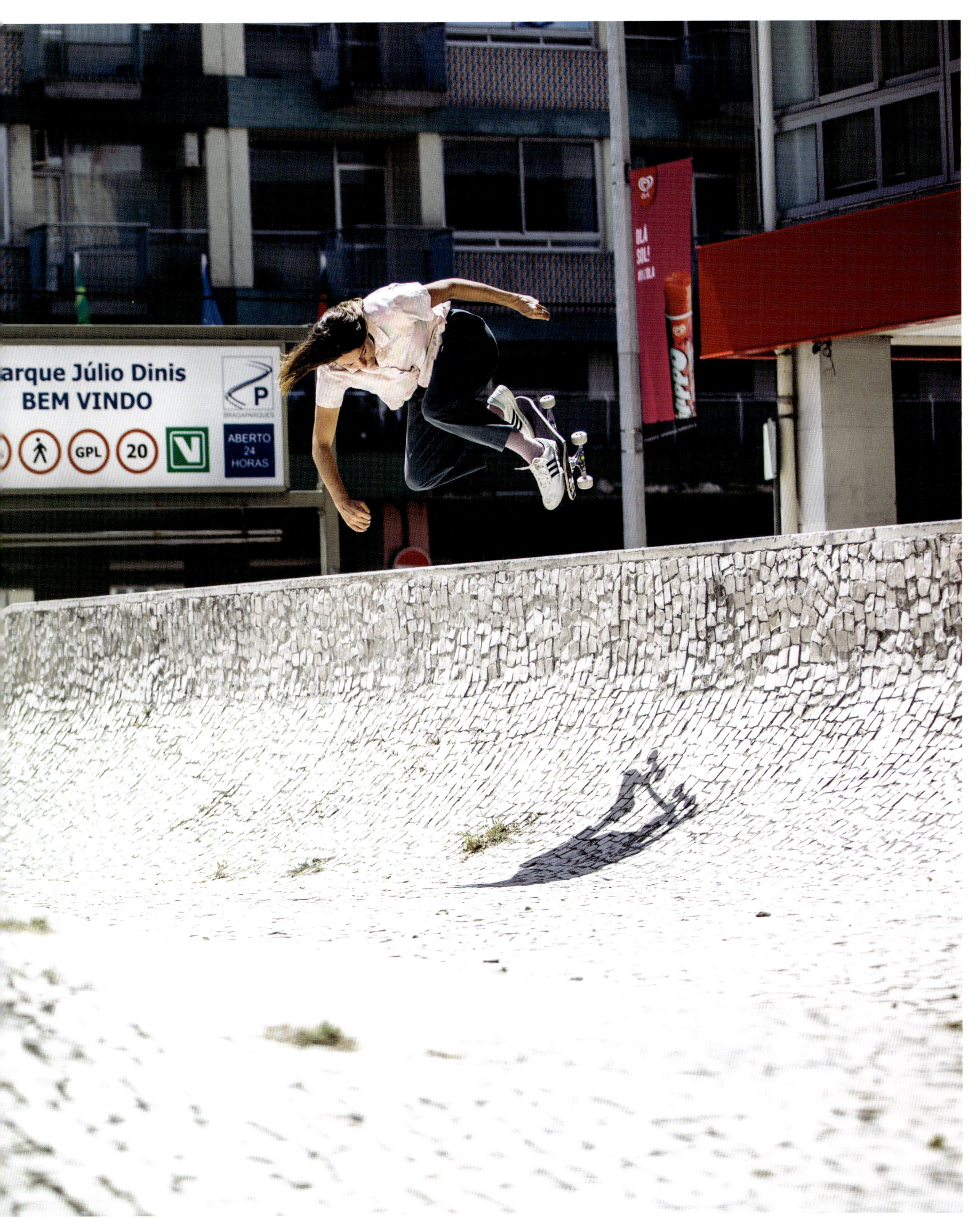
arque Júlio Dinis
BEM VINDO
P
GPL
20
ABERTO
24
HORAS
OLÁ
SOL!

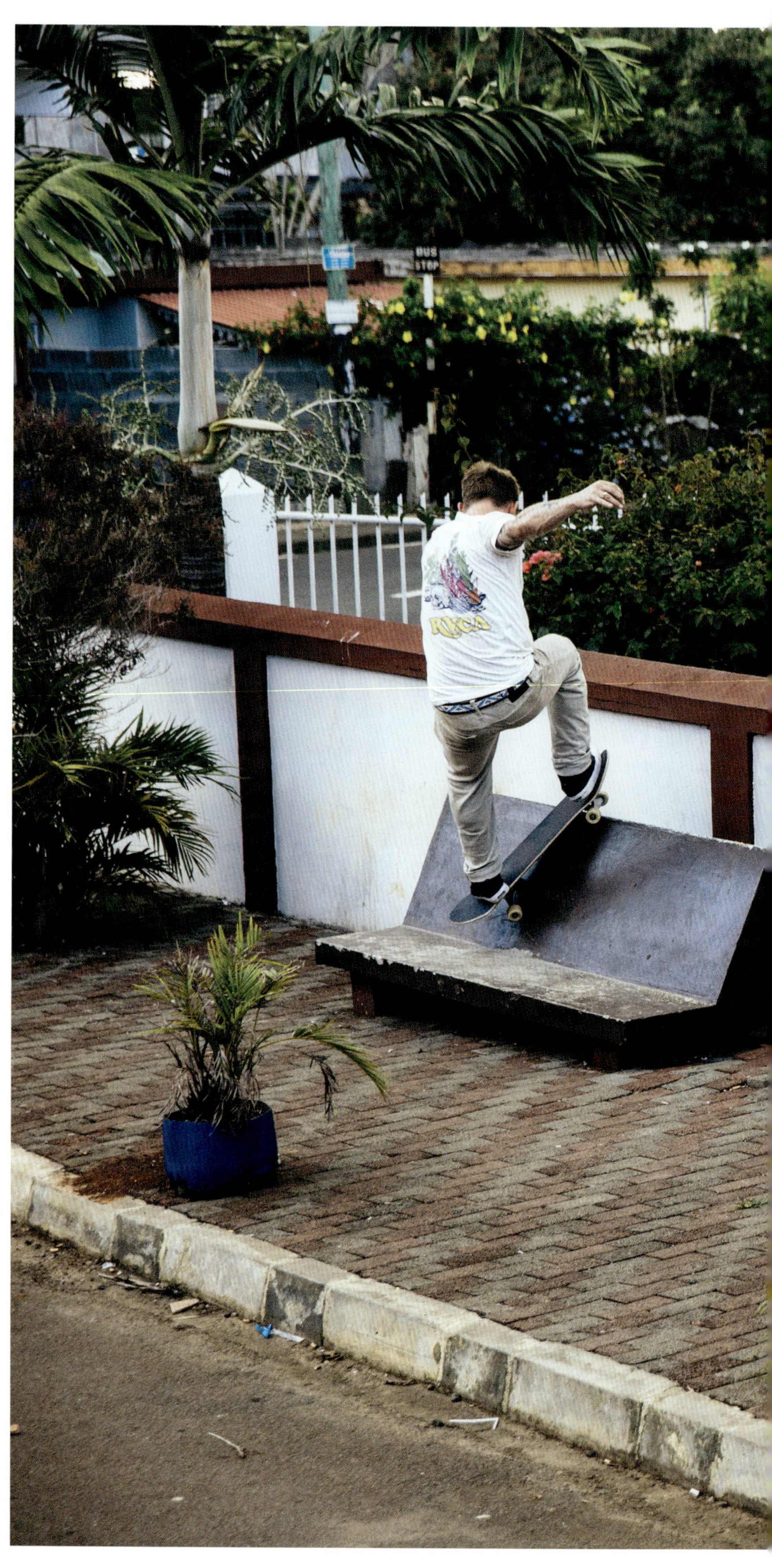
BUS STOP
RVCA

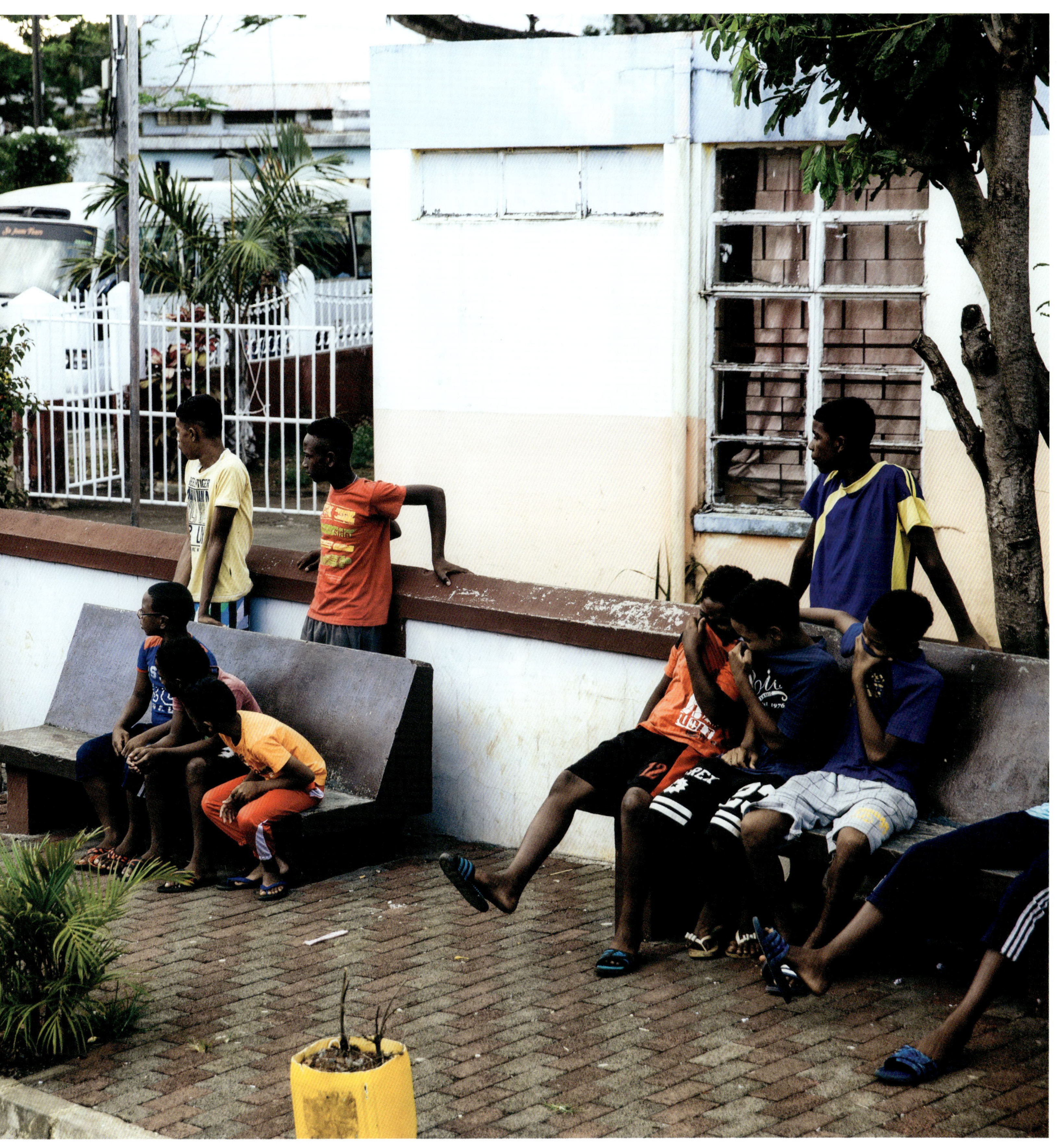

YANN HOROWITZ MAURITIUS

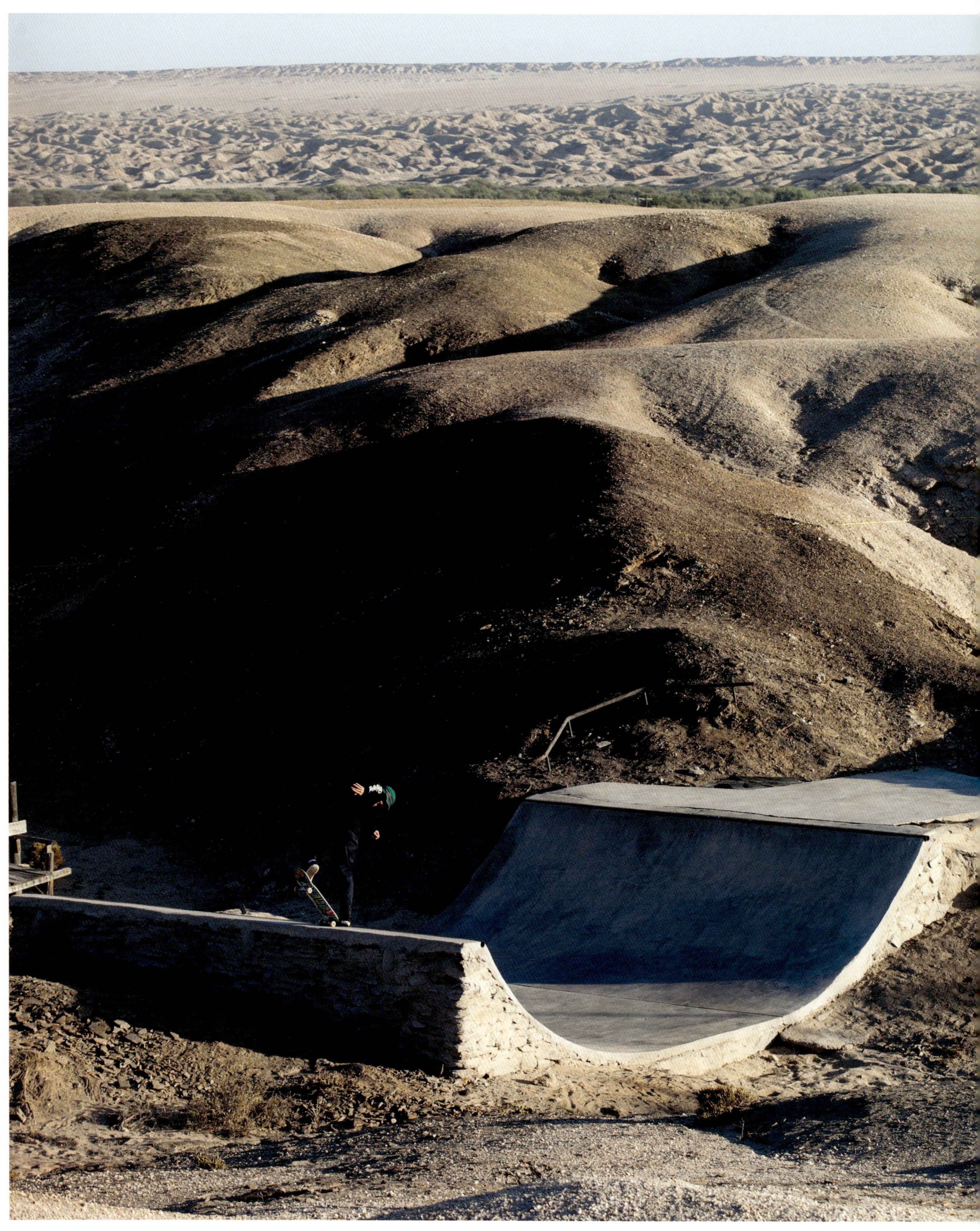

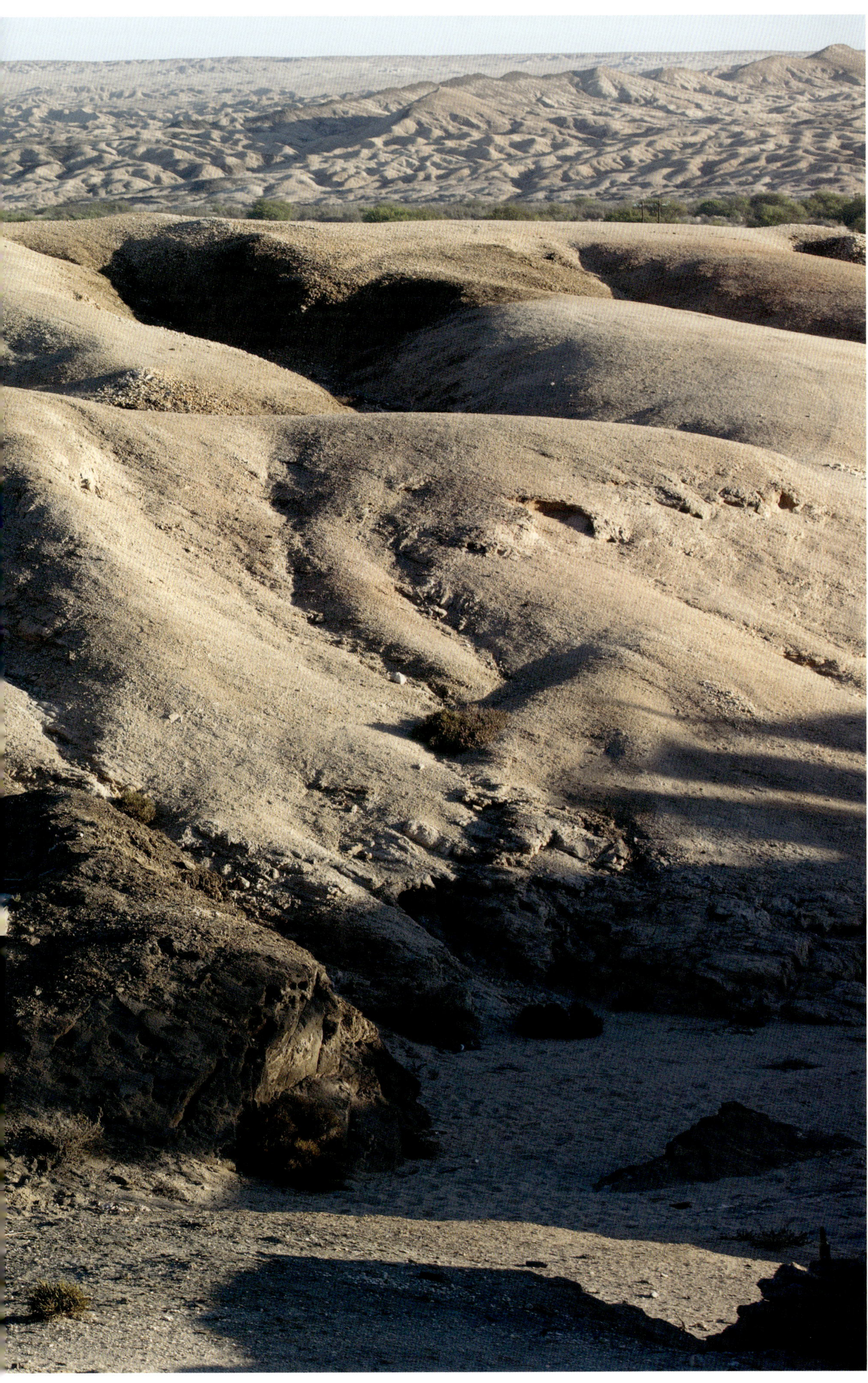

SEBO WALKER SWAKOPMUND, NAMIBIA

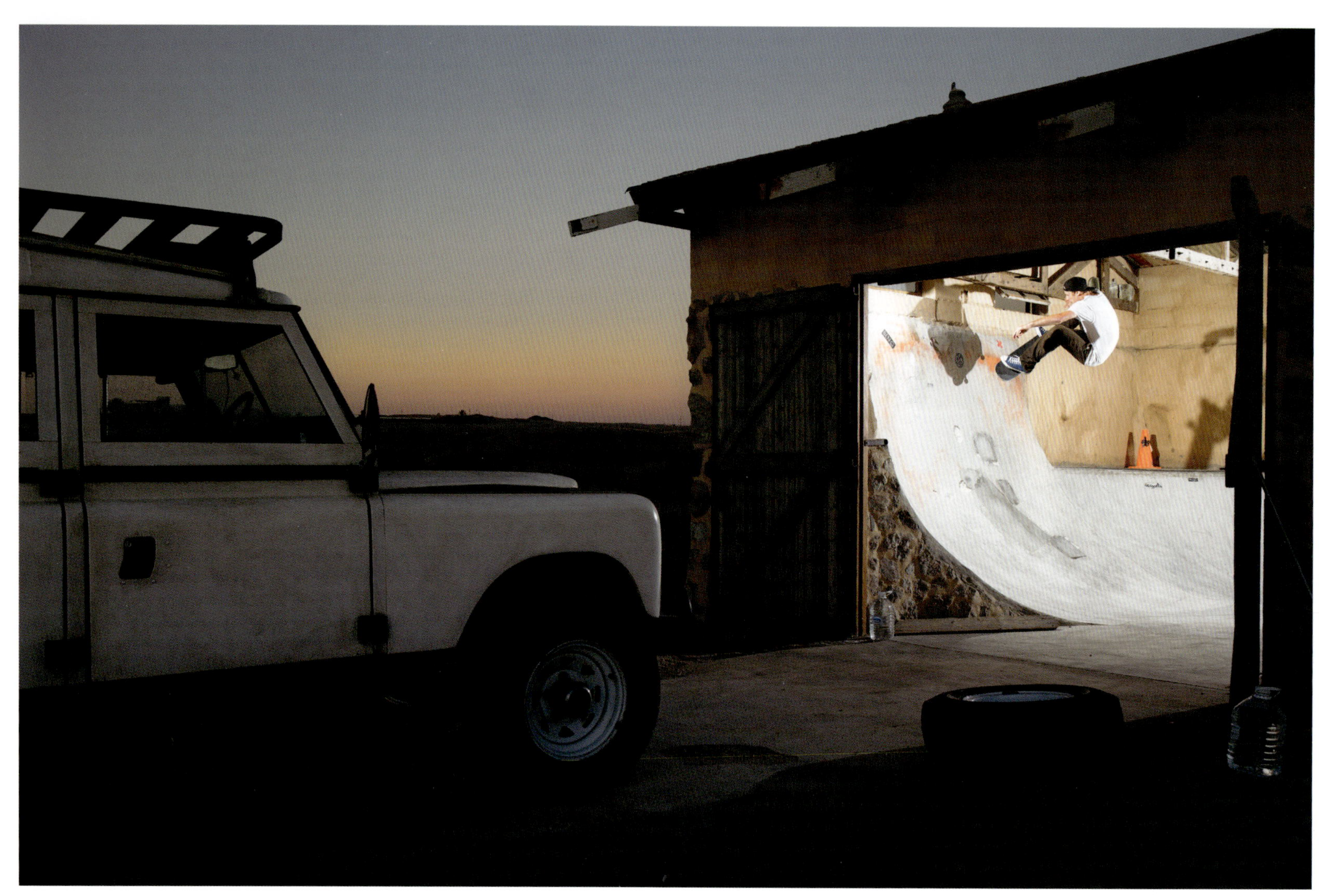

WALKER RYAN NAMIBIA

NICK GARCIA MALDIVES

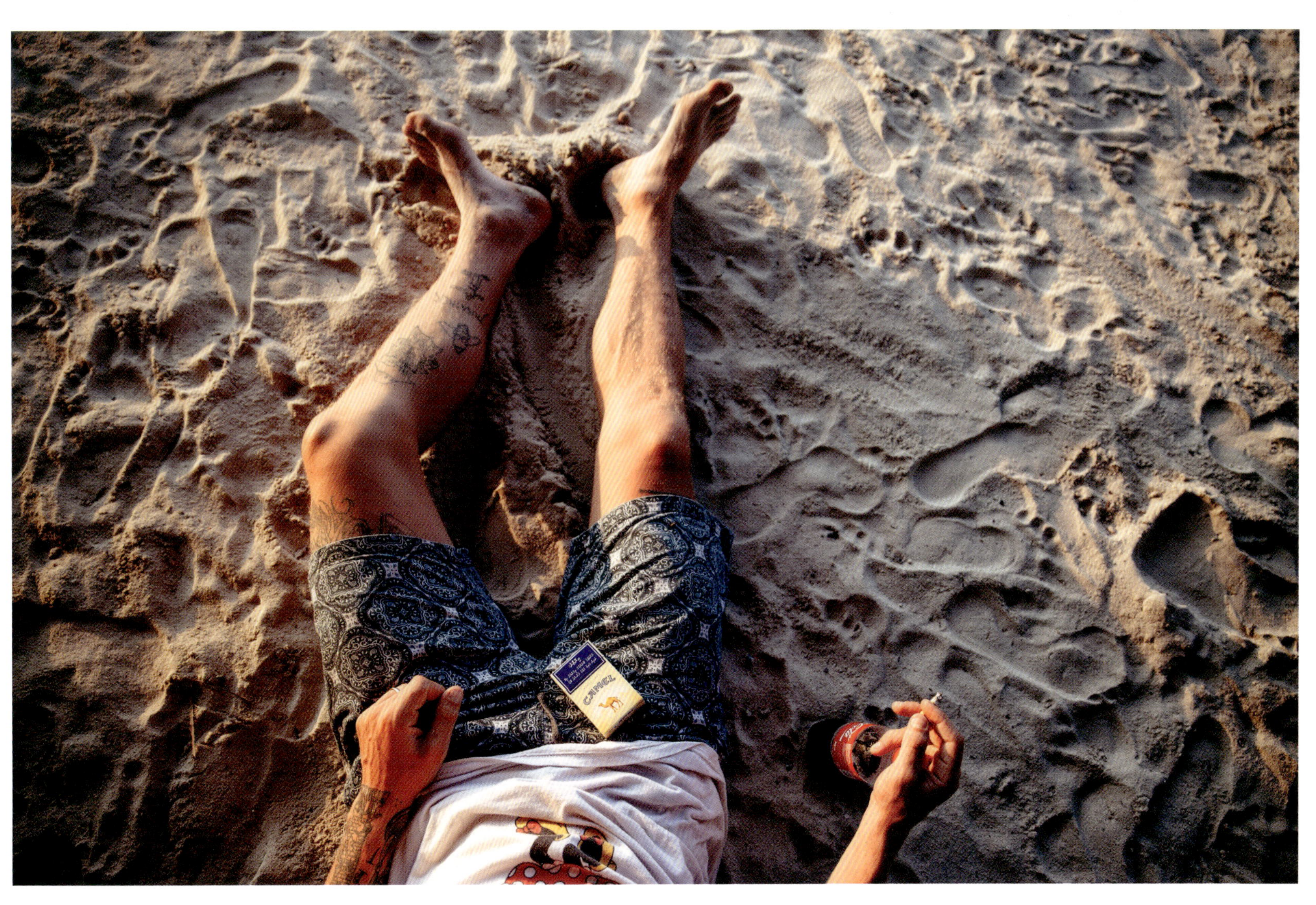

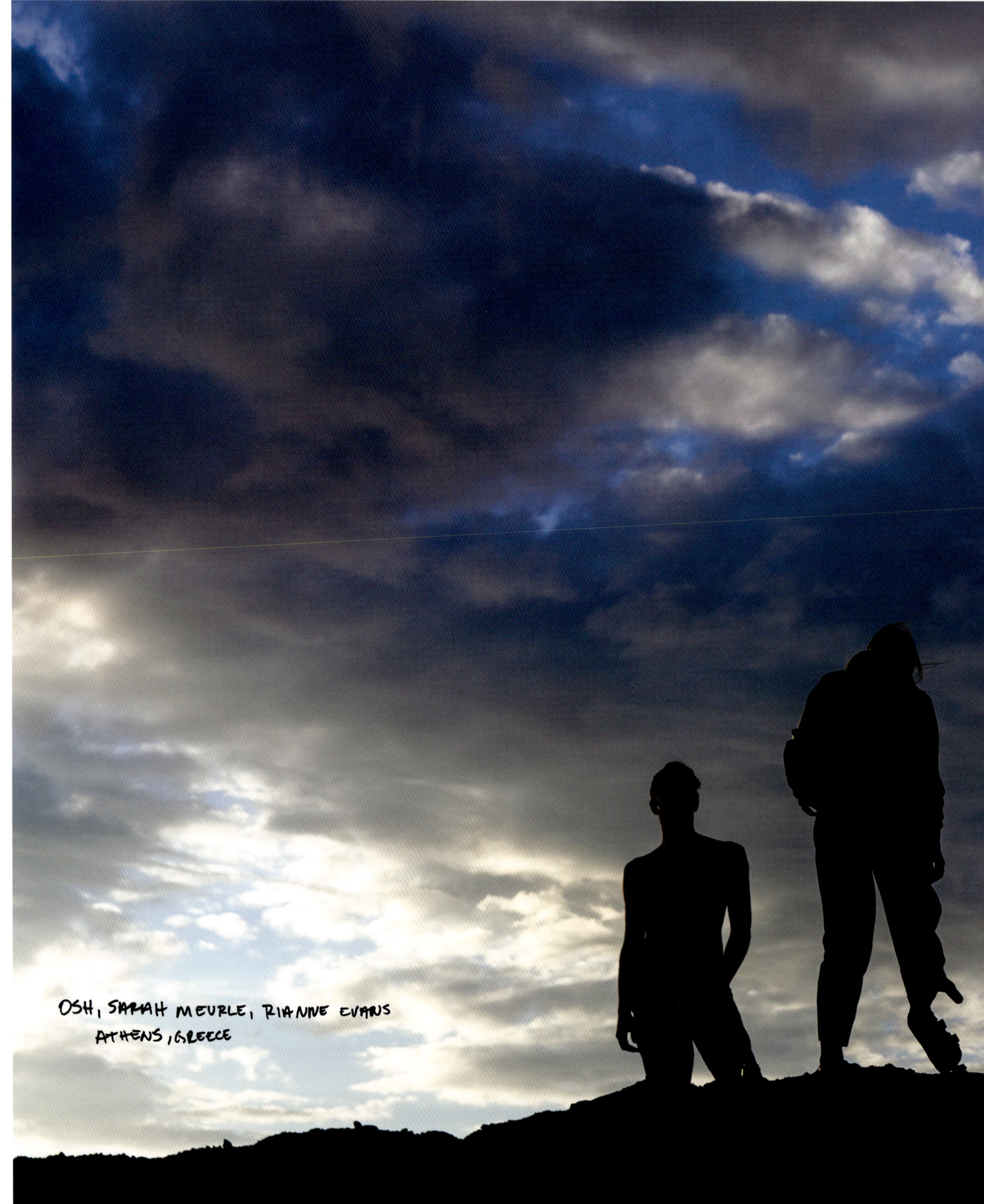

OSH, SARAH MEURLE, RIANNE EVANS
ATHENS, GREECE

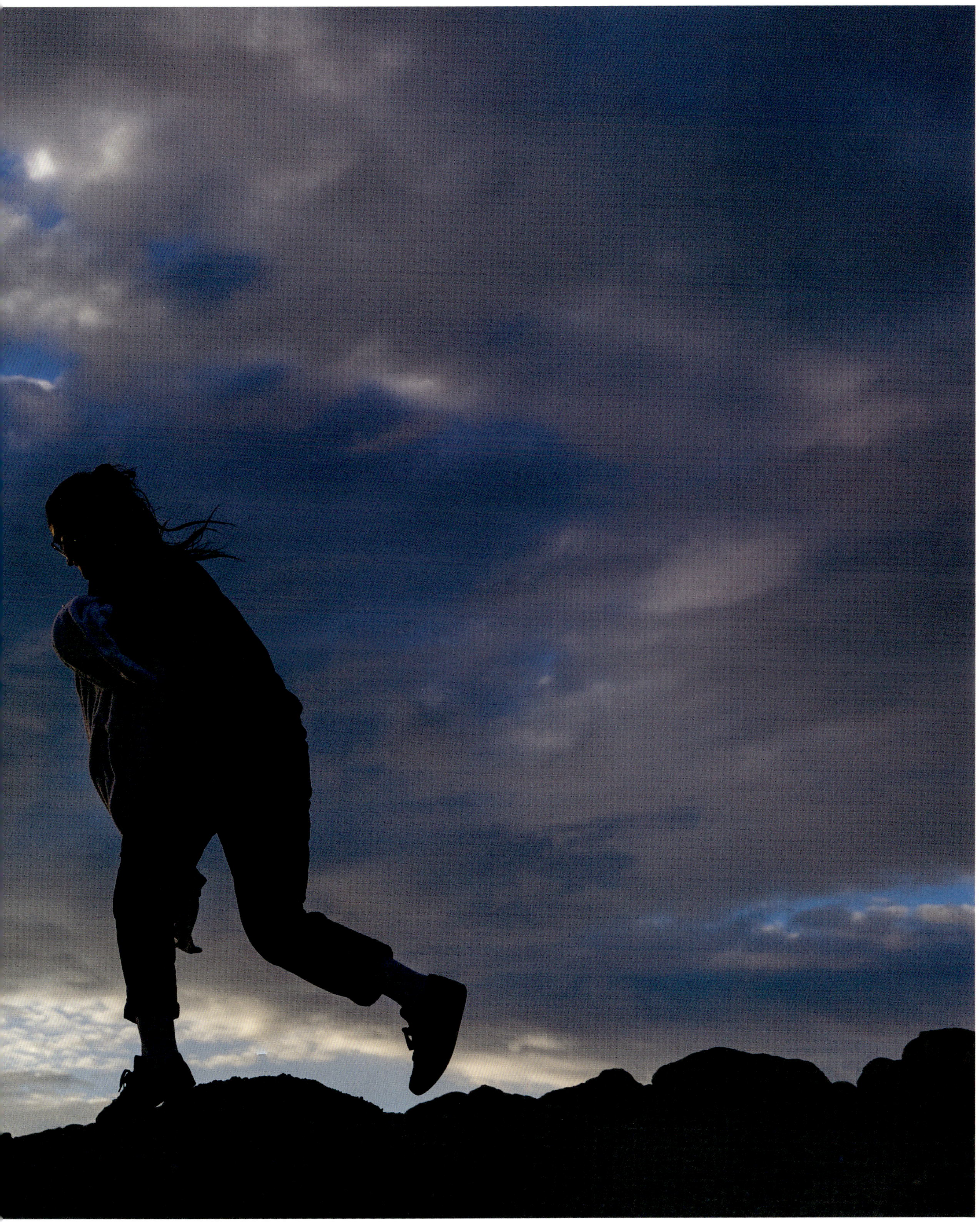

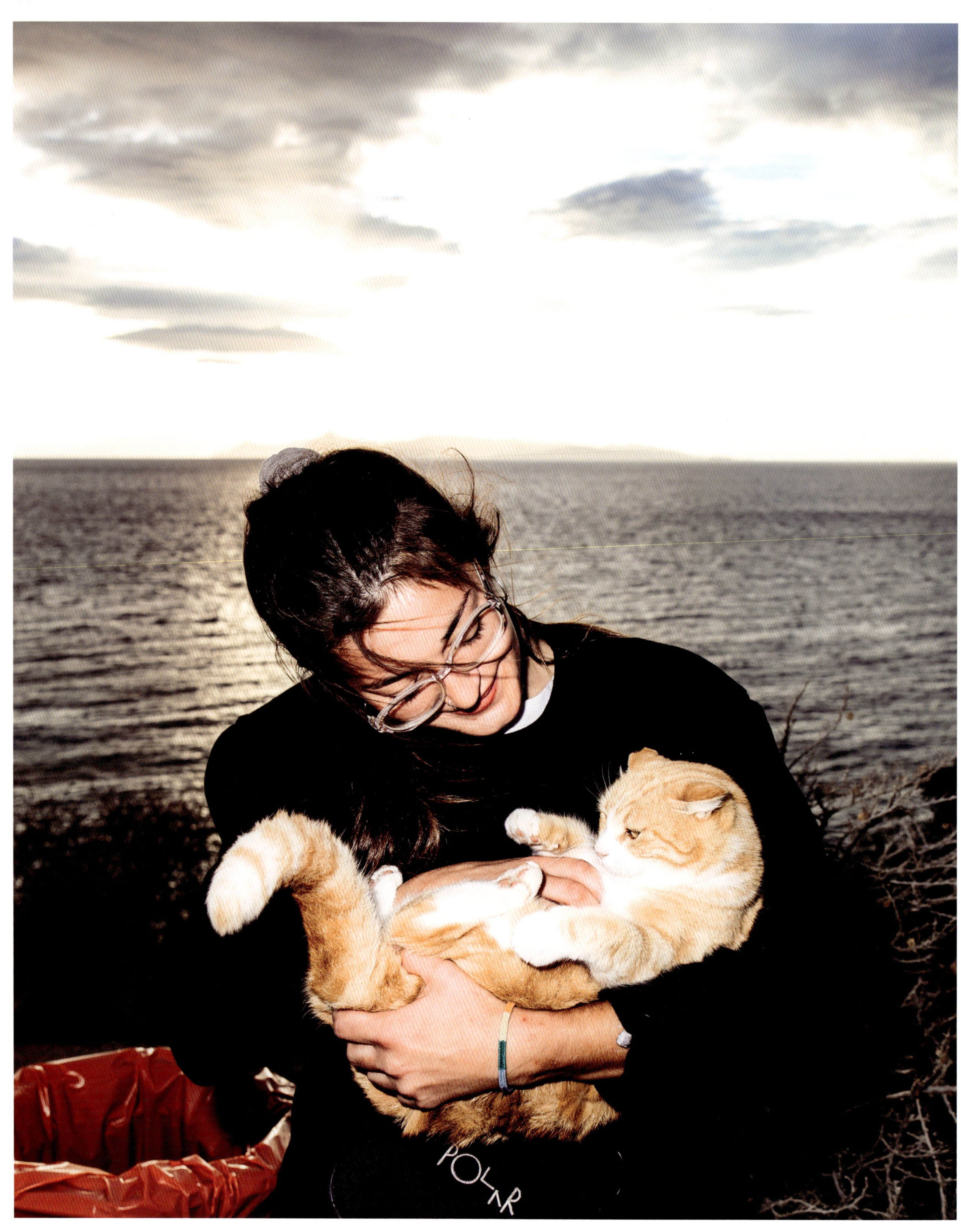
POLAR

CLIFF JUMPING ATHENS, GREECE

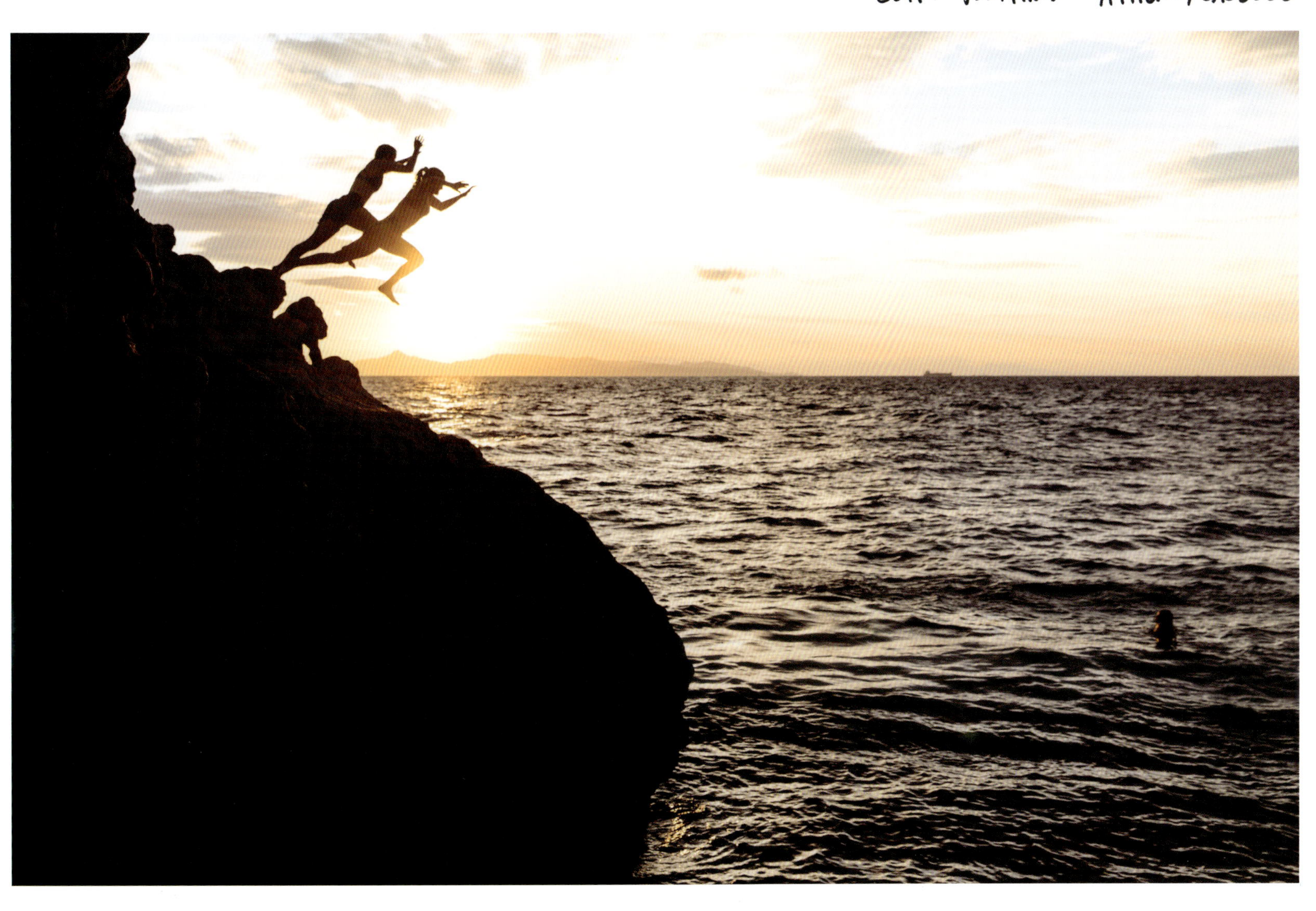

RIANNE EVANS ATHENS, GREECE

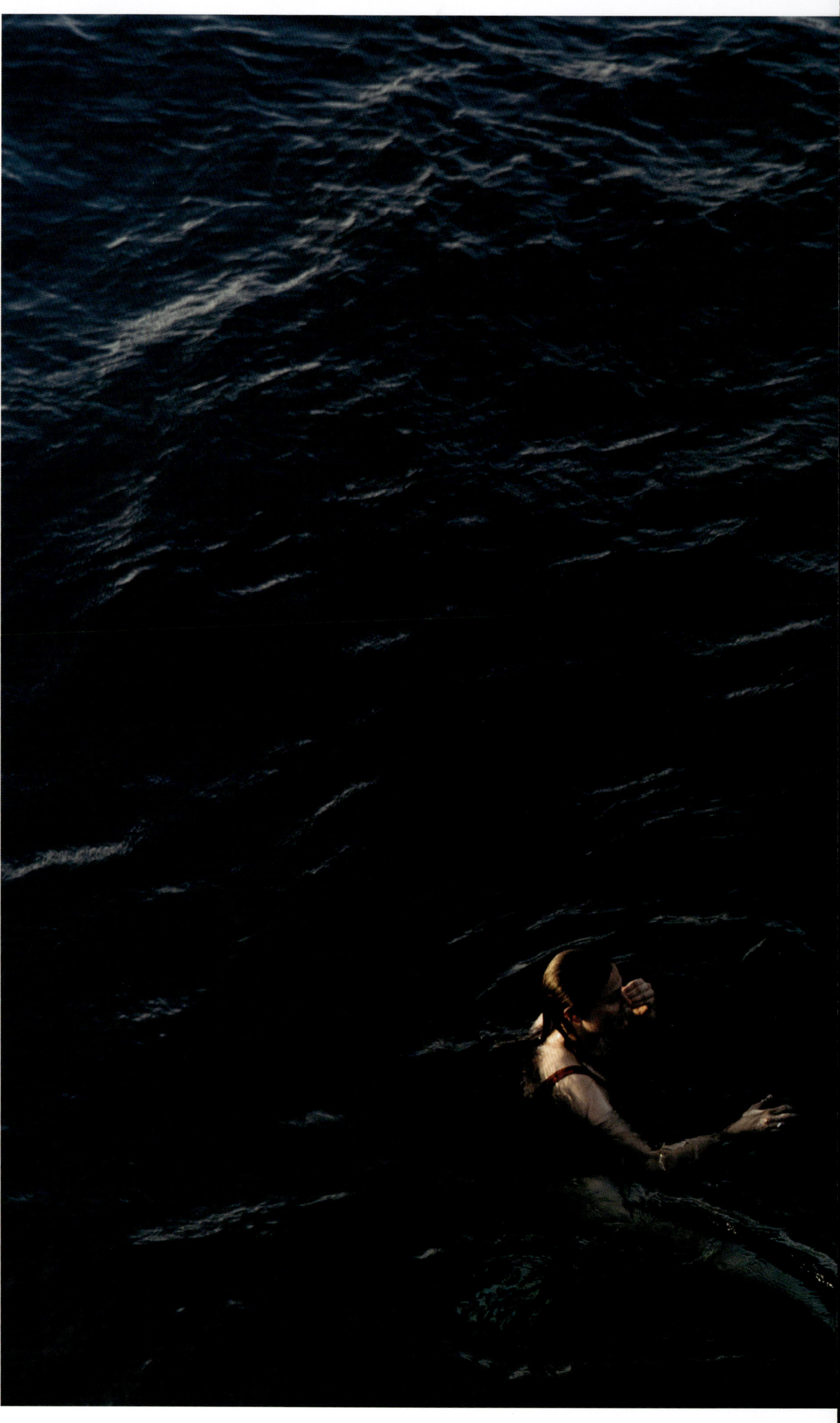

ATHENS, GREECE

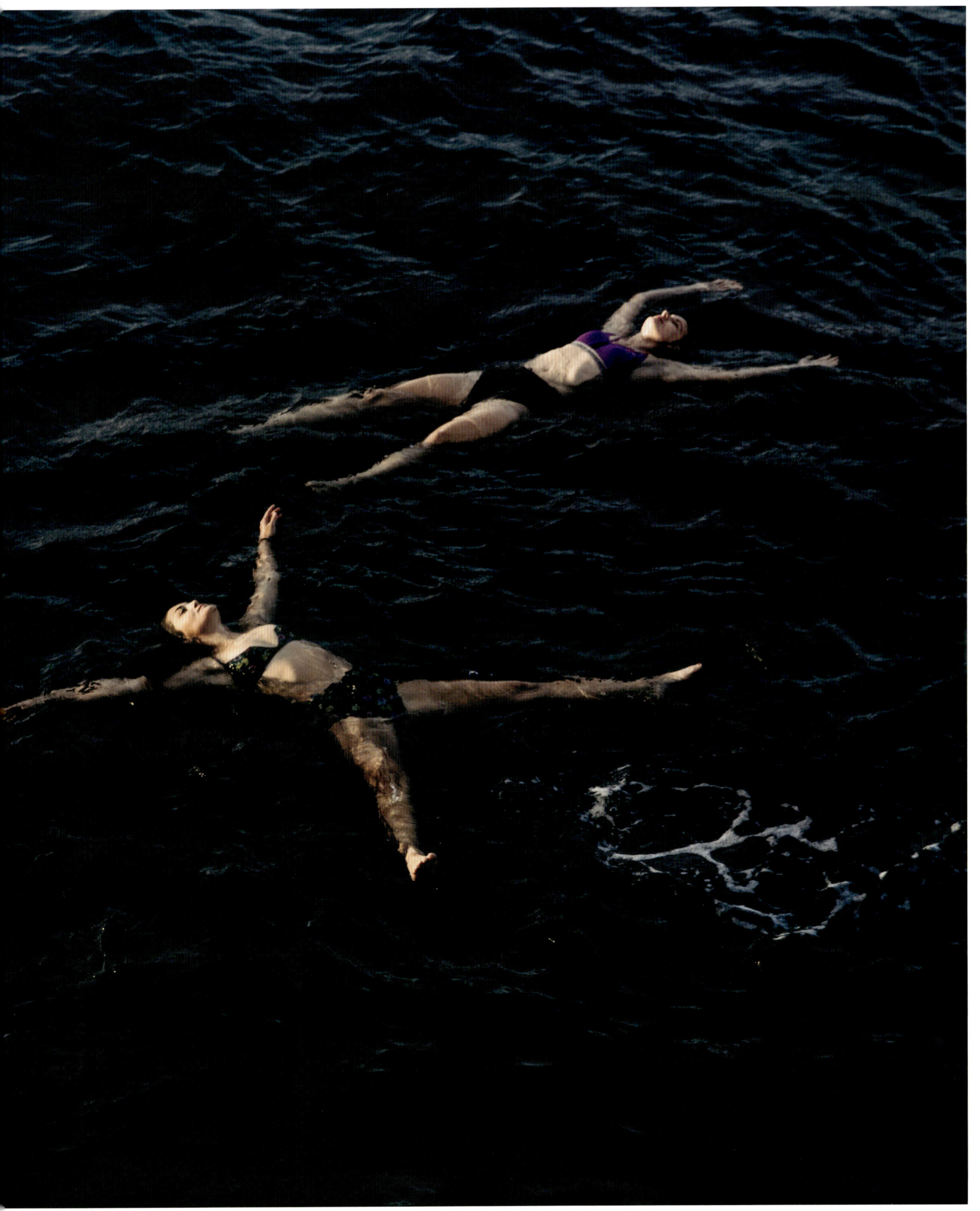

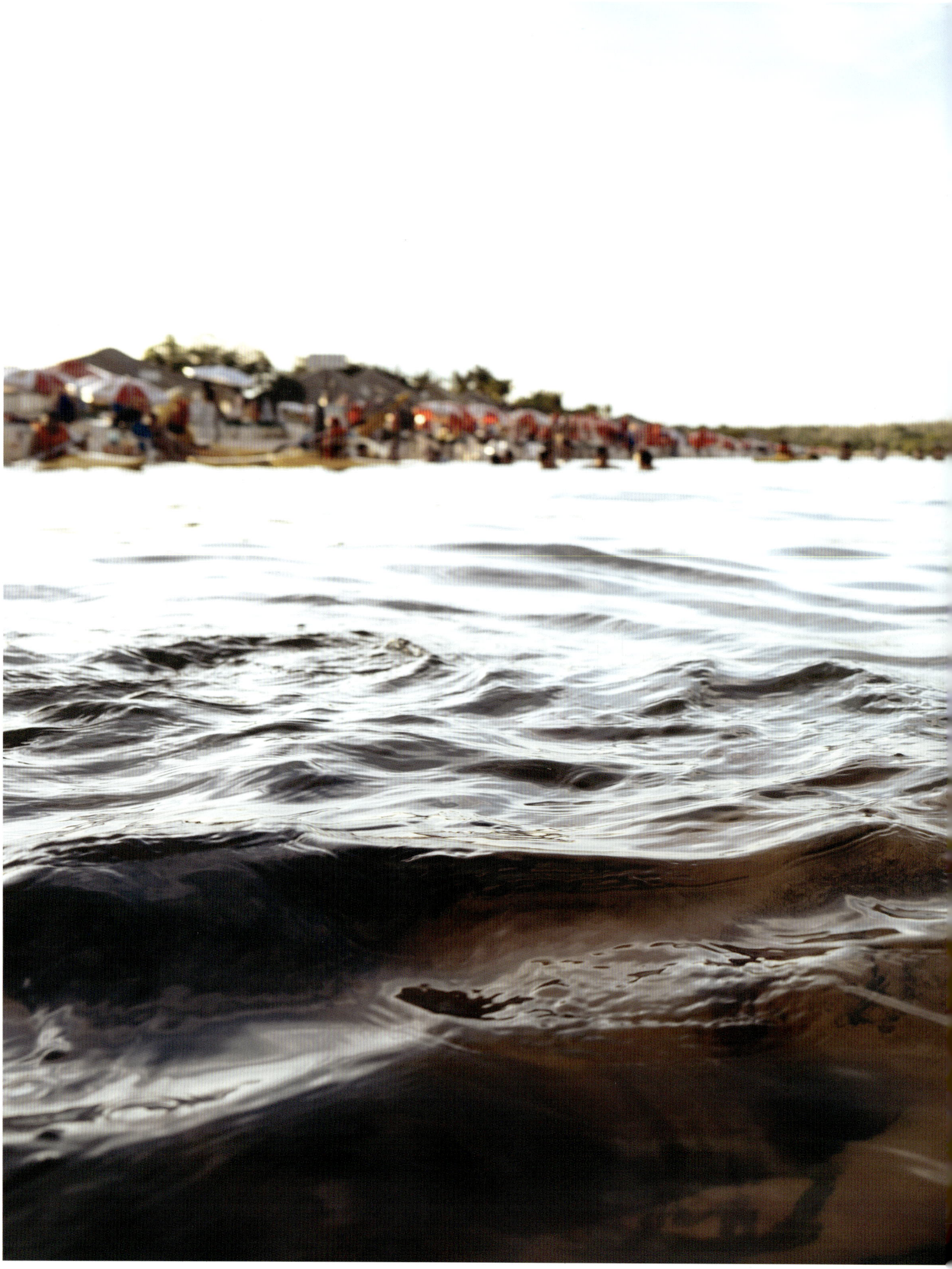

SANTAREM, BRAZIL

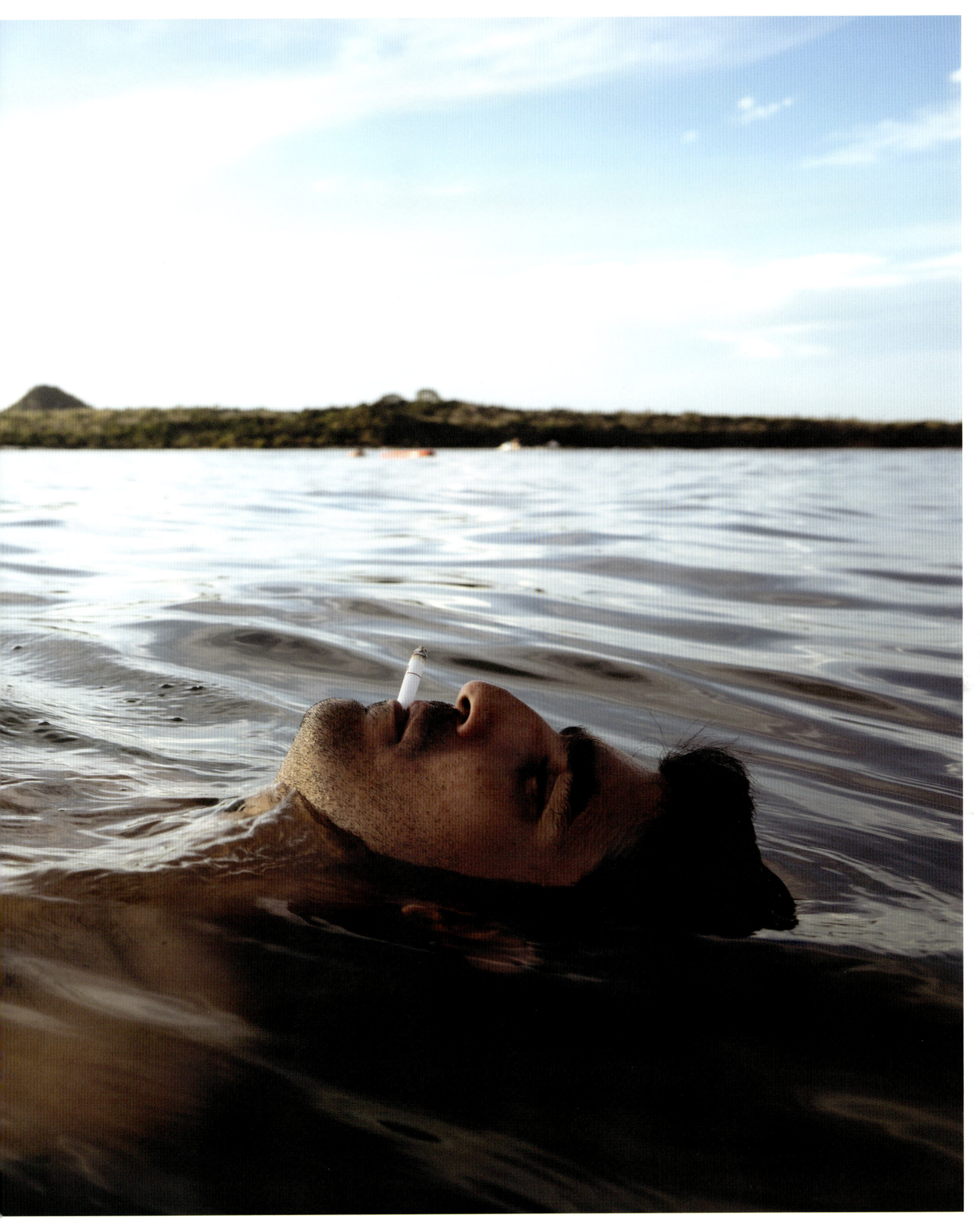

MADARS APSE ICELAND

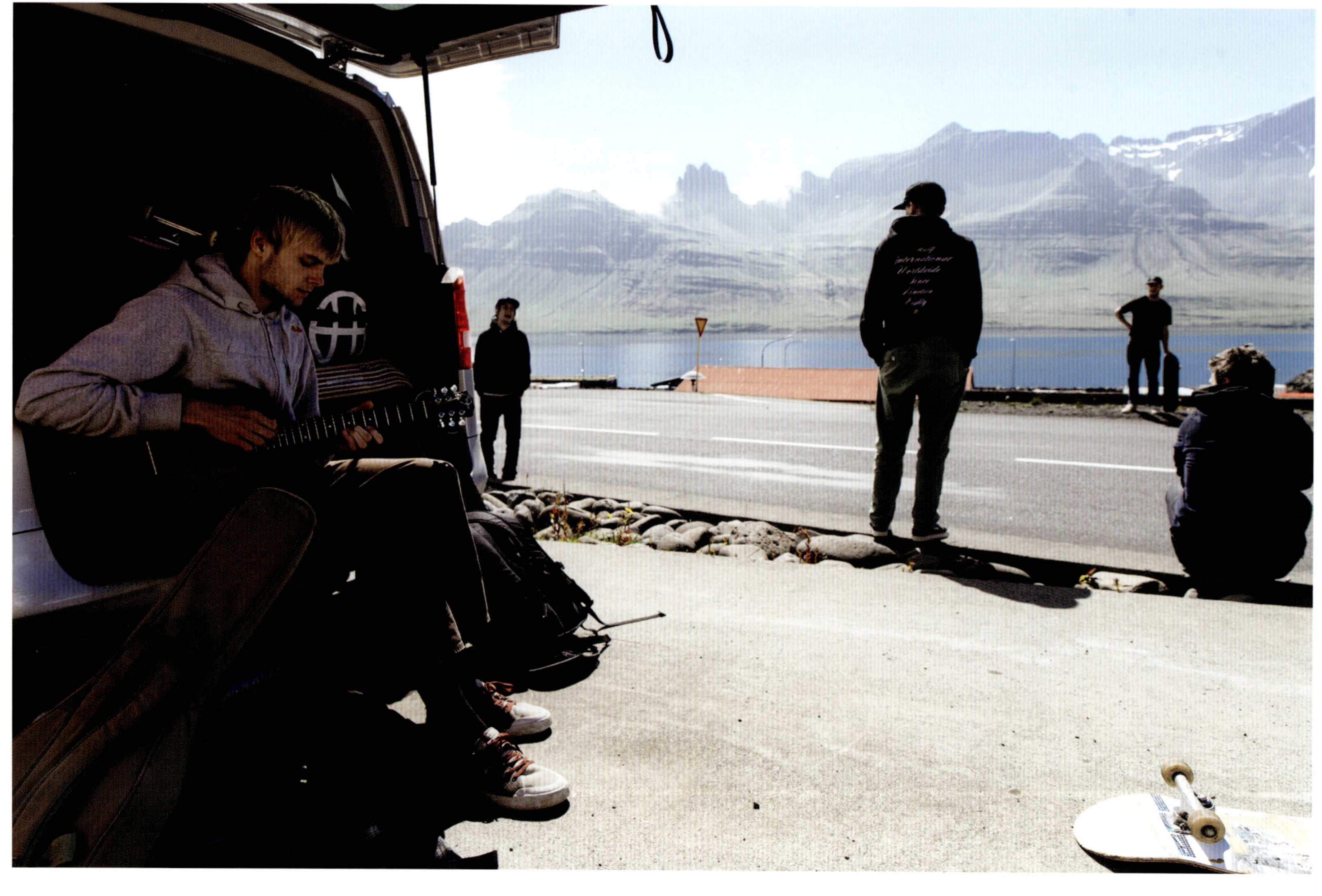

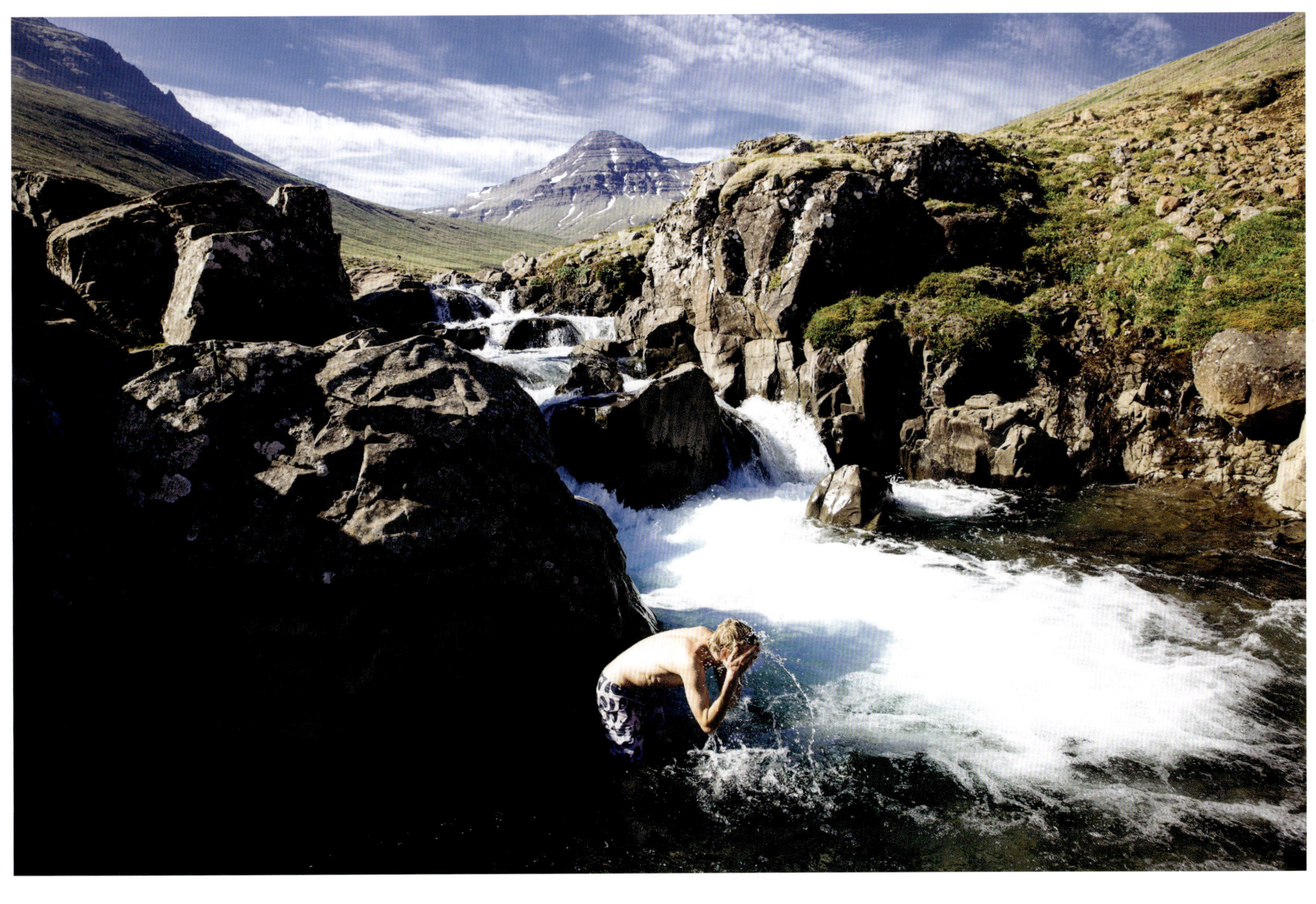

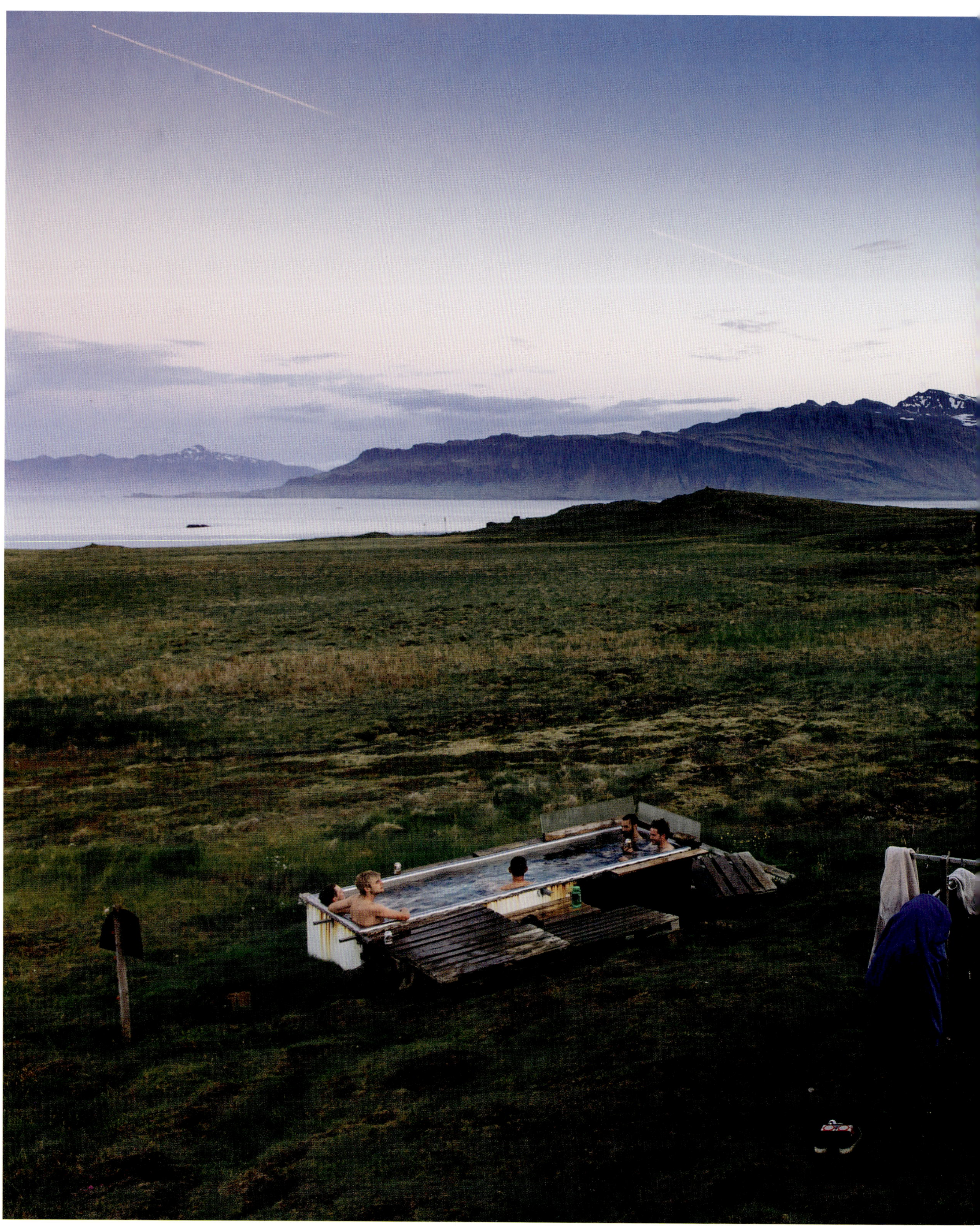

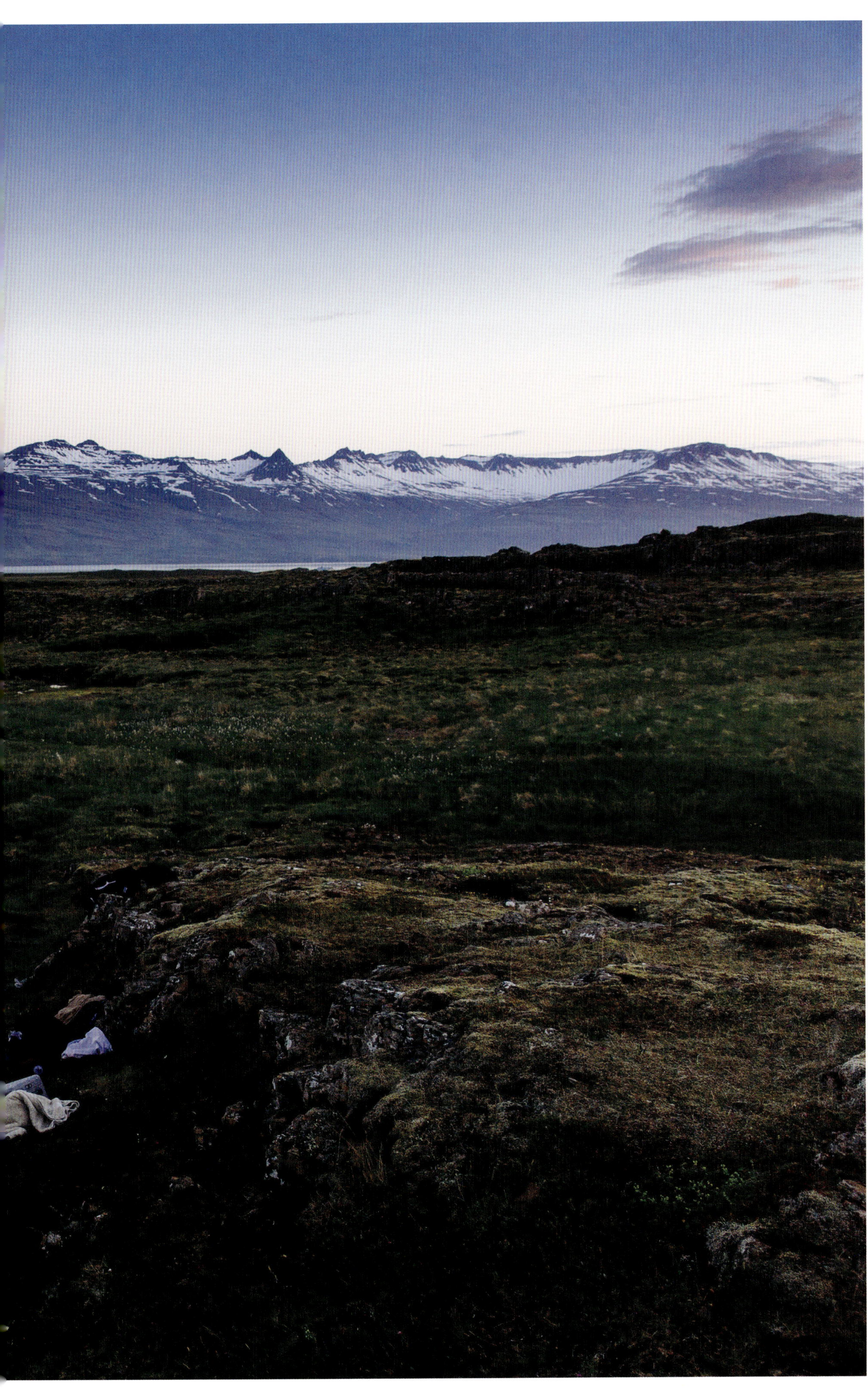

HOT SPRING Djúpivogur, Iceland

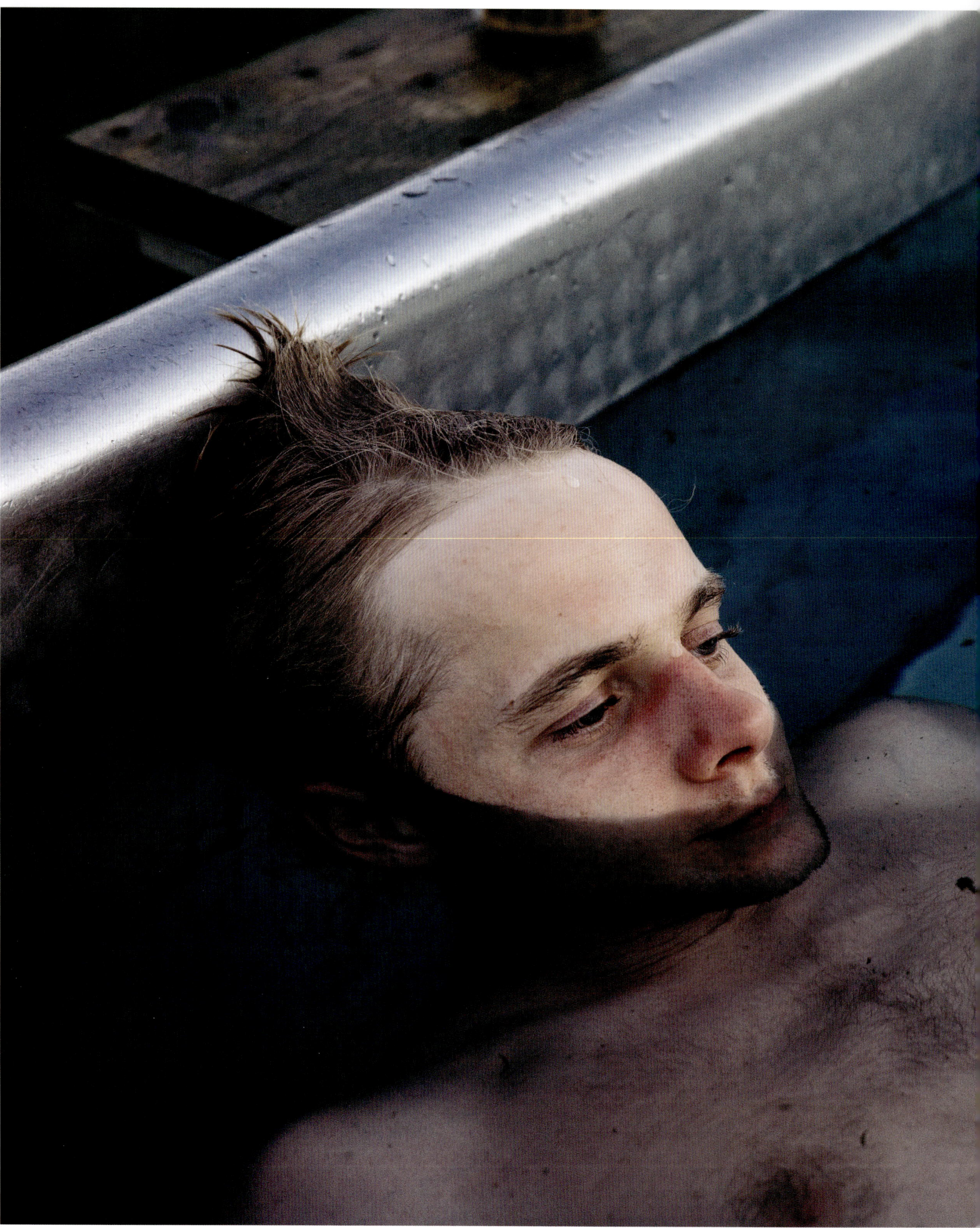

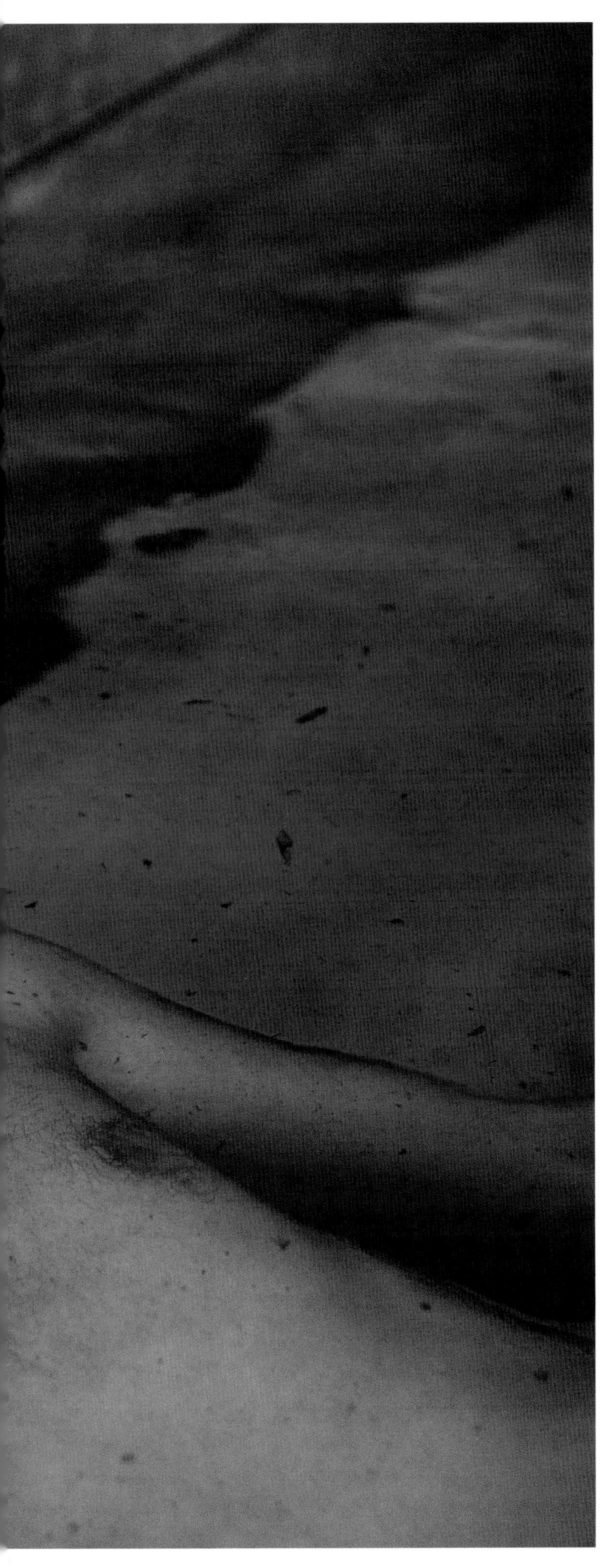

MADARS APSE Djúpivogur, Iceland

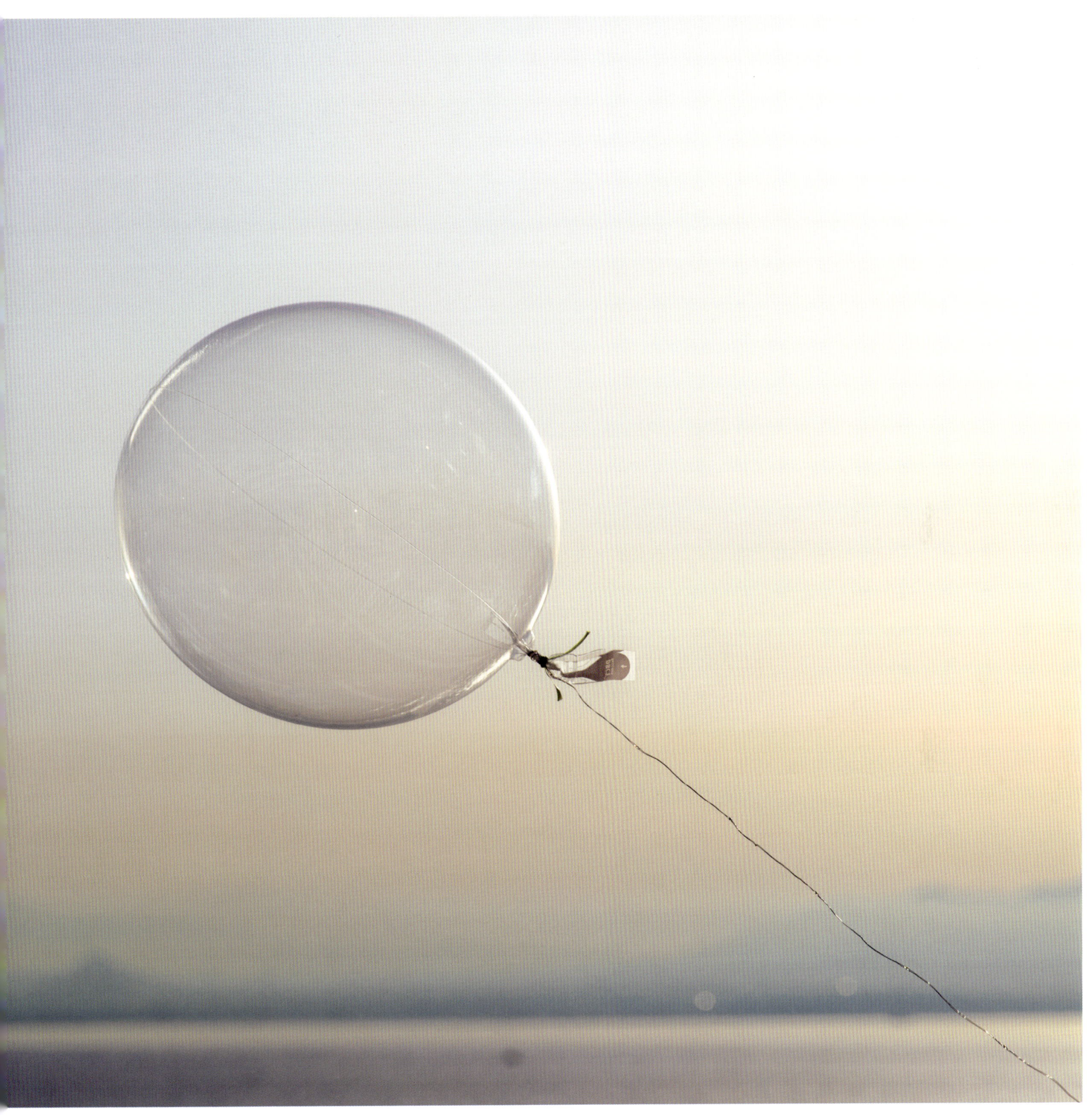

MYKONOS, GREECE

CATA DIAZ
ATHENS, GREECE

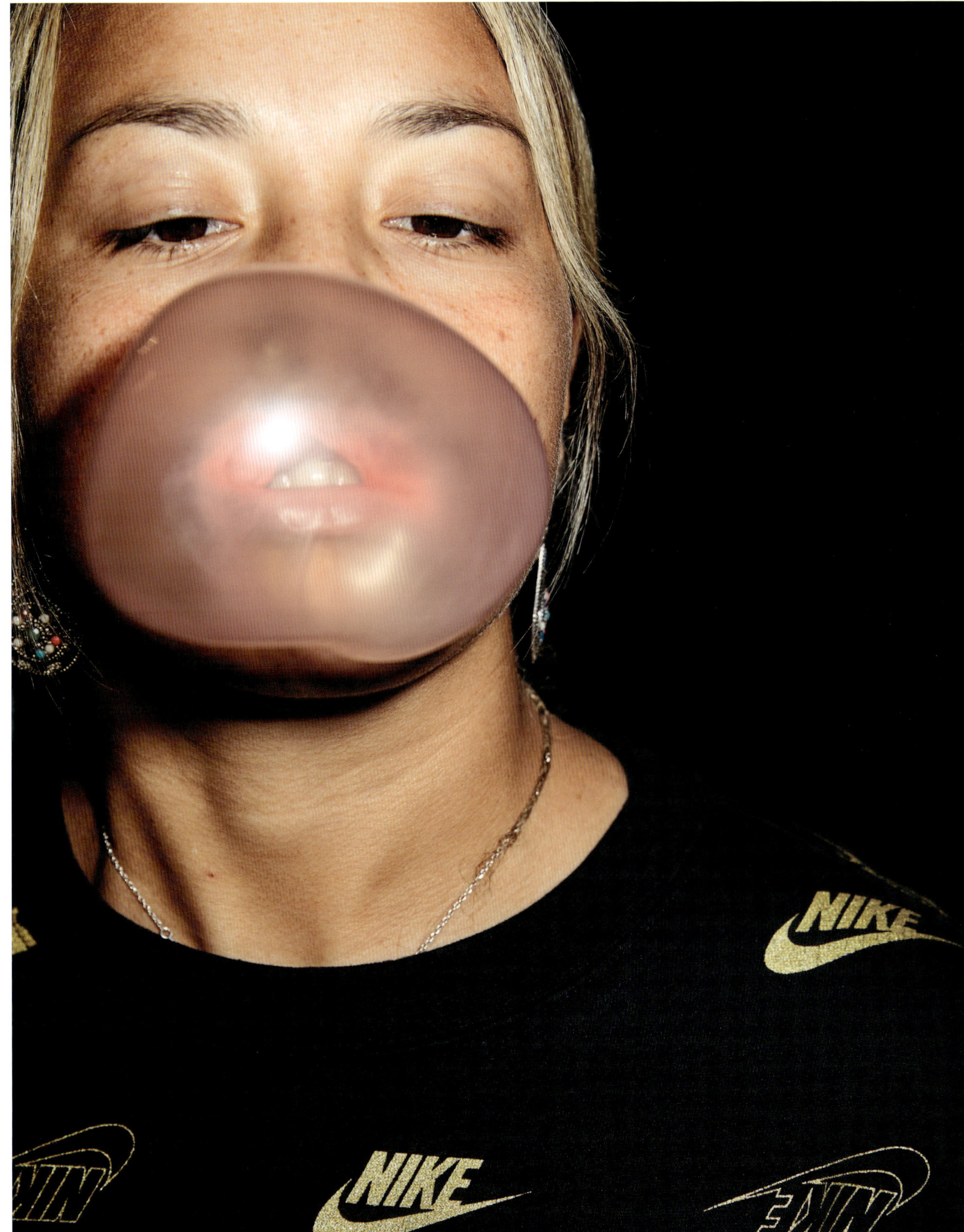
NIKE
NIKE

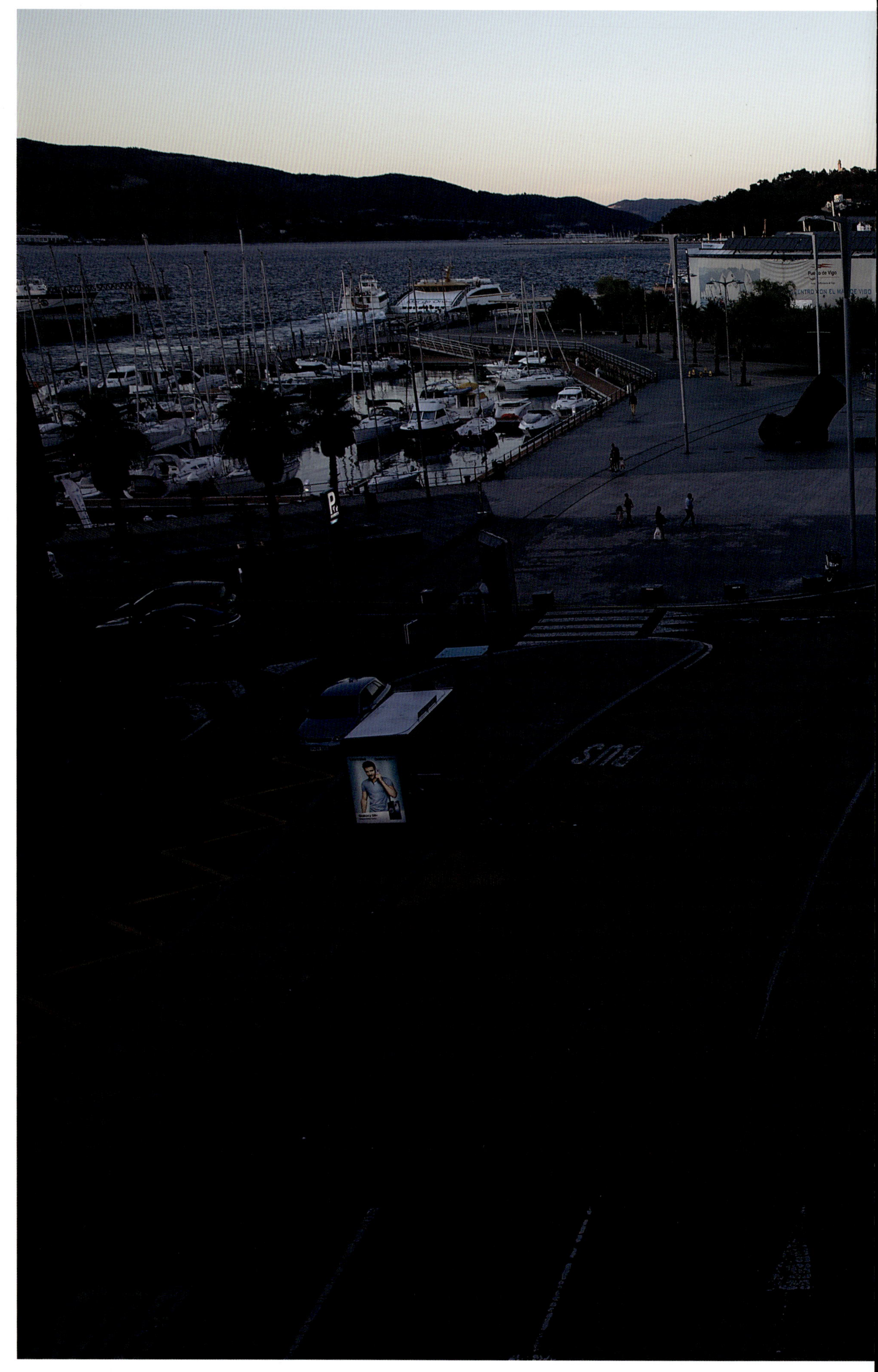

SAMARRIA BREVARD VIGO, SPAIN

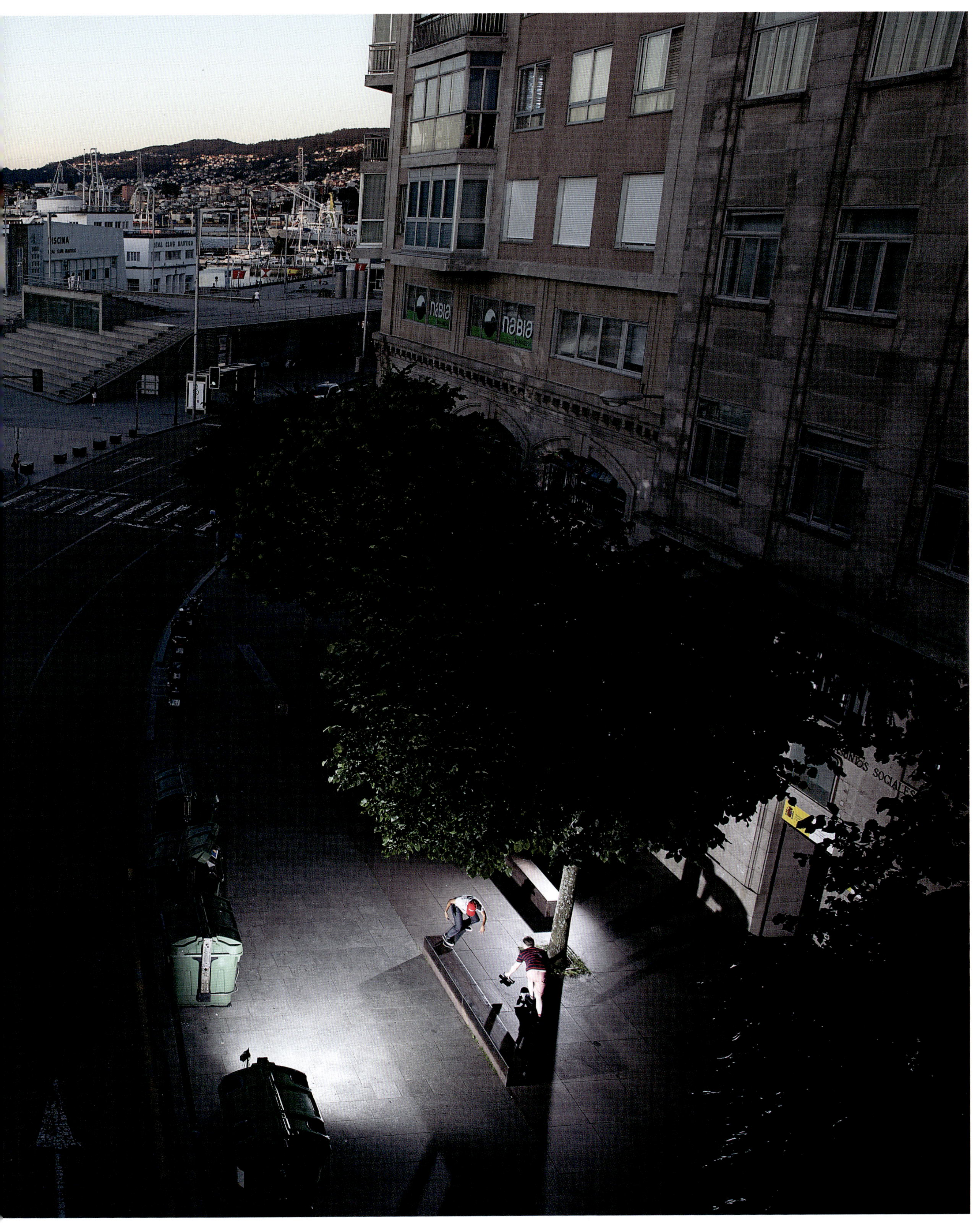
nabia
nabia

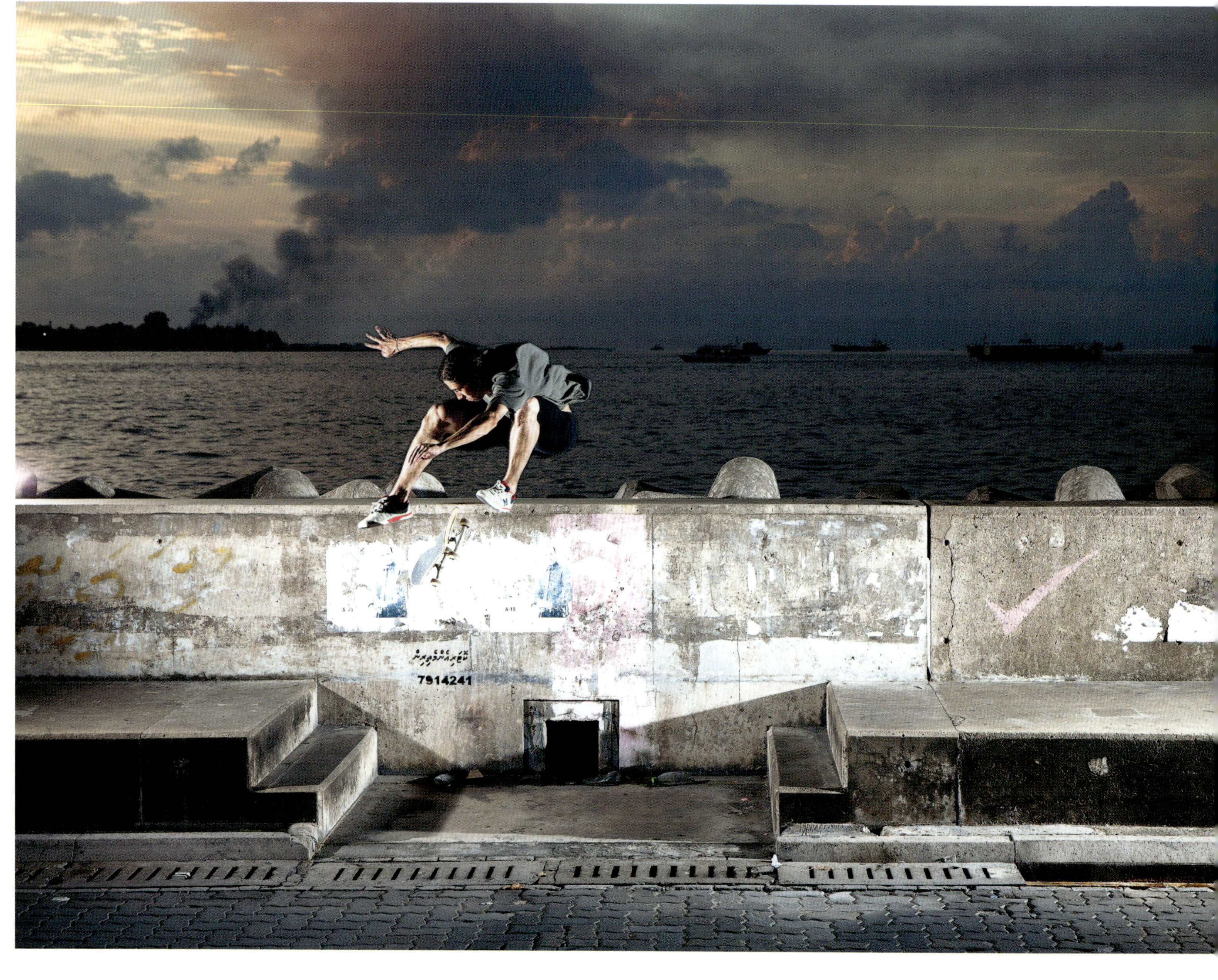
7914241

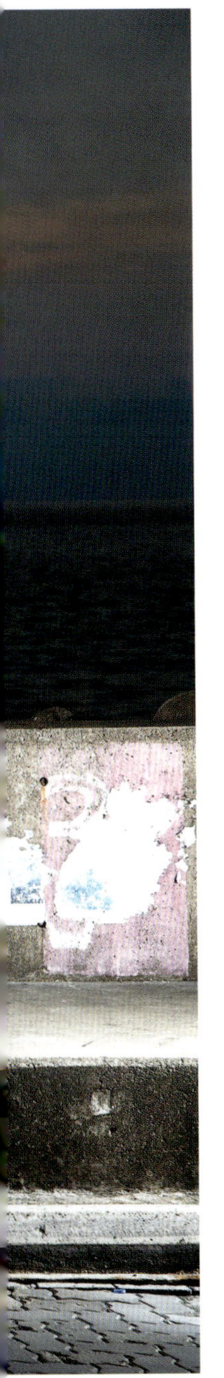

JORDAN TRAHAN
MALÉ, MALDIVES

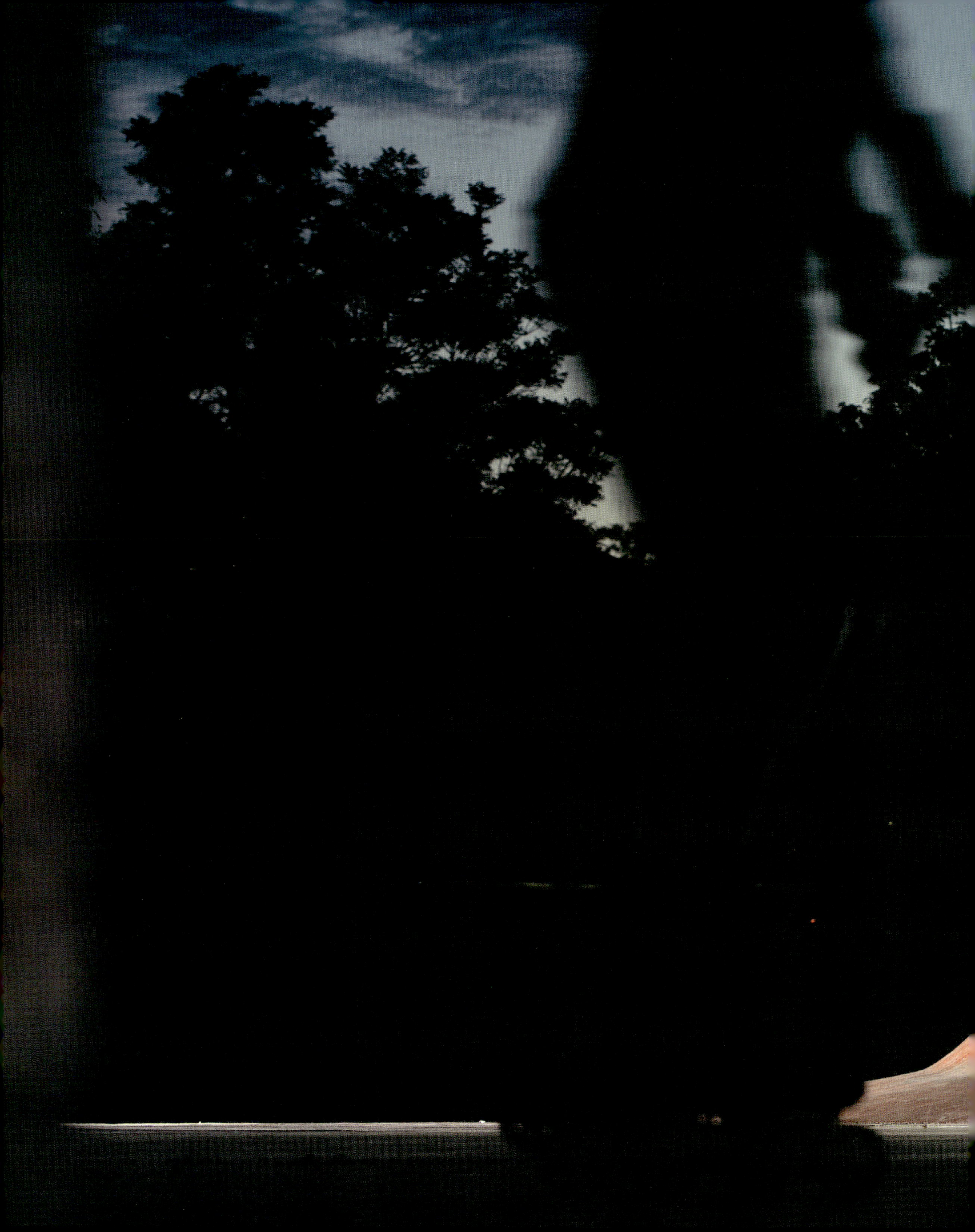

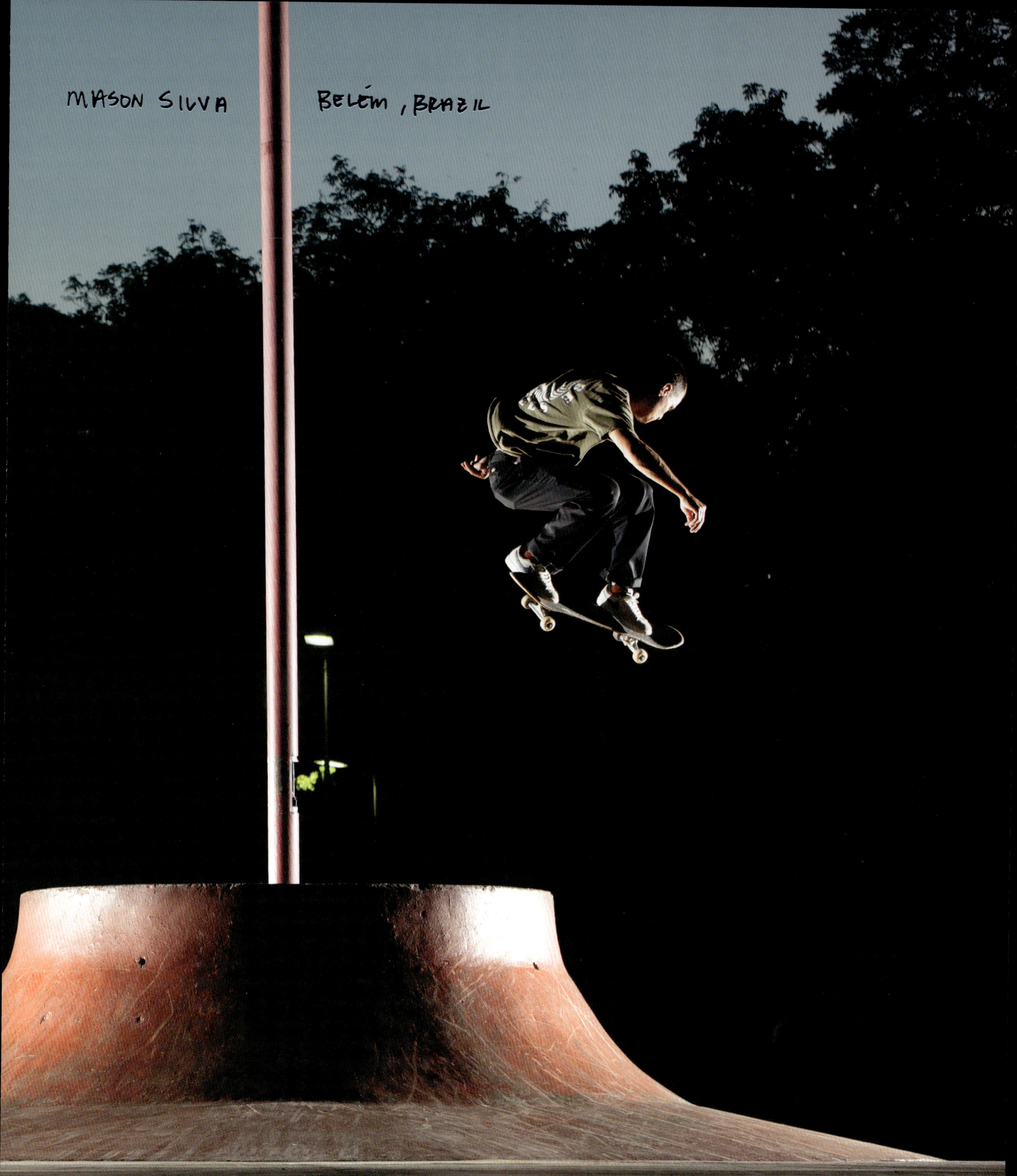

MASON SILVA BELÉM, BRAZIL

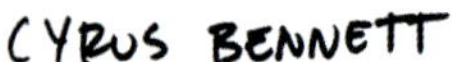

SERBIA

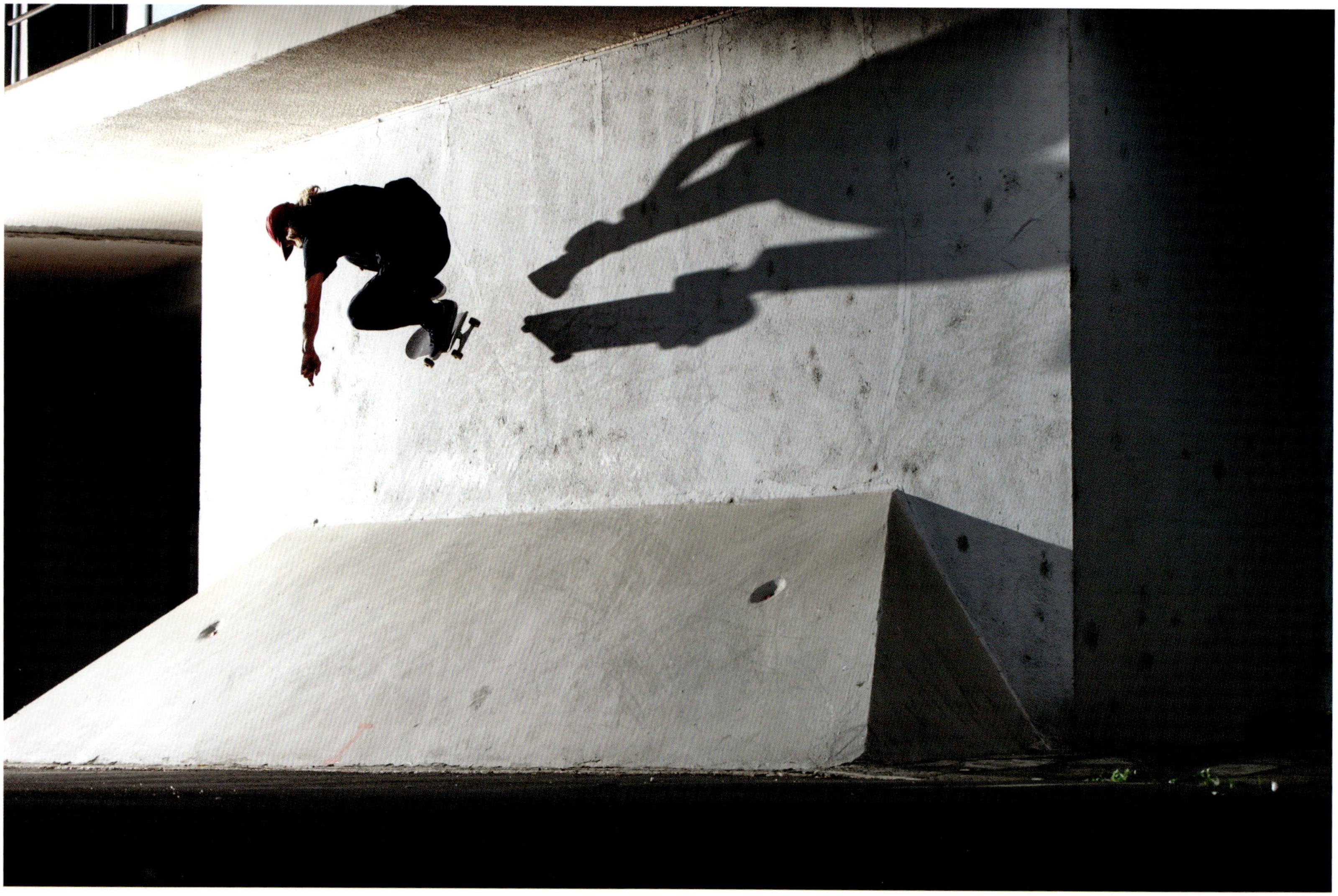

NORA VASCONCELLOS
LISBON, PORTUGAL

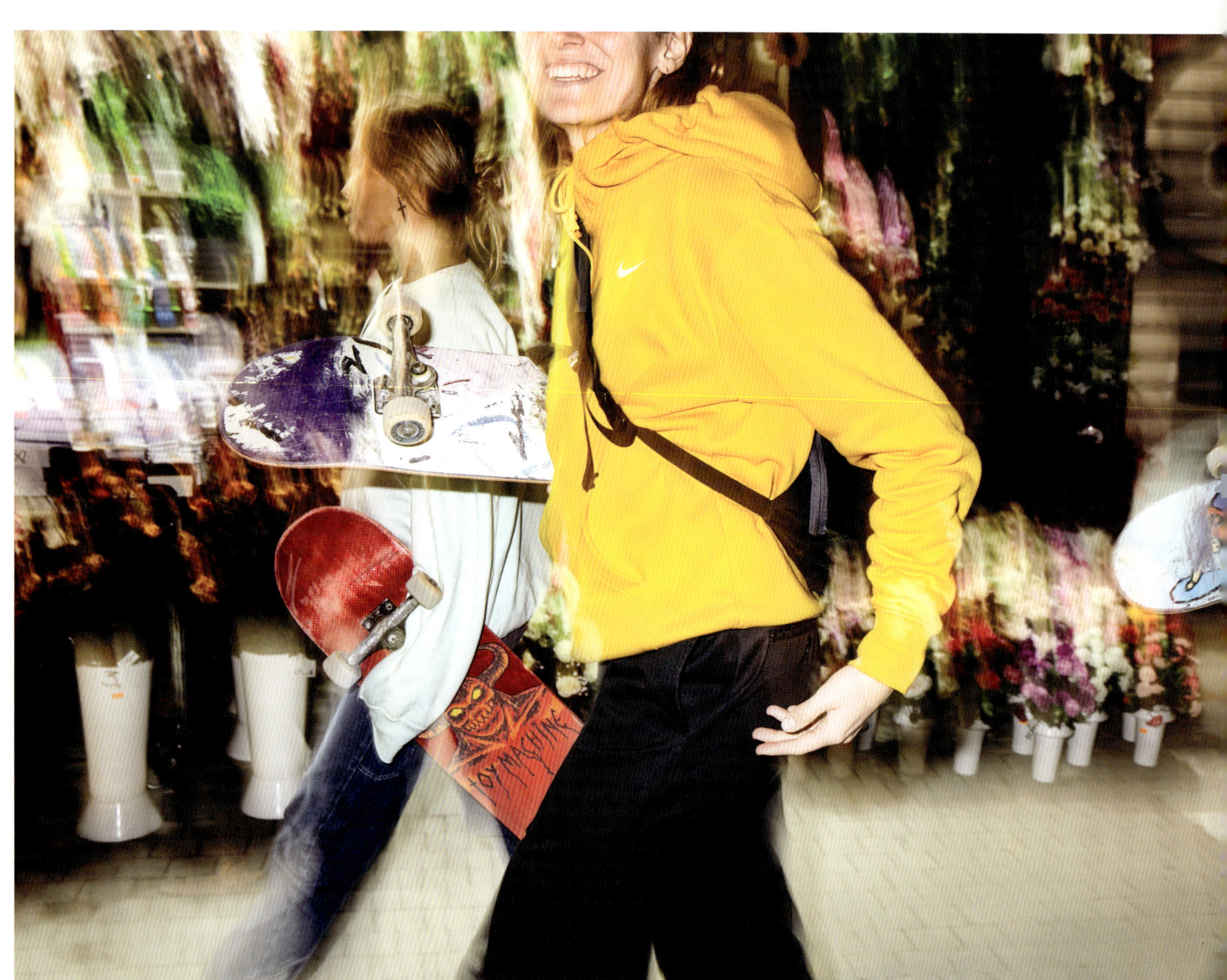

SARAH MEURLE ATHENS, GREECE

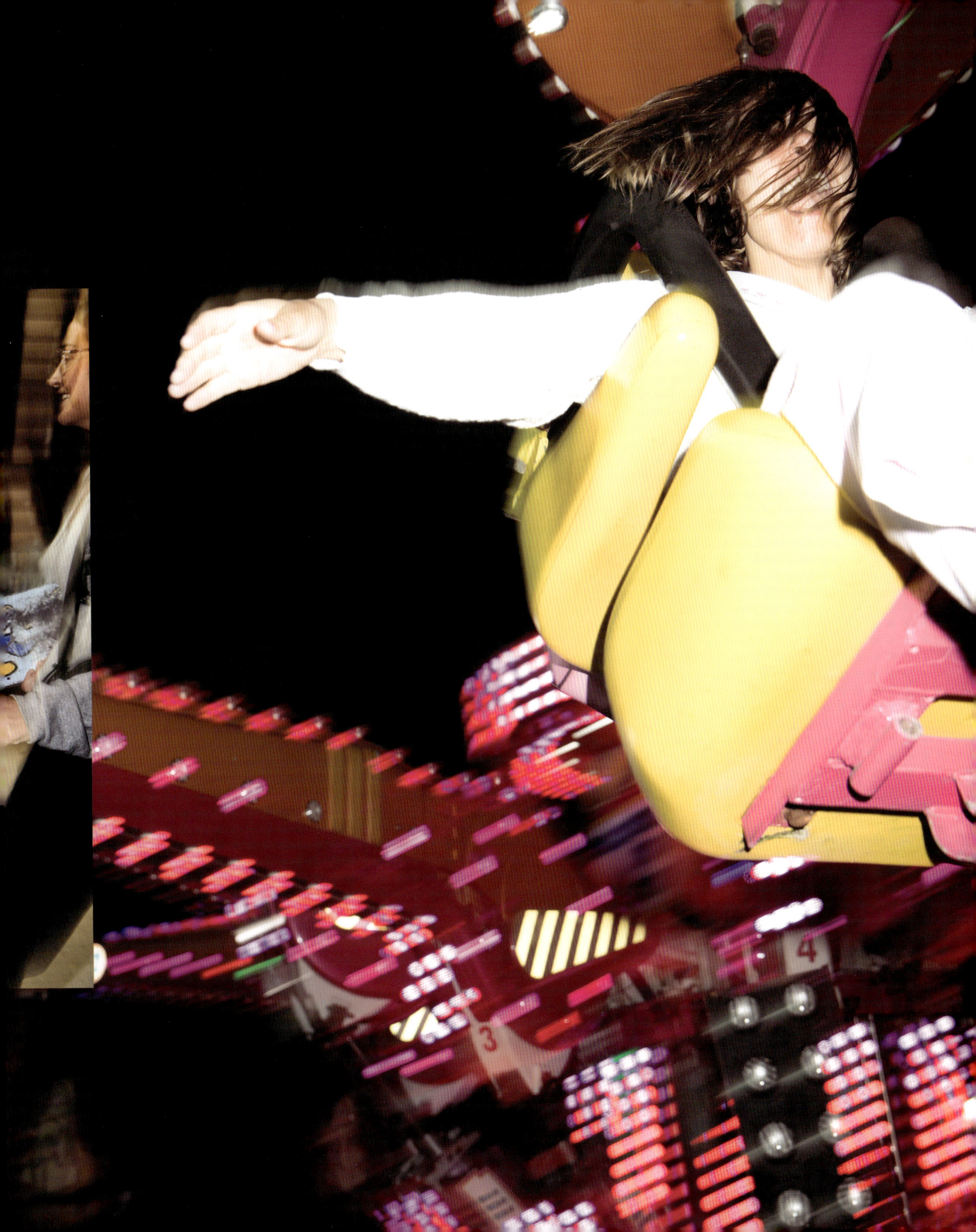

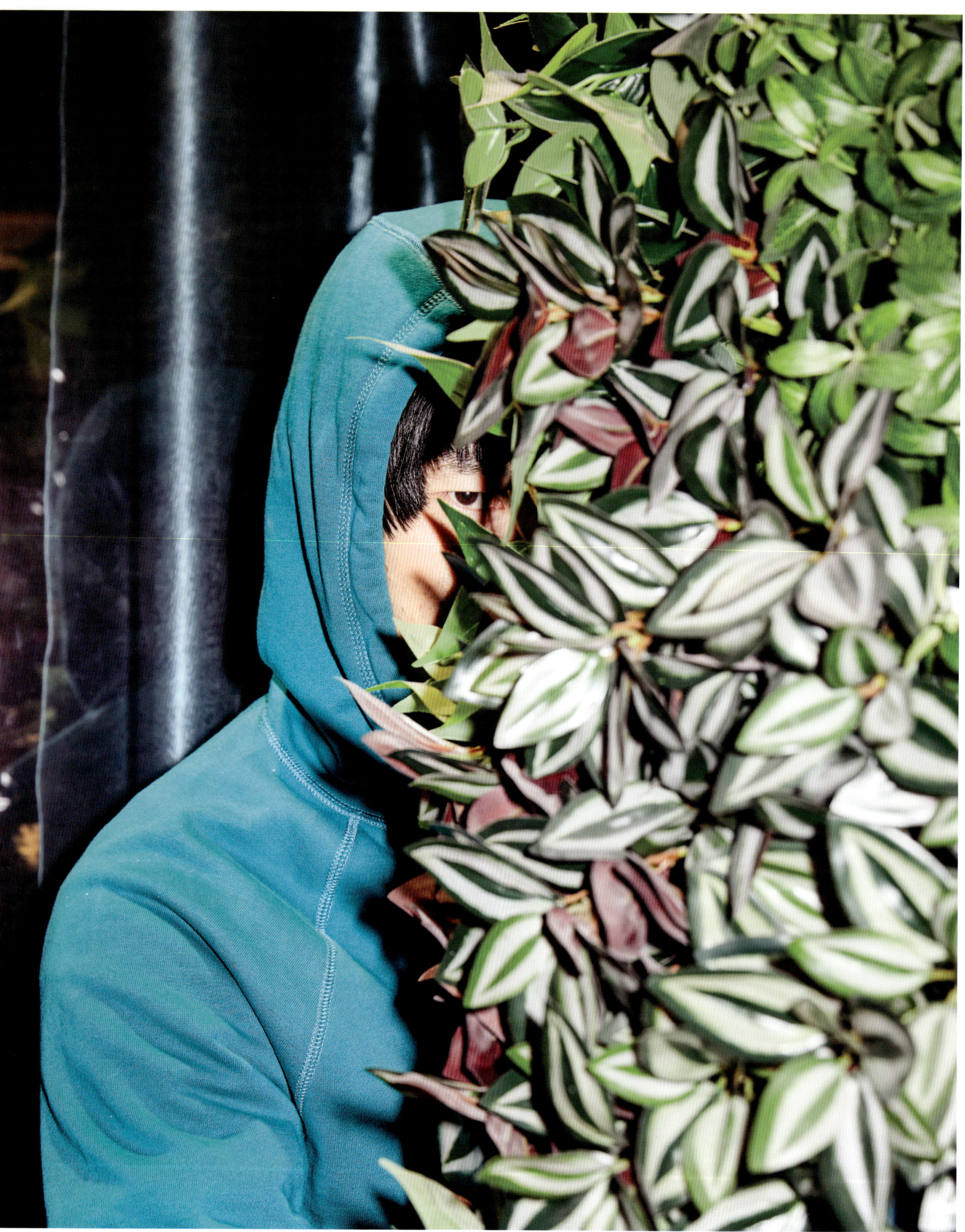

XIAO JI
SHANGHAI, CHINA

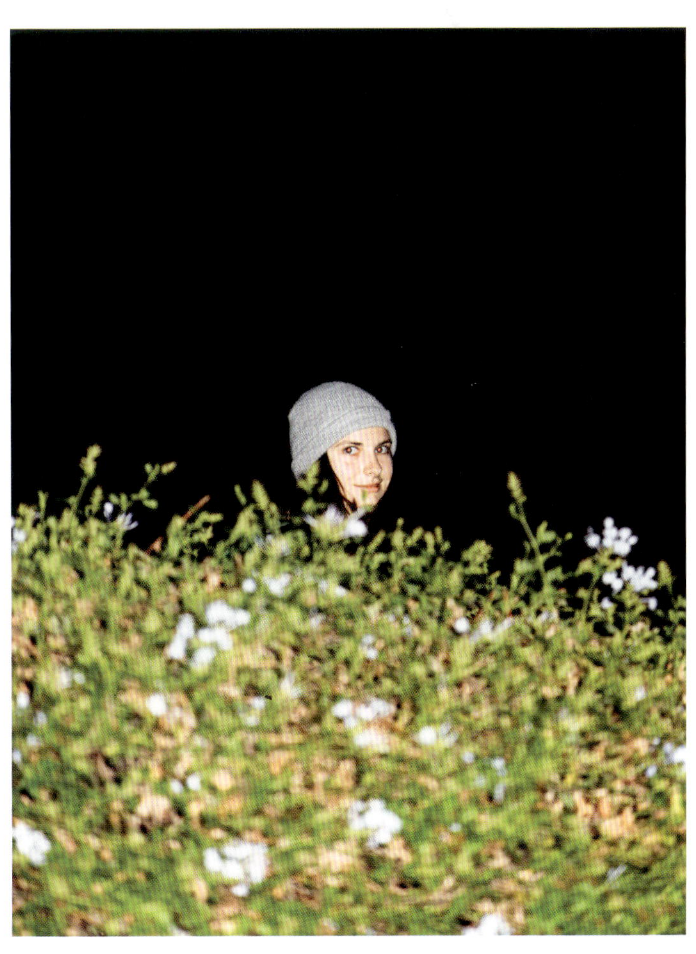

AGATA HALIKOWSKA
ATHENS, GREECE

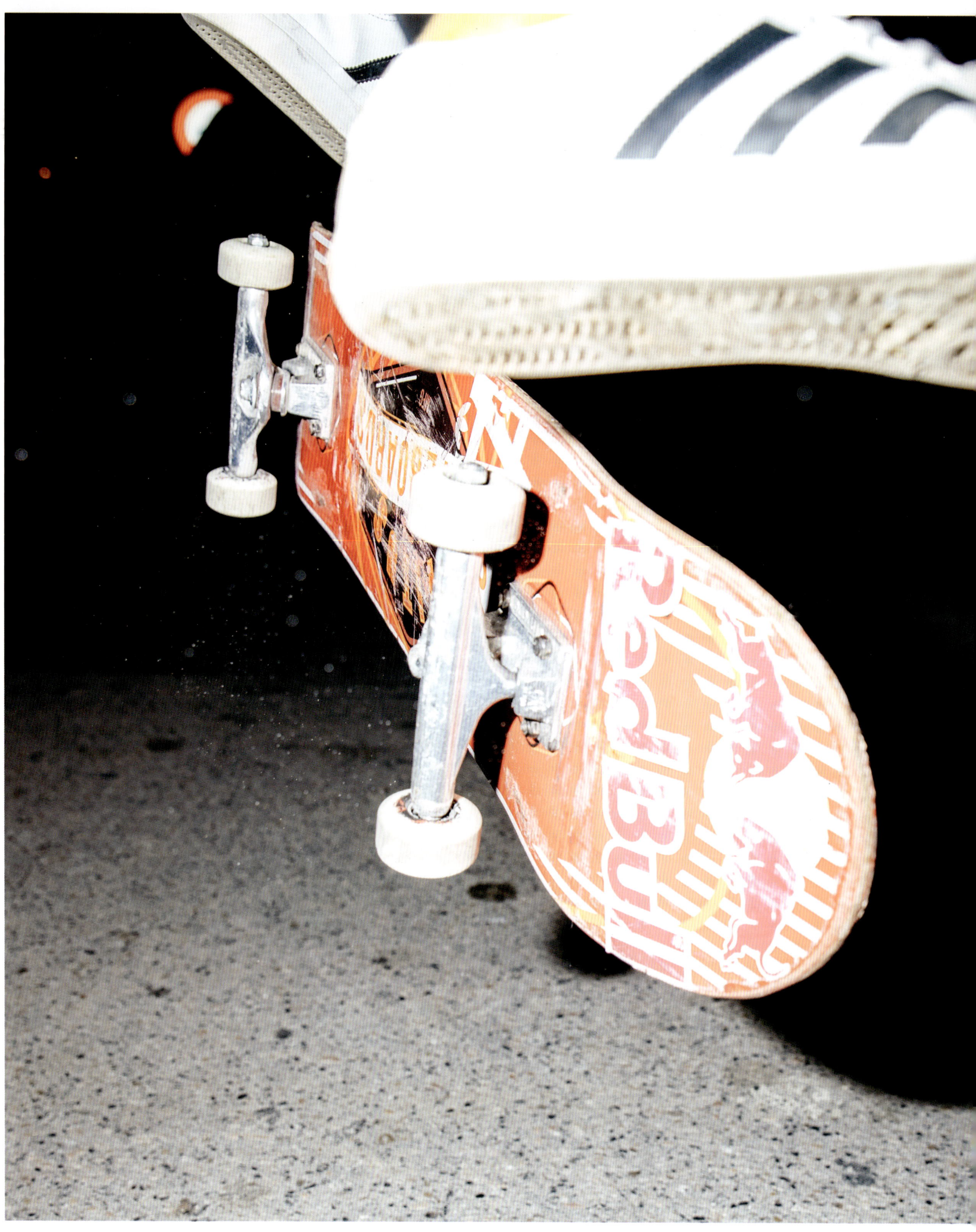

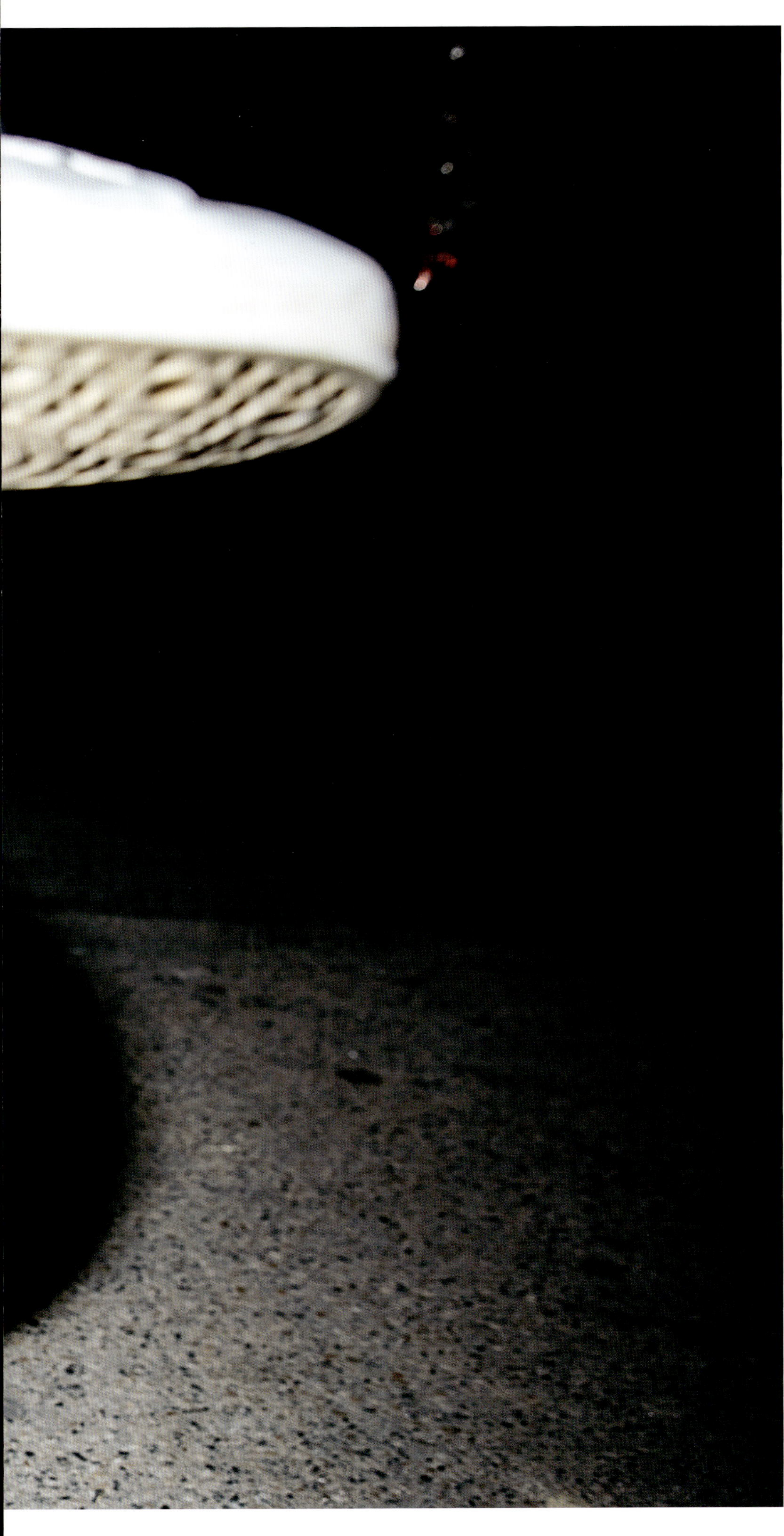

KICKFLIP TANGIER, MOROCCO

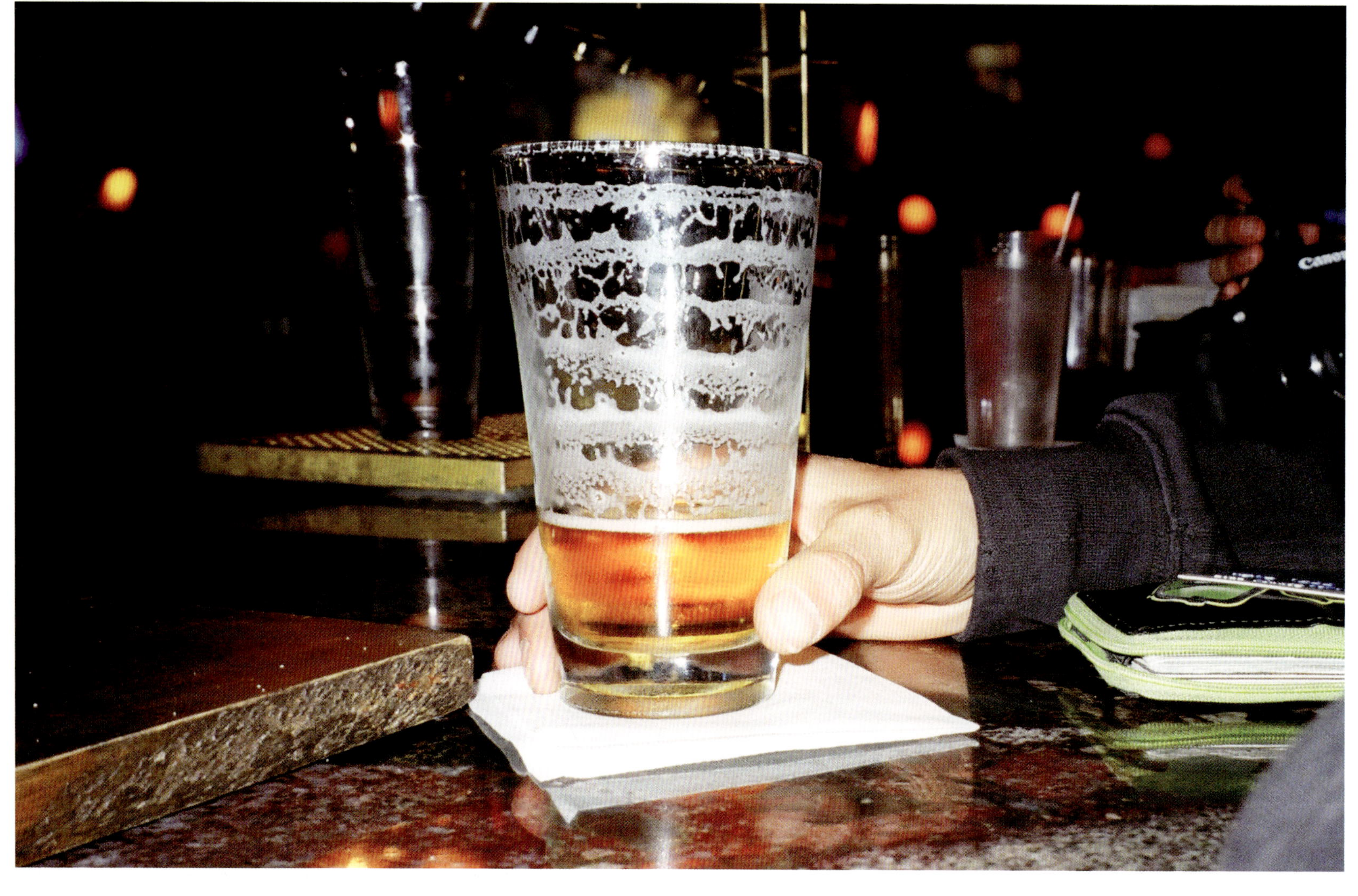

JOE TOOKMANIAN ST. JOHN'S, NEWFOUNDLAND

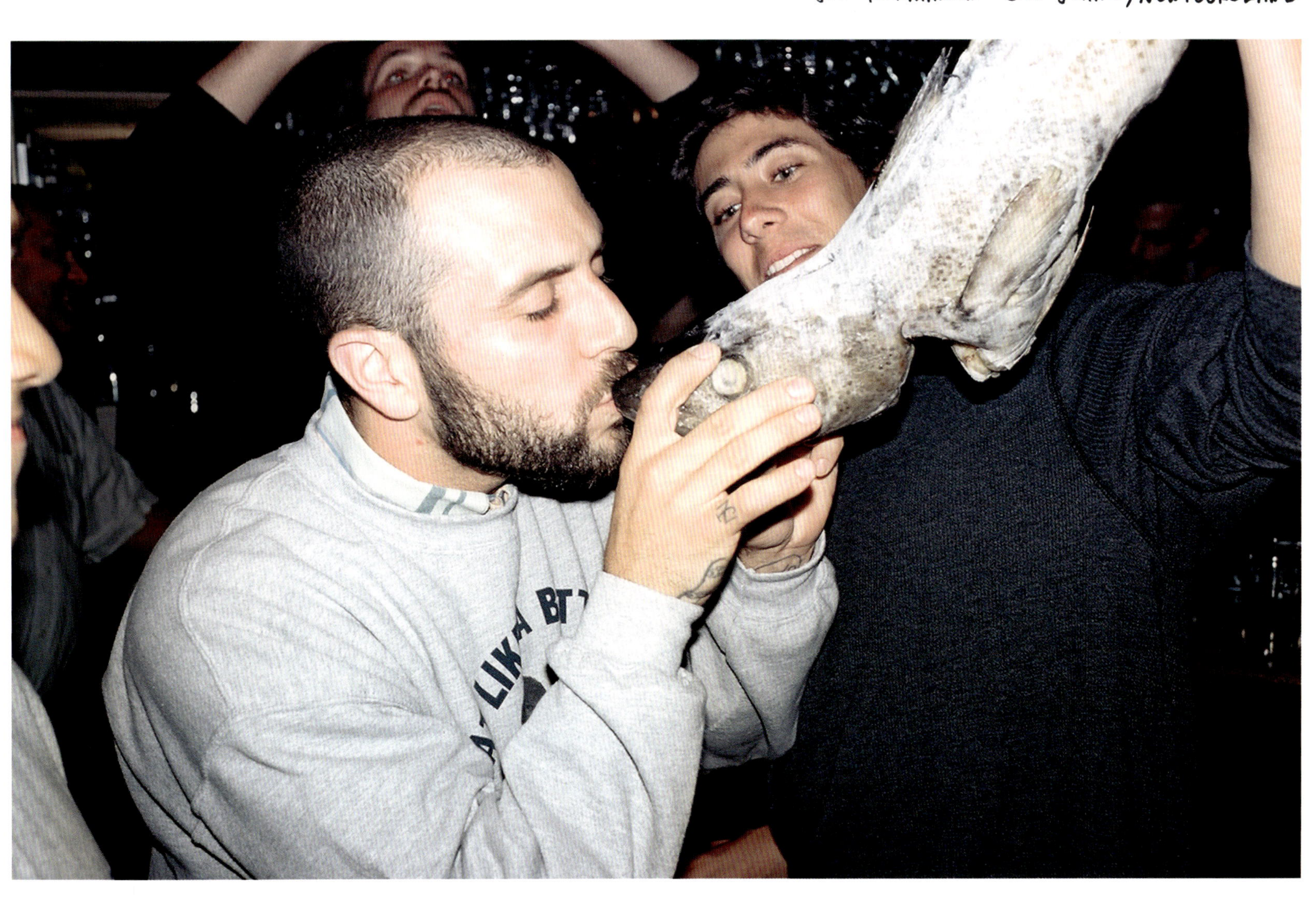

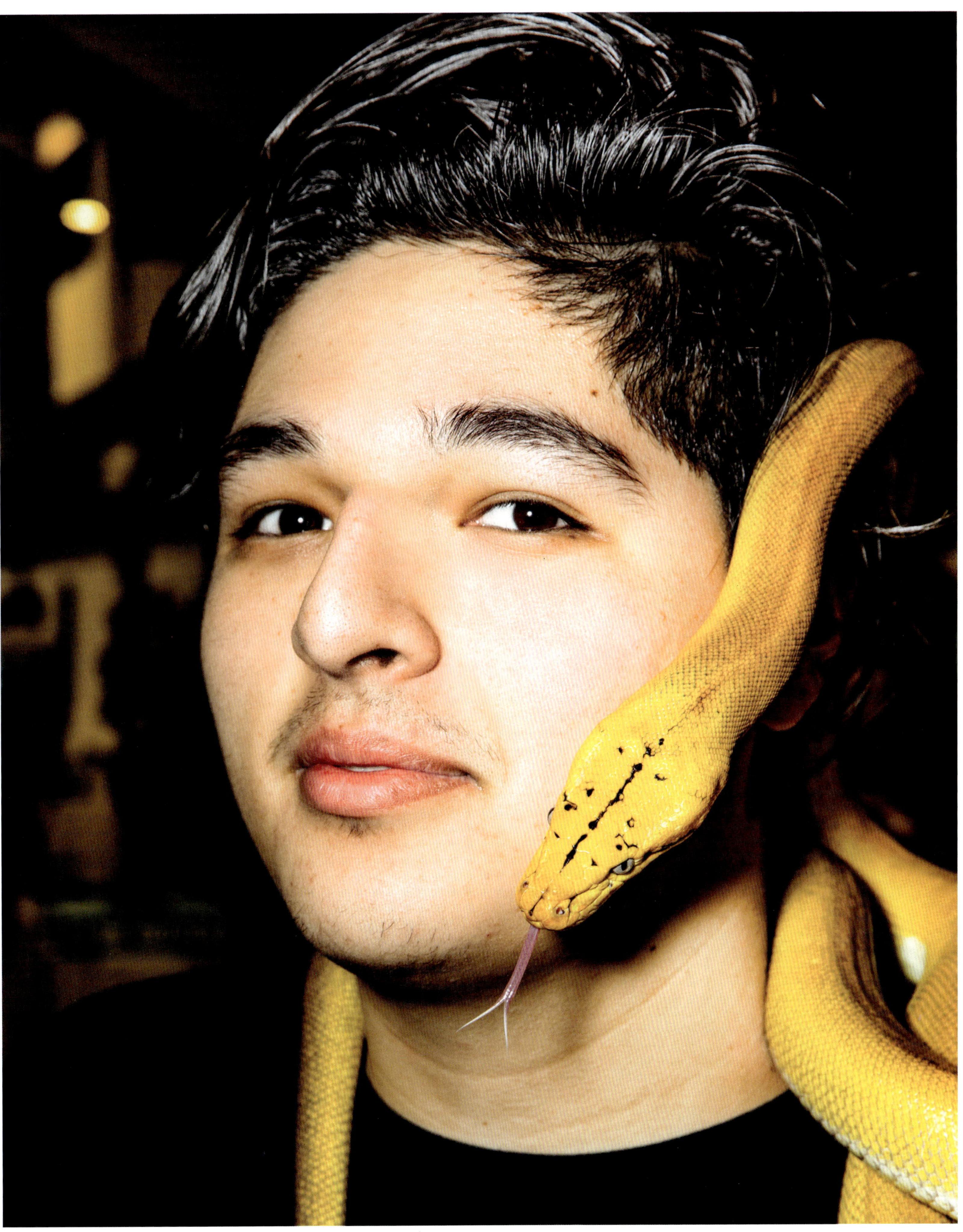

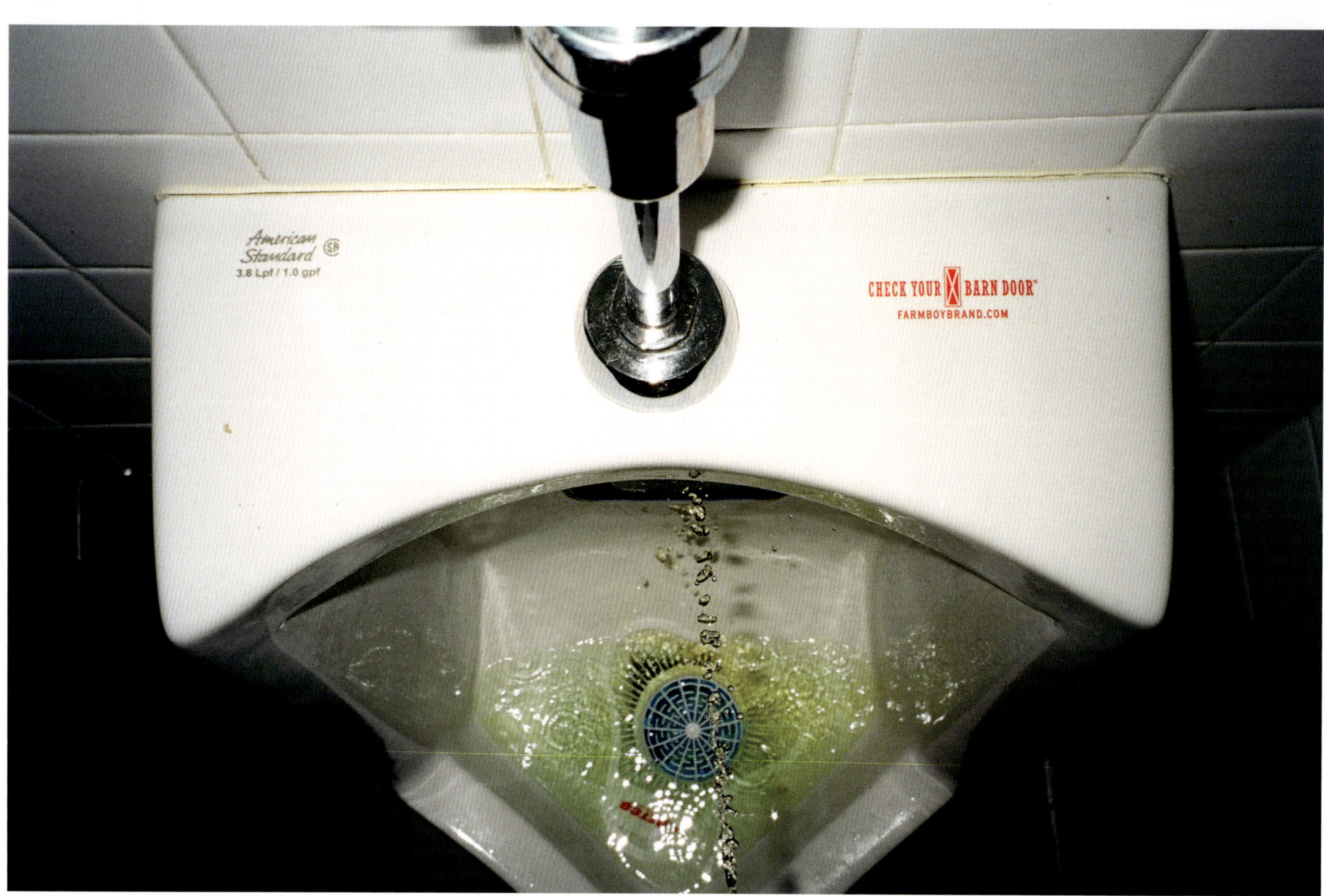
American Standard
3.8 Lpf / 1.0 gpf
CHECK YOUR BARN DOOR™
FARMBOYBRAND.COM

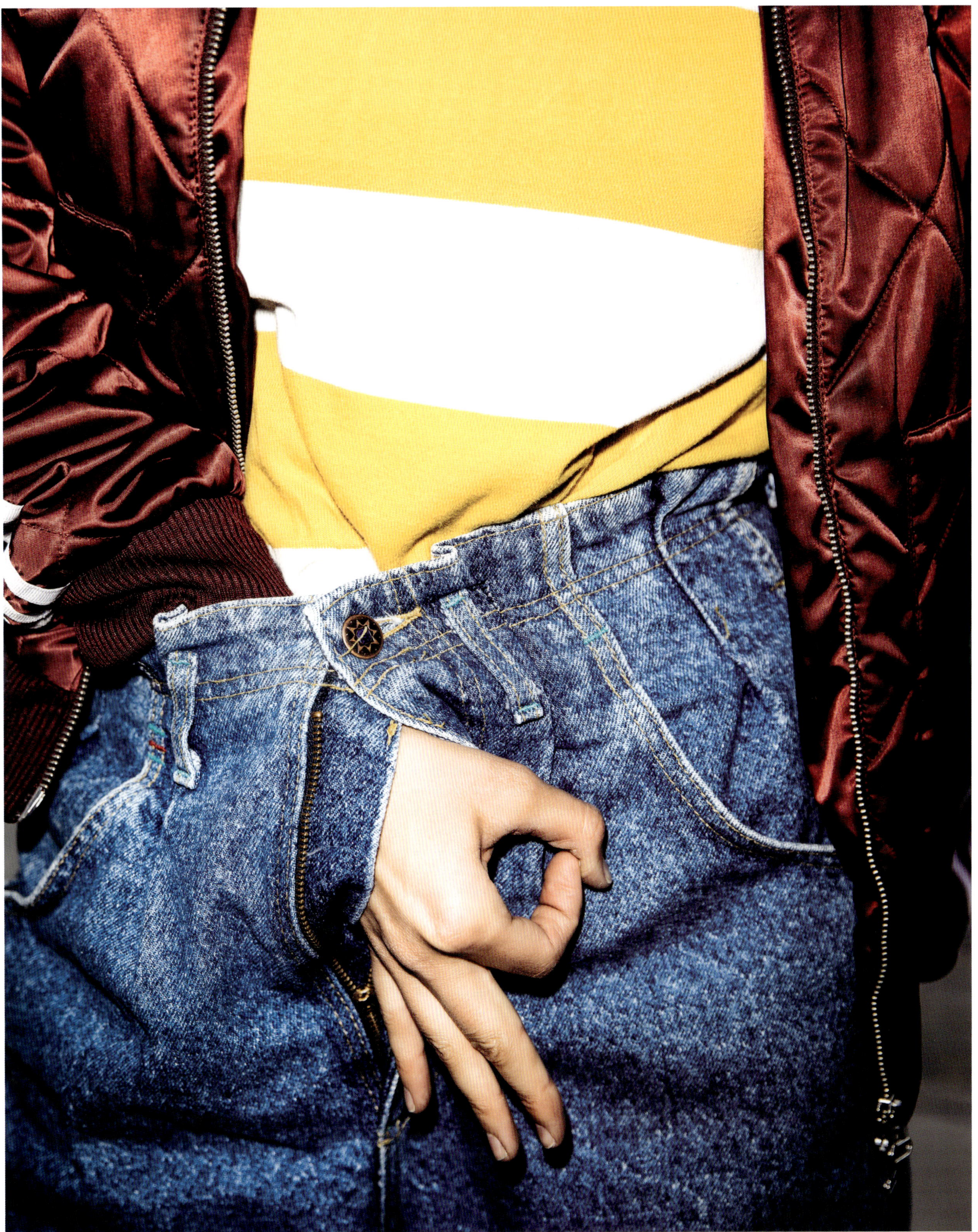

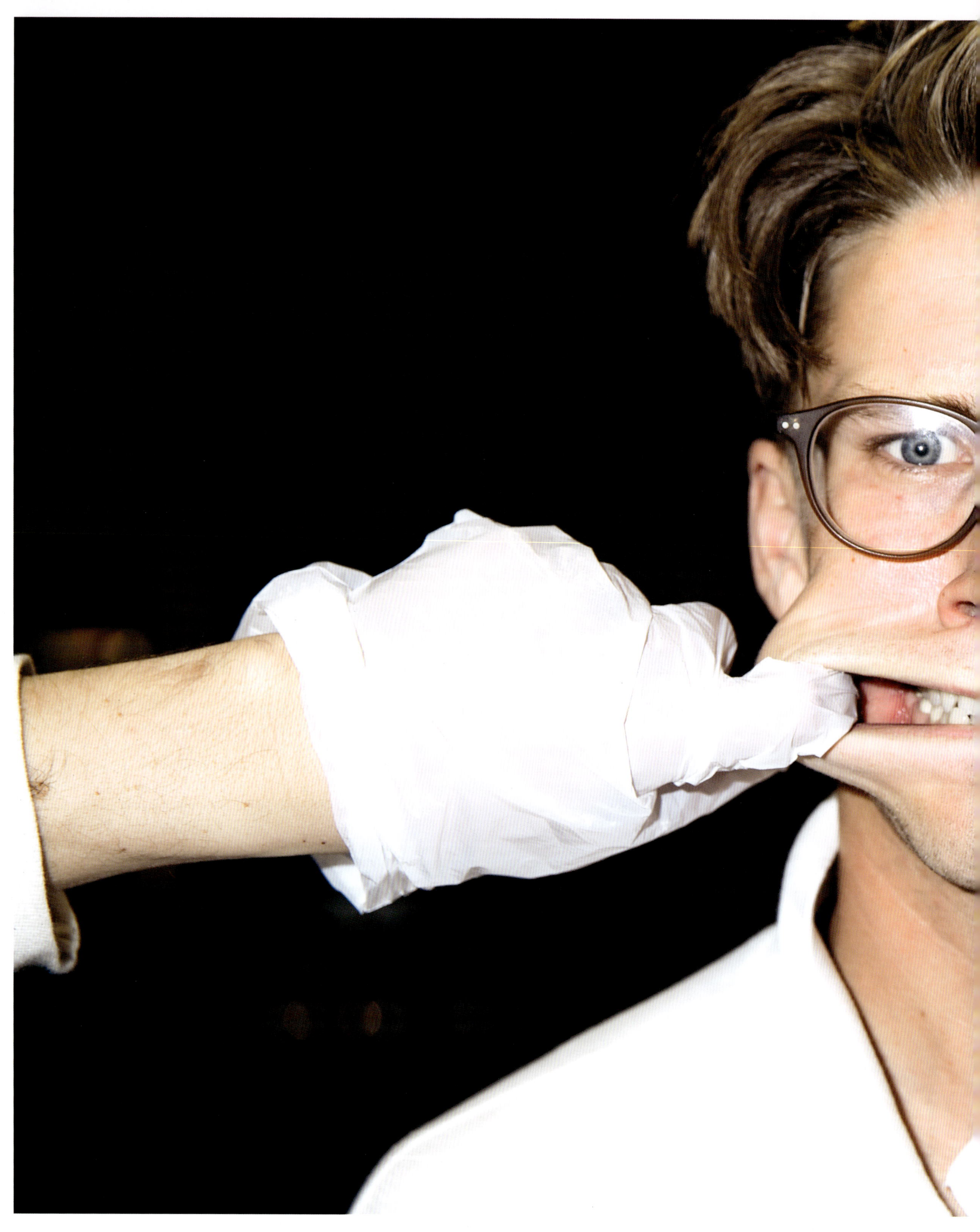

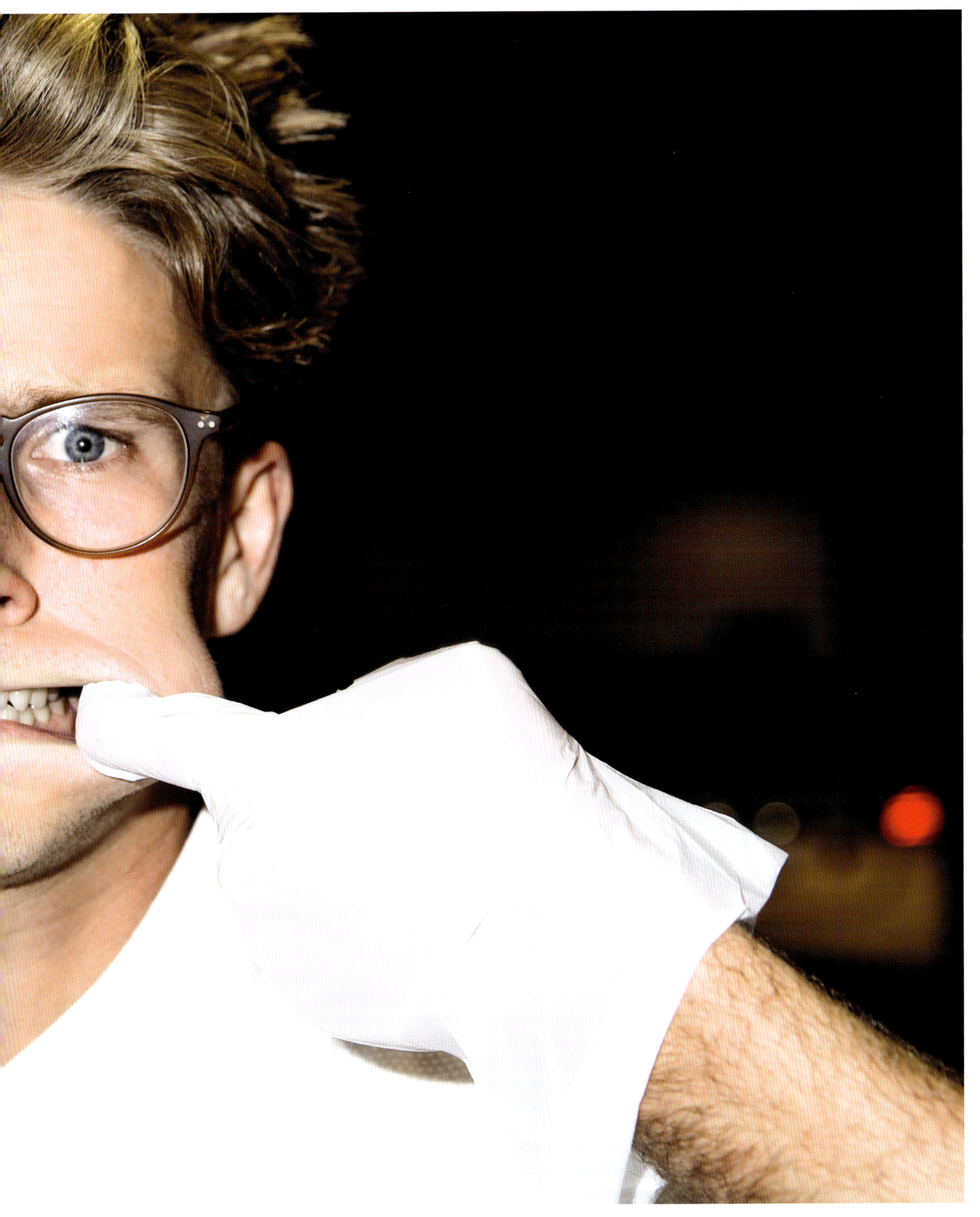

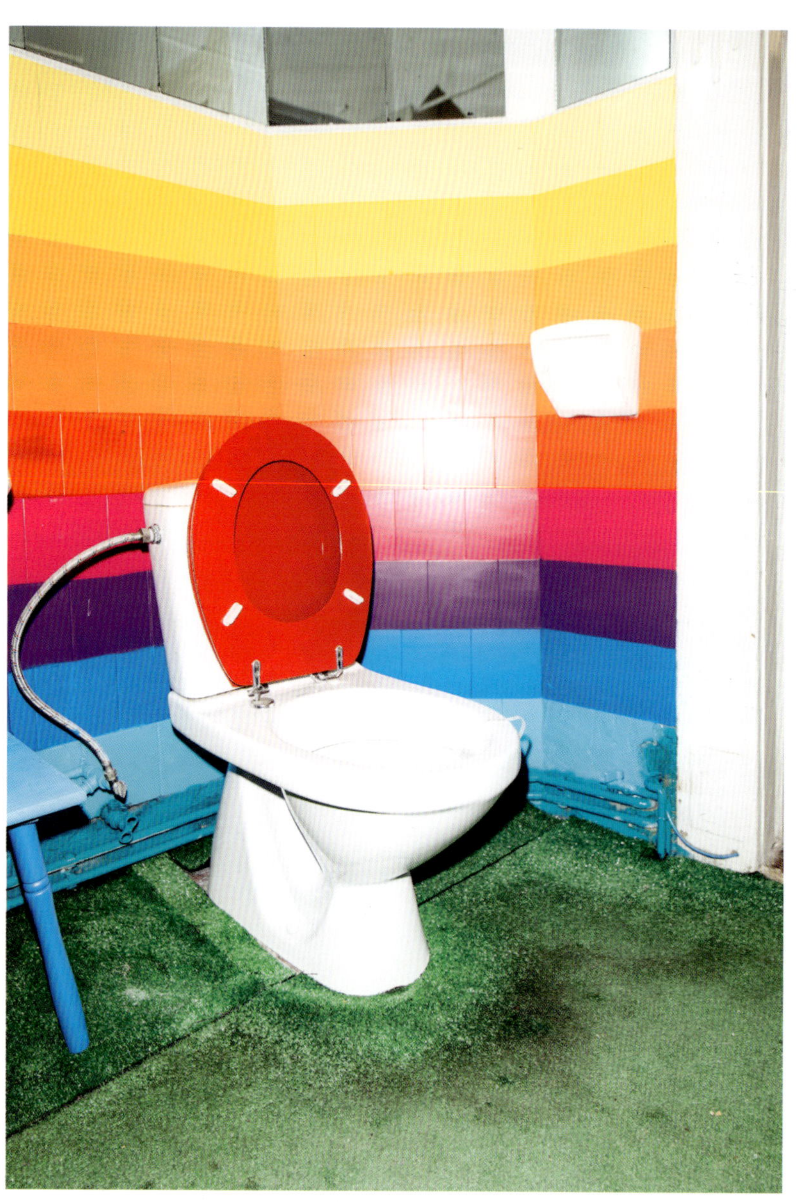

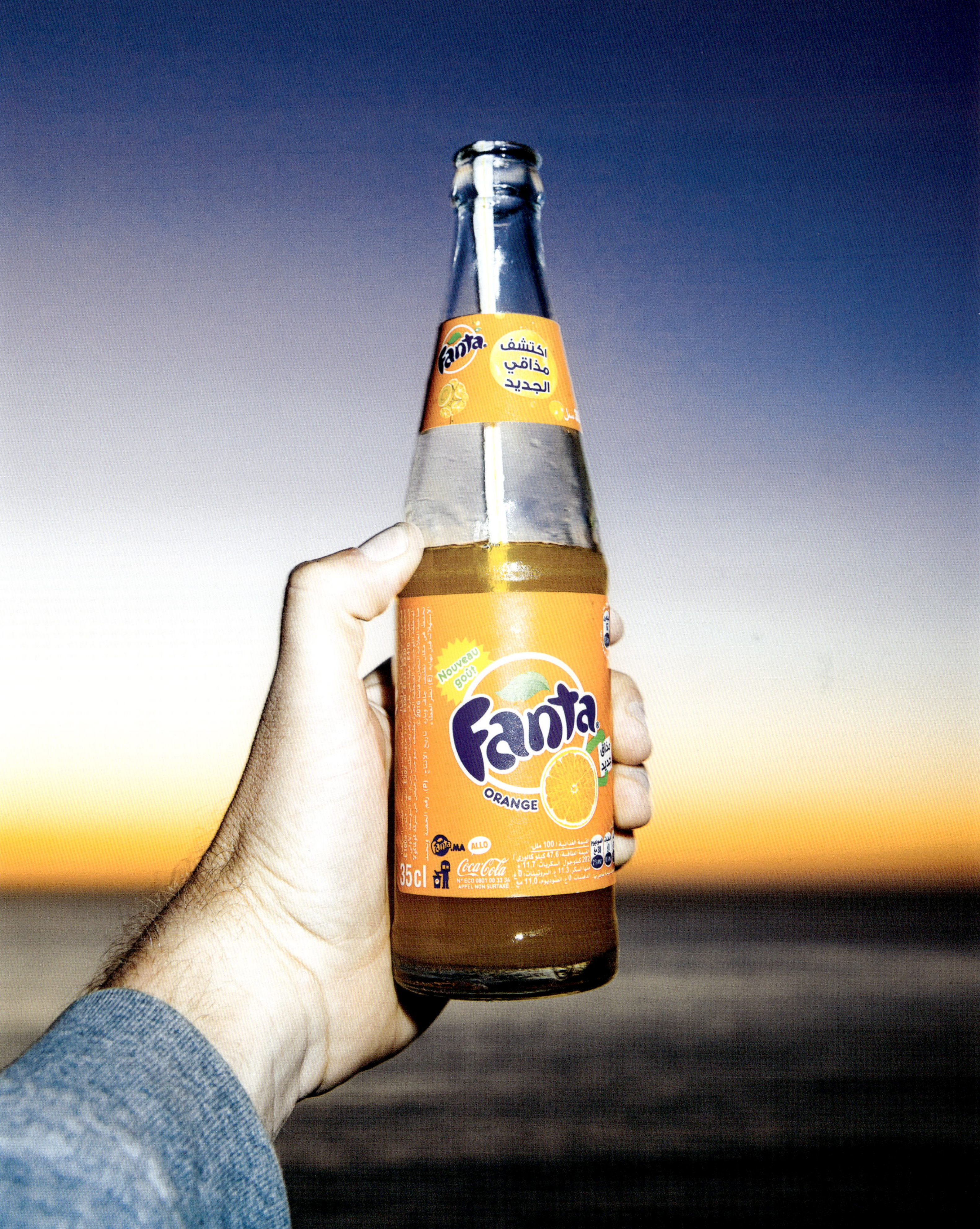

Fanta
اكتشف
مذاقي
الجديد
Nouveau goût!
Fanta
مذاق جديد
ORANGE
35cl
Coca-Cola

JOSH MATTHEWS REYKJAVIK, ICELAND

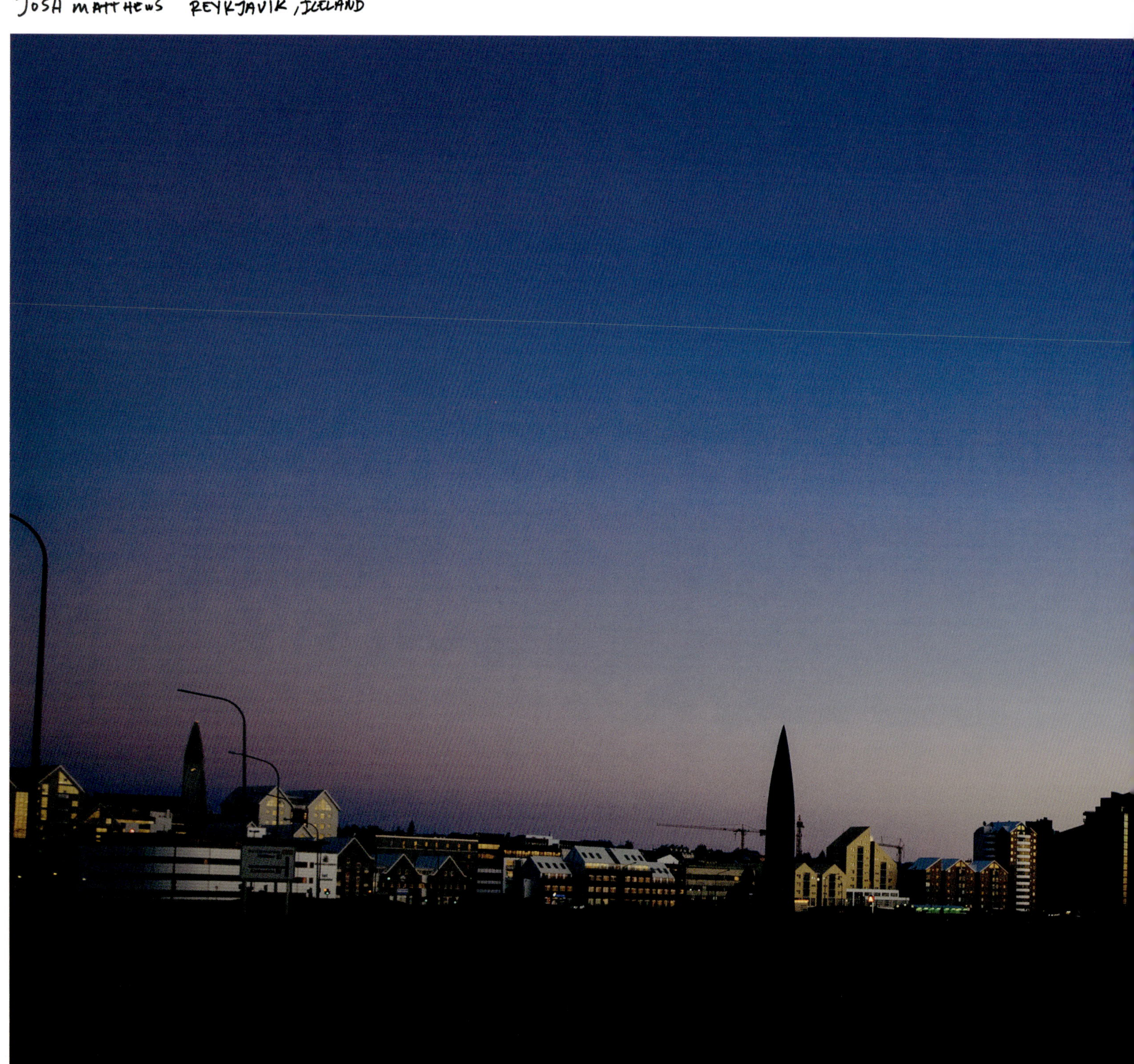

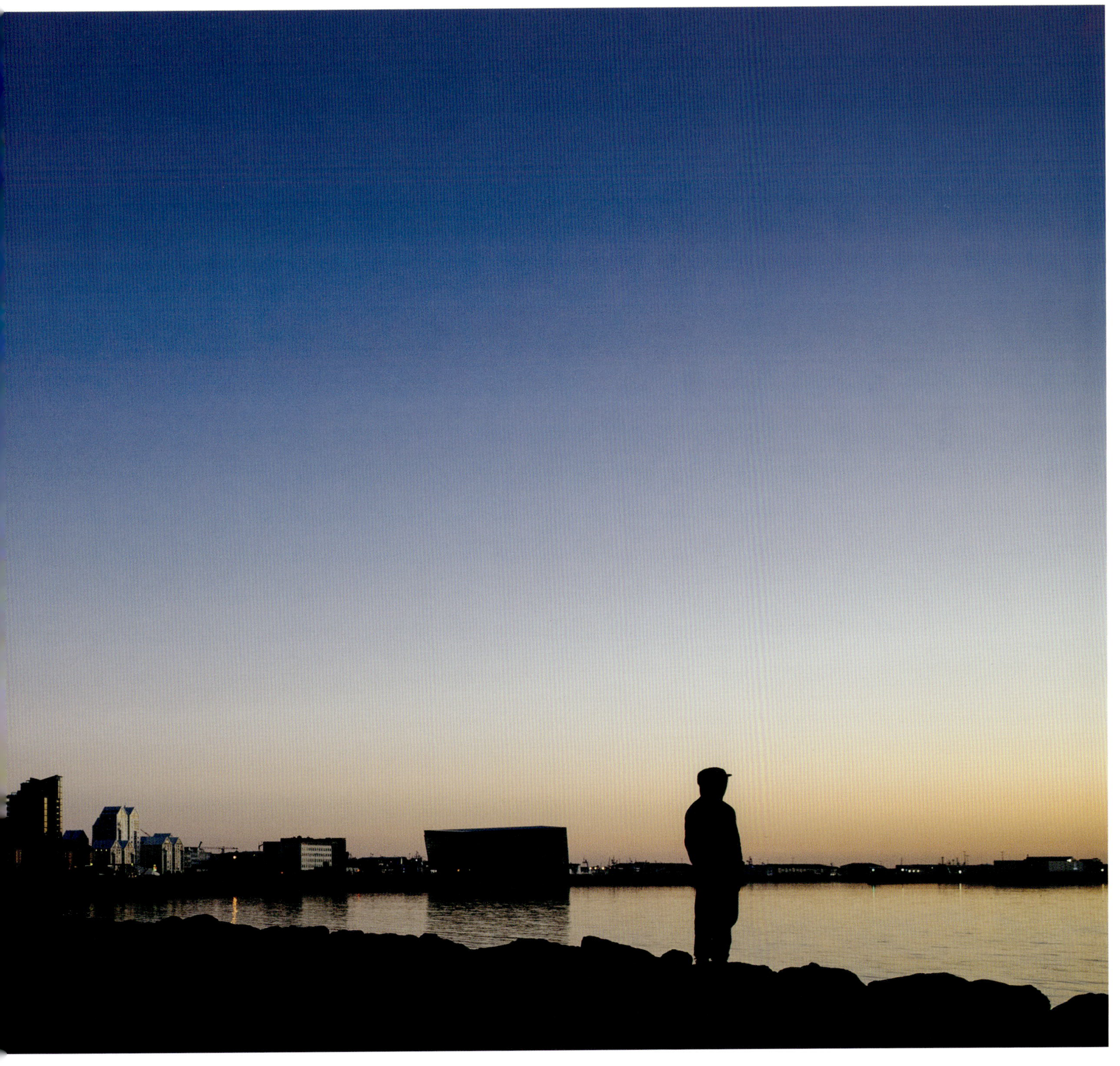

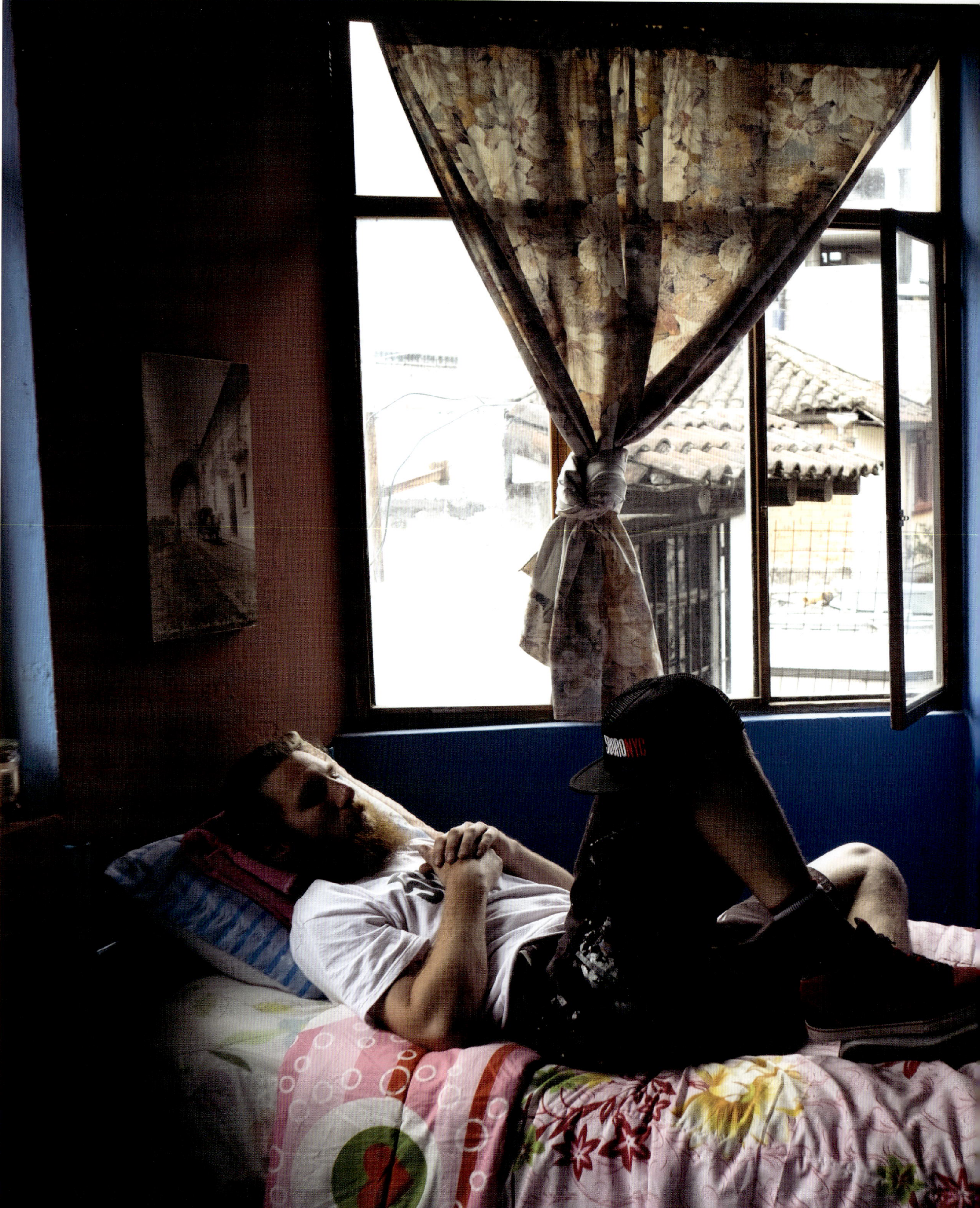
5BORONYC

WILLY AKERS QUITO, ECUADOR

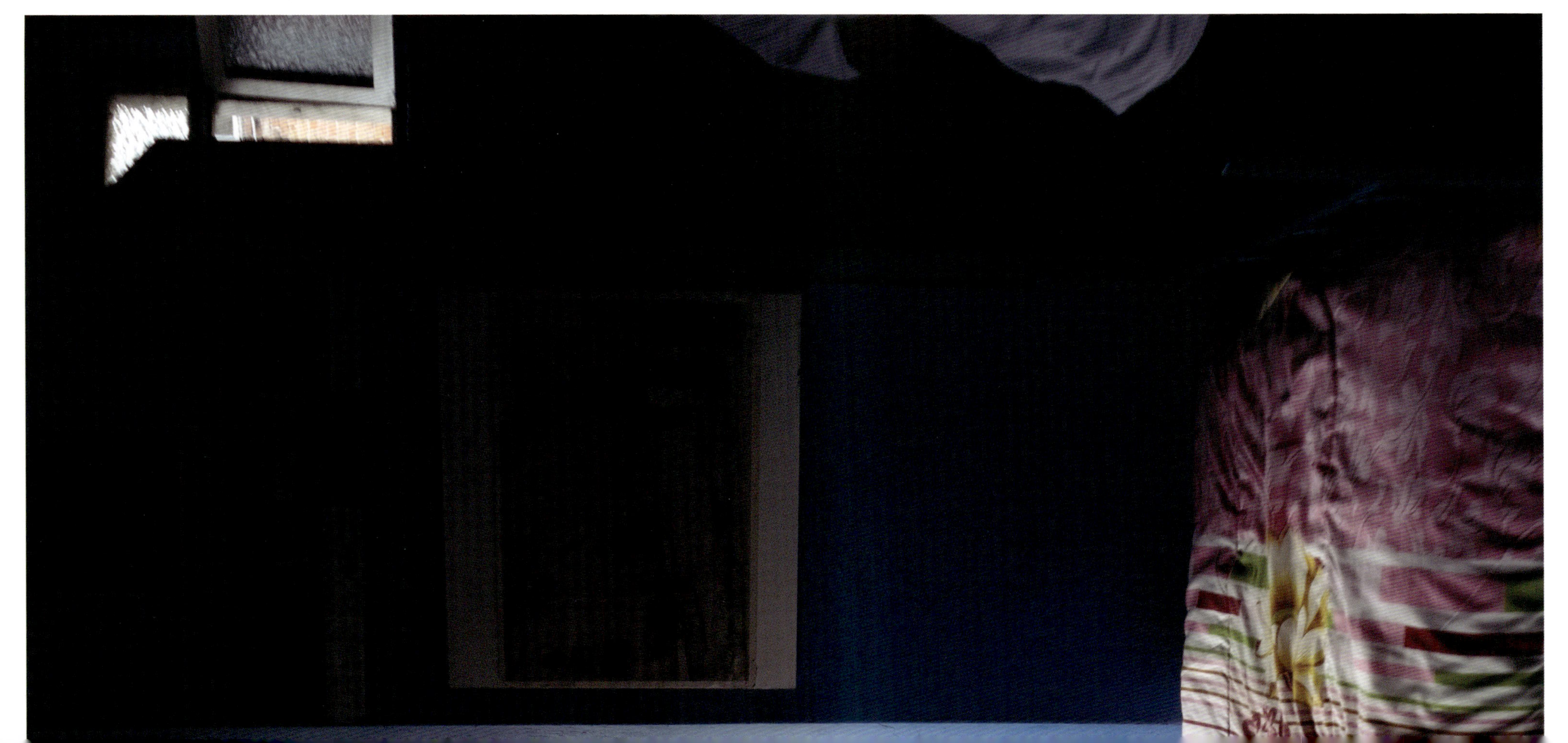

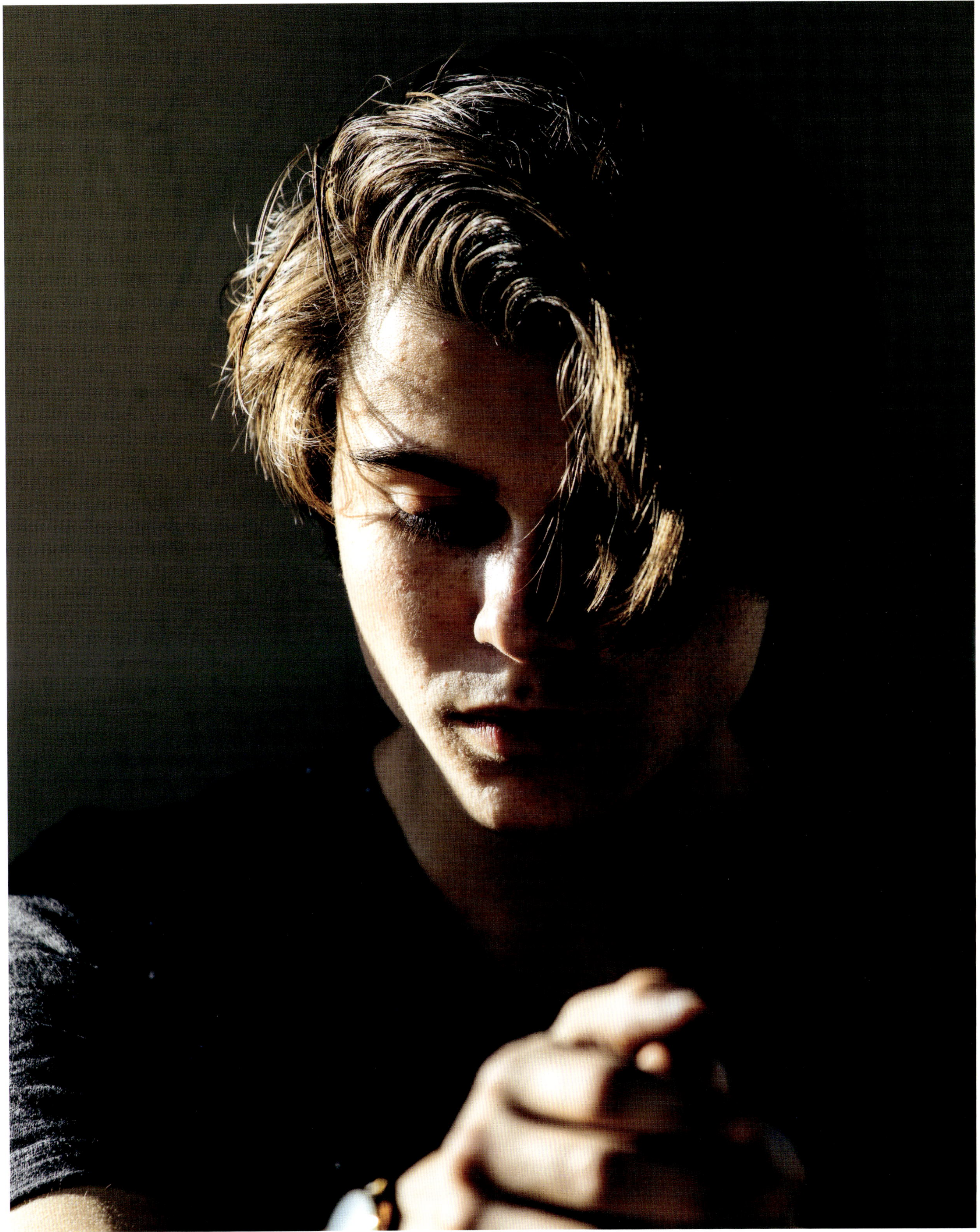

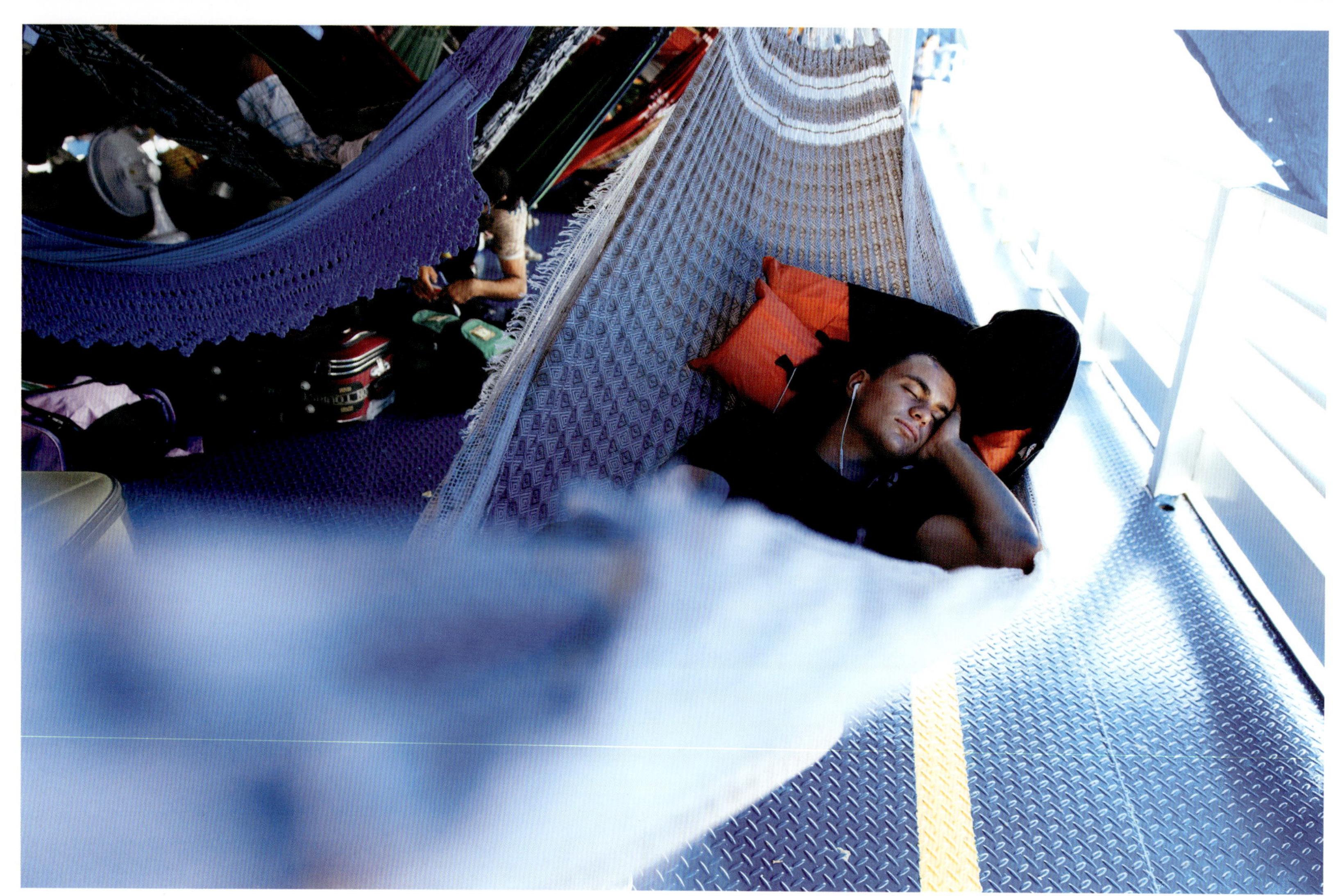

MASON SILVA   MANAUS, BRAZIL

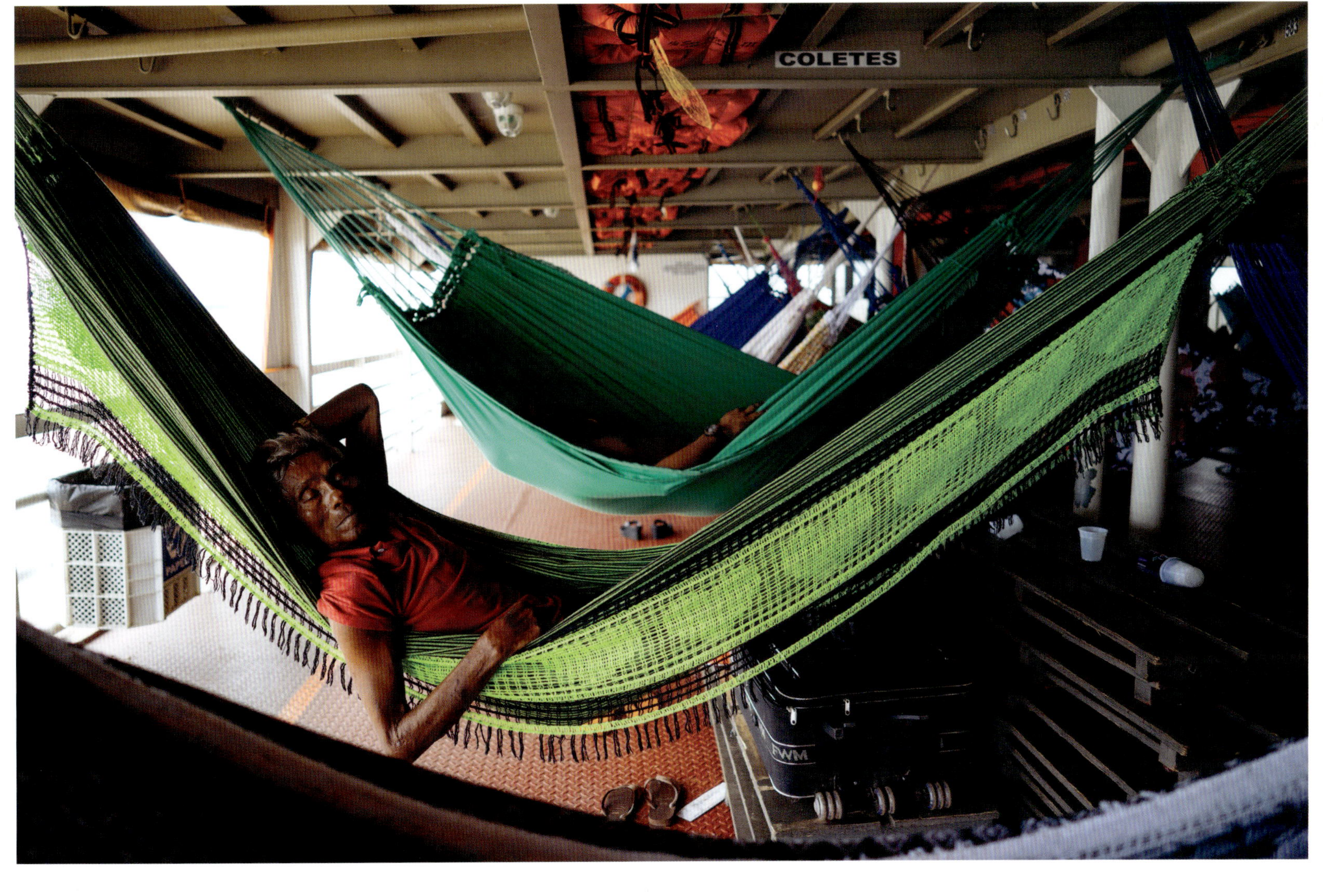
COLETES

GREECE

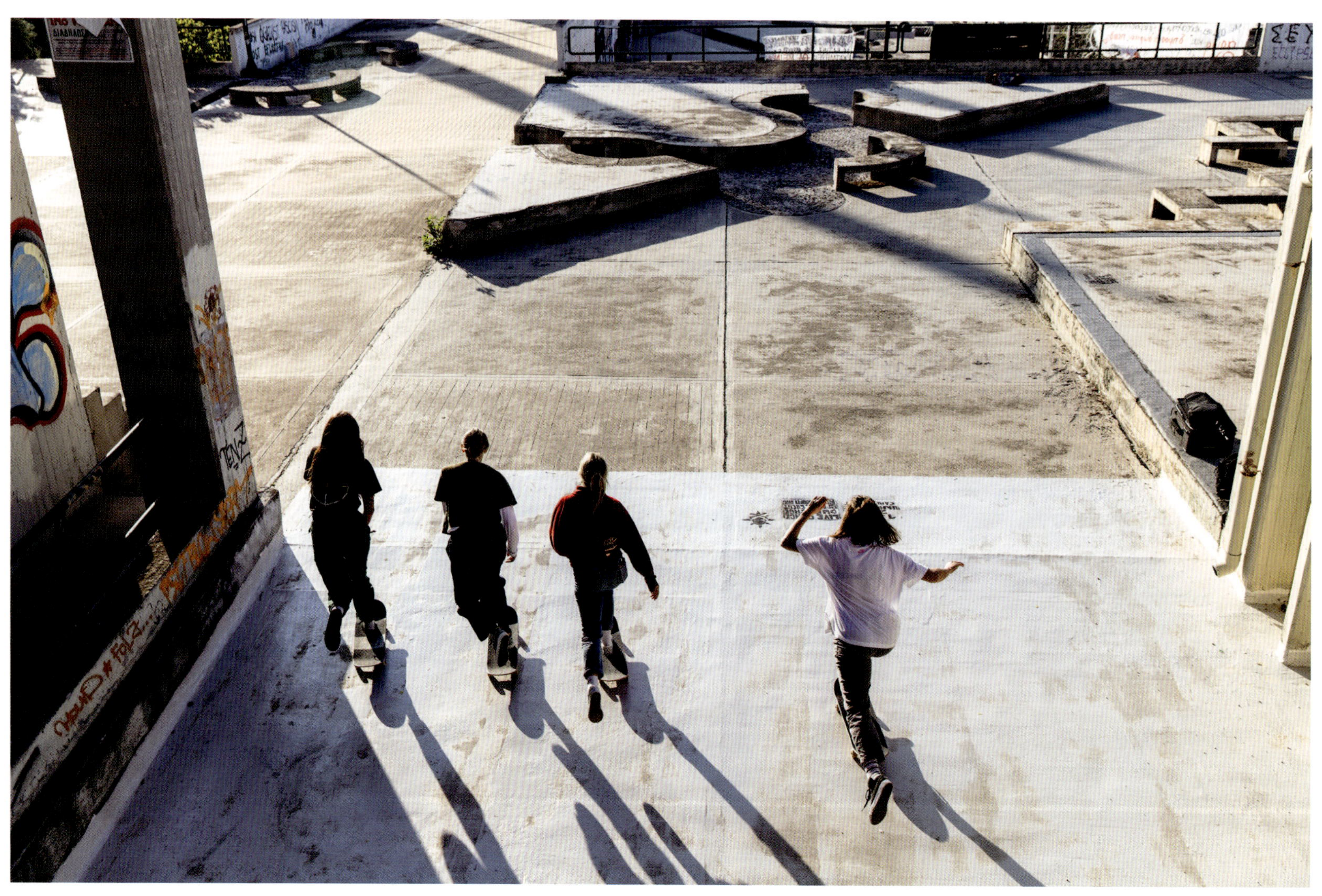

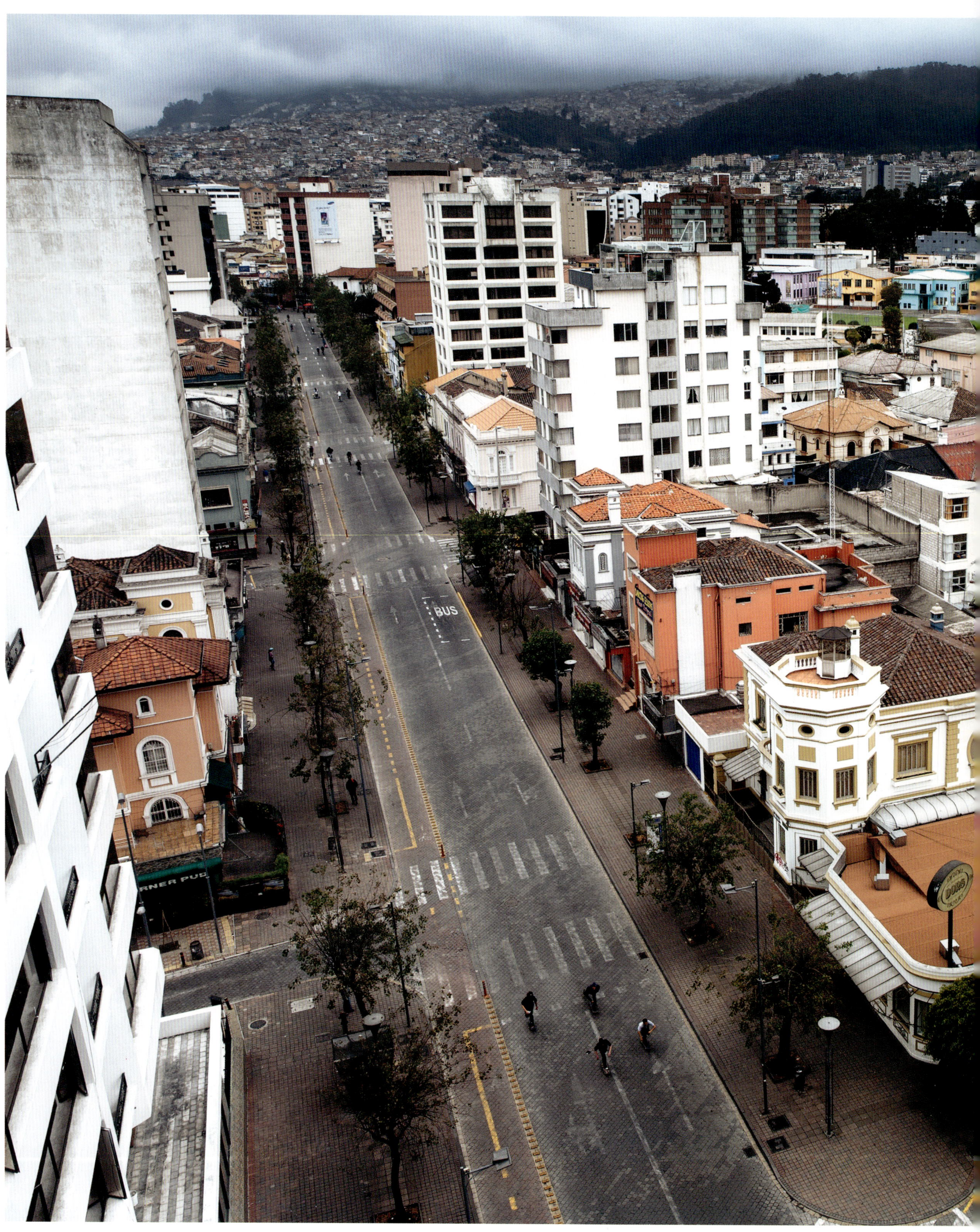
BUS

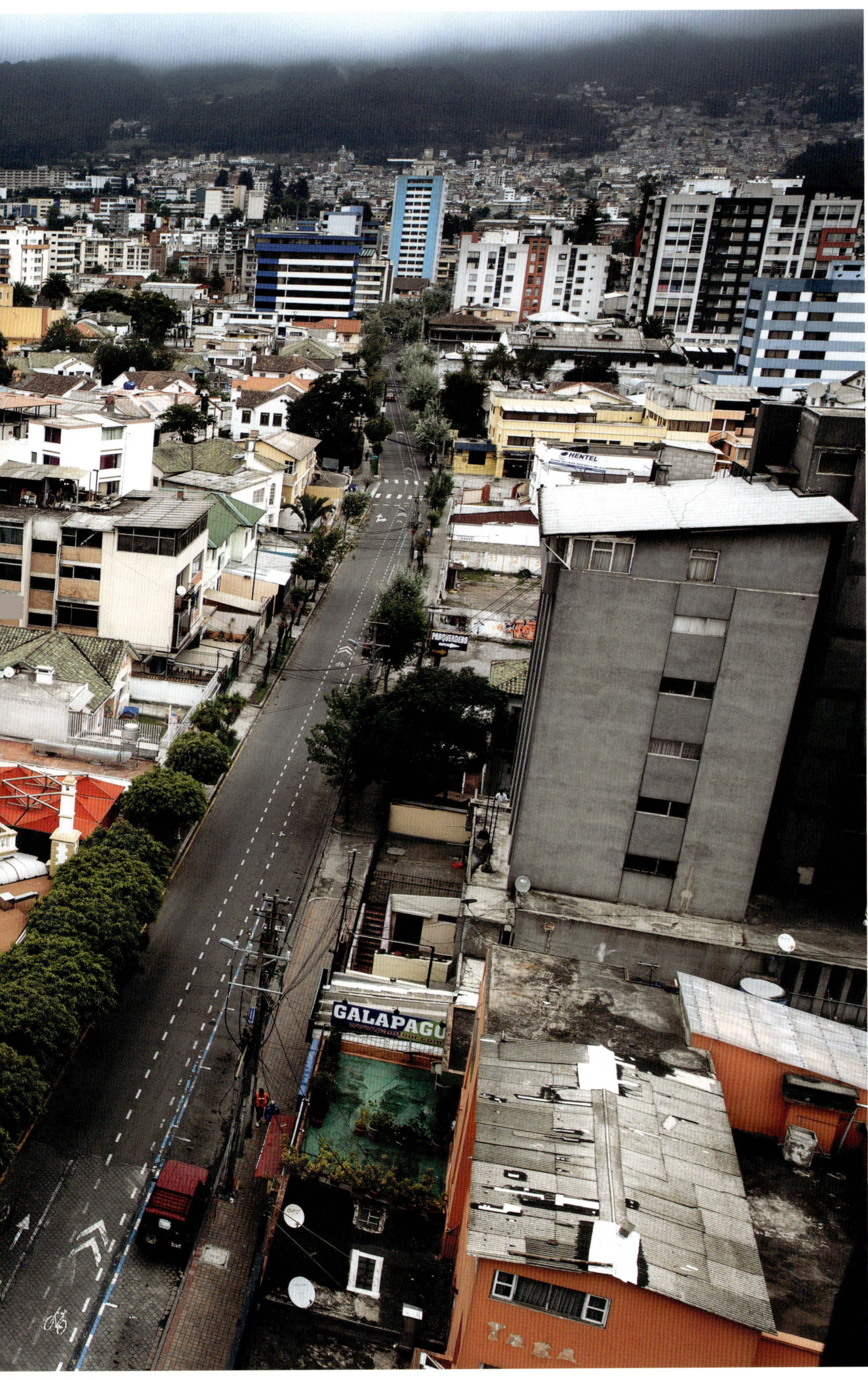
GALAPAGO
HENTEL
PARQUEADERO

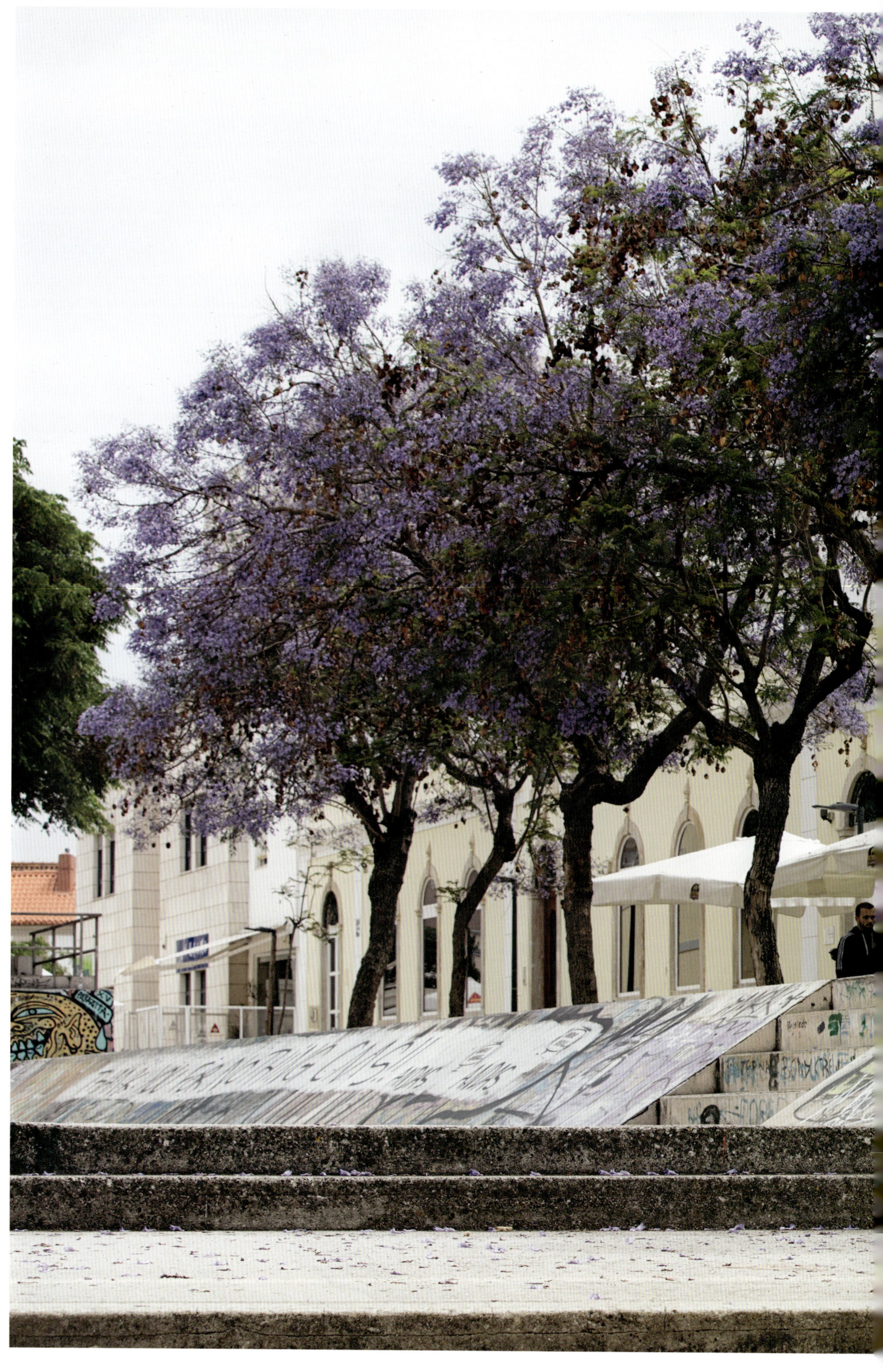

NORA VASCONCELLOS LISBON, PORTUGAL

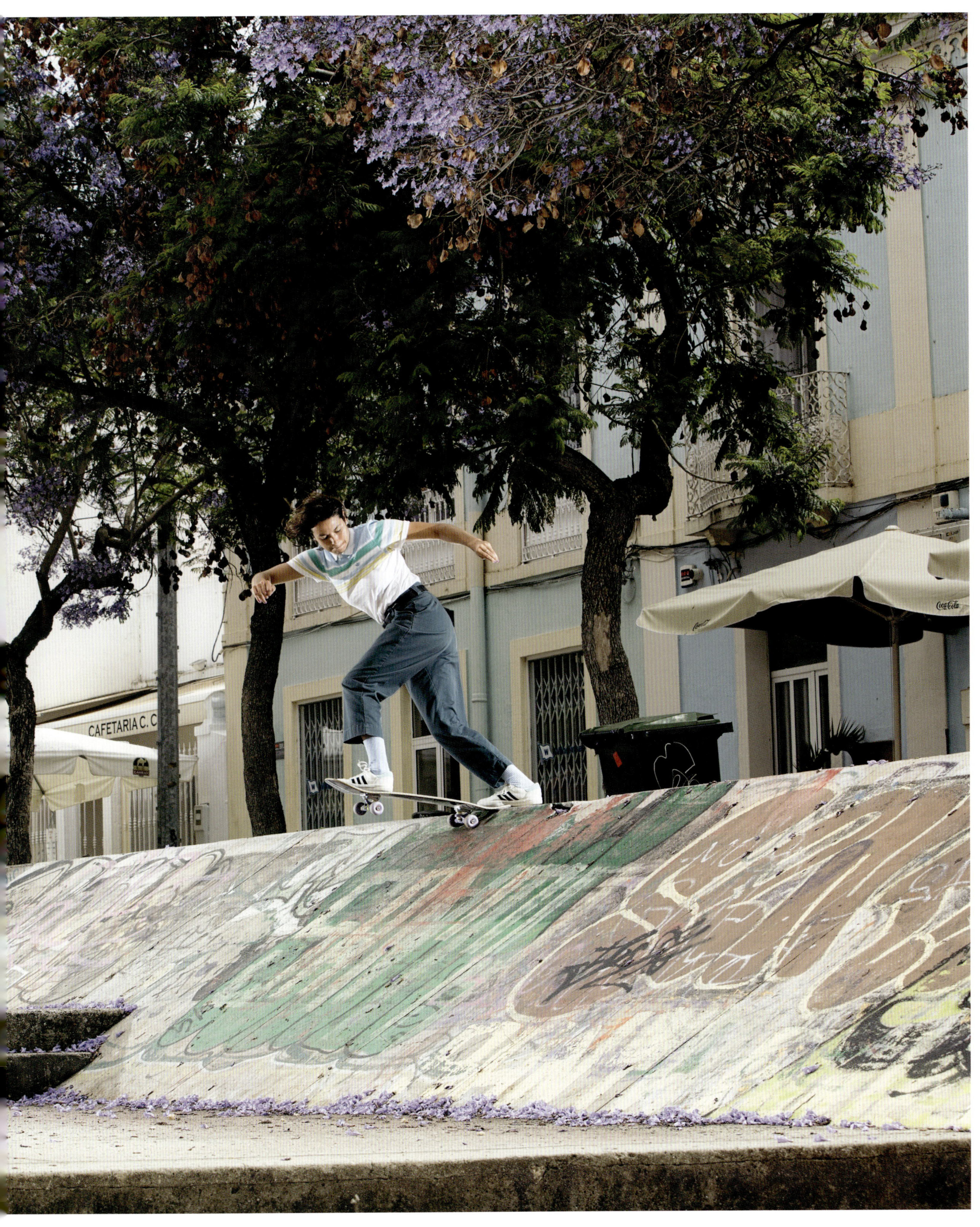
CAFETARIA C. C

T. J. ROGERS MAURITIUS

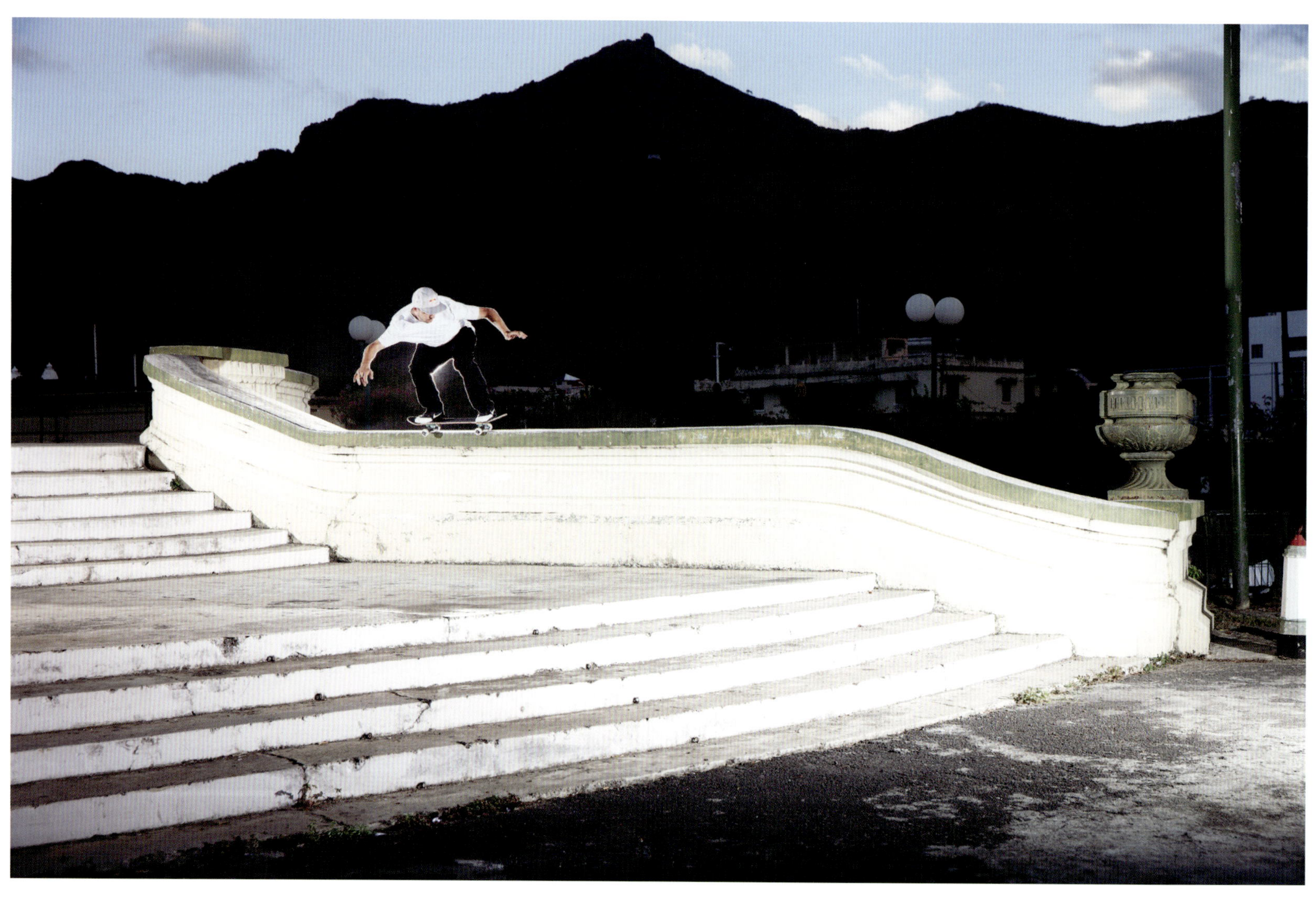

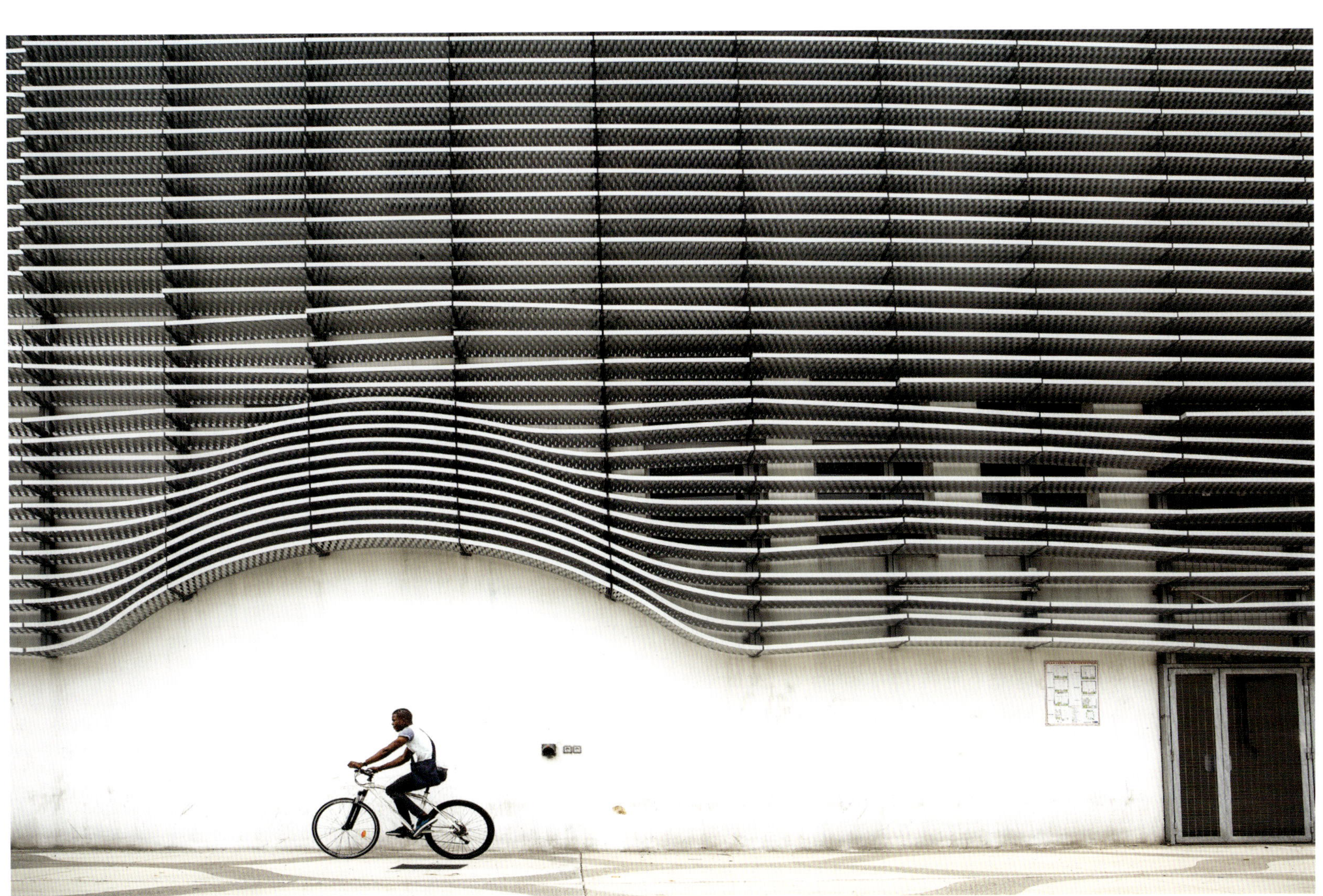

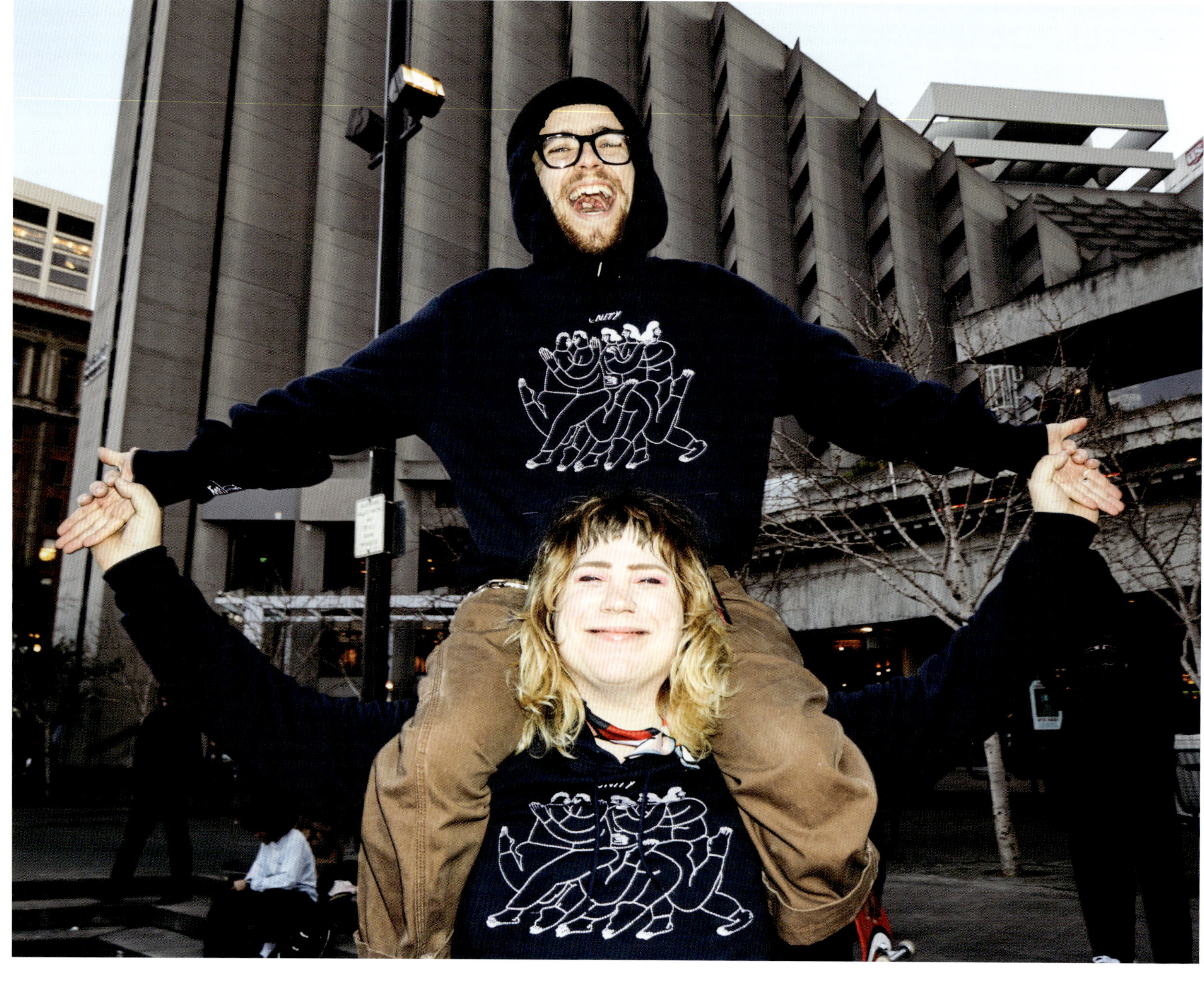

MARBIE + SMALLS SF, CA

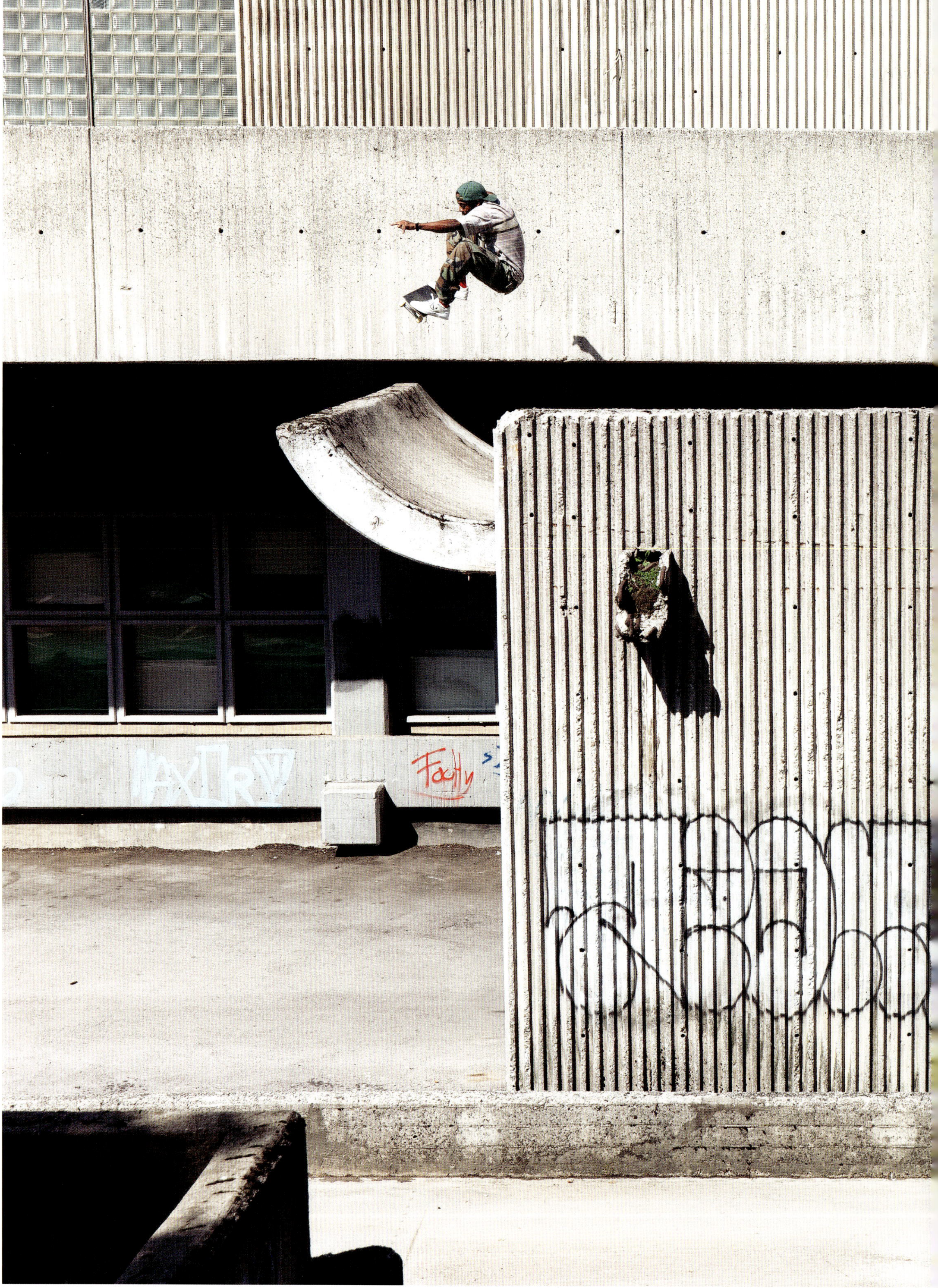

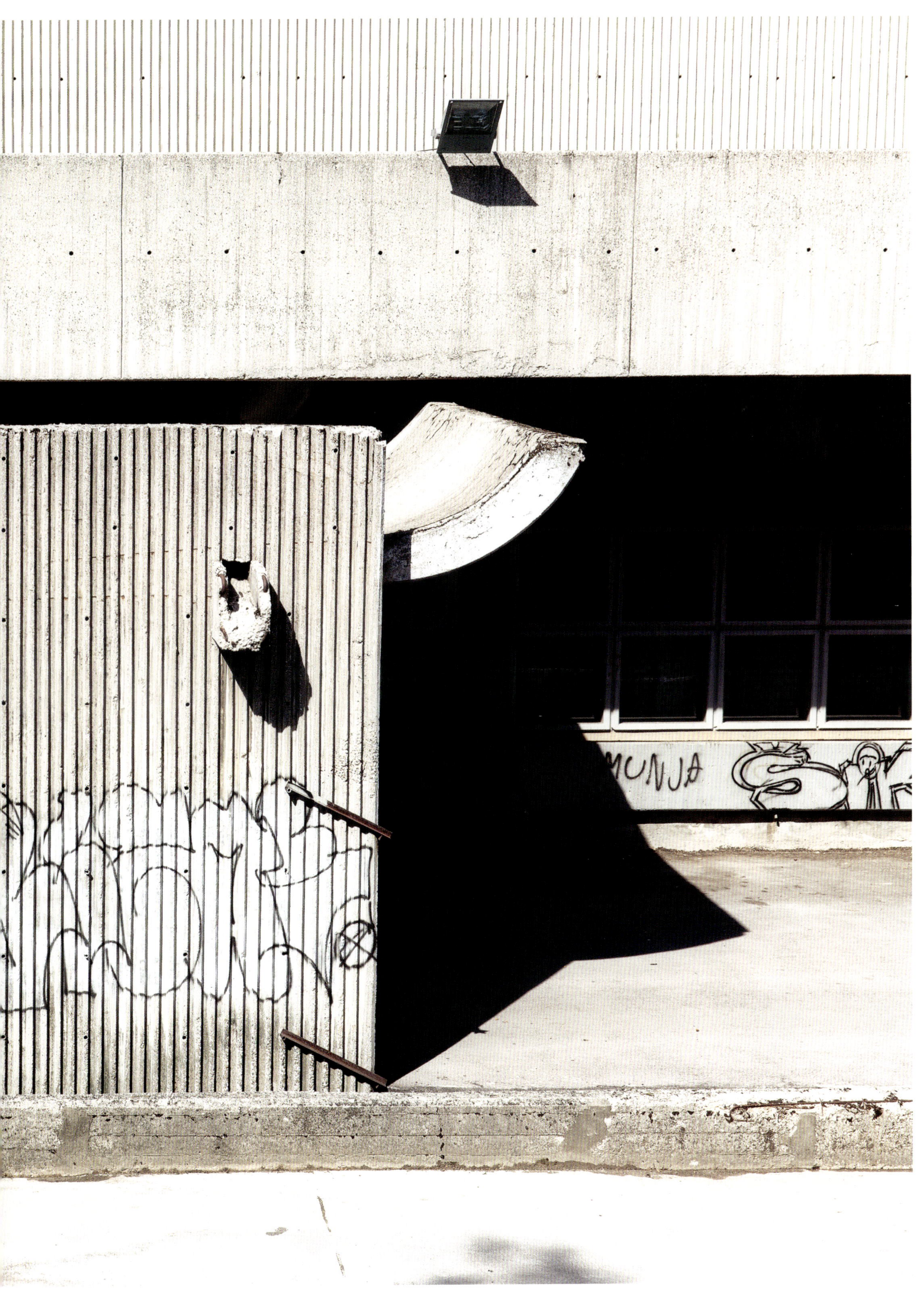

AL DAVIS SARAJEVO, BOSNIA

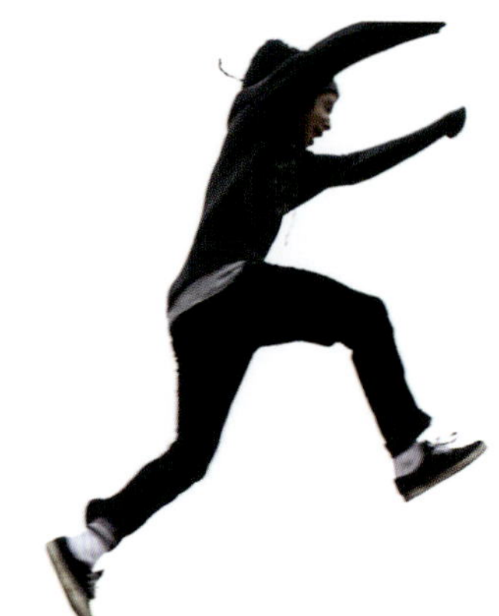

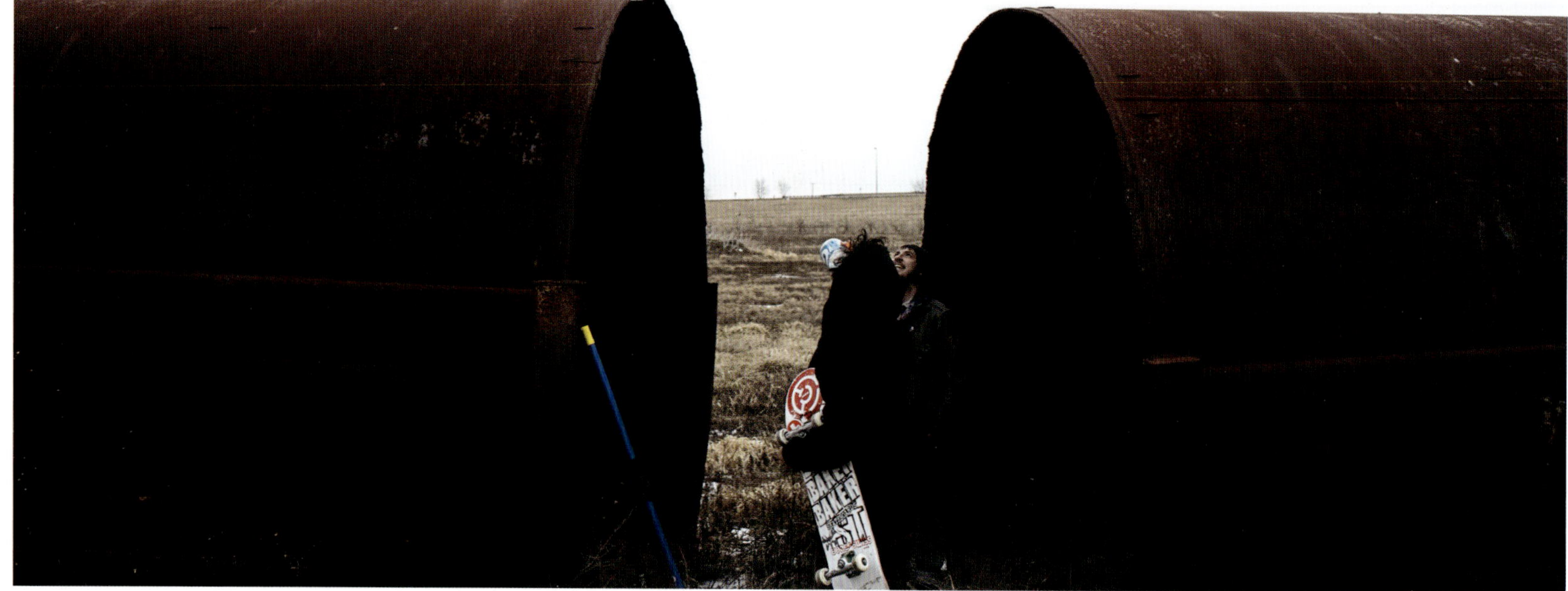

SEAN MALTO MISSOURI

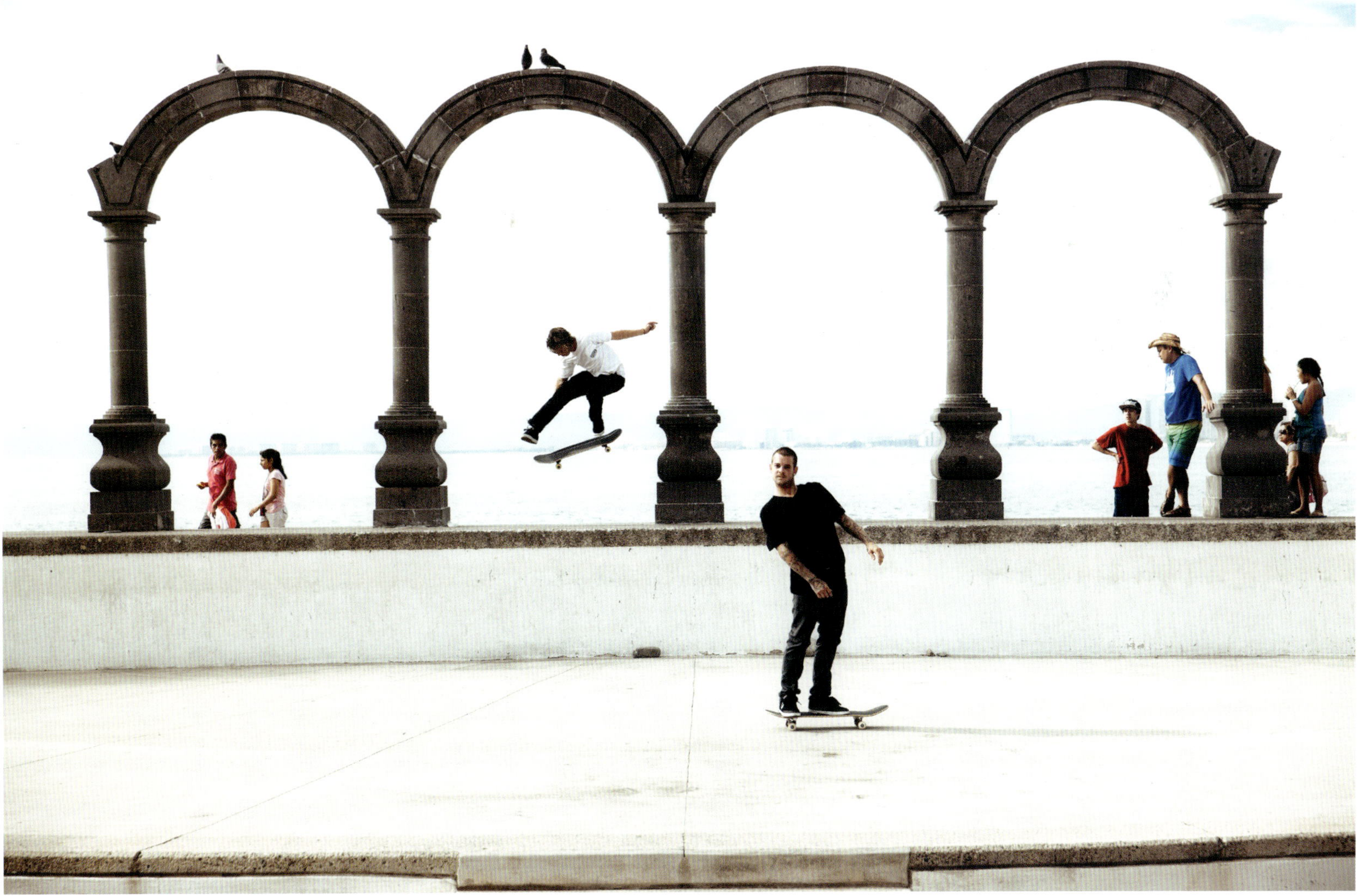

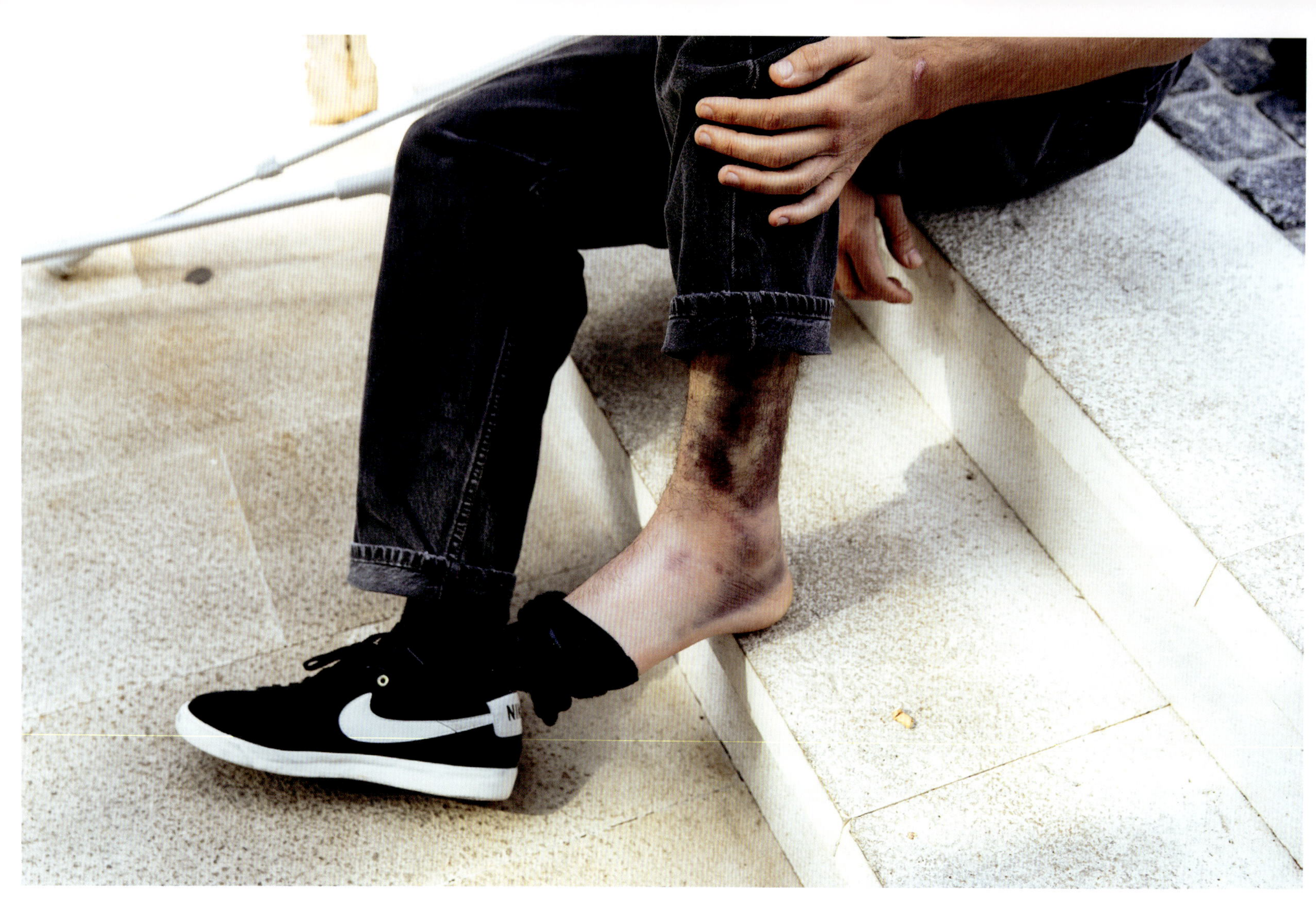

AIDAN CAMPBELL
+ RYAN SHECKLER   MEXICO

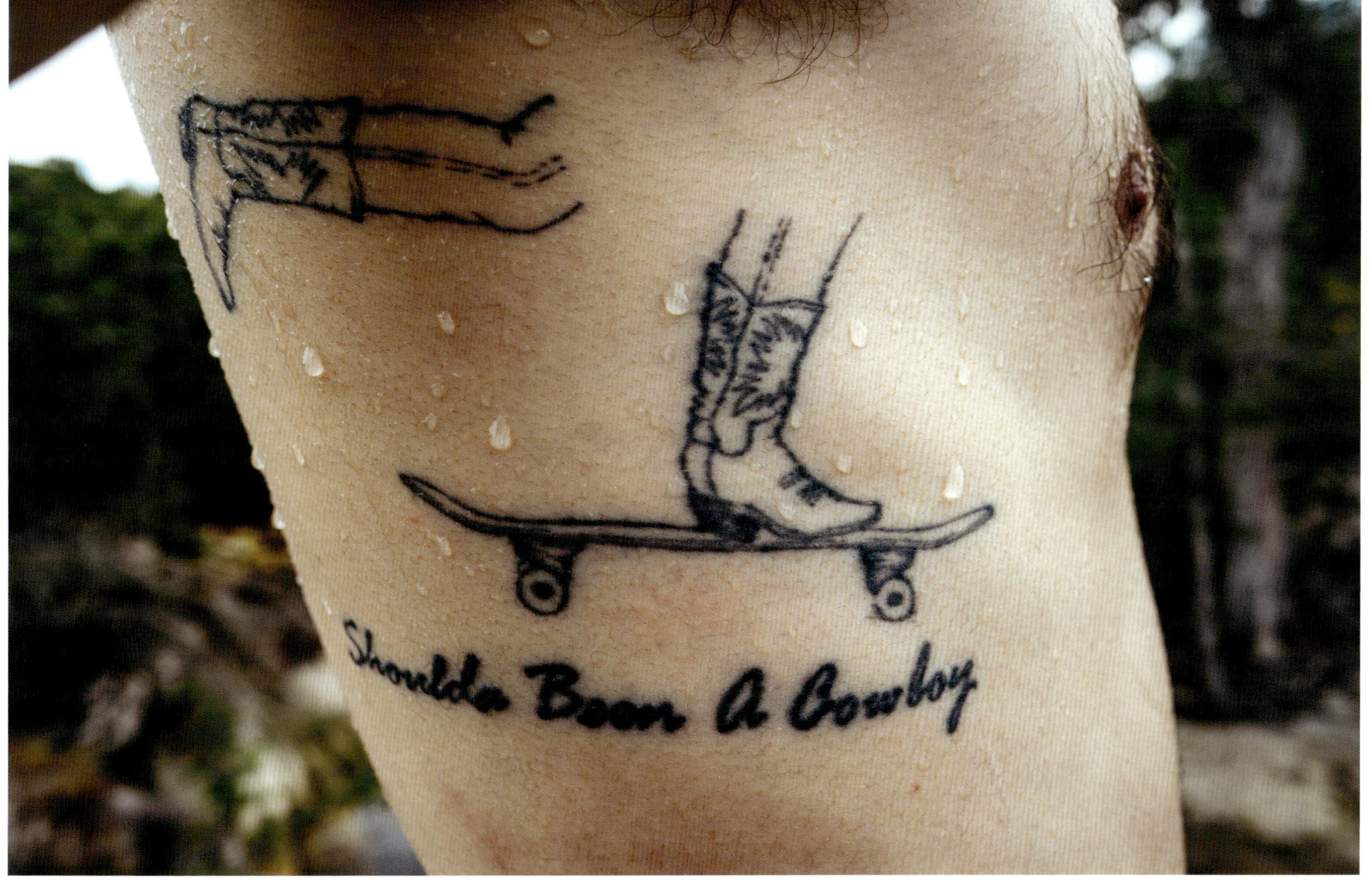
Shoulda Been A Cowboy

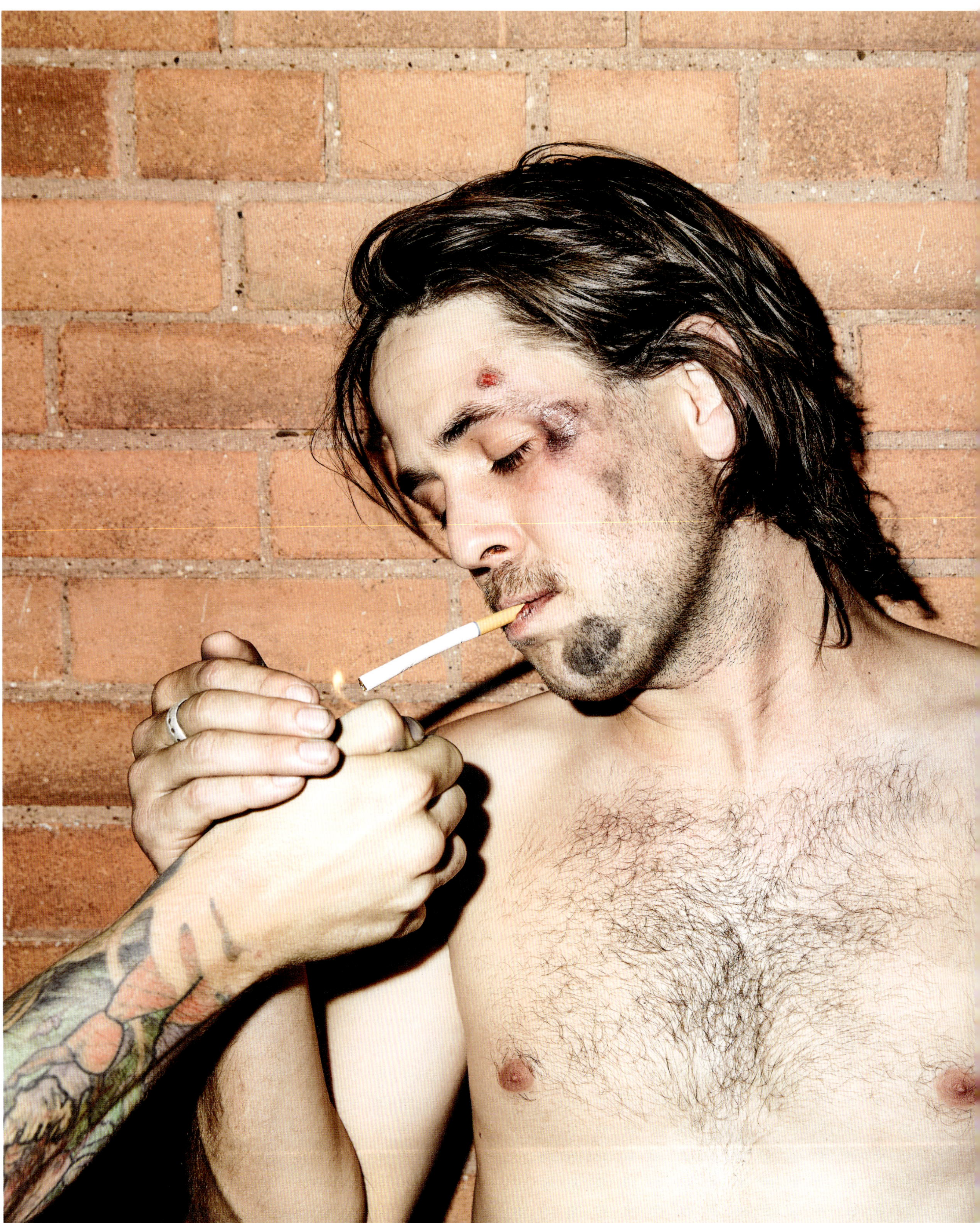

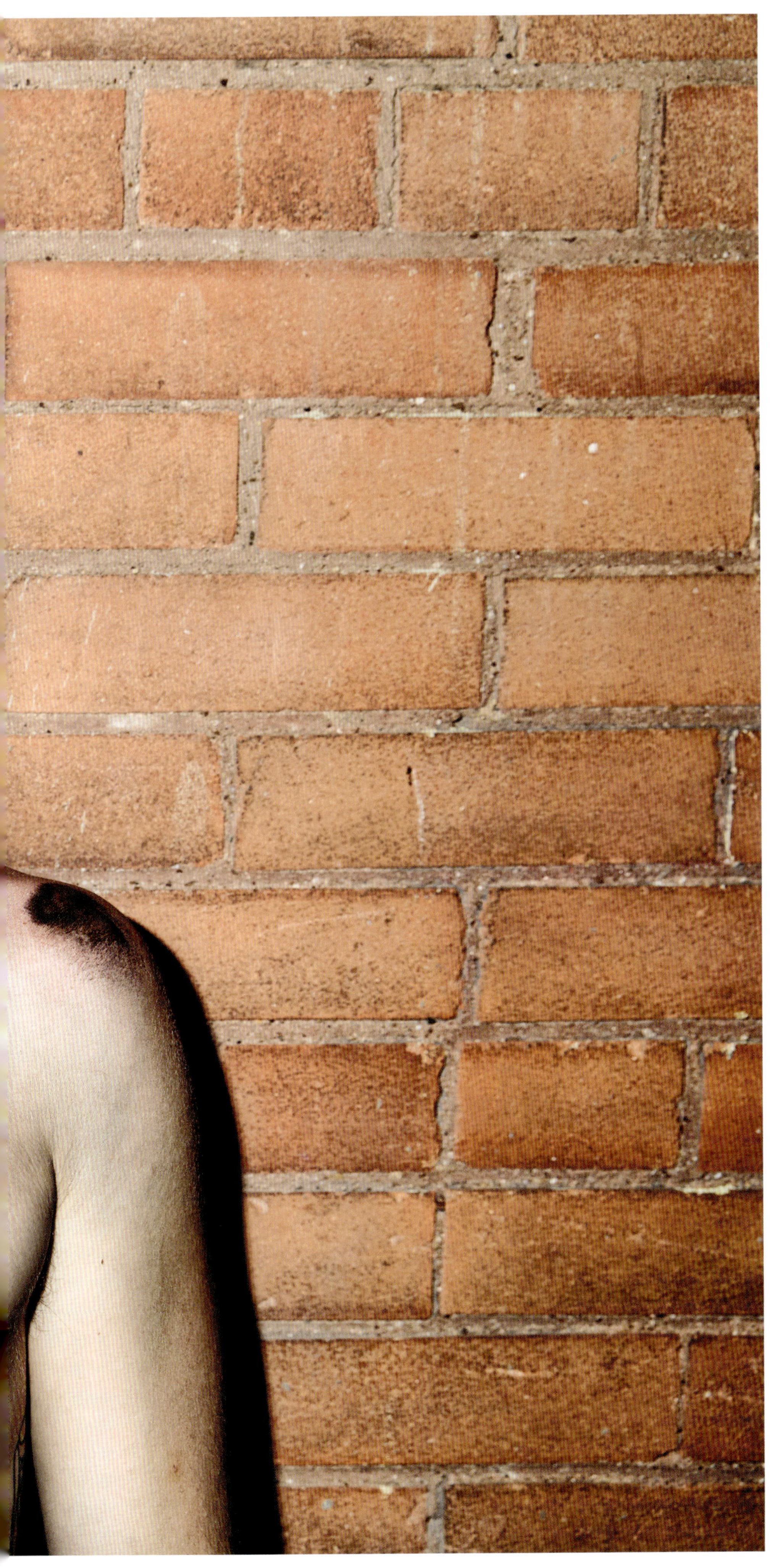

AIDAN CAMPBELL TEXAS

CHASE HAWK TEXAS

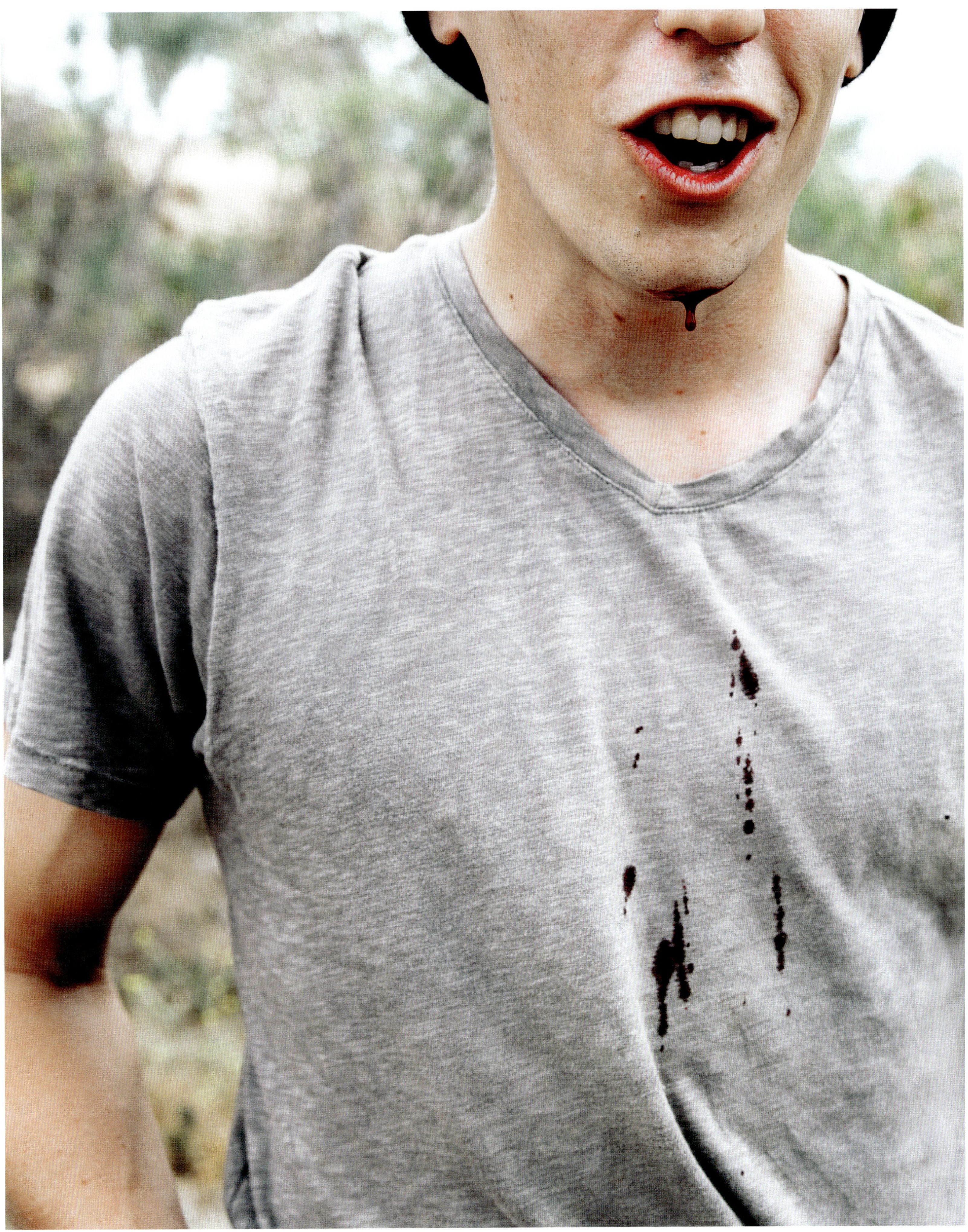

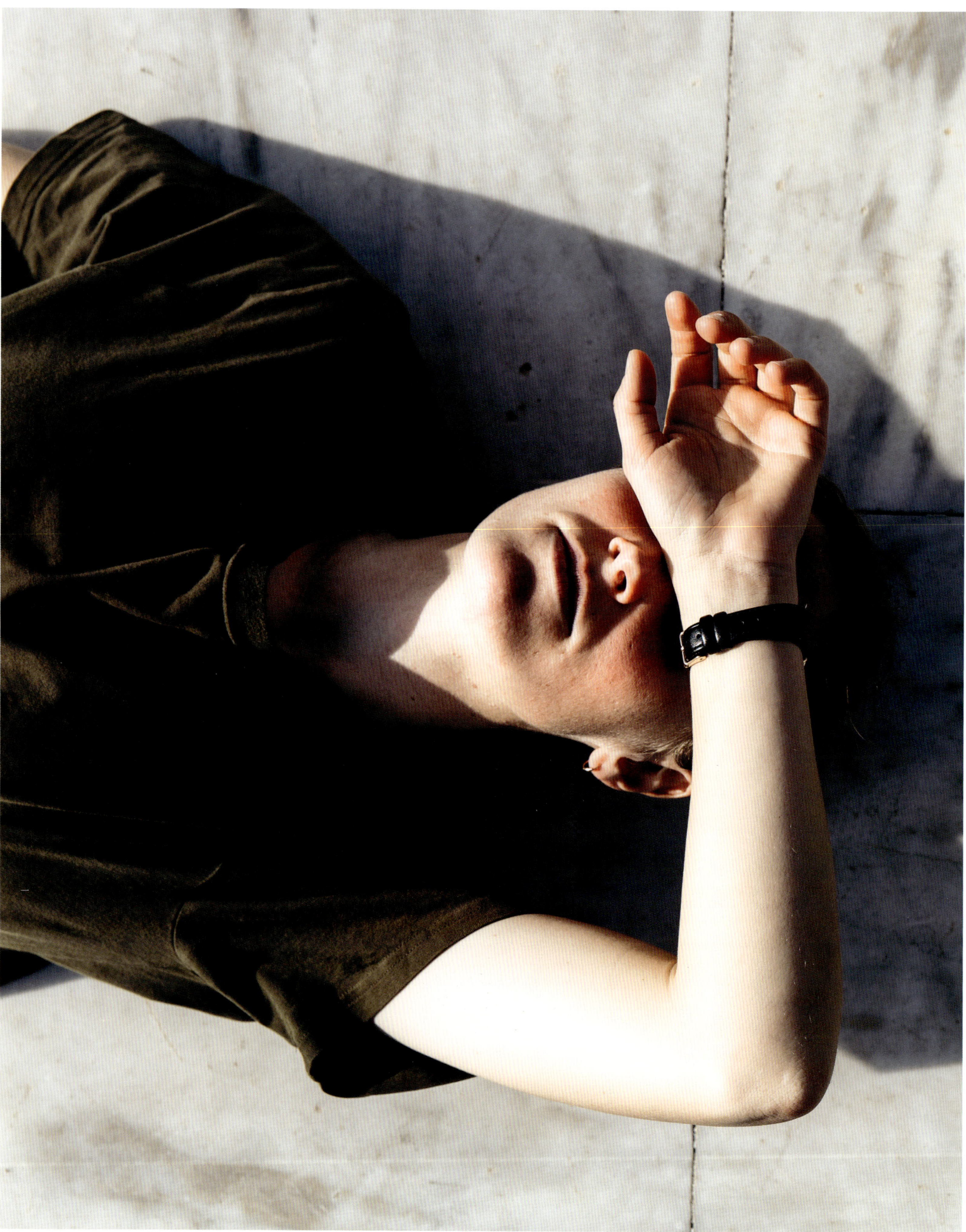

SARAH MEURLE
ATHENS, GREECE

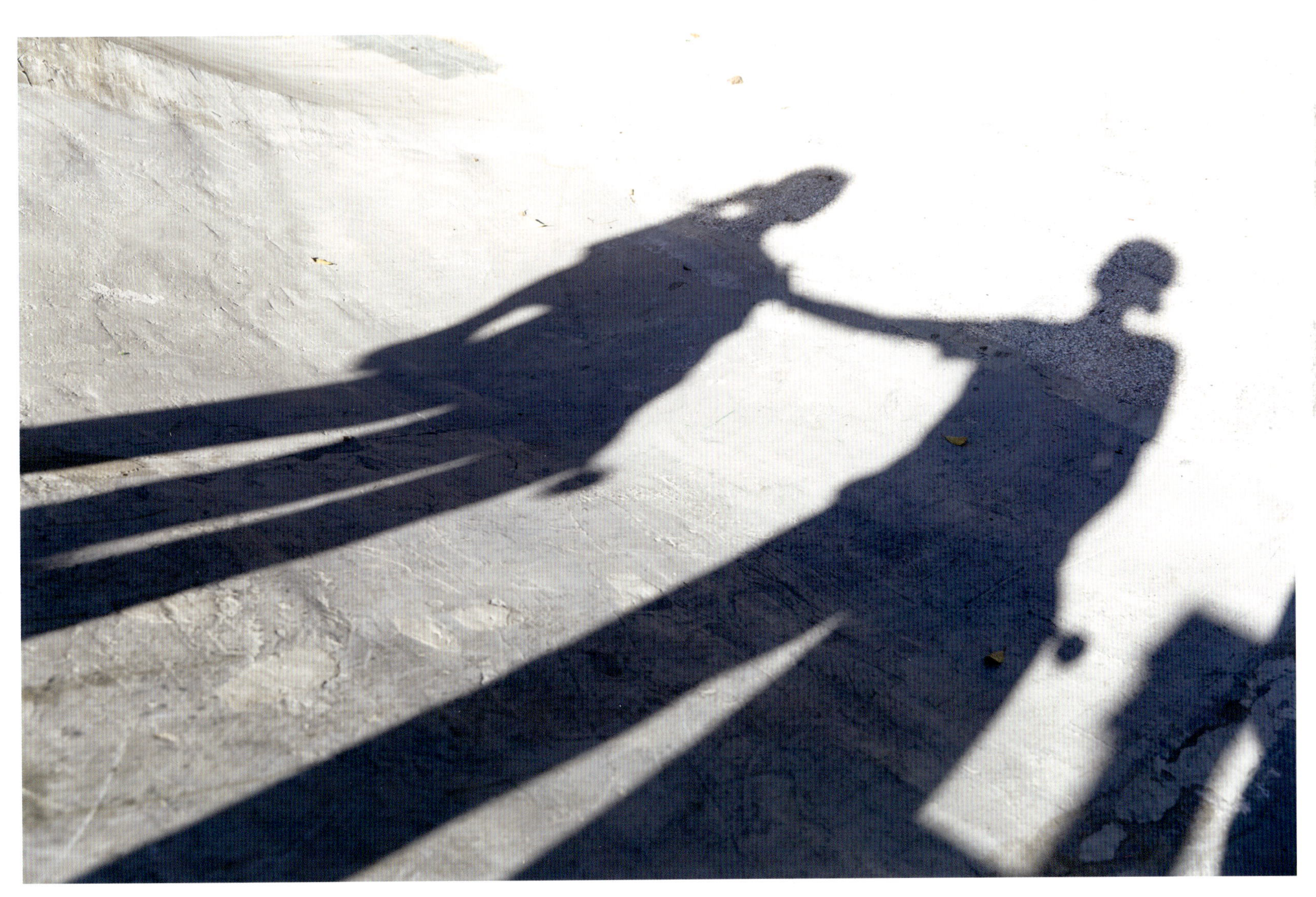

NORA VASCONCELLOS
PALM SPRINGS

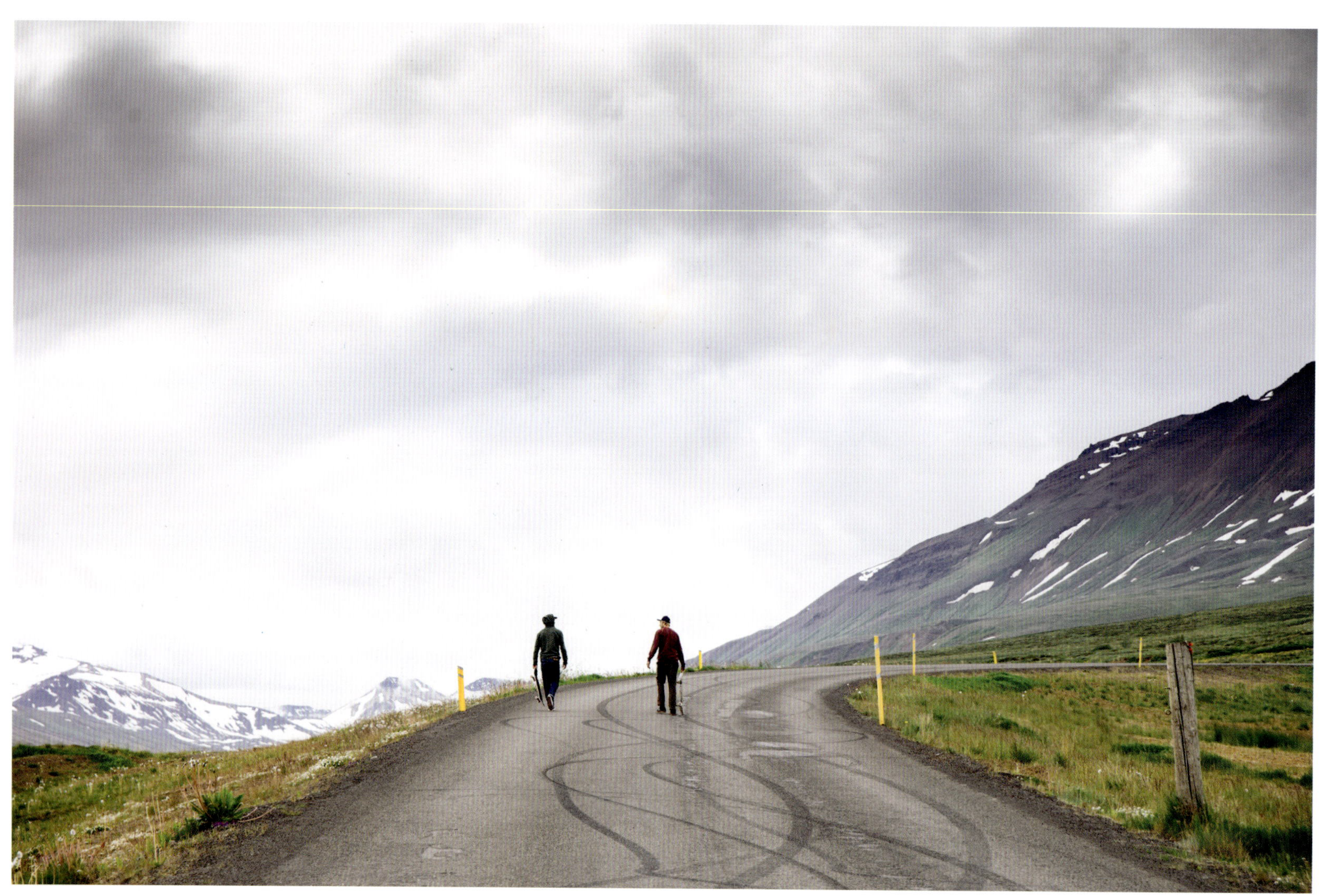

JOSH MATTHEWS + MADARS APSE
ICELAND

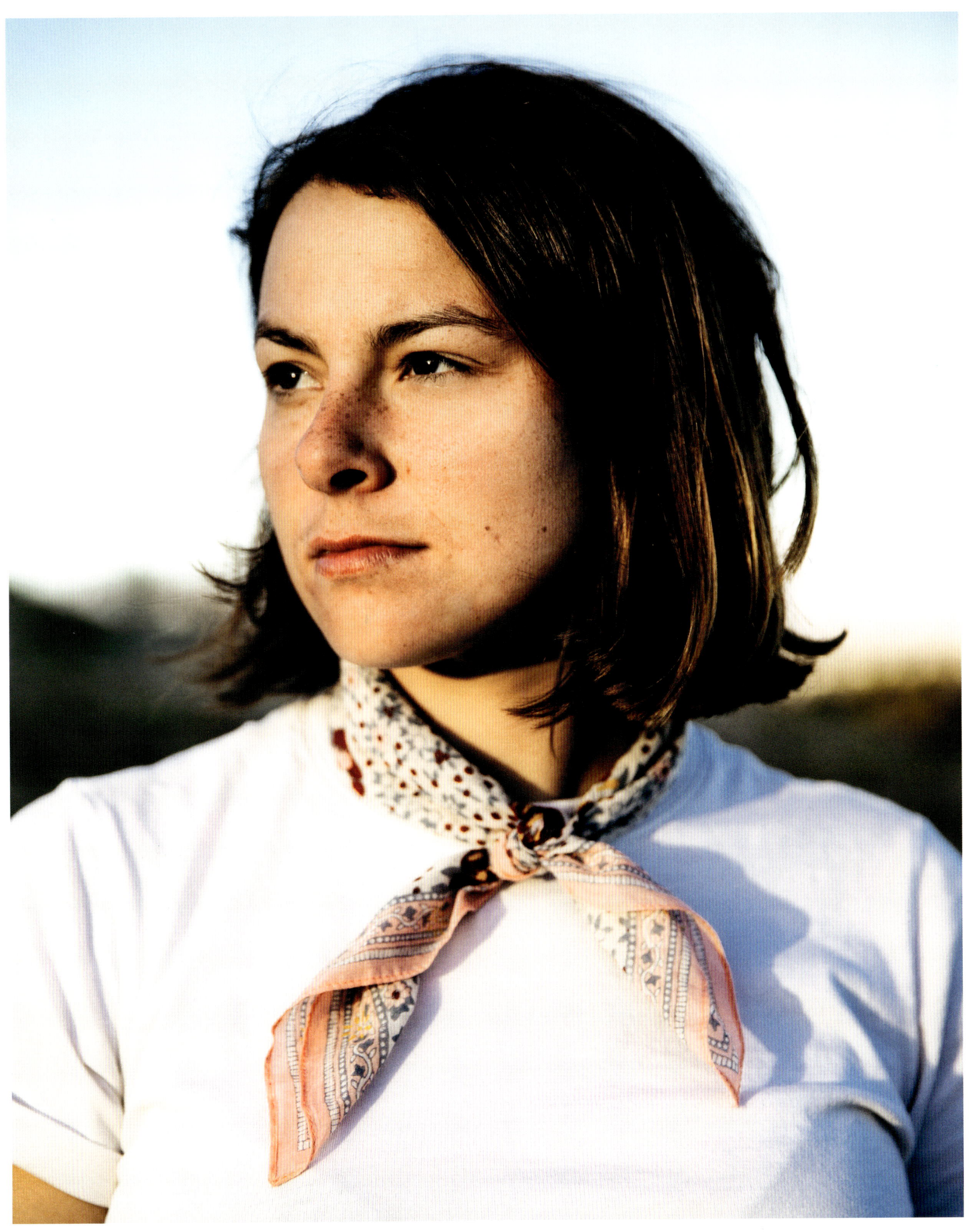

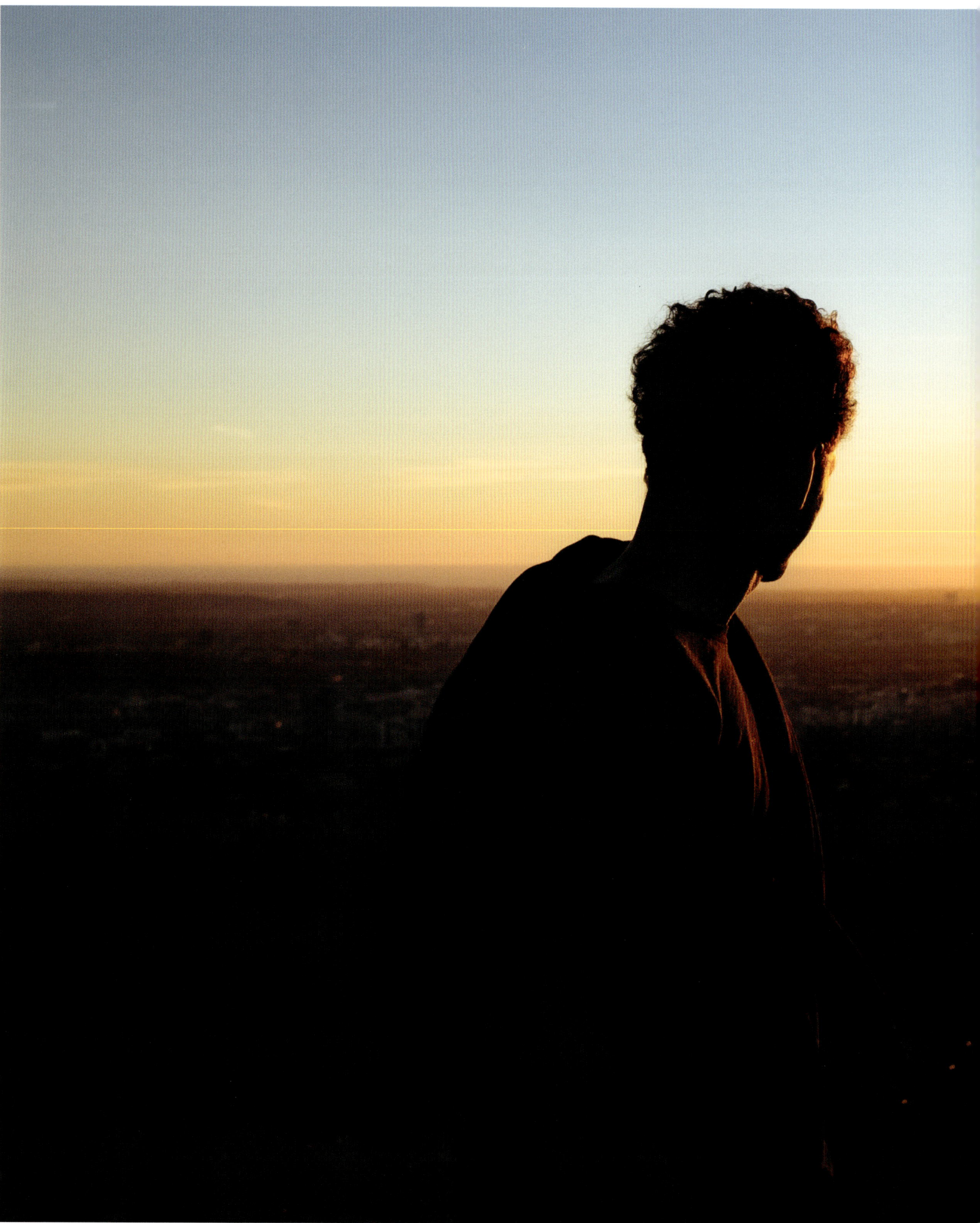

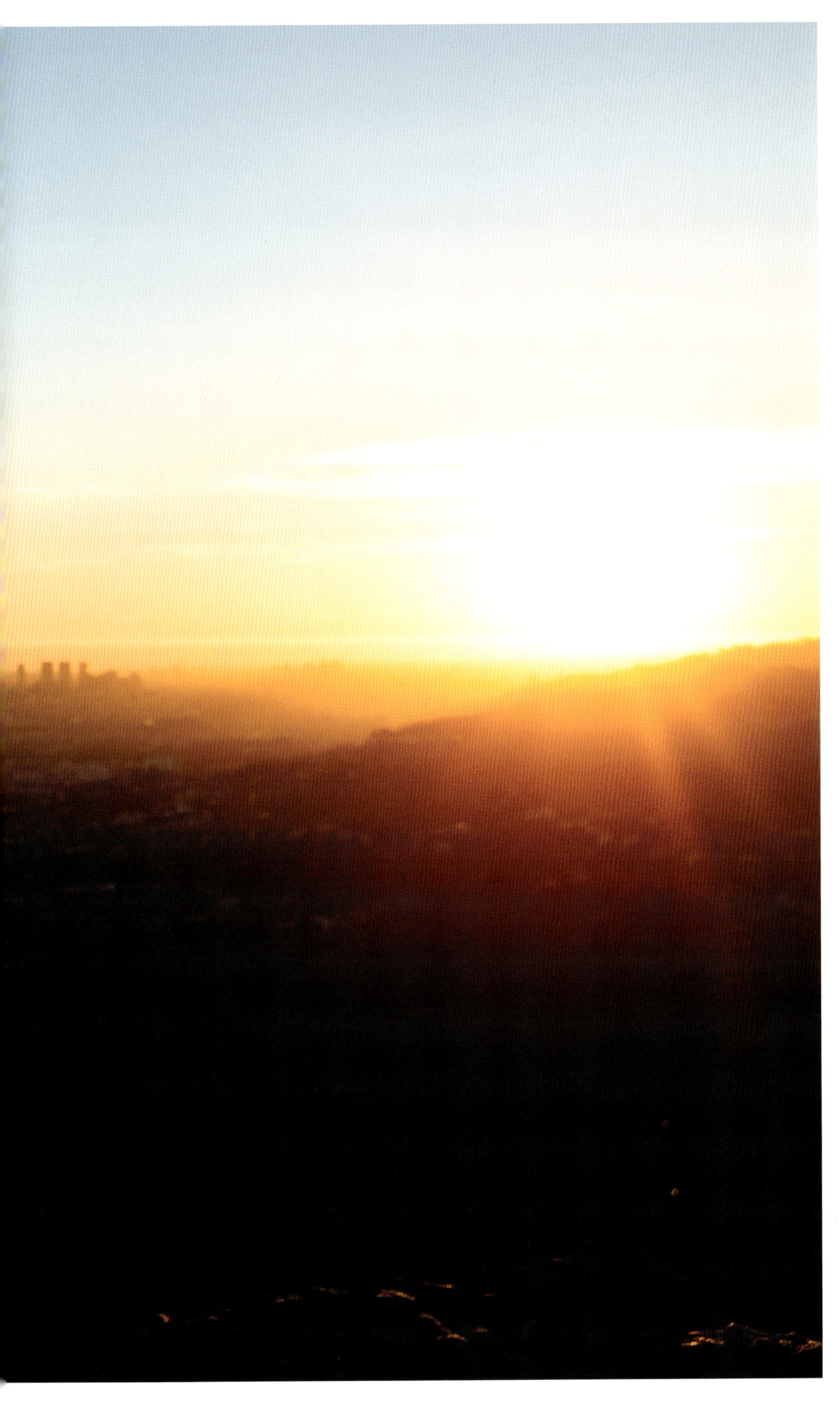

DOOGIE LA, CA

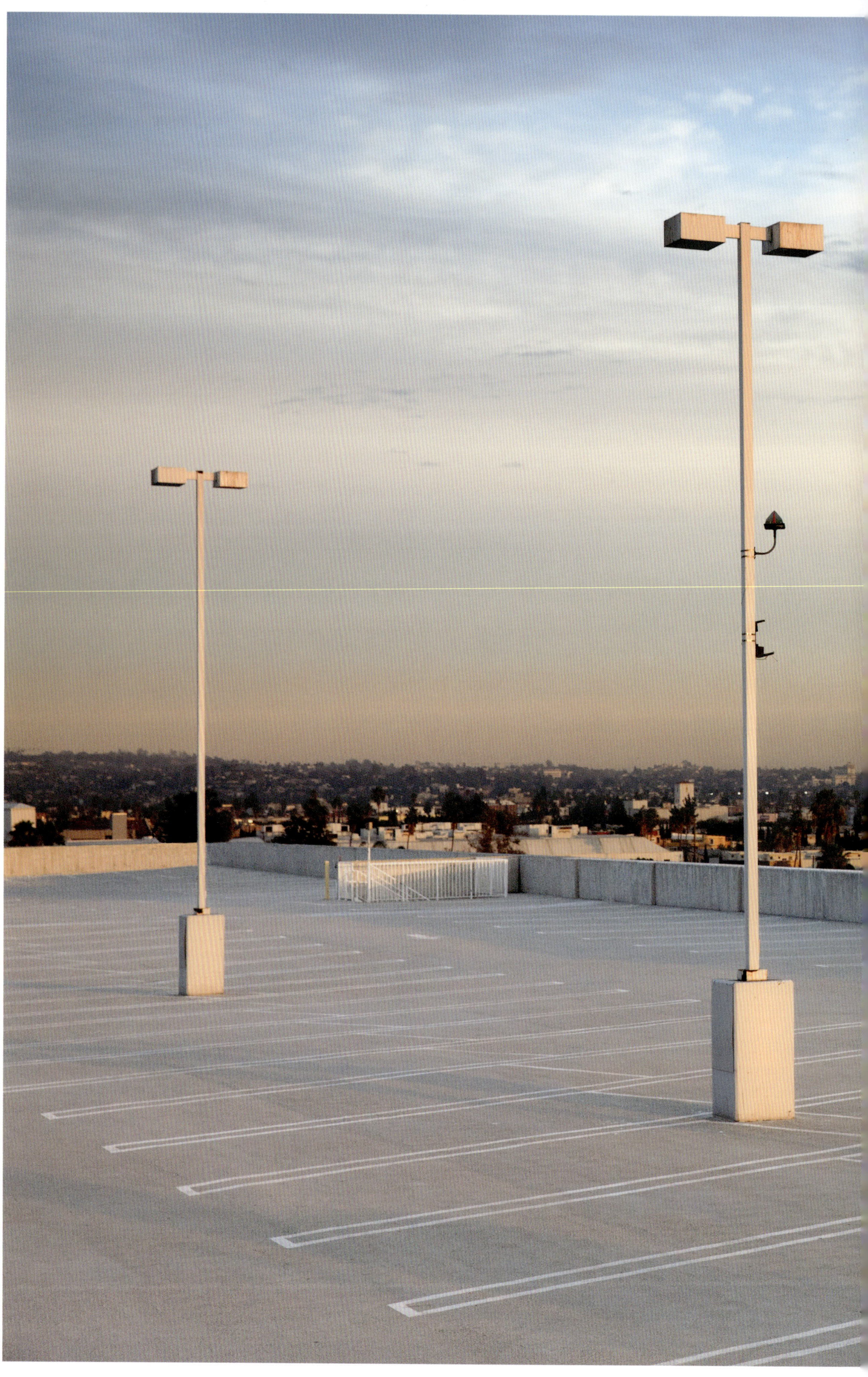

CURREN CAPLES LA, CA

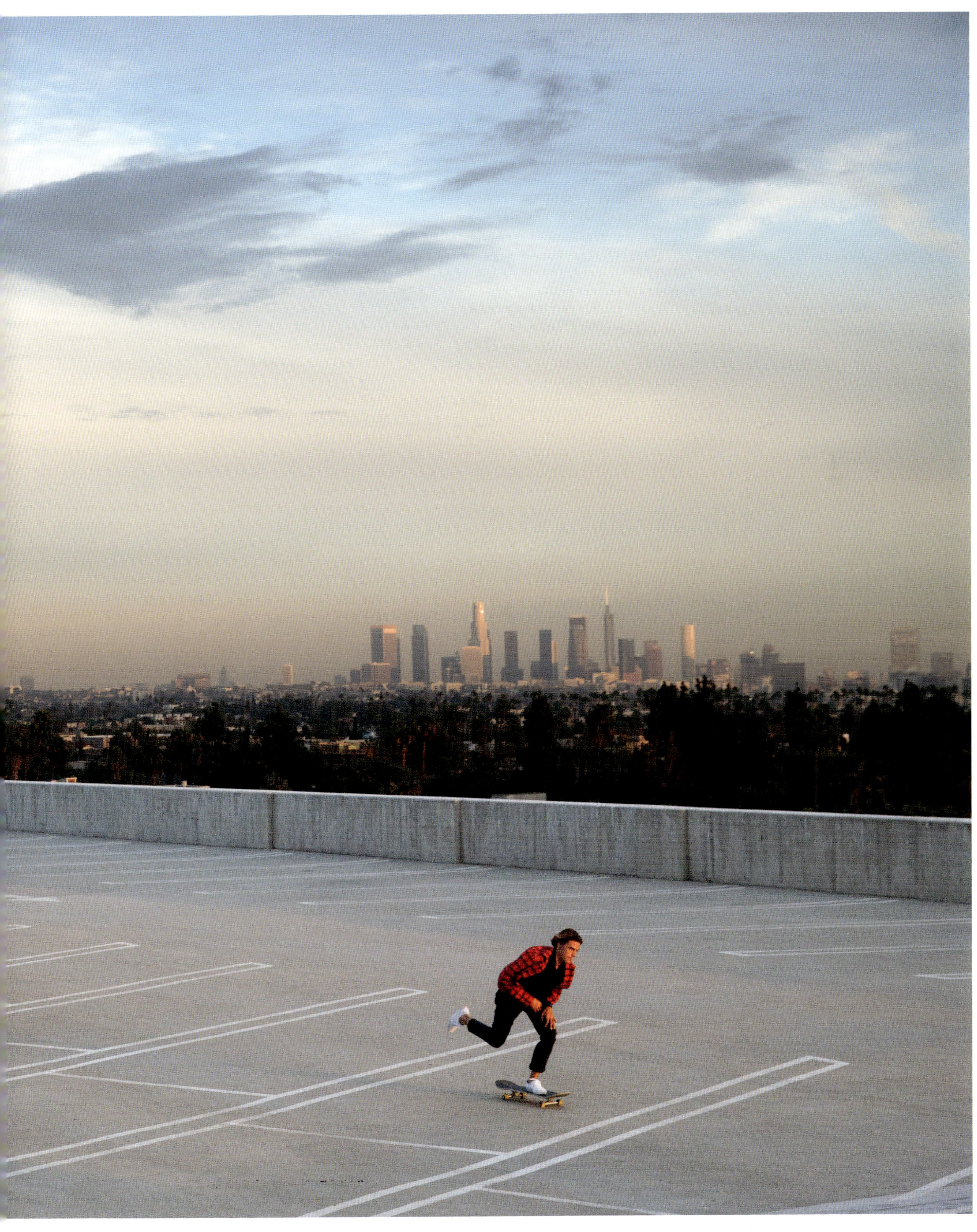

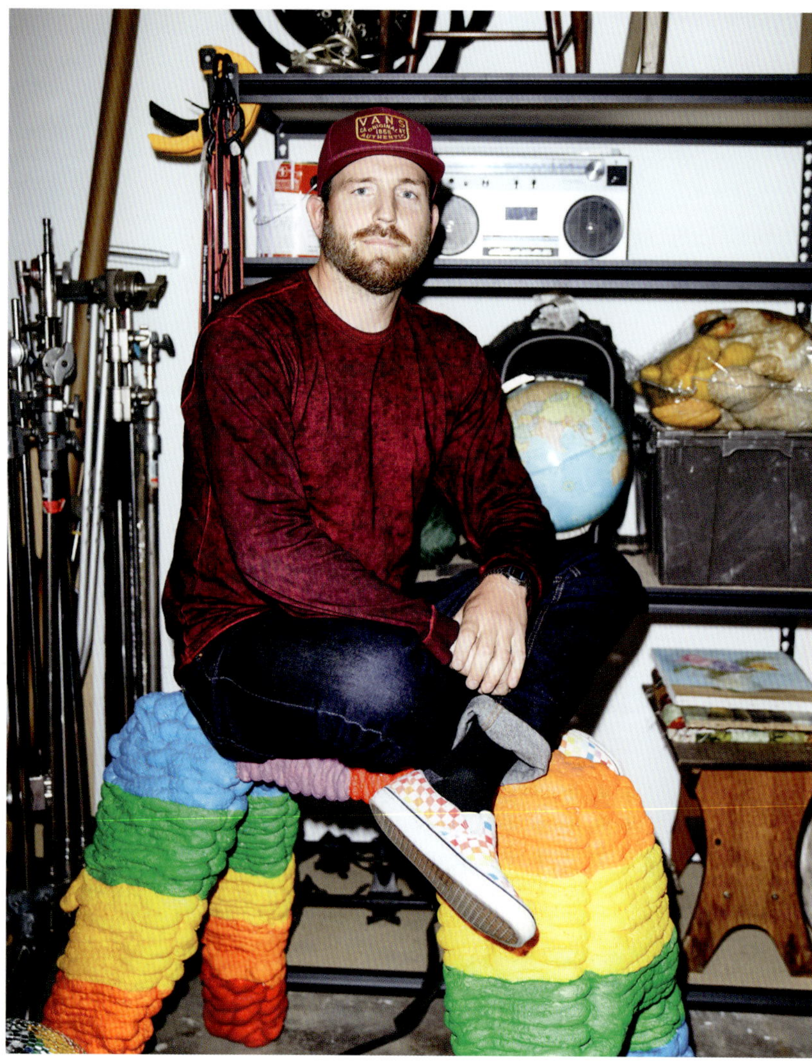

Photo: Chris Escamilla

Sam McGuire spent his younger years on a farm in his hometown of Waterloo, IA. Farm life wasn't so bad, he had a barn filled with ramps for him and his friends to skateboard in, but he longed to see all the exotic locations in the magazines he read as a kid. He wanted to see the world, and the world wasn't on the farm. So one day, he packed his things and left.

He spent the next 10 years travelling the world shooting around the worlds top professional skaters for brands like Nike, Adidas and Converse before transitioning into shooting more commercially.

In 2014 Sam came out, since then he's worked as a Queer advocate working closely to help brands become more fabulous and inclusive. He's disarming and mischievously funny, his positivity takes people off their guard during shoots. Sam inspires authenticity and is able to bring out people's most honest self. His keen eye and vibrant style help bring the color, energy and emotion of any situation.

These days, he lives in Los Angeles, CA and still spends as much time as he can on the road—to date, he's shot in over 65 countries for various commercial and editorial clients.

www.samuelmcguire.com
www.paragon-books.com